DICTIONARY OF BATTLES

DICTIONARY OF BATTLES

From the Earliest Date to the Present Time

By

THOMAS BENFIELD HARBOTTLE

AUTHOR OF "DICTIONARY OF QUOTATIONS" (CLASSICAL); "DICTIONARY OF HISTORICAL ALLUSIONS"; CO-AUTHOR OF "DICTIONARY OF QUOTATIONS" (FRENCH AND ITALIAN)

NEW YORK
E. P. DUTTON & CO.
1905

REPUBLISHED BY GALE RESEARCH COMPANY, BOOK TOWER, DETROIT, 1966

Library of Congress Card Number 66-22672

PREFACE

THE sad death of Mr. Harbottle, just as this work was going to press, has thrown upon me the onus of correcting the proofs and preparing the Index. The necessity for hurrying the work through the press has precluded comparison of the references in every instance with the original sources from which the Author had taken them ; if therefore some few printer's errors or varieties of spelling may still remain, they may, I hope, be attributed to the imperfections of one, who had to step suddenly into the breach caused by the loss of a valued friend and collaborator, whose patience in research, depth of knowledge and accuracy in compilation, he could never hope to equal.

October, 1904. P. H. DALBIAC.

DICTIONARY OF BATTLES

A

Abensberg (Campaign of Wagram.)

Fought April 20, 1809, between the French and Bavarians under Napoleon, about 90,000 strong, and the Austrians, 80,000 in number, under the Archduke Charles. On the French left, Lanne's corps drove back the Austrians, after a feeble resistance. In the centre the Bavarians were hard pressed, but eventually Napoleon succeeded in turning the Austrian flank, left exposed by the defeat of their right, and Charles was forced to retreat. The Austrians lost 7,000, the French and Bavarians about 3,000 killed and wounded.

Aberdeen (Civil War).

Fought September 13, 1644, between the Covenanters, 3,000 strong, under Lord Burleigh, and the Royalists, 1,500 strong, under Montrose. The Covenanters were put to flight, and no quarter being given, they lost heavily before reaching Aberdeen. The Royalist losses were insignificant.

Aboukir (French Invasion of Egypt).

Fought July 5, 1799, Napoleon attacking the position held by Mustapha Pasha, who had recently landed in Egypt at the head of 18,000 Turks. The French were completely successful, two-thirds of the Turkish troops being killed or driven into the sea, while 6,000, with the Pasha, surrendered.

Aboukir (British Invasion of Egypt).

Fought March 8, 1801, when 5,000 British under Sir Ralph Abercromby disembarked on the beach at Aboukir, in the face of a force of 2,000 French under General Friant. The landing was effected under a heavy musketry and artillery fire, which cost the assailants 1,100 killed and wounded, and the French were driven from their positions with a loss of 500 men.

Aboukir.

See Nile.

Abu Hamed (Soudan Campaigns).

Fought August 7, 1897, when the Dervish entrenchments outside Abu Hamed were stormed by a Soudanese Brigade, with 2 guns Royal Artillery, under Major - General Hunter. The Mahdist garrison was driven through the town, losing heavily, and their commander, Mohammed Zain, captured. The Egyptian loss was 80 killed and wounded, including 4 British officers.

Abu Klea (Soudan Campaigns).

Fought January 17, 1885,

between a British force, 1,500 strong, under Sir Herbert Stewart, and 12,000 Mahdists, of whom about 5,000 actually attacked. The British square was broken at one corner, owing to the jamming of a Gardner gun, and the Mahdists forcing their way inside, a desperate hand-to-hand conflict followed. Eventually the assailants were driven off, and the square reformed. The British loss was 18 officers, among them Colonel Fred. Burnaby, and 150 men. In the immediate vicinity of the square, 1,100 Arab dead were counted.

Abu Kru (Soudan Campaigns).

Fought January 19, 1885, between 1,200 British troops under Sir Herbert Stewart, and a large force of Mahdists. The Mahdists attacked a short distance from the Nile, and the British square moved towards the river, repelling all assaults successfully till they reached the Nile. The British losses were 121, including Sir Herbert Stewart, mortally wounded. This action is also known as the battle of Gubat.

Acapulco (Mexican Liberal Rising).

Fought August 9, 1855, between the Mexican Government troops under Santa Anna, and the Liberals under Juarez. Santa Anna was totally routed and fled from the country.

Accra (First Ashanti War).

Fought 1824, between 10,000 Ashantis and a force of 1,000 British under Sir Charles Mc-Carthy. The British were surrounded and routed by the natives, McCarthy being killed.

Accra (First Ashanti War).

Fought 1825, between 15,000 Ashantis and 400 British troops, with 4,600 native auxiliaries. The Ashantis were completely defeated, and the king compelled to abandon his designs on Cape Coast Castle.

Acragas (Second Carthaginian Invasion of Sicily).

This fortress was besieged B.C. 406 by the Carthaginians under Hannibal, the garrison being commanded by Dexippus the Spartan. Early in the siege a pestilence in the Carthaginian camp carried off Hannibal, who was succeeded by his cousin, Himilco. A relieving army of 35,000 Syracusans, under Daphnæus fought a pitched battle with the Carthaginians under the walls of the city, and succeeded in seizing and holding one of their camps, but shortly afterwards dissensions broke out in the garrison, and many of the foreign mercenaries deserting, the citizens, after a siege of eight months, left the place *en masse*. The Carthaginians at once occupied the fortress.

Acre (Third Crusade).

Siege was laid to this city by the Christians in August, 1189, and it was obstinately defended by the Saracens for two years, during which the Crusaders are said to have lost 120,000 men. In June, 1191, the besiegers were reinforced by an English army under Richard Cœur de Lion, and in the following month the garrison surrendered.

Acre.

The city remained in the hands of the Christians till 1291, when it was captured by the Moslems under Malek al Aschraf, Sultan of Egypt. The last stronghold in the Holy Land thus passed out of the keeping of the Christians.

Acre (French Invasion of Egypt).

The city was besieged March 17, 1799, by the French under Napoleon, and defended by the Turks under Djezzar, and a small force of British seamen under Sir Sidney Smith. An assault on the 28th was repulsed with loss, and then a threatened attack by a Syrian army forced Napoleon to withdraw a large portion of his troops. On the resumption of the siege, no less than seven more assaults were delivered, while the French had to meet eleven sallies of the beseiged, but they were unable to effect a lodgment, and on May 21 Napoleon reluctantly raised the siege. The fall of Acre would have placed the whole of Syria, and possibly of the Turkish Empire, in the hands of the French.

Acre (Mehemet Ali's Second Rebellion).

Mehemet Ali having refused to accept the conditions imposed upon him by the Quadrilateral Alliance, Acre was bombarded, November 3, 1840, by a combined British and Turkish fleet under Sir R. Stopford, and the town laid in ruins.

Acs (Hungarian Rising).

Fought July 2, 1849, between 25,000 Hungarians, under Görgey, and the Russo-Austrian army, greatly superior in numbers, under Prince Windischgrätz. The allies attacked the entrenched camp of the Hungarians, outside Komorn, while the Hungarians made an attempt to turn the allied left. Both attacks were repulsed, and the battle was undecided.

Actium (Mark Antony's Second Rebellion).

Fought September 2, B.C. 31, between the fleet of Antony, 460 galleys, and that of Octavius, about 250 sail, but much lighter and less well manned than those of Antony. The battle was fiercely contested, with varying fortune; but at a critical moment Cleopatra ordered the Egyptian admiral to make sail, and with 60 galleys withdrew from the fight. She was followed by Antony, and his fleet, discouraged by his flight, surrendered after ten hours' fighting. The Octavians captured 300 galleys, and 5,000 Antonians fell in the action. A few days later Antony's land army of 120,000 men laid down their arms.

Acultzingo (Franco-Mexican War).

Fought April 28, 1862, between the French, 7,500 strong, under General Lorencez, and the main Mexican army, about 10,000 in number, under General Zaragoça. The Mexicans held a strong position in the Cumbres Pass, from which they were driven by the French, and forced to retire upon La Puebla.

Admagetobriga (Gallic Tribal Wars).

Fought B.C. 61 between the Sequani under Ariovistus, and the Hædui under Eporedorix. The Hædui were defeated, with the loss of the flower of their chivalry, and were compelled to give hostages and pay tribute to Ariovistus.

Adnatuca (Gallic Wars).

Fought B.C. 53, when a Roman force of 9,000 men under Titurius Sabinus was attacked in its camps by the Eburones under Ambiorix. The assault failed, but an offer by Ambiorix of a safe passage to the nearest Roman station was accepted. On the march the Romans were treacherously attacked by the Eburones and cut to pieces, Sabinius being among the slain.

Adowa (Italian Invasion of Abyssinia).

Fought March 1, 1896, when the Italian force under General Baratieri attacked the Shoan army, strongly posted in a difficult country, and was routed with enormous loss.

Adrianople (Bulgarian Rising).

Fought April 15, 1205, between the Imperial troops under the Latin Emperor, Baldwin I, and the revolted Bulgarians under their chief, Calo-John. The Bulgarian cavalry fled, and lured the Latin horse in pursuit. Then turning upon them, they routed them with the loss of their leader, the Comte de Blois, and in the end the Imperialists were completely defeated and the Emperor captured.

Adwalton Moor (Civil War).

Fought January 30, 1643, when the Parliamentarians, numbering 4,000, with a levy of armed peasants, were defeated by 10,000 Royalists under Newcastle. Fairfax, who commanded the Parliament force, succeeded in reaching Hull.

The battle is also known as that of Atherton Moor.

Ægina (Third Messenian War).

Fought B.C. 458, between the Athenian fleet, and that of Ægina, aided by the Peloponnesian States. The Athenians were victorious, capturing 70 ships, and landing they invested Ægina, which fell into their hands after a siege of a little less than two years.

Ægospotami (Peloponnesian War).

Fought B.C. 405, between 180 Athenian triremes, under Conon, and 180 Peloponnesian ships under Lysander. The Athenian fleet was lying at Ægospotami, opposite Lampsacus, where Lysander was stationed. For four days in succession the Athenian admiral crossed the straits, and endeavoured, but in vain, to bring on a general action. On the fifth day Lysander waited till the Athenians had returned to their anchorage, and then, making a sudden dash across the straits, caught them unprepared, and seized all but twenty ships, putting to death all the Athenians who were captured. This disaster destroyed the naval power of Athens, and was soon followed by the end of the Peloponnesian War.

Ægusa (First Punic War).

Fought March 10, B.C. 241, between the Roman fleet of 200 quinqueremes under C. Lutatius Catulus, and a Carthaginian fleet under Hanno despatched to relieve the town. The action was fought in heavy weather, and the Roman sailors, being far better trained than their opponents, Catulus gained a signal victory, capturing 70 and sinking 50 of the enemy's ships. The victory ended the First Punic War.

Agedincum (Gallic War).

Fought B.C. 52, between the Romans under Labienus, and the Celts under Camalogenus. Labienus was endeavouring to effect a junction with Caesar, which the Celts were opposing, and Labienus, crossing the Marne in face of their army, inflicted upon them a severe defeat, in which Camalogenus fell.

Aghrim (Wars of the Revolution).

Fought July 12, 1691, between William III's troops, under Ginkel, and the French and Irish under St. Ruth. The English struggled in vain to carry St. Ruth's entrenchments, which were protected by a bog, but his flank was at last turned by the cavalry, which found a passage through the morass, and St. Ruth was killed. The Irish then broke and fled, and are said to have lost between 6,000 and 7,000 in the pursuit.

Agincourt (Hundred Years' War)

Fought October 25, 1415, between the French, numbering 50,000, under the Constable d'Albret, and about 15,000 English, mostly archers, under Henry V. The archers protected their front with a palisade of stakes, which broke the charge of the French men-at-arms, and the French army was routed with a loss of 10,000 slain, including the Constable and the Dukes of Alençon, Brabant and Bar, and 15,000 prisoners, including the Duke of Orleans and Marshal Boucicaut. The English lost only 1,600, among whom were the Duke of York and the Earl of Oxford.

Agnadello (War of the League of Cambrai).

Fought May 14, 1509, between 30,000 French under Louis XII and Marshal Trioulzio, and 35,000 Venetians under General Alviani. The Venetians were defeated with a loss of 6,000 men and 20 guns, Alviani being taken, and in consequence of his victory, Louis XII occupied all the territory assigned to him by the League, up to the Mincio.

Agordat (Soudan Campaigns).

Fought December 21, 1893, between 2,200 Italians, and native troops, under General Arimondi, and 11,500 Mahdists under Ahmed Ali, who had invaded Italian territory. The Mahdists were routed with a loss of about 3,000 men. The Italians lost 13, and 225 natives killed and wounded.

Agra (Farokshin's Rebellion).

Fought 1713, between the Great Mogul, Jehandar Shah, with 70,000 troops, under Zulfikar Khan, and the rebel Moguls under Jehandar's nephew, Farokshin. After a stubborn fight, the rebels overpowered the Imperial troops, and Jehandar Shah was captured and put to death by Farokshin, who ascended the throne.

Agra (Second Mahratta War).

The fortress was besieged October 4, 1803, by the British under General Lake, and was defended by a garrison of Sindhia's troops, 6,000 strong, who held the citadel, while seven additional battalions were encamped in the town. The latter force was attacked on the 10th and routed, losing 26 guns, while the survivors, 2,600 in number, surrendered on the following day. On the 17th the batteries opened fire on the citadel, and on the 18th the garrison surrendered

Agra (Indian Mutiny).

On August 2, 1857, the British garrison holding Agra sallied out to attack a body of 10,000 rebels encamped within four miles of the city. The Kotah contingent, which formed a portion of the British force, deserted to the mutineers, and the British troops, hard pressed and short of ammunition, were driven back into Agra, and forced to take refuge in the fort. In October of the same year Colonel Greathed's column of four battalions and two cavalry regiments encountered close to Agra a force of 7,000 mutineers. The rebels at first held their own, but were eventually put to flight, and pursued with great slaughter for ten miles.

Ahmedabad (First Mahratta War).

This strong fortress, garrisoned by 8,000 Arabs and Scinde Infantry, and 2,000 Mahrattas, was taken by assault, after a short bombardment, by a British force under General Goddard, February 15, 1780. The British lost 106 killed and wounded, including 12 officers.

Ahmed Khel (Second Afghan War).

Fought 1880, when a British force under General Stewart on the march to Ghuzni was attacked by about 15,000 Ghil-

zais. A rush of 3,000 Ghazis was successfully repulsed, and the enemy defeated and driven off, leaving 1,000 dead on the field. The British lost 17 only.

Ahmednugger (Mogul Invasion of the Deccan).

This place was besieged in 1599 by the Moguls under Mirza Khan, one of Akbar's generals, and defended by a garrison of Deccanis under Chand Bibi, ex-Queen of Bijapur. A practicable breach having been effected, the garrison was disposed to surrender, but Chand Bibi, heading the defenders, superintended the repair of the breach, and succeeding in holding out until a peace was signed by which the Great Mogul agreed to leave Ahmednugger unmolested.

Aiguillon (Hundred Years' War).

This fortress was besieged by the French under John, Duke of Normandy, in May, 1347, and was defended by a small English garrison under Sir Walter Manny, who held out bravely till the end of August, repelling numerous assaults. The defeat of Cressy then forced the Duke of Normandy to lead his army northward, and he was compelled to raise the siege.

Aix, Ile d' (Seven Years' War).

Fought March 4, 1758, when a British squadron of seven sail, under Sir Edward Hawke, attacked a French squadron of five ships of the line and six frigates, convoying forty transports, and drove them ashore on the Ile d'Aix. This delayed the French expedition to North America, and facilitated the capture of Cape Breton.

Aix-la-Chapelle (Wars of the French Revolution).

Fought March 3, 1795, between the French under Miranda and the Austrians under the Prince of Saxe-Coburg. The French were totally defeated, and fled in disorder, with a loss of 3,500 killed and wounded and 1,500 prisoners.

Aiznadin (Moslem Invasion of Syria).

Fought July 13, 633, between 45,000 Moslems under Khaled and 70,000 Imperial troops under Werdan. The Imperialists were routed with great slaughter, leaving Khaled to prosecute the siege of Damascus. The Moslems only admit a loss of 470.

Aladja Dagh (Russo-Turkish War).

Fought 1877, between the Russians under General Loris Melikoff, and the Turks under Mukhtar Pasha. The Russians were victorious, and Mukhtar was compelled to take refuge under the walls of Erzeroum.

Alamo, Storming of the (Texan Rising).

On February 22, 1836, General Santa Anna, with the advance guard of the Mexican army, appeared before the walls of the Alamo, a fortified mission station held by 145 Texans under Colonel Travis, who replied to a summons to surrender by a cannon shot. On March 1 the garrison was reinforced by 30 men, Santa Anna's force at this date being 4,000. On the 6th 2,500 Mexicans assaulted the fort, and at the third attempt effected an entrance. The building was defended room by room, the church within the enclosure being the last building captured, when all the survivors were put to the sword. The victory cost the Mexicans 400 killed and many wounded. " Remember the Alamo " became the watchword of the Texans.

Aland (Russo-Swedish Wars).

Fought July, 1714, between the Russian fleet of 30 ships of the line and 180 galleys under Admiral Apraxine, and the Swedish, about one-third of that strength, under Admiral Erinschild. The Swedes sought to prevent the landing of a Russian force on the island of Aland, and fought an unequal combat for three hours, when they were overpowered and forced to retire. The Czar, Peter the Great, who was serving under Apraxine as Rear-Admiral, captured Erinschild's flagship.

Alarcos (Moorish Empire in Spain).

Fought July 19, 1195, between the Moors under Yakub el Maasur, and the Spaniards under Alfonso VIII of Castile. The Spaniards were utterly routed, and very few escaped to Calatrava. The Moors claimed to have taken 30,000 prisoners.

Albuera (Peninsular War).

Fought May 16, 1811, between the allied British, Portuguese and Spanish forces, numbering 46,000, of whom 7,000 only were British infantry, the whole army being under the command of Marshal Beresford, and 33,000 French under Marshal Soult. The French attacked Beresford's position, and the

Spaniards offering but a poor resistance, defeat was only averted by the extraordinary valour of the British troops, especially of the Fusilier Brigade, which came into action when the day seemed lost, and drove the French from the field. Of the 7,000 British, but 1,800 were left standing. The French lost over 8,000, including five generals.

Alcantara (War of the Spanish Succession).

Fought 1706, when a force of British and Portuguese under Lord Galway attacked and drove out of Alcantara the garrison, consisting of a portion of Marshal Berwick's army. Ten French battalions laid down their arms, and 60 guns were captured.

Aleppo (Moslem Invasion of Syria).

This place was besieged by the Moslems under Abu Obeidah and Khaled in 638, and the city almost immediately surrendered, but the garrison retired to the citadel, where under Youkinna it maintained a stubborn defence for five months, and caused heavy loss to the besiegers. At last the citadel was taken by surprise, and Youkinna became a convert to Mohammedanism. This was the last serious resistance offered in Syria to the invading Moslems.

Aleppo (Tartar Invasion of Syria).

Fought November 11, 1400, between the Tartars under Tamerlane, and the Turks under the Syrian Emirs. Instead of standing a siege, the Emirs sallied out to meet Tamerlane in the open field, and suffered a disastrous defeat. They were driven back into Aleppo with the loss of many thousands, and a few days later the Tartars sacked the city and captured the citadel.

Aleppo (Ottoman Wars).

Fought 1516, between the Turks under Selim I, and the Egyptians under the Mameluke Sultan, Tooman Beg. After a sanguinary engagement, the Egyptians were utterly routed, and Selim added the whole of Syria to the Ottoman dominions.

Alesia (Gallic War).

Siege was laid to the town by the Romans under Cæsar, B.C. 52, and it was defended by the Gauls, numbering 80,000 infantry and 15,000 cavalry under Vercingetorix, the Romans being about 50,000 strong. An attempt was made by the Belgi, with an army of 260,000 warriors, to relieve the town, but they were met and routed by Labienus with terrific slaughter. This disaster so discouraged the garrison that the town immediately surrendered, Vercingetorix being sent a prisoner to Rome, where five years later he was beheaded as a rebellious subject of Rome.

Alessandria (Wars of the French Revolution).

Fought June 18, 1799, between the French, 14,000 strong under Moreau, and the Imperialists under Bellegarde. The French gained a signal victory, the loss of the Imperialists being 1,500 men and 5 guns.

Alexandria (Moslem Invasion of Egypt).

This city, the capital of Egypt, was besieged by the Moslems, under Amrou, in 638, and after a defence of fourteen months, in the course of which the besiegers lost 23,000 men, surrendered, leaving the victors undisputed masters of Egypt.

Alexandria (British Invasion of Egypt).

Fought March 21, 1801, between the French under General Menou, and the British expeditionary force under Sir Ralph Abercromby. The French cavalry charged the British right, but were repulsed, and after hard fighting the French were defeated and driven under the walls of Alexandria. Among those who fell was Sir Ralph Abercromby, mortally wounded.

Alexandria (Arabi's Rebellion).

Arabi Pasha having refused to cease work upon the forts of Alexandria, the Admiral, Sir Beauchamp Seymour, who had under his command a fleet of 8 battleships and 5 gunboats, decided to shell them. He opened fire on the morning of July 11, 1882, and the bombardment continued till the evening of the 12th, when the forts were totally destroyed, and the garrison abandoned the city. The gunboat *Condor*, under Lord Charles Beresford, particularly distinguished herself, running close in under the forts, and doing considerable damage.

Alford (Civil War).

Fought July 2, 1645, between the Royalists under Montrose, and the Covenanters under General Baillie. Baillie crossed the Don to attack Montrose, whom he imagined to be in retreat, but who was really waiting for him in a well-chosen position. The attack was repulsed, the Covenanters being routed with heavy loss.

Algeciras Bay (Napoleonic Wars).

Fought July 8, 1801, between a British squadron of 7 ships of the line, 1 frigate and 1 brig, under Sir James Saumarez, and a French squadron of 3 line-of-battle ships and 1 frigate, under Admiral Linois. The French were aided by the Spanish gunboats and the shore batteries, and Saumarez lost the *Hannibal*, which ran ashore, and was captured by the French. The British lost 121 killed and 240 wounded. The French lost 306 killed. On July 12, the French squadron, which had been reinforced meanwhile by 5 Spanish ships of the line, was again attacked by Sir James Saumarez, who succeeded in capturing the *St. Antoine* and blowing up the *Hermenegilda*. The British lost only 17 killed and 100 wounded ; the allies, 2,000, chiefly in the *Hermenegilda*.

Algheri.

Fought 1353, between the Aragonese under Pedro IV (the Great) and the Genoese. Pedro won a complete victory, driving the Genoese out of Sardinia, the whole of which island became an appanage of the crown of Aragon.

Algiers.

This town was attacked July 8, 1775, by a Spanish force of 51 ships of war and 26,000 men under Don Pedro de Castijon and Count O'Reilly. After a severe conflict, the . Spaniards failed to dislodge their opponents, and retired, with a loss of over 3,000 killed and wounded. The Algerines lost about 5,000.

Algiers, Bombardment of.

In 1816 Lord Exmouth, in command of 19 British war ships, and accompanied by 6 Dutch ships under Van Capellan, bombarded the forts of Algiers, mounting 500 guns. The bombardment lasted for about eight hours, and resulted in the destruction of the forts and a large part of the city. The Dey then gave way, and agreed to the total abolition of Christian slavery in his dominions. The loss of the allies amounted to 885 killed and wounded ; that of the Algerines to over 6,000.

Alhama (War of Granada).

This fortress, one of the ring of strong places protecting the Moorish capital, Granada, was surprised by a small party of Spaniards, under Juan de Ortiga, in the early morning of February 28, 1482. They scaled the ramparts unperceived, and opened the gates to the Spanish army. The garrison continued to defend the streets most obstinately, and it was only after hard fighting that the Spaniards mastered the town. An attempt was made to recapture the place by Abul Hasan, King of Granada, who set down before it, with 50,000 Moors. March 5, 1482. The garrison, under the Marquis of Cadiz, made a gallant defence, and on the 29th, Abul Hasan,

alarmed by the approach of a strong relieving army under Ferdinand, raised the siege.

Alhandega (Moorish Empire in Spain).

Fought 939, between the Moors under Abd al Rahman, and the Christians under Ramiro II of Leon. The Moors, 100,000 strong, were besieging Zamora, when they were attacked by Ramiro, who, aided by a sortie of the garrison, utterly routed them. In the battle 20,000 Moors fell, and 40,000 are said to have been drowned in the moat surrounding the city.

Alicante (War of the Spanish Succession).

On June 29, 1706, Alicante was taken by a British squadron of 5 ships under Sir George Byng. The fleet attacked the city walls, while the suburbs were occupied by a landing party of marines under Sir John Jennings. The place was captured with a loss to the British of only 30 killed and 80 wounded.

Aligurh (First Mahratta War).

This fortress, the arsenal of Sindhia of Gwalior, was captured August 29, 1803, by the 76th Highlanders under Colonel Monson, forming part of General Lake's army. The place was strongly fortified and surrounded by a ditch 100 feet wide, containing 10 feet of water. The Highlanders carried the fortress by storm, blowing in the main gate, and fighting their way from room to room till the place was captured. Two hundred and eighty-one guns were taken. The British loss amounted to 223 killed and wounded.

Aliwal (First Sikh War).

Fought January 28, 1846, between the British, 10,000 strong, under Sir Harry Smith, and 20,000 Sikhs under Runjur Singh. The troops of the Khalsa withstood three charges of the British cavalry with splendid bravery, but at last broke and fled, losing many drowned in the Sutlej, besides those left on the field. The British captured 67 guns.

Aljubarotta.

Fought August, 1385, between the Castilians, under John I, in support of the claim of Beatrix of Castile to the throne of Portugal, and the Portuguese under the Regent John. The Portuguese inflicted a crushing defeat upon the Spaniards, and John I was compelled to withdraw his troops, and renounce his sister's claim.

Alkmaar (Netherlands War of Independence).

Siege was laid to this place August 21, 1573, by 16,000 Spaniards under Don Frederico de Toledo. It was defended by a garrison of 800 soldiers and 1,300 armed burghers. On September 18, an assault was delivered, which was repulsed, with a loss to the besiegers of 1,000 men, while only 37 of the garrison fell. The opening of the dykes at last rendered the position of the Spaniards most precarious, and on October 8 the siege was raised.

Alkmaar (Wars of the French Revolution).

Fought October 2, 1799, between 30,000 British and Russians under the Duke of York, and the French, in about equal strength, under Brune. The action began by the Russians driving in the French advanced posts. Meanwhile the Duke of York had outflanked them, and as soon as he was in position a simultaneous attack on the French left and centre forced Brune to abandon the key of his position, Alkmaar, which was at once occupied by the allies.

Allia, The (First Invasion of the Gauls).

Fought July 16, 389 B.C., between the Romans, 40,000 strong, under Quintus Sulpicius, and the Gauls, about equal in numbers, under Brennus. The Romans took post on the Allia to check the advance of the Gauls on Rome. Here they were attacked by Brennus, who routed the right wing, where the younger soldiers were posted, and then broke the Roman centre and left, putting them to flight with enormous loss.

Alma (Crimean War).

Fought September 20, 1854, between the Russians, 40,000 strong, under Prince Mentschikoff, and the allied British and French armies, 26,000 strong, under Lord Raglan and Marshal St. Arnaud. The bulk of the fighting fell upon the British Second and Light Divisions and the Guards, who carried the heights held by the Russians at the point of the bayonet, and utterly routed them. The Russians lost 1,200 killed, and left 4,700 prisoners, many of them wounded, in the hands of the allies. The British loss amounted to 3,000 killed and wounded ; that of the French to 1,000.

Almanza (War of the Spanish Succession).

Fought April 25, 1707, between the French under Marshal Berwick, and the British and Portuguese under Lord Galway and the Marques das Minas. Galway, though inferior in cavalry, attacked at first with success, but the Portuguese on the right broke and fled, and the British centre, attacked in front and flank simultaneously, was routed and forced to surrender. As a consequence of this defeat, the whole of Spain was lost to Charles with the exception of Catalonia.

Almenara (War of the Spanish Succession).

Fought July 10, 1710, when the British contingent of the Archduke Charles' army, under General Stanhope, attacked and defeated the Spaniards under Philip V, after severe fighting. So complete was the rout that Philip's army was only saved by the fall of night from complete destruction.

Almorah (Gurkha War).

Fought April 25, 1815, when 2,000 British regulars under Colonel Nicolls and a force of irregular troops under Colonel Gardiner assaulted and captured the heights of the town of Almorah. The result of this victory was the surrender of the province of Kumaon and all its fortresses.

Alne (Scottish Wars).

Fought November 13, 1093, between the Scots under Malcolm Canmore and the English. The Scots were totally defeated, and Malcolm and his eldest son Edward slain in the battle.

Alresford (Civil War).

Fought March 29, 1644, between the Royalists under the Earl of Brentford and Sir Ralph Hopton, and the Parliamentarians under Sir William Waller. The Parliament forces were victorious, but their losses were so severe that Waller was unable to follow up his advantage, and the Royalists made an orderly retreat.

Alsen (Schleswig-Holstein War).

This island, in which the Danish garrison of Düppel had taken refuge, was captured by the Prussians, who crossed from the mainland in boats on the night of June 29, 1864, and under a heavy fire carried the Danish entrenchments, and compelled them to surrender. This was the last engagement of the war.

Altendorf (Thirty Years' War).

Fought August 24, 1632, between Gustavus Adolphus, with 40,000 Swedes and Germans, and the Imperialists, of about equal numbers, under Wallenstein. Wallenstein was very strongly posted on the hill and in the ruined castle of the Altenwald, and after a day spent in fruitless assaults, the King was forced to retire, having lost about 2,300 in killed and wounded. The defenders admitted a loss of 70 officers and 2,000 men killed, besides wounded and prisoners.

Alto Pascio (Guelfs and Ghibellines).

Fought 1325, between the Ghibellines under Castruccio Castracane of Lucca, and the Florentine Guelfs. The Florentines were defeated with heavy loss, among the trophies taken by Castracane being the *carroccio* of Florence.

Amakusa (Revolt of the Christians).

In 1638, the castle of Amakusa, held by 30,000 rebels under Masada Shiro, was captured after very hard fighting by the troops of the Shôgun, under Matsudaira Nobutsuna. The defenders set fire to the castle, and perished to the last man, either in the flames or by the sword.

Amalinde (Kaffir Wars).

Fought 1818 between the Gaikas and the forces of Ndlambi, in which the former were utterly routed.

Amatola Mountain (Kaffir Wars).

Fought 1846, between the Kaffirs under Sandilli, and the British and Cape troops under Colonels Campbell and Somerset. Sandilli was totally defeated, but, rallying his forces, he made a successful attack on the British baggage train, the loss of which forced them to retire.

Ambate (Conquest of Peru).

Fought 1532, between the two Peruvian chiefs Atahualpa and Huascar, in which the latter suffered a complete defeat.

Ambracian Gulf.

Fought B.C. 435, when a Corinthian fleet of 75 ships attempted the relief of Epidamnus, which was besieged by the Corcyreans, and was defeated with heavy loss by 80 Corcyrean triremes.

Ambur.

Fought 1749, between the army of Anwar-ud-din, Nawab of Arcot, 20,000 strong, and the combined forces of Muzuffer Jung and Chunda Sahib, aided by a French contingent under M. d'Auteil. Anwar-ud-din was defeated and slain, and Muzuffer Jung assumed the title of Subahdar of the Deccan, Chunda Sahib that of Nawab of Arcot.

Ambur.

This strong fortress was held by a garrison of 500 Sepoys, under Captain Calvert, and a detachment of Mysore troops under Mukhlis Khan. This man had assumed the status of an independent chief, but being suspected of intriguing with Hyder Ali, was arrested by Calvert. Hyder laid siege to the place November 10, 1767 ; but Calvert, now secure from treachery within, held out with his small garrison till December 6, when the approach of a relieving force obliged Hyder to raise the siege.

Amida (Persian Wars).

This fortress, defended by a Roman garrison, was besieged, and after a vigorous defence taken by storm by the Persians under Sapor II in 359. The garrison and inhabitants were put to the sword. The siege, which lasted 73 days, cost the Persians 30,000 men, and so weakened Sapor that he was compelled to relinquish his designs upon the Eastern Empire.

The fortress was again besieged by the Persians under Kobad in 503, being defended as before by a Roman garrison. After a defence of three months, which cost the besiegers 50,000 men, a weakly defended tower was surprised at night, and on the following day the Persians, headed by their King, scaled the walls, and massacred 80,000 of the garrison and inhabitants.

Amiens (Franco-German War).

Fought November 27, 1870, between the French under General Faure, and the Germans under Manteuffel. The French were compelled to abandon the city, but the Germans failed to secure a decisive victory. The French lost 1,383 killed and wounded, and 1,000 missing ; the Germans, 76 officers and 1,216 men.

Amoaful (Second Ashanti War).

Fought January 31, 1874, when the British expeditionary force under Sir Garnet Wolseley defeated the Ashantis after a desperate resistance, which cost the assailants 16 officers and 174 men killed and wounded. The 42nd Regiment, which led the attack, lost 9 officers and 105 men.

Amorium (Moslem Invasion of Asia Minor).

Fought 838, between the Moslems under the Caliph Motassem, and the Greeks under Theophilus. Thirty thousand Persian horsemen, serving under the Emperor, succeeded in breaking the Moslem line, but the Greeks themselves were overthrown by the Moslems, and the day ended in a complete rout of the Imperial army. Motassem then laid siege to Amorium, and after a defence of 55 days, which cost the besiegers 70,000 men, the gates were opened by treachery, and 30,000 Christians were massacred.

Amphipolis (Peloponnesian War).

Fought March 422 B.C. between 1,500 Athenians, with a contingent of allies under Cleon, and the Spartans, 2,000 hoplites, besides light armed troops, under Brasidas. Cleon advanced to attack Amphipolis, but finding the garrison preparing for a sortie, wheeled about and commenced to retreat. He was at once assailed by Brasidas, and his left fled without striking a blow. The Athenian right and centre offered some resistance, but in the end were routed with heavy loss. Both Brasidas and Cleon fell, the latter while fleeing from the field.

Amstetten (Campaign of the Danube).

Fought November 5, 1805, when the Russians retiring on Vienna fought a rear-guard action against Murat's cavalry and a portion of Lannes' corps, in which they were defeated with a loss of 1,000 killed, wounded, and prisoners.

Añaquito (Conquest of Peru).

Fought January 8, 1546, between the troops of the Viceroy, Blasco Nuñez, and those of Gonzalo Pizarro. Pizarro gained a signal victory, the Viceroy being among the slain, and in consequence the Government of Peru fell into Pizarro's hands.

Ancona (Unification of Italy).

This place was attacked, September, 1860, by the Piedmontese fleet of 13 warships under Admiral Persano, and the army of General Cialdini. It was defended by a small Papal garrison under La Moricière, and after a resistance of over a week, at the end of which time Persano forced the boom guarding the harbour, La Moricière capitulated.

Ancrum Moor (Scottish Wars).

Fought February 17, 1545, between the English under Sir Ralph Evans, and the Scots under the Earl of Angus. The Borderers who had joined the English deserted during the action, with the result that the Scots were completely victorious.

Ancyræ.

Fought B.C. 242, between the Syrians under Seleucus Callinicus, and the rebels under his brother Hierax, aided by a large contingent of Gauls. After a desperate struggle, in which Hierax nearly lost his life at the hands of his barbarian auxiliaries, Seleucus was utterly routed.

Angora (Tartar Invasion of Asia Minor).

Fought June 30, 1402, between the Tartars under Tamerlane, and the Turks under Bajazet I. The numbers engaged are variously estimated at from one to two millions, Tamerlane, it is said, having at least 800,000 men in the field. The Turks were totally defeated, Bajazet and one of his sons being captured, while another son was killed.

Angostura (Americo-Mexican War).

Fought February 21, 1847, between the Mexicans under Santa Anna and the Americans under General Scott, when the Mexicans were totally defeated.

Angostura (Paraguayan War).

Fought December 22 to 27, 1868, between the Paraguayans under Lopez, and the allied armies of the Argentine Republic, Brazil, and Uruguay. Lopez held his position for six days against the greatly superior forces of the allies, but was then compelled to retire, leaving in the hands of the enemy 1,000 prisoners and 6 guns.

Antietam (American Civil War).

Fought September 17, 1862, between the main Confederate army under General Lee, and the Federals under General M'Clellan. On the morning of the 17th Lee had only 35,000 men on the ground against M'Clellan's 95,000. The Federals strongly attacked Lee's left, and after a stubborn fight drove it back, but reinforcements arriving, Lee resumed the offensive, and recovered his lost positions. On the following day neither side was disposed to resume the struggle, and the battle was therefore indecisive. The Federals lost 12,460 men ; the Confederates about 9,000.

Antioch.

Fought B.C. 244, between the Syrians under Seleucus Callinicus and the Egyptians under Ptolemy Energetes. Seleucus was routed and compelled to take refuge within the walls of Antioch.

Antioch (Aurelian's Expedition to Palmyra).

Fought B.C. 272, between the Palmyrenians under Zenobia, and the Romans under the Emperor Aurelian. Zenobia's heavy cavalry defeated and drove from the field the Roman horse, but her infantry was unable to withstand the charge of the legionaries, and she was totally defeated.

Antioch (First Crusade).

The city was besieged, October 21, 1097, by the Crusaders under Godefroi de Bouillon, and defended by a Saracen garrison under Baghasian. The siege was unskilfully conducted, and provisions and munitions ran short in the Christian camp, with the result that the place held out till June 3, 1098, when it was taken by stratagem. An indiscriminate massacre followed, in which 10,000 of the defenders perished. On the 28th of the same month the Crusading army was attacked outside Antioch by a force of Saracens under Kirboga. Kirboga concentrated his attack against one wing of the Christians, and outflanked it, but was then assailed by the main body, and driven off with heavy loss.

Antium (War of Chiozza).

Fought May 30, 1378, when Vittorio Pisani, with 14 Venetian galleys, defeated the Genoese fleet under Fieschi. The Genoese lost 6 ships, and Fieschi was taken prisoner.

Antwerp (Netherlands War of Independence).

This city was sacked by the Spaniards, November 4, 1576. It was defended by 6,000 troops, mostly Walloons, who offered little resistance to the 5,600 Spaniards under Sancho d'Avila, who formed the attacking force. Having effected an entrance, the Spaniards proceeded to massacre the inhabitants, of whom 8,000 are said to have perished. This event is known as the Spanish Fury.

Antwerp (Liberation of Belgium).

When Holland refused to recognize the London Protocol creating Belgium into an independent State, the French laid siege to Antwerp, November, 1832. The city, which was defended by Chassé, held out till December 23, when, the citadel being demolished by the French fire, it was forced to capitulate.

Aong (Indian Mutiny).

Fought July 15, 1857, between the British relieving force under Havelock and the mutineers who were opposing their advance on Cawnpore. The rebels were defeated and driven from their entrenchments.

Aquae Sextiae (Cimbric War).

Fought B.C. 102, when the Teutones under the king, Teutobod, were totally routed by the Romans under Marius.

Aquidaban (Paraguayan War).

The last stand of the Paraguayans against the allied armies of the Argentine Republic, Brazil, and Uruguay, May 1, 1870. Lopez, with a small force of Paraguayans and 5,000 Indians, met the attack of the allies under General Camera on the banks of the Aquidaban, and after a sanguinary engagement, in which he and the Vice-President Sanchez fell, his army was cut to pieces, and the war ended. During the war the population of Paraguay was reduced from 1,500,000 to 221,000, of whom only 29,000 were males over fifteen years of age.

Aquileia (Eugenius' Usurpation).

Fought September 6 and 7, 394, between Theodosius, Emperor of the East, and Eugenius, the usurping Emperor of the West, whose army was commanded by Arbogastes. The first day's fighting went against Theodosius, who was only saved by darkness from a severe reverse, but during the night a force sent by Arbogastes to secure the passes in Theodosius' rear, deserted to his standard, and thus reinforced and aided by a dust storm which blew in the faces of his antagonists and disordered their ranks, he on the following day gained a signal victory.

Aras (First Mahratta War).

Fought May 18, 1775, between Raghunath Rao, the claimant to the Peshwaship, with 20,000 Mahrattas, and 2,500 British troops under Colonel Keating, and the army of the Mahratta chieftains, 25,000 strong under Hari Pant Phunhay. Raghunath's undisciplined levies fled, and threw the British line into confusion ; but they rallied, and after hard fighting repulsed the Mahrattas with heavy loss. The British lost 222, including 11 officers.

Arausio (Fourth Gallic Invasion).

Fought B.C. 105, when the Gauls under Boiorix totally routed two consular armies under Cæpio and Cn. Mallius Maximus. It is said that 80,000 Romans fell.

Arbela (Alexander's Asiatic Campaign).

Fought October 31, 331 B.C., between 47,000 Macedonians under Alexander the Great, and the Persian army, three or four times as numerous, under Darius Codomannus. Alexander, who led the Macedonian right wing, forced a passage between the Persian left and centre, and attacked the centre on the flank. After a stubborn resistance, and though meanwhile the Macedonian left had been hard pressed, the Persians gave way, and Darius taking to flight, the whole army fled in confusion, and was routed with enormous loss, especially at the passage of the Lycas, which barred their retreat. This victory made Alexander master of Asia.

Arcis-sur-Aube (Allied Invasion of France).

Fought March 21, 1814, between 23,000 French under Napoleon, and 60,000 allies under Schwartzenberg. The French made a gallant stand against superior numbers, and in the end effected an orderly retreat, with a loss of about 2,000. The allies' losses were considerably heavier.

Arcola (Napoleon's Italian Campaigns).

Fought November 15, 16, and 17, 1796, between the main Austrian army under Alvinzi, and the French under Napoleon. Napoleon's object was to drive back Alvinzi before he could effect a junction with Davidowich, who was descending from the Tyrol. The village of Arcola was occupied on the 15th, after severe fighting, in which Napoleon was in great personal danger on the bridge, but it

c

was evacuated during the night. On the 16th Napoleon again attacked the village, but the Austrians held their ground. On the 17th he turned the position, and Davidowich still remaining inactive, Alvinzi was driven back, with losses variously estimated at from 8,000 to 18,000. The French also lost heavily.

Arcot.

This fortress was captured by Clive, with a force of 200 Europeans and 300 Sepoys, in August, 1751. The garrison, 1,100 strong, offered no resistance, but marched out on Clive's approach. In the course of the autumn Arcot was beleaguered by an army of 10,000 natives, and 150 Frenchmen under Chunda Sahib, the French nominee for the Nawabship of Arcot. Against this overwhelming force, Clive, whose garrison had been reduced by sickness to 120 Europeans, and less than 200 Sepoys, held out for seven weeks, till the approach of a Mahratta army forced Chunda Sahib to raise the siege. The garrison had 45 Europeans and 30 Sepoys killed.

Argaum (Second Mahratta War).

Fought November 28, 1803, between the British under Wellesley (the Duke of Wellington) and the forces of the Rajah of Berar, under Sindhia of Gwalior. Three of Wellesley's battalions, which had previously fought well, on this occasion broke and fled, and the situation was at one time very serious. Wellesley, however, succeeded in rallying them, and in the end defeated the Mahrattas, with the loss of all their guns and baggage. The British lost 346 killed and wounded. This victory ended the Second Mahratta War.

Argentaria (Invasion of the Alemanni).

Fought May, 378, between the Romans under Gratianus and the Alemanni under Priarius. The Alemanni were overwhelmed by the Roman legionaries, though they stood their ground bravely, and only 5,000 escaped from the field. Priarius was slain.

Argentoratum.

Fought August, 357, between 13,000 Romans under Julian, and a vastly superior army of Alemanni under Chnodomar. The Romans attacked the German lines shortly before nightfall, after a long march, and though the right wing, under Julian, was at first driven in, they were rallied by their general, and the left and centre pressing on, the Alemanni were totally routed, with a loss of 6,000, in addition to those who fell in the flight. The Romans lost 4 tribunes and 243 soldiers only. Chnodomar was taken prisoner.

Arginusæ (Peloponnesian War).

Fought B.C. 406, between 150 Athenian triremes under Thrasyllus and other generals, and 120 Peloponnesian ships under Callicratidas. The Peloponnesians were routed, with a loss of 70 vessels, sunk or taken, and Callicratidas slain. The Athenians lost 25 ships with their crews, and the generals were brought to trial for not having taken proper steps to rescue the men of the disabled ships. They were convicted, and six of them, including Thrasyllus, executed. This victory temporarily restored to Athens the command of the sea.

Argos (Roman Invasion of Greece).

Fought B.C. 195, between Nabis of Sparta, with 15,000 men, and 50,000 Romans and Macedonians under Flaminius. Nabis was totally defeated, and though allowed to retain Sparta, was compelled to restore to the Achæan league all his foreign possessions.

Arikera (Second Mysore War).

Fought May 13, 1791, between the British under Lord Cornwallis, and the forces of Tippu Sahib. The latter was encamped between Arikera and Seringapatam, and was attacked by Cornwallis, who attempted to surprise him by a night march, but was foiled by heavy rain. A frontal attack on Tippu's position was, however, successful, and, aided by a flank movement under Maxwell, resulted in the total defeat of the Mysore troops, with a loss of over 2,000. The British loss amounted to 500. This is also known as the battle of Carigat.

Arius, The.

Fought B.C. 214, between the Syrians under Antiochus the Great, and the Parthians and Bactrians under Arsaces III, and Euthydemus. Antiochus was severely wounded, but remained at the head of his troops, and completely routed the enemy with enormous loss.

Arkenholm (Douglas Rebellion).

Fought May 12, 1455, between the troops of James II of Scotland and the rebels under the Douglas brothers. The rebels were completely defeated. Archibald Douglas was killed, Hugh captured, and James, Earl of Douglas, forced to take refuge in England.

Arklow (Irish Rebellion).

Fought 1798, when General Needham, with about 1,400 Militia and Volunteers, defended the town from the attack of 27,000 rebels led by Father John Murphy. The rebels were beaten off with great slaughter, and their intended advance on Dublin prevented.

Armada, The Invincible.

The fight with the Spanish Armada in the Channel began on Sunday, July 21, 1588, and lasted with intervals until the 30th. The Armada consisted of 130 ships, many of large size, under the command of the Duke of Medina Sidonia. The English fleet numbered 197 in all, but only 34 were Queen's ships, and of these but 8 were over 600 tons burden. Lord Howard of Effingham commanded, with Drake and Hawkins as his lieutenants. The English vessels hung on to the flanks of the Spanish ships as they sailed up channel, harassing them in every way, and doing considerable damage, until the Armada anchored in Calais roads. Here many of their finest vessels were captured or destroyed by fire-ships, and finally on the 30th, Medina Sidonia decided to attempt to escape northwards. His fleet was scattered by storms, and many wrecked on the Scotch and Irish coasts, and in the end only about one-half of the Armada returned to Spain.

Arnee.

Fought 1751, shortly after the relief of Arcot, between 900 British troops, under Clive, with 600 Mahratta horse under Basin Rao, and a French force of 4,800, including 300 Europeans, who were in charge of a convoy of treasure. Clive took up a position in swampy ground, crossed by a causeway along which the convoy must pass. The French were thrown into disorder, and forced to retreat, but night saved them from complete destruction. The treasure was captured.

Arnee (First Mysore War).

An indecisive action fought June 7, 1782, between the British under Sir Eyre Coote, and the Mysore troops under Hyder Ali.

Arques (Eighth Civil War).

Fought September 23, 1589, between 5,000 Huguenots under Henri IV, and 30,000 Leaguers under the Duc de Mayenne. Henri had taken up a strong position, defended by marshy ground, and of such a nature that Mayenne could only bring against the king 5,000 troops at a time, thus neutralizing the disparity of numbers. He repulsed attack after attack, with heavy loss to the assailants, and eventually Mayenne was forced to withdraw, with the loss of about half his army.

Arrah (Indian Mutiny).

A house in Arrah was, in 1857, defended by Mr. Boyle, with 16 Englishmen and 60 Sikh police, against the attacks of three revolted native regiments, led by a Zemindar named Kur Singh. This small garrison held out from July 25 till August 3, when they were relieved by a small field force under Major Vincent Eyre.

Arras (Wars of Louis XIV).

This place, held by a French garrison, was besieged August, 1654, by the Spaniards under the Great Condé. On the 24th a relieving army under Turenne attacked the Spanish lines, and totally routed them with a loss of 3,000 men. Condé succeeded in rallying the remainder of his army, and made a masterly retreat to Cambray.

Arretium (Etruscan War).

Fought B.C. 283, when the consular army of L. Cæcilius Metellus, marching to the relief of Arretium, which the Etruscans were besieging, met with a disastrous defeat. Thirteen thousand, including Metellus, were slain, and the rest made prisoners.

Arroyo Grande (Uruguayan War of Independence).

Fought 1842, between the Argentine troops under Oribe, and the Uruguayans under Ribera. Ribera was totally defeated, and Oribe proceeded to lay siege to Montevideo.

Arsouf (Third Crusade).

Fought 1192, between the English Crusaders under Richard Cœur de Lion, and the Saracens, 300,000 strong under Saladin. The Saracens made a desperate onslaught on the English, and both their wings gave way, but the centre under the king stood firm and finally drove back the Moslems in great disorder, with a loss of 40,000 men.

Ascalon (First Crusade).

Fought August 19, 1099, between the Crusaders under Godefroi de Bouillon, and the Saracens under Kilidj Arslan. The Crusaders gained a signal victory, and for a time the Moslem resistance to the Christian occupation of the Holy Land came to an end.

Asculum (Pyrrhus' Invasion of Italy).

Fought B.C. 279, between 45,000 Romans under Sulpicius Saverrio and P. Decius Mus, and the Epirots, with their Italian allies, in about equal force. The Romans fought to raise the siege of Asculum, but were finally routed by the Epirot cavalry and elephants, and driven back to their camp with a loss of 6,000. The Epirots lost 3,000.

Asculum (Social War).

Fought B.C. 89, between 75,000 Romans under Strabo, who was besieging the town, and 60,000 Italians under Judacilius, who had marched to its relief. The Romans were victorious, but Judacilius succeeded in throwing a considerable portion of his army into the beleagured city.

Ashdown (Danish Invasion).

Fought 871, between the West Saxons under Æthelred and the Danes under Bag Secg and Halfdene. Largely owing to the brilliant leading of Alfred (the Great), who commanded one of the wings, the Danes, after a desperate conflict, which lasted throughout the day, were finally put to flight, having lost one of their kings and five jarls.

Ashtee (Third Mahratta War).

Fought February 19, 1818, between the army of the Peshwá, Baji Rao, under Gokla, and the British under General Smith. The Peshwá fled before the action began, and Gokla, charging at the head of his cavalry, was killed, whereupon the Mahrattas broke and fled in confusion.

Asirghur (Third Mahratta War).

This fortress, held by Jeswunt Rao, with a strong Mahratta garrison, was besieged by a British force under Sir John Malcolm and General Doveton, March 18, 1819. On the 21st the garrison was driven into the upper fort, and after a continuous bombardment, Jeswunt Rao surrendered April 7. The British loss during the siege was 313 killed and wounded ; that of the garrison somewhat less.

Askultsik (Ottoman Wars).

Fought 1828, between 30,000 Turks and the Russians, 17,000 strong, under General Paskiewitch. The Turks were routed, and their camp, with all artillery and baggage, captured. Paskiewitch then laid siege to the town, which was defended by a garrison of 50,000 men, and after a siege of three weeks, carried it by storm, August 28.

Aspendus.

Fought B.C. 191, between the Syrian fleet of Antiochus the Great, under Hannibal, and a Rhodian squadron under Eudamus. Though Hannibal was in superior force, he suffered a severe defeat.

Aspern (Campaign of Wagram).

Fought May 21 and 22, 1809, between 36,000 French under Napoleon, and 70,000 Austrians under the Archduke Charles. The battle commenced about four p.m. on the 21st by an attack on the French position at Aspern, and at nightfall the Austrians had established a lodgment in the village. On the 22nd, both armies having been reinforced during the night, the combat was renewed round Aspern, which was taken and retaken ten times, while Essling was the scene of an equally desperate conflict. Towards evening the bridge by which Napoleon had crossed the Danube was swept away, and Napoleon was compelled to retire. Each side lost about 20,000 men, and both claimed the victory. Among the French who fell were Marshal Lannes and General St. Hilaire.

Aspromonte (Garibaldi's Rising).

Fought August 29, 1862, between a small force of " Red Shirts " under Garibaldi, and the royal troops under General Pallavicini. After a short engagement, in which Garibaldi was wounded, the " Red Shirts," largely outnumbered and surrounded, laid down their arms.

Assandun (Danish Invasion).

The last of the five battles fought in 1016 between the English under Edmund Ironside and the Danish invaders under Knut. Owing to the treachery of Ædric, who crossed over with the Hereford men in the course of the battle, the English were defeated, and shortly afterwards Knut was proclaimed King of England.

Assaye (First Mahratta War).

Fought September 23, 1803, when General Wellesley (the Duke of Wellington) with 4,500 British and native troops routed the army of Sindhia of Gwalior, over 30,000 strong. All the camp equipment and 100 guns were taken. The Duke always considered this the bloodiest action, for the numbers engaged, that he ever witnessed. The British loss amounted to 1,566, or more than one-third of Wellesley's entire force.

Astrakhan.

Siege was laid to this town, 1569, by the Turks under Selim II, who required it as a base for his projected invasion of Persia. It was held by a small Russian garrison, which made an obstinate defence, and was finally relieved by an army despatched to its assistance by Ivan the Terrible, which attacked the Turkish lines, and utterly routed them.

Atahualpa (Conquest of Peru).

Fought 1531, between 160 Spaniards under Pizarro, and 30,000 Peruvians, forming the escort of the Inca, Manco-Capac. The battle was nothing but a butchery, Pizarro, who had invited the Inca to visit him, falling upon the unsuspecting Peruvians, seizing Manco-Capac, and slaughtering 4,000 men, without the loss of a single Spaniard.

Atbara (Soudan Campaigns).

Fought April 8, 1898, between

the British and Egyptian army, 14,000 strong, under Sir Herbert Kitchener, and 18,000 Mahdists under Mahmad. The Mahdists occupied an entrenched zareeba on the Atbara, where they were attacked and utterly routed, with a loss in the zareeba of 5,000 killed and 1,000 prisoners, while many more fell in the pursuit. Mahmad was captured. The Anglo-Egyptian losses were 570 killed and wounded, including 29 British officers.

Athenry (Conquest of Ireland).

Fought 1316 between the English under William de Burgh and Richard de Bermingham, and the O'Connors under their chieftain, Feidlim. The O'Connors were defeated, 11,000 of the sept falling in the battle. This is the last appearance of the O'Connors as a clan in Irish history.

Atherton Moor.

See Adwalton Moor.

Auerstadt.

See Jena.

Augsburg.

Fought 900, between the Germans and the invading Hungarians. The Christians fought gallantly, but were overwhelmed by the numbers of the barbarian cavalry, and in the end suffered a signal defeat.

Auldearn (Civil War).

Fought May 9, 1645, when Montrose and his Highlanders defeated a largely superior force of Covenanters under Sir John Hurry, who was marching northward to raid the lands of the Gordons.

Auray.

Fought September 27, 1364, between the partisans of John de Montfort, and those of Charles of Blois, the rival claimants to the Dukedom of Brittany. The English party, under Sir John Chandos, were besieging Auray, when they were attacked by the French, who were led by Bertrand du Guesclin. Chandos' position, however, was very strong, and the French were unable to make any impression upon it. Meanwhile they were thrown into utter confusion by an attack on their flank, and were ultimately routed, with heavy loss, Charles of Blois being among the slain. Bertrand du Guesclin was captured. De Montfort was shortly afterwards acknowledged by Charles V of France as Duke of Brittany.

Aussig (Hussite War).

Fought 1426, between the Germans under the Emperor Sigismund, and the Taborites, the extreme section of the Hussites, under John Zisca. The Germans were signally defeated.

Austerlitz (Campaign of the Danube).

Fought December 2, 1805, between 50,000 Russians and 25,000 Austrians under Kutusoff, and 75,000 French under Napoleon. An attempt to turn the French flank failed, and led to the left of the allies being entirely cut off from their centre. Their left and centre were thus beaten in detail, and the right, which had at first held its own, was surrounded, and driven in disorder across a partially frozen lake, where many perished. The allies lost 20,000 killed, wounded, and prisoners, and a large number of guns. The French lost about 5,000. The battle is called the Battle of the Three Emperors, those of Russia, Austria, and France being all present with their respective armies.

Avaricum (Gallic War).

This place was made the head-quarters of the revolted Gauls under Vercingetorix, B.C. 53, and was besieged by Cæsar, with 50,000 Romans. The place was strongly defended, but supplies ran short, and Vercingetorix attempted to withdraw his troops. In this he was unsuccessful, and the Romans, delivering a vigorous assault, took possession of the town, and massacred the garrison and inhabitants.

Avus (Second Macedonian War).

Fought B.C. 198, between 20,000 Macedonians under Philip, and two Roman legions under T. Quinctius Flamininus. A force of 4,000 legionaries penetrated to the rear of Philip's camp, and when Flamininus attacked in front, they fell upon the Macedonian rear, and completely routed them, with a loss of 2,000.

Axarquia (War of Granada).

Fought March 20, 1483, between a Spanish force of 3,000 knights, and about 2,000 infantry, under the Marquis of Cadiz, and a strong Moorish force under Abul Hasan. The Spaniards were marching through the defile of Axarquia, on their way to attack Malaga, when they were assailed in front and flank, and totally routed, losing 800 killed and 1,600 prisoners. Among the killed were 400 men of rank.

Ayacucho (South American War of Independence).

Fought December 9, 1824, between the South American patriots, 5,780 strong, under Sucre, and the Spaniards, 9,310 in number, under Laserna. The latter were routed with a loss of 2,100 killed and wounded, and over 3,500 prisoners, including Laserna, in addition to 15 guns. The Patriots lost 979. This engagement, which is also know as the Battle of Candorcanqui, practically decided the question of South American independence.

Aylesford (Jutish Invasion).

Fought 456, between the Jutes under Hengist and Horsa, and the Britons under Vortigern. Horsa was slain in the battle, but the Jutes were victorious.

Azimghur (Indian Mutiny).

Fought April 15, 1858, between a British column, composed of three regiments of infantry and three of Sikh cavalry, under Sir Edward Layard, and the Dinapur mutineers, about 5,000 strong, under Kur Singh. The rebels were routed and dispersed, Kur Singh falling mortally wounded.

Azores.

In 1591, a fleet of 7 ships under Lord Thomas Howard was driven from Floris by the Spanish fleet under Don Alfonso Bassano. The action was chiefly remarkable for the gallant fight made by Sir Richard Grenville in the *Revenge*, which maintained an unequal struggle for nine hours, when her gallant commander was mortally wounded, and she surrendered at daybreak.

B

Badajos (Peninsular War).

On March 17, 1812, this fortress, held by a garrison of French, Hessians and Spaniards, 5,000 strong, under Phillipon, was invested by Wellington. The breaches were declared to be practicable on April 5, and an assault was ordered. After terrible slaughter, the town was taken, with a loss to the assailants of 3,500, the total British losses during the siege exceeding 5,000. Fearful excesses were committed after the assault, and for two days the troops were completely out of hand.

Baduli-ki-Serai (Indian Mutiny).

Fought June 8, 1857, when a British force, under Sir Henry Barnard, defeated a large body of mutineers, who were opposing their march to Delhi. All the rebels' guns were captured.

Bagdad (Tartar Invasion of Mesopotamia).

This city was captured by the Tartars under Tamerlane, July 23, 1401.

Bagradas (Civil War of Cæsar and Pompey.)

Fought B.C. 49, between the Cæsareans under Curio and the Numidians under Juba and Saburra, who adhered to the fortunes of Pompey. The Roman cavalry was cut to pieces, before the legionaries could come to its assistance, and eventually the Romans were surrounded, and cut down to a man, Curio being amongst the slain. This victory left the Pompeians masters of Africa.

Bahur (Seven Years' War).

Fought August, 1752, between the French, numbering 2,500, including natives, under M. Kirkjean, and 2,000 British troops, with 4,000 of Mohammed Ali's levies, under Major Lawrence. The French were totally defeated, losing heavily in men, guns and stores. This victory determined the Mahrattas, who were wavering, to throw in their lot with the British.

Balaclava (Crimean War).

Fought October 25, 1854, between 30,000 Russians under Prince Mentschikoff, and the British under Lord Raglan. The Russians, having driven the Turks from their redoubts at Kadikoi, entered the valley of Balaclava, where they were encountered and driven back by the Heavy Cavalry Brigade under General Scarlett. Later in the day, acting under a mistaken order, Lord Cardigan at the head of the Light Brigade, charged the Russian guns at the head of the valley, and captured their batteries. Being, however, shelled from all sides, he was compelled to retire with heavy loss. Of this famous feat of arms, General Pelissier is reported to have said, " C'est magnifique, mais ce n'est pas la guerre." Another feature of this singular battle was the repulse by the Highland Brigade, in line, of a charge of the Russian cavalry. The British losses were small, except in the case of the Light Brigade, whose casualties amounted to 272 out of 673 who took part in the charge.

Balls Bluff (American Civil War).
Fought October 21, 1861, between the Federals under General Stone, and the Confederates under General Evans. The Federals crossed the Potomac to attack the Southern position, but were repulsed, and driven back over the river in confusion losing 1,100 killed and wounded, 700 prisoners and the only three guns which they had succeeded in taking across. The Confederates lost 155 only.

Ballymore (Irish Rebellion).
Fought June 3, 1798, when Colonel Walpole, with 500 Royal troops, on the march to Enniscorthy, was surprised and overpowered by a body of rebels under Father Murphy. Walpole and the majority of his force were cut to pieces.

Baltimore (Second American War).
This city was attacked September 11, 1814, by a British fleet of ten sail, under Admiral Sir Alexander Cochrane, and a land force of 3,270 under General Ross, who fell during the action. The Americans, 17,000 strong, under General Winder, were defeated, but the British retired on the evening of the 13th. The British lost 46 killed and 300 wounded, the Americans, 20 killed, 90 wounded, and 200 prisoners.

Bamian (Tartar Invasion of Kharismia).
This city was invested by the Mongols under Genghiz Khan in 1221, and after an obstinate defence, lasting several months, was taken by storm. Genghiz, who had seen a favourite grandson killed during the progress of the siege, gave orders that neither woman nor child was to be spared, and the whole city with its inhabitants was wiped out.

Banda (Indian Mutiny).
Fought April 19, 1858, between a force of rather over 1,000 British troops under General Whitlock, and 7,000 mutineers under the Nawab of Banda. After an obstinate conflict the rebels were totally routed.

Banda Islands (Wars of the French Revolution).
These islands, forming part of the Dutch East Indian possessions, were captured March 8, 1796, by a British squadron under Admiral Peter Rainier.

Bands, The (Danish Invasion).
Fought 961, between the Scots under their king, Indulph, and the Danish pirates. The Danes were defeated, but Indulph fell in the battle.

Bangalore (Second Mysore War).
This place was besieged by the British under Lord Cornwallis, March 5, 1791, and notwithstanding numerous efforts to relieve it on the part of Tippu Sahib, it was taken by storm on the night of the 21st, Tippu's final attempt being beaten off by the reserve with heavy loss. The British casualties were few.

Bannockburn (Scottish Wars).
Fought June 24, 1314, between the Scots under Robert Bruce, and the English invaders under Edward II. Bruce's position was partly covered by

a marsh, and further strengthened by pitfalls, in which the English cavalry were entrapped, and defeated with great loss. The king escaped with difficulty and the invasion was abandoned.

Bapaume (Franco-German War).

Fought January 3, 1871, between the French under General Faidherbe, and the Germans under Von Goeben. The result was indecisive, and though the French gained some tactical successes, the result strategically was an advantage to the Germans, as General Faidherbe was compelled to desist from his attempt to raise the siege of Péronne. The Germans lost 52 officers and 698 men ; the French 53 officers and 1516 men killed and wounded, and 550 prisoners.

Barbosthenian Mountains (Wars of the Achæan League).

Fought 192 B.C. between the Spartans under Narbis, and the Achæan League under Philopœmen. Nabis was totally routed, with the loss of three-fourths of his troops.

Barcelona (War of the Spanish Succession).

This city, which was held for Philip V of Spain by a Spanish garrison, was besieged September 14, 1705, by the British under the Earl of Peterborough. After a short bombardment, the place surrendered, October 9.

Barnet (Wars of the Roses).

Fought April 14, 1471, between the Yorkists under Edward IV, and the Lancastrians under the Earl of Warwick. Warwick prepared to attack the king as he issued from Bar-

net, but Edward came out during the night and took up a position opposite Warwick unseen. The left of the Yorkists was outflanked and beaten, but their right outflanked and defeated the Lancastrian left, and then fell upon and routed the centre. Warwick was slain. The losses on the two sides are said to have amounted in all to 1,000 killed.

Barosa (Peninsular War).

In the course of the operations for the relief of Cadiz, General Graham, with 4,000 British troops, defeated Marshal Victor with 9,000 French, March 5, 1811. The French lost 2,000 killed and wounded, including two generals, 6 guns, 2 eagles, and 400 prisoners. The British losses amounted to 50 officers and 1,160 rank and file. A large Spanish force under La Peña stood idly by, and took no part in the action.

Barquisimeto (South American War of Independence).

Fought 1813, between the Colombian patrots under Simon Bolivar, and the Spanish Royalists, Bolivar gaining a complete victory.

Basing (Danish Invasion).

A victory of the Danish invaders in 871 over the West Saxons.

Bassano (Napoleon's Italian Campaigns).

Fought September 8, 1796, when Napoleon, who had on the previous day destroyed the Austrian vanguard at Primolano, fell upon the main body of Wurmser's army. The assault on the town of Bassano was delivered by Augereau's division on the right, and Masséna's on the left, and the French utterly routed the Austrians, Wurmser narrowly escaping capture. Six thousand men laid down their arms, and when Wurmser collected his scattered forces, he had but 16,000 left out of the 60,000 with which he had commenced the campaign.

Bassein (First Mahratta War).

This place, held by a Mahratta garrison, was besieged by a British force under General Goddard, November 13, 1780. A serious attempt was made to relieve the garrison, but the defeat of the relieving force by Colonel Hartley at Dugaar, on December 10, completely discouraged the defenders, and they surrendered on the following day.

Bassorah (Arab Revolt).

Fought in 665 between the Caliph Ali, at the head of 29,000 Moslems, and the rebel Arabs in superior force, under Telha and Zobin. The rebels were defeated with heavy loss, Telha and Zobin being slain, and Ayesha, the widow of the prophet, who had espoused their cause, captured. This victory is known to Moslems as the Day of the Camel, 70 men, who in succession held the bridle of the camel on which Ayesha was mounted, being killed in the fight which raged round her.

Batavia (Napoleonic Wars).

This town was captured by the British under Sir Samuel Auchmuty, with 10,000 troops, August 26, 1811. The French and Dutch garrison had abandoned the town, and occupied a strong position at Fort Cornelius, in the immediate neighbourhood. The British stormed the entrenchments, with a loss of 872 killed and wounded, whereupon the survivors of the garrison laid down their arms.

Batoche (Riel's Second Rebellion).

Fought May 9 to 12, 1885, when 750 Canadians under General Middleton gradually drove back and finally defeated Riel's force of half-breeds and Indians, with a loss of 224. The Canadians lost only 54 killed and wounded. Riel surrendered on the 15th.

Batowitz.

Fought 1653 between 40,000 Poles under John II, and the Wallachians under Bogdan. The Poles, who were waiting to intercept the passage of the Wallachians, were thrown into disorder by a furious charge headed by Bogdan in person, and almost completely annihilated.

Bautzen (Campaign of Leipzic).

Fought May 20 and 21, 1813, between 150,000 French under Napoleon, and the Prussians and Russians, 100,000 strong, under Blucher and Count Wittgenstein. The allies were strongly posted in and around Bautzen, while their front was protected by the Spree. On the 20th Napoleon forced the passage of the Spree, and seized Bautzen after severe fighting, driving the allies from their first line of defence. On the 22nd he attacked the second line, while a flank march of Ney's corps drove in their right flank, and captured all their positions. The allies retired in good order, lack of cavalry preventing Napoleon from pushing his advantage. The allies lost 15,000 killed and wounded in the two days ; the French, 1,300.

Bavay (Gallic War).

Fought B.C. 57 between the Romans, 50,000 strong, under Cæsar, and a large force of Gauls, drawn from the Nervii, Viromandui, Atrebates and other tribes. The Gauls attacked as the Romans were pitching their camp on the banks of the Sambre, but, although surprised, the legionaries stood their ground, and utterly routed their assailants. The Nervii, in particular, were practically annihilated.

Baylen (Peninsular War).

Fought July 19, 1808, between 15,000 Spaniards under Castaños, and 20,000 French under Dupont. The French were totally defeated with a loss of over 2,000 men, and Dupont surrendered with his whole army.

Baza (War of Granada).

This fortress, one of the outposts of Granada, was besieged by Ferdinand, with 95,000 Spaniards, in June 1489, and was defended by a strong Moorish garrison under Sidi Yahye. The town was very strong, and was gallantly defended, and the siege lasted until December, when the place was surrendered on honourable terms.

Beachy Head (War of the Revolution).

A naval action fought June 30, 1690, between a combined English and Dutch fleet of 73 sail under Torrington, and a French fleet of 78 ships under de Tourville, which had been despatched to create a diversion in favour of James II in Ireland. The allies were defeated, the Dutch losing six and the British one ship.

Beaugé (Hundred Years' War).

Fought March 22, 1421, between the English under the Duke of Clarence, and the Armagnacs, aided by the Scottish mercenaries, resulting in one of the few defeats sustained by the English during the French wars. The Duke and his immediate following, charging ahead of his troops, vigorously attacked the Scottish outposts, and, becoming separated from the main body, was surrounded and slain, all his gentlemen being either killed or captured. The bodies were afterwards recovered by the English archers, but the defeat was complete.

Beaumont (Franco - German War).

Fought August 30, 1870, between the Fifth French Corps d'Armée under General de Failly, and the Fourth and Twelfth German Army Corps under the Crown Prince of Saxony. The French were surprised in their cantonments, and were driven back upon Monzon, with a loss of 4,800 men and 42 guns. The Germans lost about 3,500.

Beaune-la-Rolande (Franco-German War).

Fought November 28, 1870, between 9,000 Germans under the Grand Duke of Mecklenburg, and 60,000 French under General Crouzat. The French assailed the German position, but, notwithstanding the disparity of numbers, the Germans succeeded in maintaining their ground, after a desperate encounter, driving off their assailants with a loss of 8,000 men. The Germans lost 37 officers and 817 men only.

Beauséjour (Seven Years' War).

This fort in Nova Scotia, held by a garrison of 460 men under Duchambon de Vergor, was invested June 4, 1755, by 2,000 Massachusetts volunteers and a small force of regulars under Colonel Monckton. On the 14th the besiegers opened fire, and on the 16th the garrison surrendered.

Beaver's Dam Creek. *See* Seven Days' Battle.

Bedr (Mohammed's War with the Koreish).

Fought in 623, and notable as the first military exploit of Mohammed, who, with only 313 followers, routed a force of 950 Koreish, who had been sent out to meet and protect a caravan of 1,000 camels, with which was their chief, Abu Sophian. After his victory, Mohammed pursued and captured the caravan.

Bedriacum (Revolt of Vitellius).

Fought April 14, 69, between the legions of the Emperor Otho and the Vitellians under Valens. The Imperial troops were utterly routed, and driven back to their camp, which they surrendered to the Vitellians on the following day.

Bega (Ottoman Wars).

Fought 1696, between the Turks, under Mustapha II, and the Imperialists, when the Turks gained a complete victory.

Belgrade (Ottoman Wars).

Siege was laid to this city by a large Turkish army under Mohammed II, the defence being in the hands of John Hunyady. After a gallant resistance of 40 days, the Turks were compelled to raise the siege, September 4, 1456. This was Hunyady's last exploit, and he died a month later. Mohammed was wounded in the course of the siege.

Belgrade (Ottoman Wars).

Fought August 16, 1717, between 40,000 Austrians under Prince Eugene, and 180,000 Turks under the Grand Vizier, Ibrahim Pasha. The Turks were entrenched in and around Belgrade, and were attacked by Eugene at night. His right wing lost touch and were in danger of being overwhelmed, but was rescued by the Prince. The main attack was completely successful, and the Turks were driven out of their positions with a loss of 20,000 killed and wounded, and 166 guns. The Austrians lost almost as heavily, among those who fell being Marshal Hauben.

Belgrade (Ottoman Wars).

On October 8, 1789, the city was surrendered by the Turks, after a brief siege, to an Austrian army under General Laudon.

Belle Isle (Seven Years' War).

Fought November 20, 1759, between a British fleet of 27 ships of the line and 6 frigates under Sir Edward Hawke, and a French fleet of 20 ships of the line and 6 frigates under Admiral de Conflans. The French were completely defeated, losing 6 ships and a large number of men. The British lost 2 ships ashore, and 58 killed and 251 wounded.

Belle Isle (Seven Years' War).

On June 7, 1761, the island was captured by 8,000 British troops under General Hodgson, convoyed by the fleet under Admiral Keppel. After a first repulse, the troops made good their landing, and the garrison of Palais, the principal town, at once capitulated.

Belle Isle (Wars of the French Revolution).

Fought June 23, 1795, between a British fleet of 17 battleships under Lord Bridport, and a French squadron. The French endeavoured to escape, but the British gave chase, and captured three ships, with a loss of 3 killed and 113 wounded. The French lost about 700.

Bellevue (Franco-German War).

Fought October 7, 1870, when Marshal Bazaine attempted to break through the lines of the Germans investing Metz. He was unsuccessful, and was driven back into the city with a loss of 64 officers and 1,193 men. The Germans lost 75 officers and 1,703 men.

Belmont (Second Boer War).

Fought November 23, 1899, between a Boer commando, about 3,000 strong, occupying a strong position on the hills near Belmont, and Lord Methuen's division of 7½ battalions of infantry and a regiment of cavalry. The Boer position was carried by a frontal attack, which cost the assailants 28 officers and 270 men. The Boers lost about 300 killed and wounded, and 50 prisoners.

Benburb (Great Irish Rebellion).

Fought June 5, 1646, when 5,500 Irish rebels under O'Neill, totally routed the Scottish army under Monro. The Scots left 3,000 dead upon the field, and the fugitives were ruthlessly butchered by the Irish in their flight.

Bender (Ottoman Wars).

This place, held by a Turkish garrison, was besieged by the Russians under Count Panin, August, 1768. After a defence of two months, the place was taken by storm, and the garrison put to the sword.

Benevento (Italian Wars).

Fought February 26, 1266, between the Neapolitans, under Mainfroy, the usurper of the crown of the Two Sicilies, and the French under Charles of Anjou. After a sanguinary engagement, in which Mainfroy was slain, the Neapolitans were utterly routed, and Charles of Anjou remained in undisputed possession of the throne.

Beneventum (Pyrrhus' Invasion of Italy).

Fought B.C. 275, when Pyrrhus with a strong force of Epirots and Italians made a night attack upon the consular army of M. Carius Dentatus, encamped in a strong position near Beneventum. Pyrrhus was repulsed with considerable loss, including eight elephants. Encouraged by this success, the Romans shortly afterwards advanced to meet Pyrrhus in the open plain, and were at first driven back by the elephants, but rallying, they drove these back through Pyrrhus' lines, and disordered the Epirot phalanx, and a charge of the legionaries completed the rout. This was Pyrrhus' last serious attack against the Roman power, and he soon afterwards left Italy.

Beneventum (Second Punic War)

Fought B.C. 214, between 18,000 Carthaginians under Hanno, and 20,000 Romans under Tiberius Gracchus. Hanno's troops were routed, his infantry being cut to pieces, and he himself escaping with difficulty, with a portion of his cavalry.

Beneventum   (Second   Punic War).

Fought B.C. 212, when a Roman consular army under Cn. Fulvius, stormed Hanno's camp, three miles from Beneventum, at daybreak, and surprising the Carthaginians, routed them with heavy loss and captured all the corn and supplies intended for the revictualling of Capua.

Bennington (American War of Independence).

Fought August 10, 1777, between a British force under Colonel Baum, and the New Hampshire troops under General Stark. Baum had been ordered to seize the American magazines at Bennington, but found the place too strong, and asked for reinforcements. Meanwhile they were surrounded and attacked by Stark. The British fought till their ammunition was exhausted and then surrendered, while Baum was killed trying to cut

his way through the American lines.

Berea (Kaffir Wars).

Fought December 20, 1852, between the British under General Cathcart, about 2,500 strong, and the Basutos, many thousands in number, under Moshesh. The British, after hard fighting, succeeded in holding their ground, but were obliged on the following day to retreat to the entrenched camp on the Caledon, having suffered a loss of 37 killed and 15 wounded.

Beresina (Moscow Campaign).

On November 28, 1812, the French Grande Armée, in retreat from Moscow, was attacked by the Russians under Tchitchakoff and Wittgenstein. The former on the right bank, assailed Napoleon, who had already crossed the river, while Wittgenstein attacked Victor's corps, which formed the French rear-guard. The attack on Napoleon was repulsed, but on the other side of the river the Russian onslaught caused a panic among those who were waiting to cross, and though the rear-guard made a brave resistance, the losses among the stragglers and others were enormous. The official Russian report says that 36,000 bodies were recovered from the Beresina after the thaw.

Berestecko.

Fought 1653, between the Poles, 100,000 strong under John II, and a large army of Wallachians, Lithuanians, and Ukraine Tartars, 300,000 in all, under Bogdan of Wallachia. After a sanguinary battle, the Poles were completely victorious, defeating Bogdan with enormous loss.

Bergen (Seven Years' War).

Fought April 13, 1759, between the French under the Duc de Broglie, and the Hanoverians, about 40,000 strong, under Ferdinand of Brunswick. The French gained a signal victory, and retained possession of Bergen, the recapture of which was the object of Ferdinand's advance.

Bergen-op-Zoom (War of the Austrian Succession).

This fortress, held by a garrison of Dutch and English under Cronstrun, was besieged July 15, 1747, by 25,000 French under Count Lowendahl. The besieged made numerous vigorous sorties, inflicting heavy losses upon the French, but on September 17 the besiegers, by an unexpected assault, effected a lodgment, and after severe fighting captured the place. The French lost 22,000 men during the siege ; the garrison 4,000. A Scottish brigade in the Dutch service specially distinguished itself, losing 1,120 out of a strength of 1,450.

Bergen-op-Zoom (Wars of the French Revolution).

On March 8, 1875, Bergen, which was held by a French garrison 6,000 strong, under General Bizouet, was attacked by a British force, 4,000 strong under General Cooke. The force was divided into four columns, one of which, approaching the town from the harbour side, at low water, effected an entrance, while two of the others gained the top of the battlements but could get no further. At dawn

on the 9th, as there was no prospect of ultimate success, the assailants retired, having suffered a loss of 300 killed and 1,800 prisoners, many of whom were wounded.

Bergen-op-Zoom (Wars of the French Revolution).

In the outskirts of the town a battle took place September 19,1799, between 35,000 British and Russians under the Duke of York, and the French under Vandamme. The Russians on the right met with disaster, their commander, Hermann,with nearly all his division, being taken prisoners, but the British repulsed the French attack with heavy loss. The victory, however, was not of much advantage to the allies, who were forced to continue their retreat to Zijp. The French lost about 3,000 killed and wounded, and the British 500 only, but the Russian casualties amounted to 3,500, while they also lost 26 guns.

Bergfried (Campaign of Friedland).

Fought February 3, 1807, when Leval's division of Soult's corps forced the bridge of Burgfried, and carried the village, driving out the Russians after a short and sharp encounter, with a loss of about 1,200 men. The French lost 700.

Béthune (War of the Spanish Succession).

This small fortress, held by a French garrison of 3,500 under M. du Puy Vauban, was invested July 14, 1707, by the Imperialists, with 30 battalions under Count Schulemburg. Vauban made a most skilful and gallant defence, lasting 35 days, when, the garrison being reduced to 1,500 men, he was compelled to surrender. This little place cost the allies 3,500 in killed and wounded.

Betioca (South American War of Independence).

Fought 1813, between the Colombian patriots under Simon Bolivar, and the Spanish royalists, Bolivar gaining a complete victory.

Betwa, The (Indian Mutiny).

Fought April 1, 1858, between 1,200 British under Sir Hugh Rose, forming part of the force besieging Jhansi, and 20,000 rebels, chiefly belonging to the Gwalior contingent, under Tantia Topi. The enemy was thrown into confusion by a charge of cavalry on the flank, and, being then attacked with the bayonet, broke and fled, leaving 1,000 dead on the field and all their guns.

Beylan (Mehemet Ali's First Rising).

Fought 1831, between the Syrians and Egyptians under Ibrahim Pasha, and the Turks, the latter being completely defeated.

Beymaroo (First Afghan War).

Fought November 23, 1841, when a detachment of General Elphinstone's force, under Brigadier Shelton, attempted to dislodge a large body of Afghans, posted near Beymaroo village. The detachment had one gun only, which, being well served, did considerable execution, but it broke down, whereupon the Afghans attacked, and a charge of Ghazis caused a panic and a

disorderly flight to the British camp.

Bezetha (Jewish War).

Fought October, 66, when the Romans under Cestius Gallus were attacked by the populace of Jerusalem, and driven out of their camp, with a loss of 6,000 men and all their baggage and siege train.

Bhurtpur (Second Mahratta War).

This city, garrisoned by about 8,000 of the Rajah's troops, was besieged by General Lake, January 4, 1805. Finding that his siege train was inadequate to reduce the town by the ordinary methods, Lake determined to carry it by storm. Four successive assaults were made, but without success, and on April 21 Lake was obliged to withdraw, having lost 3,200 men during the siege.

Bhurtpur, Second Siege of.

The city was again besieged by the British under Lord Combermere in 1827, a dispute having taken place as to the succession, and the Rajah who was under British protection having been expelled. After a bombardment of two months, which had little effect on the fortress, it was taken by assault.

Biberac (Wars of the French Revolution).

Fought October, 1796, between the French under Moreau, and the Austrians under the Archduke Charles, who had previously defeated Jourdan at Warzburg, and now turned upon Moreau, who was retreating through the Black Forest. Moreau severely defeated the

Austrians, and continued his retreat unmolested.

Bibracte (Gallic War).

Fought B.C. 58, between the Romans under Cæsar and a largely superior force of Helvetii. The battle was a momentous one, for a defeat to Cæsar meant destruction. He therefore sent away all his officers' horses, giving them to understand that they must stand their ground to the last. In the event, the Helvetii were totally routed, and compelled to submit to the domination of Rome.

Bilbao (First Carlist War).

This fortress was besieged by the Carlists November 9, 1836, and was defended by a small Christino garrison. The besiegers took possession of some of the suburbs, which were recaptured by a sortie. Finally, after several unsuccessful attempts, Espartero, at the head of about 18,000 Christinos, drove off the besiegers, December 25, and relieved the city, capturing the Carlist artillery of 25 pieces. In the action the Christinos lost 714 killed and wounded, while the losses of the garrison during the siege amounted to about 1,300.

Bingen (Gallic Revolt).

In the year 70, Petilius Cerialis, who, with four Roman legions, had crossed the Alps from Switzerland, surprised the revolted Gauls under Tutor, in their camp at Bingen. The Gallic legionaries in Tutor's army deserted to the Romans, and Tutor was totally defeated.

Biruan (Tartar Invasion of Kharismia).

Fought 1221, between 80,000 Tartars under Katuku, and the troops of Jellalladin, Sultan of Kharismia, 60,000 strong. The Tartars were routed and driven from the field in confusion.

Bithur (Indian Mutiny).

Fought August 16, 1857, when 4,000 mutineers, strongly posted, were attacked and routed by the relieving force under General Havelock. When driven from their position, the rebels had to cross a stream in their rear by a small bridge, and had Havelock possessed an adequate cavalry force, but few could have escaped.

Bitonto (War of the Polish Succession).

Fought May 25, 1734, between the Imperialists, 10,000 strong, and the Spaniards under Mortemar. The Imperialists were driven from a strong position, with heavy loss, and the victory resulted in the establishment of Spanish rule throughout the Neapolitan provinces.

Blackheath (Flammock's Rebellion).

Fought June 22, 1497, between the royal troops under Henry VII, and the rebels under Flammock and Lord Audley. The rebels were defeated with a loss of 2,000 killed, and all their leaders were captured and executed.

Black Rock (Second American War).

Fought 1814, between 1,400 British troops under General Riall, and a force of 2,000 American Indians, occupying a strong position at Black Rock. The British stormed the entrenchments and dispersed the enemy, following up their success by the seizure of Buffalo.

Blackwater (O'Neill's Rebellion).

Fought 1598, between 5,000 Irish rebels under Hugh O'Neill, and 5,000 English under Sir Henry Bagnall, the English Marshal. Bagnall was defeated with a loss of 1,500 and all his ammunition and baggage, while he himself was killed by O'Neill.

Bladensburg (Second American War).

Fought August 24, 1814, between the British under General Ross, and the Americans under General Winder, who was opposing the British advance upon Washington, and had taken up a positon which commanded the only bridge over the Potomac. Ross attacked with a portion of his force, under Thornton, and, having carried the bridge, a combined assault upon the main position resulted•in a signal defeat of the American army, which broke and fled. Ross entered Washington the same evening.

Blanquefort (Hundred Years' War).

Fought November 1, 1450, when the English made a sally from Bordeaux to repel a marauding band under Amanien. The English cavalry, advancing too rapidly, became separated from the main body, and was cut off. Amanien then fell upon the infantry, who, being unsupported, were overwhelmed and almost annihilated. So great was the slaughter that the day was long known in Bordeaux as the "Male Journée."

Blenheim (War of the Spanish Succession).

Fought August 13, 1704, between the British and Imperialists under Marlborough and Prince Eugene, and the French and Bavarians under Marshals Tallard and Marsin, and the Elector of Bavaria. The French numbered 60,000, the allies 52,000. Tallard had massed his best troops in the village of Blenheim, and Marlborough, seeing the weakness of his centre, hurled his cavalry against it, and cut the French line in two. Prince Eugene meanwhile had withstood the attack of Marsin and the Elector, and, after Marlborough's charge, he assumed the offensive, and the French right and centre were totally routed. The French lost 40,000, including 1,600 prisoners, amongst whom was Marshal Tallard. The allies lost about 11,000.

Bloore Heath (Wars of the Roses).

Fought September 23, 1459, between the Yorkists under the Earl of Salisbury, and the Lancastrians under Henry VI. The former, who were inferior in numbers, were attacked by Henry, who crossed a brook before the assault. As the Lancastrians were reforming after the crossing, the Yorkists charged down upon them, and dispersed them with heavy loss.

Blueberg (Napoleonic Wars).

On January 8, 1806, a British force 6,600 strong, under General Baird, which had just landed at Saldanha Bay, was attacked by the Dutch and French under General Janssens, issuing from Cape Town. The British gained a signal victory, in which they lost 212 killed, wounded and missing, while their opponents' losses amounted to about 300. Baird at once occupied Cape Town.

Boadicea, Defeat of (Roman Occupation of Britain).

In the year 61, Suetonius, with 10,000 legionaries, totally routed an enormous host of Britons under Boadicea, Queen of the Iceni, who had sacked Camelodunum, and taken Londinium and Verulamium. The Britons lost 80,000 killed, and Boadicea took poison on the battlefield.

Bois-le-Duc (Wars of the French Revolution).

Fought November 12, 1794, between the French and Austrians under the Duke of York, and the French under Moreau. Moreau's object was to enter Holland at a period when the dykes would be no obstacle to his advance, and for the purpose endeavoured to cross the Meuse at Fort Crèvecœur, near Bois-le-Duc. The allies however, disputed his passage so vigorously that Moreau was forced to retire, and give up his project.

Bokhara (Tartar Invasion of Kharismia).

This city was besieged by the Tartar army under Genghis Khan in March, 1220, and was held by a Kharismian garrison. On the approach of the Tartars, however, the Kharismian general, with the whole garrison, 20,000 strong, fled from the place, and the Bokhariots, having no means of defending themselves, opened the gates to Genghis. The Governor held out for a short time in the citadel, which was finally fired and destroyed.

Boomplaats.

Fought August 29, 1848, between the British, 800 strong, with 250 Griquas, under Sir Harry Smith, and a force of 1,000 Transvaal Boers under Commandant Jan Kock. The British stormed the Boer position and drove out the defenders, at a cost of 22 killed and 38 wounded. The Boers stated their losses at 5 killed and 9 wounded.

Borghetto (Napoleon's Italian Campaigns).

Fought May 30, 1796, in the course of Napoleon's pursuit of Beaulieu. The French crossed the Mincio at Borghetto, having previously repaired the bridge under a heavy fire, and forced the Austrians to evacuate Peschiera, with a loss of 500 prisoners, besides killed and wounded.

Bornholm (Dano-Swedish Wars).

Fought 1676, between the fleet of Charles XI of Sweden, and a combined Dutch and Danish squadron. The Swedes were utterly routed, a disaster which was followed by the loss of Helsingborg, Landscroon, and other fortresses.

Bornhoven.

Fought 1227, between the Danes under Valdemar II, and the insurgents of the province of Dithmarsh, who had risen against the Danish dominion. The royal troops were totally routed, and, as a consequence, the province was lost to the Danish crown.

orodino (Moscow Campaign).

Fought September 5, 1812, between 120,000 Russians under Kutusoff, and the French in equal force under Napoleon. The Russians, who were intrenched in a very strong position, were attacked soon after daybreak, and their first line of redoubts was carried and held by the French till the end of the day, but the victory was far from decisive, as at nightfall Napoleon retired to his original position, leaving the Russians in possession of the field. The French lost 10,000 killed, including 8 generals, and 20,000 wounded, including 30 generals. The Russians lost about 45,000. This battle is also called the Battle of the Moskowa.

Boroughbridge (Rebellion of the Marches).

Fought 1322, between the Royalists under Edward II, and the rebels under Hereford and Lancaster. The rebels, falling back before the king, were surprised by a force under Sir Andrew Harclay while crossing the bridge at Boroughbridge, and were utterly routed. Hereford was killed, and Lancaster, with several hundred barons and knights, surrendered.

Borysthenes, The (Russo-Polish Wars).

Fought 1512, when the Poles under Sigismund I defeated an army of Muscovites, 80,000 strong, with enormous slaughter.

Bosra (Moslem Invasion of Syria).

This strong fortress was besieged, 632, by 4,000 Moslems under Serjabil. A sortie of the garrison nearly caused their destruction, but they were rescued by the arrival of 1,500 horse under Khaled. After a brief interval, the whole of the garrison marched out of the city to give battle, but were defeated by Khaled with a loss to his troops of 250 men only, and the city was shortly afterwards betrayed by Romanus, the Governor.

Bosworth Field (Wars of the Roses).

Fought August 21, 1485, between Richard III and Henry Duke of Richmond (Henry VII). Richmond had received a promise from Lord Stanley and his uncle that they would desert during the battle, and, after holding aloof for some time, they came over, with their followers, at a critical moment of the engagement, and Richard was routed and slain. He fought to the end, and among others who fell with him were the Duke of Norfolk and Lord Ferrers.

Bothwell Bridge (Covenanters' Rising).

Fought June 22, 1679, when the Royal troops, under the Duke of Monmouth, defeated the Covenanters with great slaughter.

Boulogne.

Siege was laid to the town by the English under Henry VIII, September 14, 1544. It was defended with great gallantry, and, in the face of enormous difficulties, for two months, when it was forced to surrender, the inhabitants being allowed to march out with their arms and property.

Bourbon (Napoleonic Wars).

On July 8, 1810, this island was captured by a British squadron of five ships under Commodore Rowley, with a detachment of troops under Colonel Keatinge. The British lost 22 killed and 79 wounded.

Bouvines (Wars of Philip Augustus).

Fought 1214 between the French under Philip Augustus, and the Germans, Flemish and English under Otho IV, the numbers engaged on both sides being considerable. The French gained a signal victory, which broke up the coalition and rendered the position of Philip Augustus secure on the throne of France.

Bovianum (Sceond Samnite War).

Fought B.C. 307 between the Romans under Titus Minucius, and the Samnites under Statius Gellius. Gellius attempted to relieve Bovianum, which the Romans were besieging, and was totally defeated, though Minucius fell in the battle. This defeat broke the Samnite power, and they sued for peace in the following year, leaving Rome without dispute the first power in Italy.

Boyaca (South American War of Independence).

Fought August 17, 1819, between the Colombian patriots under Bolivar, and the Spanish Royalists, 2,500 strong, under Colonel Barreiro. Bolivar crossed the Cordilleras, under incredible difficulties, and, eluding Barreiro, took up a position at Boyaca, cutting him off from his base at Bogota. The Spaniards attacked him, and were routed with heavy loss, Barreiro and 1,600 men being captured. The patriots lost 66 only.

Boyne, The (War of the Revolution).

Fought July 1, 1690, between the forces of William III, and the Irish under James II. William and the elder Schomberg attacked the front of James's position, while the younger Schomberg crossed the Boyne a few miles higher up, and attacked him in flank. William forced the passage of the river, and drove the Irish from their entrenchments at a cost of 500 killed and wounded, including the elder Schomberg. The Irish lost 1,500.

Braddock Down (Civil War).

Fought January 19, 1643, between the Royalists under Sir Ralph Hopton, and the Parliamentary forces under Ruthven. The latter had crossed the Tamar and occupied Liskeard, without adequate support, and was defeated by the Royalists with heavy loss.

Bramham Moor (Northumberland's Rebellion).

Fought February 20, 1408, when Sir Thomas Rokeby, High Sheriff of Yorkshire, defeated the Earl of Northumberland, who had again raised the standard of rebellion in the North. The Earl was slain, and the rebellion subsided.

Brandywine (American War of Independence).

Fought September 11, 1777, between 18,000 British under General Howe, and 8,000 Americans under Washington. The

British General made a flank movement with a large portion of his force, whereupon Washington attacked the British in the front, but, being ill supported by his lieutenant, Sullivan, he was driven back, and forced to retreat, with a loss of 900 killed and wounded and 300 prisoners. The British lost 590 killed and wounded.

Brechin (Douglas Rebellion).

Fought 1452, between the revolted Douglasses under the Earl of Craufurd, and the Royal troops under the Earl of Huntly. The Douglasses were defeated.

Bregenz (War of the League Above the Lake).

Fought January 1408, between the troops of the League Above the Lake and the burghers of Constance, aided by the Suabian nobles. The Leaguers were totally routed, with the result that the League was shortly afterwards dissolved.

Breitenfeld, First Battle. *See* Leipsic.

Breitenfeld, Second Battle (Thirty Years' War).

Fought November 2, 1642, between the Imperialists under the Archduke Leopold and Piccolomini, and the Swedes under Torstenson. The latter, who were in retreat, were caught by the pursuing Austrians at Breitenfeld, but turning upon them, they offered a desperate resistance, and finally drove them from the field, totally routed, with a loss of 10,000 men.

Brenneville.

Fought August 20, 1119, between a small body of English cavalry under Henry I, and a similar French force under Louis VI. Though only about 900 men were engaged, and very few killed, the fight was considered a decisive victory for the English, and Louis shortly afterwards made peace, conceding Henry's terms.

Brentford (Civil War).

Fought November 12, 1642, between the Royalists under Prince Rupert, and a Parliamentary force under Denzil Holles. Three regiments stationed at Brentford were driven out of their entrenchments by the Royalists, losing 1,500 prisoners and 11 guns.

Brescia (Italian Rising).

This city, where the populace had risen and shut up the small Austrian garrison in the citadel, was carried by assault by Genera Haynau, with about 4,000 Austrians, March 31, 1849. Carrying the Porta Torrelunga, he fought his way from barricade to barricade, till, by the evening of April 1, the resistance of the citizens was overcome. The Austrians lost 480 killed, including General Nugent, and many wounded. The wholesale executions ordered by Haynau after the capture earned for him the sobriquet of the Hyæna.

Breslau (Seven Years' War).

Fought November 22, 1757, between 90,000 Austrians under Prince Charles of Lorraine, and 25,000 Prussians under the Prince of Bevern. The Prussians, who were encamped under the walls of Breslau, were driven into the city with a loss of 5,000 killed and wounded, 3,600 prisoners, including the Prince of

Bevern, and 80 guns. They evacuated the city at once, leaving a garrison of 6,000, which surrendered two days later. The Austrians lost 8,000 killed and wounded.

Brest (War of the Holy League).

Fought August 10, 1512, between the English fleet of 45 sail under Lord Edward Howard, and the French fleet of 39 sail under Jean de Thenouënel. The French ships were driven into Brest, or along the coast, with heavy loss. The English lost 2 ships and 1,600 men.

Bridge of Dee (Civil War).

Fought June 18, 1639, between the Covenanters, 2,300 strong, and the Royal troops under Lord Aboyne. The bridge itself was barricaded and held by 100 sharpshooters, under Colonel Johnstone, and Montrose, who led the Covenanters, finding the defences too strong, succeeded by a stratagem in drawing off the main body of the defenders, whereupon he forced a passage. The losses on both sides were very small.

Brienne (Allied Invasion of France).

Fought January 29, 1814, between 18,000 French under Napoleon, and about 30,000 Russians and Prussians under Blucher. The allies were driven from their positions, and the Château de Brienne taken. After nightfall a determined attempt to retake the château was made by the Russians under Sachen, but they failed to dislodge the French. The allies lost about 4,000 ; the French 3,000 killed and wounded.

Brihuega (War of the Spanish Succession).

Fought 1710 between the British under Stanhope, and the French under the Duc de Vendôme. Stanhope, who was retreating from Madrid to Catalonia, was surprised and surrounded, and, though he made a gallant stand, fighting till all his powder was spent, and then leading a bayonet charge, his force was at last reduced to 500 men, when he surrendered.

Brill (Netherlands War of Independence).

This fortress was captured from the Spaniards by the Beggars of the Sea, about 400 strong, under De la Marck and Treslong, April 1, 1572. It was the first success of the Netherlands patriots in their struggle against Spanish rule, and may be said to have laid the foundation of the Dutch republic.

Brittany, Action off (Gallic War).

This, the first sea fight in the Atlantic, was fought B.C. 56, between the Roman fleet under Brutus, and the fleet of the Veneti, consisting of 220 galleys. The Romans were victorious, and the surrender of the Veneti and the whole of Brittany quickly followed.

Bronkhorst Spruit (First Boer War).

The opening engagement of the war, when, on December 20, 1880, a British column, 259 strong, under Colonel Anstruther, was ambushed by 150 mounted Boers under Joubert, and defeated with a loss of 155 killed and wounded. The Boers stated their losses at 2 killed and 5 wounded only.

Brooklyn (American War of Independence).

Fought August 27, 1776, between 30,000 British under Sir William Howe, and the Americans, about 11,000 strong, under General Putnam. The Americans were completely defeated, with a loss of about 2,000 killed and wounded. The British lost 65 killed and 255 wounded.

Brunanburh (Danish Invasion).

Fought 937, when Æthelstan defeated with great slaughter the combined armies of Anlaf the Dane, Owen of Cumberland, and Constantine III of Scotland.

Bucharest (Ottoman Wars).

Fought 1771, between the Turks under Mousson Oglou, and the Russians under General Romanzoff. The Turks were totally defeated.

Buena Vista (Americo-Mexican War).

Fought February 22, 1846, between 18,000 Mexicans under General Santa Anna, and 4,500 Americans under General Zachary Taylor. The Americans occupied a series of heights commanding the Angostura pass, and were there attacked by Santa Anna, who failed to dislodge them, the day ending with the combatants occupying the same ground as in the morning. On the 23rd, however, Santa Anna retired. The Americans lost 746 killed and wounded ; the Mexicans admitted a loss of 1,500 killed, but it was probably heavier.

Buenos Ayres (Napoleonic Wars).

This city was captured June 27, 1806, by a *coup de main,* by a British force, 1,700 strong, under General Beresford, aided by a small squadron under Sir Home Popham. Beresford, however, was not strong enough to hold the place, and before reinforcements could arrive he was defeated by the South Americans under General Liniers, with a loss of 250 killed and wounded, and compelled to surrender with his whole force.

Buenos Ayres (Napoleonic Wars).

Fought July 5, 1807 when 9,000 British troops under General Whitelocke assaulted the city. They penetrated into the streets, but suffered terrible losses from the defenders' fire from windows and roofs, and, General Whitelocke proving a most incapable leader, were forced to surrender and evacuate the whole of the River Plate region.

Buenos Ayres (Mitre's Rebellion).

Fought November 6, 1874, between the Argentine Government troops under Sarmiento, and the rebels under Mitre and Aredondo. The rebels were defeated, and Mitre forced to surrender.

Bull Run (American Civil War).

Fought July 21, 1861, between 40,000 Federals under General M'Dowell, and 30,000 Confederates under General Beauregard. The Confederates occupied a position extending for about nine miles along the southern bank of the Bull Run, and an attempt to turn and drive in their left was at first successful, but, being rallied by General Beauregard, they assumed the offensive, and totally routed the Northerners, with a loss of 1,492 killed and wounded, 1,600 prisoners, and 28 guns. The Confederates lost 1,752.

Bull Run, Second Battle (American Civil War).

Fought August 30, 1862, between the Confederates under Stonewall Jackson, and the Federals under General Pope. The Federals attacked Jackson's position, which he maintained till evening, when, the Federal left giving way, he ordered a general advance, and drove the enemy from the field with heavy loss. Over 7,000 prisoners were taken.

Bunker's Hill (American War of Independence).

Fought June 17, 1775, when 2,000 British troops, forming a portion of General Gage's army, dislodged the Americans holding Breeds Hill and Bunker's Hill, on the outskirts of Boston. The position was stubbornly contested, the assailants losing 800 men.

Burlington Heights (Second American War).

Fought May 5, 1813, when the British under Colonel Procter were attacked by 1,300 Americans under General Clay, while engaged with another American force holding Burlington Heights. The Americans broke the British line and seized their guns, but Procter, who had only 1,000 men, with some Indian auxiliaries, rallied his troops and routed Clay, with a loss of nearly 1,000 killed, wounded and captured.

Burns Hill (Kaffir Wars).

Fought 1847, between the Kaffirs under Sandilli, and a small British force sent to arrest that chief. The British were greatly outnumbered, and were defeated and forced to retreat.

Busaco (Peninsular War).

Fought by Wellington, September 29, 1810, to secure his retreat to Torres Vedras. He occupied the heights of Busaco with 25,000 men and was attacked by 40,000 French under Masséna. The actual assault was delivered by the corps of Ney and Reynier, but they could make no impression, and were repulsed with a loss of about 4,500. The British lost 1,300 killed and wounded

Buxar.

Fought October 23, 1764, between 7,000 British troops and sepoys under Major Monro, and the army of Oude, 40,000 strong, under Surabjah Daulah, who was accompanied by the Great Mogul, Shah Allum. The British gained a signal victory, Surabjah Daulah abandoning his camp with a loss of 4,000 men and 130 guns. The British lost 847 killed and wounded.

Buzenval (Franco-German War).

A sortie from Paris under General Trochu on January 19, 1871. The French, advancing under cover of a fog, established themselves in the Park of Buzenval, and occupied St. Cloud, where they maintained their position throughout the day. At other points, however, they were less successful, and, on the morning of the 20th, the force at St. Cloud, finding itself unsupported, was obliged to retire, and all the captured positions were abandoned. The

Germans lost 40 officers and 570 men ; the French 189 officers and 3,881 men. This sortie is also known as the Battle of Mont Valérien.

Byzantium.

Fought 318 B.C., between the Macedonian fleet under Antigonus, and that of the Asiatic rebels under Clytus. The Asiatics were surprised at anchor, most of the crews being ashore, and, after a feeble defence, the whole of their fleet was destroyed or captured, with the exception of the admiral's galley, in which Clytus succeeded in escaping.

Byzantium (War of the Two Empires).

In 323 the city was besieged by Constantine the Great after his victory over Licinius at Hadrianopolis. Licinius, finding the place difficult of defence, crossed into Asia and collected an army to raise the siege. He was, however, defeated at Chrysopolis, and Byzantium surrendered in 324. Constantine was proclaimed Emperor of the united Empire, and Byzantium, under its modern name of Constantinople, was made the capital.

C

Cabala (Second Carthaginian Invasion of Sicily).

Fought B.C. 379, between the Syracusans under Dionysius, and the Carthaginians under Mago. The latter were totally defeated and Mago slain.

Cabria (Third Mithridatic War).

Fought B.C. 72, between three Roman legions under Lucullus,

and the Pontic army under Diophantus and Taxiles. The Pontic cavalry, on which Mithridates chiefly relied, was overwhelmed by Fabius Hadrianus, and the king was driven out of Pontus, which was erected into a Roman province

Cadesia (Moslem Invasion of Persia).

Fought 636, between 30,000 Moslems under Said, the lieutenant of the Caliph Omar, and 120,000 Persians under Rustam. Throughout the first day the Persians, superior in numbers, but far inferior in warlike qualities, sustained the attacks of the Moslems without losing ground, but on the following day Rustam was slain, and his followers, losing heart, were driven headlong from the field, with fearful slaughter. The Moslems lost 7,500 in the battle.

Cadiz.

On April 19, 1587, Sir Francis Drake, with between 30 and 40 English ships, entered Cadiz Bay, and destroyed over 100 Spanish vessels. This exploit Drake described as " Singeing the King of Spain's beard."

Cadsand (Hundred Years' War).

Fought November 10, 1357, between 2,500 English under the Earl of Derby, and 5,000 Flemings in the French service. The Flemings were defeated with a loss of 1,000 men.

Cairo (Ottoman Wars).

Fought 1517, between the Turks under Selim I, and the Egyptians under the Mameluke Sultan, Toomaan Bey. The Egyptians were utterly routed and Cairo taken, 50,000 of the inhabitants being massecred. Toomaan Bey, the last of the Mamelukes, was hanged before the city gates, and Egypt annexed to the Ottoman Empire.

Cajwah.

Fought January 8, 1659, between the Moguls of Delhi, under Aurungzebe, the Great Mogul, and the army raised by his brother Shuja, in support of Dara, the rightful heir to the throne. After an obstinate conflict, Shuja was driven from the field with heavy losses in men, leaving behind him 114 guns.

Calafat (Crimean War).

This position, strongly entrenched and held by 30,000 Turks under Ahmed Pasha, was invested by the Russians, 40,000 strong, under General Aurep, about the middle of February, 1854. The Russians delivered assault after assault upon the place, without effect, and finally withdrew their forces in May ; having suffered a loss from disease, privation, and battle of 20,000 men. The Turks lost 12,000.

Calais (Hundred Years' War).

Siege was laid to this fortress in August 1346 by the English under Edward III. The citizens made a gallant defence, holding out for nearly a year, but at last were forced to surrender August 4, 1347. In the course of the siege, six burgesses offered themselves to the king as ransom for their fellow citizens ; but their lives were spared on the intercession of Queen Philippa.

Calais.

The last English stronghold in France was captured by the French under the Duc de Guise, January 8, 1558, after a siege of seven days only. Mary is said to have exclaimed, on hearing the news, that at her death the word " Calais " would be found engraven on her heart.

Calatafimi (Unification of Italy).

Fought May 15, 1860, between Garibaldi's " Thousand Volunteers," with a few thousand Sicilian " Picciotti " and 4,000 Neapolitans under General Landi. The Neapolitans were driven back with heavy loss, and retreated in disorder to Palermo. Garibaldi lost, of his thousand, 18 killed and 128 wounded.

Calcutta.

Siege was laid to the city June 16, 1756, by Sarabjah Daulah, Nawab of Bengal, with a large force. The garrison, consisting of 514 regulars and militia, and 1,000 matchlock men, under Captain Minchin, was quite inadequate to man the defences, and it was decided to abandon the city, remove all non-combatants to the ships, and only defend the fort. The Governor, Mr. Drake, was among those who left the place, and he was accompanied by Captain Minchin, who deserted his post, as did many of the militiamen, with the result that only 190 remained for the defence of the fort. An assault was repulsed, with a loss to the defenders of 95 killed and wounded, but on the 20th the little garrison surrendered. The survivors were thrust into a small room, known as the Black Hole, and used as a soldiers' prison, and out of 146 only 23 survived the horrors of the night.

Caldiero (Napoleon's Italian Campaigns).

Fought November 11, 1796, between the French under Napoleon and the Austrians under Alvinzi. Napoleon attacked the Austrian position, and, for the first time in the campaign, suffered a reverse, being unable to carry the enemy's lines, and eventually, after severe fighting, retiring with a loss of 3,000. Within the week, however, this defeat was avenged by the victory of Arcola.

Caldiero (Napoleon's Italian Campaigns).

On November 30, 1800, Masséna, with 50,000 French, encountered the Austrians, 80,000 strong, under the Archduke Charles, strongly posted in the village and on the heights of Caldiero. Masséna attacked and carried the heights, but the village held out until nightfall. During the night the Archduke removed his baggage and artillery, leaving a corps of 5,000 men, under General Hillinger, to protect his retreat, which force was on the following day captured *en bloc*. The Austrians lost 3,000 killed and wounded, and, including Hillinger's corps, 8,000 prisoners ; the French about 4,000 killed and wounded. Thus, though the battle was indecisive, Masséna gained a considerable strategic victory.

Calicut (Second Mysore War).

Fought December 10, 1790, between 9,000 Mysore troops under Hussein Ali, and a British force of one European and two native regiments under Colonel Hartly. Hussein Ali occupied a strong position in front of Calicut, which was attacked and carried by Hartley with a loss of 52 only. The enemy lost 1,000 killed and wounded, and 2,400 prisoners, including their commander.

Callao (South American War of Independence).

On the night of November 5, 1820, Lord Cochrane, who with three Chilian frigates was blockading the Spaniards in Callao, rowed into the harbour with 240 seamen and marines, and cut out the Spanish frigate *Esmeralda* from under the 300 guns of the shore batteries. He lost in the enterprise 41 killed and wounded, while the whole of the crew of the *Esmeralda*, including the Spanish Admiral, was captured or killed.

Callao.

The town was bombarded by the Spanish fleet of 11 warships, May 2, 1866. The Peruvian batteries replied vigorously, and, after severe fighting, drove off the Spanish ships with a loss of 300. The Peruvians lost 1,000 killed and wounded.

Calpulalpam (Mexican Liberal Rising).

Fought December 20, 1860, between the Mexican Government troops under Miramon, and the Liberals under Juarez. The Liberals won a signal victory, which opened the way to Mexico, and brought about the downfall of Miramon's administration.

Calven, The (Swabian War).

Fought March 22, 1499, between 6,300 men of the Grisons under Benedict Fontana, and 15,000 Imperialists under Maximilian I. The Swiss carried the Austrian entrenchments, and drove them out with heavy loss.

Cambuskenneth. *See* Stirling.

Camden (American War of Independence).

Fought August 16, 1780, between the British under Cornwallis, and the Americans under Gates and de Kalb. Cornwallis had concentrated about 2,000 men at Camden, and though the Americans numbered 5,000, they were of very inferior quality. After a small affair of outposts, the British attacked the American levies, who were unable to face the steady attack of the regulars, and fled with heavy loss. Among the killed was de Kalb. The British lost 312 killed and wounded.

Camelodunum (Second Invasion of Britain).

Fought 43, between the Romans under the Emperor Claudius, and the Britons under Caractacus. The Britons were routed, and Camelodunum, Caractacus' capital, taken.

Camerinum (Third Samnite War).

Fought B.C. 298, between two Roman legions under Lucius Scipio, and the Samnites under Gellius Equatius, aided by a force of Gauls. Scipio, who had been stationed near Camerinum to watch the pass through which the Gauls were expected to cross the Apennines, was unable to prevent the junction of the two armies, and was totally defeated, one of his legions being cut to pieces.

Campaldino (Guelfs and Ghibellines).

Fought June 11, 1289, between the Guelfs of Florence and the Ghibellines who had been expelled from the city. The latter were utterly routed, and this defeat put an end to their power in Florence. The battle is notable for the presence of Dante in the ranks of the victors.

Campen (Seven Years' War).

Fought October 18, 1759, between the Prussians under the Prince of Brunswick, and the French under General de Castries, when the Prussians were defeated with a loss of 1,600 men.

Campo Santo (War of the Austrian Succession).

Fought February 8, 1743, between the Spaniards under Mortemar, and the Imperialists under Count Traum. Mortemar was endeavouring to effect a junction with the army of the Prince de Conti, and though the action was undecided, its results were in favour of the Imperialists, who prevented the two armies from joining hands.

Campus Castorum (Revolt of Vitellius).

Fought in 69 between the revolted legionaries, 70,000 strong, under Valens and Cæcina, and the army of the Emperor Otho under Suetonius Paulinus. The Imperial troops gained some advantage, but Suetonius did not consider himself strong enough to follow it up, and was relieved of his command by Otho.

Camperdown (Wars of the French Revolution).

Fought between the British fleet, 16 line of battle ships, under Admiral Duncan, and the Dutch, in equal force, under Admiral de Winter, October 11, 1797. The Dutch fleet was on its way to co-operate with the French in a landing in Ireland, and was intercepted by Duncan, who at once gave battle. The British fleet, in two lines, broke through the Dutch line, and, in the general action which followed, captured eight ships, including the flagship, the *Vrijheid*. The British lost 1,040 killed and wounded, the Dutch 1,160 and 6,000 prisoners.

Candia (Candian War).

Siege was laid to this place by the Turks under Jussuf, the Capitan Pasha, in 1648, and was defended by a small garrison of Venetians, under Luigi Moncenigo. So vigorous was the defence that the Turks lost 20,000 men in the first six months of the siege. The siege lasted over twenty years, the place being from time to time revictualled and reinforced by the Venetians and the French, but it was finally surrendered by Morosini, September 27, 1669.

Canea (Candian War).

This place was besieged June 24, 1644, by 50,000 Turks under Jussuf, the Capitan Pasha, and defended by a small force of Venetians and Candians, who held out until August 22, repulsing numerous assaults, which cost the Turks 20,000 men.

Cannæ (Second Punic War).

Fought August 2, B.C. 216, between 90,000 Romans under Varro, and about 50,000 Carthaginians under Hannibal. Hannibal, though outnumbered in infantry, was much superior in cavalry. The Romans were drawn up with the sea in their rear, and were attacked and broken by the Carthaginian horse. The infantry followed up the attack, and, flight being impossible, the Romans were slaughtered where they stood, 80,000 falling, including the Consul Æmilius, 25 superior officers, and 80 senators. The Carthaginians lost 6,000.

Cape Bona (Invasion of the Vandals).

Fought 468, between the Roman fleet of 1,100 galleys and transports under Basiliscus, and the fleet of the Vandals under Genseric. The Romans were lying at anchor, having landed their troops, and Genseric, taking advantage of a favourable wind, sent in a fleet of fireships, following them up by a determined attack. More than half the Roman ships were destroyed, Basiliscus escaping with difficulty.

Cape Finisterre (War of the Austrian Succession).

Fought May 3, 1747, between a British fleet of 16 sail under Admiral Anson, and a French fleet of 38 sail under Admiral de la Jonquière. The French were completely defeated, losing 10 ships and nearly 3,000 prisoners.

Cape Finisterre (War of the Austrian Succession).

Fought October 14, 1747,

when a British fleet of 14 ships under Admiral Hawke attacked a French fleet of 9 battleships under Admiral de Letendeur. The French were signally defeated, losing four ships. The British lost 598 killed and wounded.

Cape Finisterre (Napoleonic Wars).

Fought July 22, 1805, between a British fleet of 15 sail of the line under Sir Robert Calder, and the combined French and Spanish fleets returning from the West Indies, under Admiral Villeneuve. The French fleet, consisting of 20 battleships, was attacked by Calder, who captured 2 ships. Fogs and light airs prevented him from following up his advantage next day, for which he was tried by court-martial and most unjustly censured. The British loss was 183 killed and wounded, the French losing 149 killed and 327 wounded.

Cape Henry (American War of Independence).

Fought March 16, 1781, between a British fleet of eight ships of the line and three frigates under Vice-Admiral Arbuthnot, and a French squadron stronger by one frigate. The French were forced to retire, the British losing 30 killed and 64 wounded.

Cape Passaro (War of the Quadruple Alliance).

Fought July 31, 1718, between a British fleet of 21 ships under Sir George Byng, and a Spanish fleet of 29 ships under Don Antonio Castañeta. Admiral Byng attacked the Spaniards in the Straits of Messina, and,

after a very severe action, in which both sides lost heavily, captured or destroyed no less than 15 of the Spanish ships. Castañeta died of wounds received in the action. This battle is also known as the Battle of Messina.

Cape St. Vincent (Wars of the French Revolution).

Fought February 14, 1797, between a British fleet of 15 ships of the line and 5 frigates under Sir John Jervis, and a Spanish fleet of 26 sail of the line and 12 frigates. In spite of their superior numbers, the Spaniards were totally defeated, losing 4 ships and over 3,000 prisoners, in addition to heavy losses in killed and wounded. The British lost 74 killed and 227 wounded. For this signal victory, Jervis was created Lord St. Vincent.

Caprysema (First Messenian War).

Fought B.C. 743, between the Spartans and Corinthians, and the Messenians with their allies from other Peloponnesian states under Cristomenes. The Spartans were routed, and, but for the eloquence of Tyrtacus, would have abandoned the struggle.

Capua (Second Punic War).

This place was besieged in the autumn of B.C. 212, by 60,000 Romans under Q. Fulvius and Appius Claudius. The Romans formed a double wall of circumvallation round the city, and, early in the winter, their defences were attacked by the garrison from within and Hannibal from without, but with no success. Hannibal then

E

attempted to draw the be-
siegers from their position by
marching upon Rome, but only
a small portion of the besieging
force followed him.   It being
thus found impossible to relieve
the city, it shortly afterwards
surrendered.

Carabobo (South American War of Independence).

Fought June 24, 1821, be-
tween the Colombian patriots,
8,000 strong, under Bolivar, and
the Spanish Royalists, about
4,000 in number, under La
Torre.   The Royalists were
utterly routed, barely 400
reaching Porto Cabello.   This
battle determined the independence of Colombia.

Caracha (South American War of Independence).

Fought 1813, between the
Colombian Patriots under Bolivar and the Spanish Royalists, Bolivar gaining a complete
victory.

Caraguatay (Paraguayan War).

Fought August 1869, between
the Paraguayans under Lopez,
and the Brazilians under the
Comte d'Eu.   After a stubborn
engagement the Brazilians were
victorious.

Carbisdale (Civil War).

Fought April 27, 1650, between the Royalists of Orkney,
1,000 strong, with 500 Swedish
mercenaries, and a small Parliamentary force under Colonel
Strachan.   Montrose, who commanded the Royalists, saw his
troops broken by the Parliamentary horse, only the Swedes
offering any serious resistance.
The Royalists lost 396 killed
and wounded and over 400

prisoners, while Strachan only
had lost 2 wounded.   This was
Montrose's last fight, and he was
soon afterwards captured.

Carénage Bay (American War of Independence).

Fought 1778, between the
French under the Comte
d'Estaing, and the English under
Admiral Barrington and General
Meadows.   After a severe encounter, the French were defeated, and the British took
possession of the island of St.
Lucia.

Carigat. *See* Arikera.

Carlisle (Rebellion of the Forty-five).

This city was besieged by the
Jacobites under the Young
Pretender, November 9, 1745,
and was defended by the
Cumberland and Westmoreland
Militia, with small force of
regulars, under Colonel Durand.
The besiegers opened fire on the
13th, and on the evening of the
14th, under pressure of the
inhabitants, Durand surrendered.

Carnoul (Persian Invasion of India).

Fought 1739, between the
Persians under Nadir Shah, and
the Moguls under the Emperor
Mohammed Shah and his Grand
Vizier, Nizam-ul-Mulk.   The
Persian veterans completely defeated the raw Mogul levies,
and Nadir Shah shortly afterwards occupied and sacked
Delhi, carrying off, it is said,
jewels and coin to the value of
thirty millions sterling.

Carpi (War of the Spanish Succession).

Fought July 1701, between
the Imperialists under Prince

Eugene, and the French army in Lombardy, under Marshal Catinat. The French were signally defeated, and, in consequence, Catinat was recalled from the command.

Carrhæ (Parthian War).

Fought B.C. 53, between the Romans, 52,000 strong, under Publius Crassus, and the Parthians under Sillaces. The Parthians, who were entirely cavalry, adopted their usual tactics of retiring and drawing their foes in pursuit. As the heavily armed legionaries became strung out across the plain, they turned upon them and cut them down in detail. Of the division, 6,000 strong, which actually came into action, 500 were made prisoners, and the rest, including Crassus, slain.

Carrical (Seven Years' War).

An action was fought off this place August 2, 1758, between a British squadron under Admiral Pococke, and the French under Comte d'Aché. After a severe engagement, the French fleet drew off, but the English pursuit, owing to damaged rigging, was ineffectual, and d'Aché reached Pondicherry without the loss of a ship.

Carthage (Third Punic War).

In B.C. 152 siege was laid to this city by a Roman consular army under Manius Manilius, aided by a fleet under L. Censorinus. The Carthaginian army under Hasdrubal was encamped outside the walls, and greatly hindered the operations of the Romans, who would have made little progress but for the efforts of Scipio Æmilianus, then a military tribune. In B.C. 148,

Scipio was made consul, and appointed to the command, and he succeeded in completely blockading the city, which, after an obstinate resistance lasting six years, was captured B.C. 146 and razed to the ground.

Carthage (Invasion of the Vandals).

Fought September 14, 533, between the Vandals under Gelimer, about 160,000 strong, and the Romans under Belisarius, far inferior in numbers. Gelimer divided his army into three, of which he led one portion to attack the main body of the Romans. The action was precipitated, however, by the hasty attack by Ammatas of the vanguard, wherein he was routed with heavy loss. Gelimer then fell upon the pursuing Romans, but Belisarius coming up, the Vandals were put to flight, and the Romans gained a complete victory. On the following day Carthage opened her gates to the victors.

Carthagena (War of the Austrian Succession).

This port was blockaded March 9, 1741, by a British fleet under Admiral Vernon. An unsuccessful attack was made upon the forts, and eventually Vernon, having lost 3,000 men during the operations, withdrew April 9.

Casal (Wars of Louis XIV).

Fought April 1640, between the French, 10,000 strong, under Harcourt, and the Spaniards, numbering 20,000, who were besieging Casal. Harcourt pierced the Spanish lines and totally defeated them, with a loss of 3,000 killed and wounded, 800 prisoners, and 18 guns.

Casilinum (Second Frank Invasion of Italy).

Fought 554, between 18,000 Imperial troops under Narses, and the Franks and Alemanni, 30,000 strong, under Buccelin. The Romans won a signal victory, and are said by the chroniclers to have exterminated the invading army with a loss to themselves of 80 only. Buccelin fell in the battle.

Cassano (War of the Spanish Succession).

Fought August 16, 1705, between the French under the Duc de Vendôme, with 35 battalions and 45 squadrons, and the Imperialists under Prince Eugene. The Prince, with greatly inferior numbers, attacked the French in a strong position, which he succeeded in carrying as the night fell. The Imperialists lost about 4,000 ; the French about 5,000.

Castalla (Peninsular War).

Fought April 13, 1813, between 17,000 allied troops under Sir John Murray, and 15,000 French under Suchet. The French were defeated. The allies lost 600 killed and wounded ; the French, according to Suchet, 800, according to Murray, 3,000, but the former figure is probably nearer to the truth.

Castelfidardo (Unification of Italy).

Fought September 18, 1860, between the Papal troops under General La Moricière, about 8,000 strong, and the Sardinians, 40,000 strong, under General Cialdini. The Papal army was totally routed, and, after the action, La Moricière was only able to assemble about 300 infantry, with which remnant he made his way to Ancona.

Castelnaudary.

Fought September 1, 1632, between the troops of Louis XIII and the rebel nobles under the Duc de Montmorenci, son of the Constable. The rebels were utterly routed, and Montmorenci taken prisoner.

Castiglione (War of the Spanish Succession).

Fought September 8, 1706, between the Imperialists under the Prince of Hesse, and the French under General de Medavi. The Prince was besieging Castiglione, when he was attacked by the French, and totally defeated, with a loss of 8,000 killed, wounded, and missing.

Castiglione (Napoleon's Italian Campaigns).

Fought August 3, 1796, between the French under Napoleon, and the Imperialists under Wurmser. Napoleon, with 25,000 men, advanced upon Lonato, while Augereau moved upon Castiglione. Lonato was carried by assault, and the Austrian army cut in two. One part under General Bazalitch effected a retreat to the Mincio, but the other section was cut up by a French division under Guyeaux and Junot's dragoons, near Salo, losing 3,000 prisoners and 20 guns.

In the portion of the action fought near Castiglione, the Austrians were defeated with a loss of 2,000 men, after a desperate encounter, and driven back upon Mantua. On the 4th, Napoleon at Lonato, with only 12,000 men, was summoned to surrender by a portion of Bazalitch's force, 4,000 strong. Napoleon, however, succeeded in making the messenger think that he was in the middle of the main French army, and consequently the whole Austrian detachment laid down their arms.

Castillejos (Moroccan War).

Fought January 1, 1860, when the advance guard of the Spanish army, under General Prim, defeated a strong force of Moors, after severe fighting. The victory opened the road to Tetuan.

Castillon (Hundred Years' War).

This was the last battle of the Hundred Years' War, and was fought July 17, 1453. The English under Talbot, Earl of Shrewsbury, marched to the relief of Castillon, and attacked the lines of the besiegers, but were taken in flank by a sortie from the French entrenchments and totally defeated, Talbot being slain. On October 19 following, Bordeaux opened her gates to the French.

Catana (Second Carthaginian Invasion of Sicily).

Fought B.C. 387 between 200 Syracusan galleys under Leptines, and a vastly superior Carthaginian fleet. The Syracusans were utterly routed, partly owing to their inferior numbers, but also in part to the bad generalship of Leptines, who dispersed his ships too widely, allowing them to be overwhelmed in detail. The victors at once entered upon the siege of Syracuse.

Caudine Forks (Second Samnite War).

Fought B.C. 322, when four Roman legions, under T. Veturius Calvinus and Spurius Postumus were entrapped by the Sabines under Pontius, in the narrow pass of Caudium. The Romans fought till nightfall, suffering heavy loss, and next day, finding every exit from the pass barred, the survivors surrendered.

Cawnpur (Indian Mutiny).

The Residency of Cawnpur was invested by the mutineers June 6, 1857, and defended by a small garrison until June 24, when the survivors, about 450 in number, surrendered under promise from the Nana Sahib of a safe conduct to Allahabad. They were, however, fired upon as they took to the boats, and only a few escaped. The survivors of this massacre were afterwards murdered in cold blood by order of the Nana Sahib.

Cawnpur (Indian Mutiny).

Fought December 6, 1857, between the British under Sir Colin Campbell, and 25,000 rebels, including the Gwalior contingent. The mutineers were routed at all points, and fled, pursued by the cavalry for 14 miles, suffering heavy loss. Out of 36 guns, 32 were captured. The British lost 99 only.

Cecryphalea (Third Messenian War).

A naval action, fought B.C. 458 between the Peloponnesians and the Athenians, in which the latter were victorious.

Cedar Creek (American Civil War).

Fought October 17, 1864, between 10,000 Confederates under General Early, and about 40,000 Federals under General Sheridan. Under cover of a fog, Early turned Sheridan's right, capturing 18 guns, but Sheridan, rallying his broken right wing, totally routed the Confederates, who had been engaged in plundering the captured camp. The Federal losses were the heavier, but Sheridan captured 22 guns, besides retaking the 18 he had lost at the beginning of the action.

Cedar Mountain (American Civil War).

Fought August 9, 1862, between 15,000 Confederates under Jackson, and about 20,000 Federals under General Pope. The strong Confederate position was assailed at 5 p.m., and successive attacks were repulsed until late in the evening, when the fighting ceased. The Federals lost about 2,800 killed, wounded, and missing ; the Confederates, 800 or 900.

Cepeda.

Fought October 23, 1859, between the troops of the Argentine Confederation under Urquiza, and those of the State of Buenos Ayres, under Mitre. Urquiza was victorious, and in the following month Buenos Ayres entered the Confederation.

Cephisus.

Fought 1307 between the Catalan " Great Band," 9,500 strong, and the troops of Walter de Brienne, Duke of Athens, 15,000 in number. The Catalans surrounded their camp with an artificial inundation, into which the Duke's cavalry rode

unsuspectingly, and were cut to pieces, de Brienne being amongst the slain.

Cerignola (Neapolitan War).

Fought 1503 between the Spaniards under Gonsalvo de Cordova, and the French under the Duc de Nemours. The French were totally defeated and Nemours slain.

Cerisolles (Wars of Charles V).

Fought 1544, between the French under François de Bourbon, and the Imperialists under du Gast, the French gaining a complete victory.

Chacabuco (South American War of Independence).

Fought February 12, 1817, between the Chilian patriots under San Martin, and the Spanish royalists. The Chilians won a complete victory.

Chæronea (Amphictyonic War).

Fought August B.C. 338 between the Macedonians under Philip, and the Athenians and Thebans under Chares and Theagenes respectively.[1] Philip had 30,000 foot and 2,000 horse, the latter led by Alexander, then a lad of eighteen ; the allies were slightly fewer in number. Philip reinforced his right wing, which was opposed by the Athenians, and sent his heavy cavalry against the Thebans, on the allied right. Their charge broke the Theban ranks, and they then attacked the Athenians in flank and rear. A hopeless rout ensued, the Theban " Sacred Band " dying where they stood. The Athenians lost 6,000 killed and 2,000 prisoners. The Thebans were almost annihilated.

Chæronea (First Mithridatic War).

Fought B.C. 86, between the Romans under Sulla, 30,000 strong, and the troops of Pontus, 90,000 in number, under Archelaus. The Romans were completely victorious.

Chalcedon (Third Mithridatic War).

Fought B.C. 74, between the Roman fleet, under Rutilius Nudo, and that of Pontus. The Romans sallied out of the harbour, but were driven back, and the Pontic fleet then broke the chain protecting the entrance and destroyed the whole of the Roman ships, 70 in number.

Chalgrove Field (Civil War).

A cavalry skirmish fought June 18, 1643, between the Royalists under Prince Rupert, and the Parliamentarians under Hampden, and notable only for the fact that Hampden was killed in the affair.

Châlons (Revolt of the Legions of Aquitaine).

Fought 271, between the troops of the Emperor Aurelian, and the revolted legions under Tetricus. Tetricus, who was only a puppet in the hands of his soldiers, concerted measures with Aurelian for their destruction, and so posted his forces as to give the Emperor the advantage, after which he deserted, with a few followers. The revolted legionaries fought desperately, but were cut to pieces.

Châlons (Invasion of the Alemanni).

Fought July 366 between the Romans under Jovinus, and the Alemanni under Vadomair.

After an obstinate engagement, lasting throughout the day, the Alemanni were routed with a loss of 6,000 killed and 4,000 prisoners. The Romans lost 1,200.

Châlons (Invasion of the Huns).

Fought 451 between the Romans and the Visigoths under Actius and Theodoric respectively, and the Huns under Attila. The battle was fought on an open plain, and while the right and centre of the allies withstood Attila's onslaught, the Visigoths on the left made a furious charge, in which Theodoric fell, and totally routed the right of the Huns. Attila then withdrew to his camp, having suffered heavy loss, and prepared to resist the attack of the allies on the following day. Actius, however, did not renew the conflict, and allowed Attila to retreat unmolested.

Châlons.

Arising out of a tournament in 1274, in which the life of Edward I was endangered by foul play, a fight in earnest took place between the English and French knights present. The French were worsted, and a considerable number slain. This fight is called the " Little " Battle of Châlons.

Champ-Aubert (Allied Invasion of France).

Fought February 10, 1814, when Napoleon with his main army, by an extraordinary forced march through a difficult country, fell upon Blucher's army marching upon Paris, viâ Châlons. Blucher was advancing in three divisions, and Napoleon attacked the second of these, under Alsusieff, and completely dispersed it, taking 2,000 prisoners and all the guns. On the following day he encountered Sachen, who with 20,000 men formed the advance guard, and defeated him at Montmirail, with a loss of 6,000, forcing him to abandon the main road and retire on Château Thierry. On the 13th he encountered General d'York, with 30,000 Russians and Prussians at Château Thierry, driving him out with heavy loss, including 3,000 prisoners, while finally on the 14th he turned on the main body under Blucher himself, who, not being sufficiently strong to face the main French army, was compelled to retire, which he did in good order, after losing 3,000 in killed, wounded, and prisoners. This flank march is considered one of Napoleon's most brilliant achievements.

Chancellorsville (American Civil War).

Fought May 2, 3, and 4, 1863, between 53,000 Confederates under Lee, and 120,000 Federals under Hooker. Lee, though largely outnumbered, detached half his force under Jackson to turn Hooker's right, while he contained the Federals with the rest of his army. Jackson's march was successfully carried out, and on the afternoon of the 2nd he commenced his attack, routing the Federal 11th Corps. This success, however, cost the Confederates dear, for Jackson's staff was mistaken in the dusk for that of a Federal general, and was fired into by a South Carolina regiment, and Jackson mortally wounded. On the 3rd the attack was renewed in front and flank, with further success for the Confederates, while on the 4th the Federals were driven off, and Hooker forced to recross the Rappahannock on the 5th. The Confederates lost about 10,000 men ; the Federals about 18,000, including 7,650 prisoners.

Chanda (Third Mahratta War).

This fortress, the chief stronghold of the Rajah of Nagpur, was besieged by a British force under Colonel Adams, May 9, 1818. It was defended by over 3,000 of the Rajah's troops, but after two days' bombardment the place was taken by storm, with small loss to the assailants, while the garrison had 500 killed, including the commandant.

Chandernagore (Seven Years' War).

This place was besieged March 14, 1757, by Clive, with 2,000 Company's troops, and defended by 600 Frenchmen and 300 Sepoys. On the 19th three British ships under Admiral Watson arrived, and on the 24th a joint attack by sea and land resulted in the capture of the place.

Charasiab (Second Afghan War).

Fought October 6, 1879, when Sir Frederick Roberts attacked a force of Afghans and Ghilzais, who were massed on the road by which a convoy was approaching from Zahidabad, under General Macpherson. The enemy was routed and dispersed, and the convoy reached camp safely.

Charenton (War of the Fronde).

Fought February 8, 1649, between the Royal troops, 8,000 strong, under the Great Condé, and the forces of the Paris Parliament under Clauleu. Condé gained a complete victory, driving the Frondeurs from all their entrenchments, and forcing them back upon Paris with heavy loss, including 100 officers. Among the slain was Clauleu.

Charleston (American Civil War).

The siege of this place may be considered to have commenced April 6, 1863, on which day the Federal fleet crossed the bar. On the 7th an attack was made upon fort Sumter by nine ironclads under Admiral Dupont, which was repulsed with a loss of 1 ship and the disabling of several others. The defenders lost 2 men only. On July 10th and 11th a land force attacked Fort Wagner, but was repulsed with loss. On the 18th an assault by three brigades under General Seymour was also repulsed with enormous loss ; and preparations were then made for a sap. On September 5, after a very heavy bombardment, Fort Wagner proved to be untenable, and, with the works on Morris Island, was abandoned, but the besiegers failed in all their attempts on Fort Sumter, and the inner defences. From this time the siege became a mere blockade of the port, until, on the approach of Sherman's army, the garrison, then 9,000 strong, evacuated the city, February 18, 1865.

Châteauguay (Second American War).

Fought 1813, between the Americans, 7,000 strong, under General Hampton, and a force of Canadian Militia, far inferior in numbers, who were strongly posted near Châteauguay. The Americans attempted to storm the Canadian lines, but the Canadians made a most gallant defence, and repulsed them with heavy loss.

Châteauneuf-Raudon (Hundred Years' War).

This fortress was besieged 1380 by the French under Du Guesclin, and was defended by an English garrison under de Ros. After an obstinate defence the town surrendered, July 4, but the siege was fatal to Du Guesclin, who succumbed to his fatigues and privations.

Château Thierry. *See* Champ-Aubert.

Chattanooga (American Civil War).

Fought November 24 to 27, 1863, between 80,000 Federals under Grant, and the Confederate Army of the West, 40,000 strong, under Bragg. The attack on the Confederate lines commenced on the 27th, the Federals capturing Look Out Mountain, on their extreme left. They advanced unseen through a thick fog, to the upper slopes, and drove out the defenders, whence this action is known as the " Battle above the Clouds." On the following day Bragg's centre was pierced, while the fighting of the 26th and 27th was in the nature of severe rearguard actions. The Federals lost 5,286 killed and wounded, and 330 missing. The Confederates lost fewer in killed and wounded, but they left in the hands of the Federals 6,142 prisoners, 40 guns and 7,000 rifles. Also called the " Battle of Missionary Ridge."

Che-mul-pho (Russo-Japanese War).

Fought February 8, 1904, between a Japanese squadron of four protected cruisers, convoying transports, under Admiral Uriu, and a Russian cruiser and gunboat which sought to oppose the landing. After a smart action the cruiser was blown up to avoid capture, and the gunboat destroyed, the Russians losing 504 killed and wounded. The Japanese suffered no material damage.

Cheriton (Civil War).

Fought March 29, 1644, when the Royalists under Lord Firth were defeated by the Parliamentarians under Waller. This defeat prevented the threatened Royalist incursion into Kent and Sussex.

Chetaté (Crimean War).

Fought January 6 to 9, 1854. On the 6th the advanced Russian post of 6,000 men at Chetaté under General Fischbuch was attacked by 6,000 Turks under Ahmed Pasha, and after heavy fighting, in which the Russians lost 3,000 killed and wounded, and many prisoners, and the Turks 1,000, was driven out of the village. On the following days the Russians made desperate attempts to recover the position, General Anrep, on the 9th, bringing up some 20,000 men from Cragova. All their efforts, however, failed, and the three days' fighting cost them a further 2,000 men, the Turks losing about 1,000.

Chevilly (Franco-German War),

Fought September 30, 1870, when a sortie from Paris under General Vinoy was repulsed by the Sixth German Corps under Von Tümpling, with a loss of 74 officers and 2,046 men. The Germans lost 28 officers and 413 men killed and wounded.

Chevy Chace. See Otterburn.

Chiari (War of the Spanish Succession).

Fought September 1, 1701, between the Imperialists, about 28,000 strong, under Prince Eugene, and the French and Spaniards under the Duke of Savoy. The Prince occupied the small town of Chiari, where he was attacked by the allies, who, after two hours' hard fighting, were repulsed with a loss of nearly 3,000. Owing to the strength of their position, the Imperialists lost 117 only.

Chickahominy (American Civil War).

Fought June 3, 1864, between the Federal Army of the Potomac under Grant, and the Confederate army of Virginia under Lee. Grant attacked the Southerners' entrenchments, with the object of forcing the passage of the Chickahominy, and his first onslaught met with some success, but the Confederates, rallying, drove back their assailants to their original position with heavy loss. All further attempts on Lee's lines failed, and the Federals were finally repulsed with a loss of over 13,000 killed, wounded and missing. The Confederates lost about 6,000.

Chickamauga (American Civil War).

Fought September 19 and 20, 1863, between the Confederate Army of the West under General Bragg, and the Federals under General Rosecrans. On the 19th the Confederates attacked along the whole line and drove back their opponents, cutting them off from the river, and forcing them to bivouac for the night in a waterless country. On the 20th the attack was renewed, and though Bragg's right was repulsed, he was elsewhere successful, and by nightfall Rosecrans was in full retreat. Bragg however, failed to follow up his victory, and allowed Rosecrans to retire on Chattanooga unmolested. The Federals lost 16,351 men and 36 guns ; the Confederates about 12,000.

Chillianwallah (Second Sikh War).

Fought January 14, 1849, between the British under Lord Gough, and the Sikhs, 40,000 strong, under Shere Singh. The battle was very evenly contested, and though in the end Lord Gough drove the Sikhs from the field, his own position was so insecure that he was himself compelled to retire after the action.

Chiloe (South American War of Independence).

On January 19, 1826, the small group of islands, held for the Spanish crown by a garrison under Quintanella, was surrendered to a force of Chilians, 4,000 strong, with a small squadron of warships under Freyre.

Chingleput (Seven Years' War).

This fortress, defended by a French garrison of 40 Europeans and 500 native troops, was captured, 1752, by Clive, with a force of about 700 recruits and Sepoys.

Chios (Social War).

Chios having risen against Athenian rule in B.C. 357, a fleet of 60 ships under Chabrias and Chares was sent to reduce it. A force having been landed, a joint attack was made by the fleet and the army, but in attempting to enter the harbour, the galley of Chabrias, which led the way, was surrounded and overpowered, Chabrias falling The troops were then withdrawn, and the attack abandoned.

Chios.

Fought B.C. 201 between the Macedonian fleet, 48 triremes and some smaller vessels under Philip, and the combined fleets of Rhodes and Pergamus under Theophiliscus and Attalus. Philip was defeated with the loss of half his ships, 3,000 killed and 5,000 prisoners. The allies lost 6 ships and 800 men.

Chiozza (War of Chiozza).

This city, which had been captured by the Genoese from Venice, was besieged by the Venetians under Pisani and defended by Doria, who was killed during the siege. The place made an obstinate resistance, but was forced to surrender June 24, 1380, the Venetians capturing 19 Genoese galleys and 4,000 prisoners. This disaster broke the power of the Genoese Republic for many years.

Chippewa (Second American War).

Fought July 6, 1814, between 4,000 Americans under General Jacob Brown, and 2,400 British, 1,500 being regulars, under General Riall. Riall attacked

Brown in a strong position at Chippewa, and was repulsed with considerable loss.

Chitor.

Towards the end of the thirteenth century this fortress was besieged by the Pathans under Ala-ud-Din, and was defended by the Rana, Lakhsman. The first attack was repulsed, though the Rajputs suffered terribly, but at the second attempt the Pathans overpowered the defenders, who were mercilessly put to the sword. All the Rajput women in the place committed suttee, to avoid captivity. Lakhsman Singh and eleven out of his twelve sons fell in the defence.

The second sack of Chitor took place in 1535, when the Rana Bikrmajit made a gallant but unavailing defence against the Gujeratis under Bahadur Shah. Thirteen thousand women were slain by the remnant of the garrison, before they opened the gates, and rushed out to fall fighting. Only one small child of the Royal line escaped the massacre, namely Udai Singh. It was during the reign of this Udai Singh that the third sack took place in 1568, by the Delhi Moguls under Akbar. Udai Singh deserted his capital, which was defended by a garrison of 8,000 Rajputs under Jagmal. The siege was scientifically conducted, and, a breach having been effected, an assault was ordered. A mine, however, was exploded in the breach, killing 500 of the assailants, and the assault was repulsed. Shortly afterwards Jagmal was killed, and a second assault proved successful, the garrison, refusing to surrender, being put to the sword.

Chitral (Chitral Campaign).

On March 3, 1895, the Chitral garrison, consisting of 90 Sikhs and 280 Kashmir Imperial Service troops, with 7 British officers under Captain Campbell, was attacked by a large force of Chitralis and Bajauris under Shere Afzal, the Pretender to the Chitral throne, and Umrar Khan of Bajaur. A sortie was repulsed, with a loss of 58, including 2 British officers, and General Baj Singh, who commanded the Kashmiris, but in spite of a series of attacks, and continual mining operations, the garrison held out until April 18, when it was relieved by Colonel Kelly. One fifth of the garrison was killed or wounded.

Chizai (Hundred Years' War).

Fought July 1372, between the French under Du Guesclin, and the English under Thomas Hampton. Du Guesclin, who was engaged in the siege of Chizai, was attacked by the English, in about equal force to his own, and, after a long and bloody engagement, totally defeated them, and captured the town. The reverse cost Edward III Saintonge and Poitou.

Choczim (Ottoman Wars).

Fought 1769, between the Russians under Galitzin, and the Turks under Mohammed Emin Pasha. The Russians, who were endeavouring to capture Choczim by a *coup de main*, were met and defeated by the Turks with considerable loss.

Chong-ju (Russo-Japanese War).

The first encounter between the land forces of Russia and Japan, April, 1904, when the advanced guard of the First Japanese Army came in contact with a force of Cossacks under General Mischtchenko, and after a brisk engagement drove them back and occupied Chong-ju. The losses on both sides were small.

Chorillos (Peruvio-Chilian War).

Fought January 13, 1861, between the Chilians under General Baquedano and the Peruvians under General Caceres. The Peruvians were totally defeated with a loss of 9,000 killed and wounded, and 2,000 prisoners. The Chilians lost 800 killed and 2,500 wounded.

Chotusitz (War of the Austrian Succession).

Fought May 17, 1742, between the Austrians under Prince Charles of Lorraine, and the Prussians under Frederick the Great. The numbers were about equal, but the steadiness of the Prussian infantry eventually wore down the Austrians, and they were forced to retreat, though in good order, leaving behind them 18 guns and 12,000 prisoners. The killed and wounded numbered about 7,000 on each side, and the Austrians made 1,000 prisoners. The Prussian cavalry delivered several desperate and unsuccessful charges, and were almost destroyed.

Christianople (Dano-Swedish Wars).

The first military exploit of Gustavus Adolphus of Sweden, who, during the war of 1611,

made a night assault on this fortress with 1,500 men, and blowing in the gate, captured the place without losing a man.

Chrysopolis (War of the Two Empires).

Fought 323 between 60,000 troops under Licinius, Emperor of the East, and a force detached by Constantine from the siege of Byzantium. Licinius was totally defeated, with a loss of 25,000, and surrendered. The result of this victory was the re-union of the whole of the Roman Empire under one head.

Chrystlers Farm (Second American War).

Fought November 11, 1813, between 800 British under Colonel Morrison, and about 3,000 Americans under General Boyd. The Americans were defeated with a loss of 249 killed and wounded and 100 prisoners. The British lost 203.

Chunar.

This fortress, which was held for Shir Khan Sur, Nawab of Bengal, was besieged by the Moguls under Humayun in 1538. This is the first siege in Indian history which was conducted according to the rules of war, and was notable for the use made of artillery by both sides. After a siege lasting several months, the garrison was forced by famine to surrender.

Cibalis (War of the Two Empires).

Fought October 8, 315, between Constantine the Great, with 20,000 men, and Licinius, Emperor of the East, with 35,000. Constantine was posted in a defile, where he was attacked by Licinius. The attack was repulsed, and Constantine followed the enemy into the open plain, where Licinius rallied his troops, and resumed the offensive. The day seemed lost, when a charge of the right wing, under Constantine in person, once more broke the Illyrians, and Licinius having lost 20,000 of his best troops, abandoned his camp during the night and retreated to Sirmium.

Ciudad Rodrigo (Peninsular War).

This town was invested by Wellington January 8, 1812, and carried by assault twelve days later. The besiegers lost during the siege 1,290 killed and wounded, of whom 710, including Generals Craufurd and Mackinnon, fell in the storm. The French lost 300 killed and wounded, 1,500 prisoners, and 150 guns.

Ciuna (Second Samnite War).

Fought B.C. 315, between the Romans under Caius Mænius and the Samnites under Pontius. The Romans gained a signal victory.

Civitella (Norman Invasion of Italy.

Fought 1033, when 3,000 Normans under Robert Guiscard assailed and totally routed a miscellaneous force of Germans and Italians under Pope Leo IX. Only the Germans offered any serious resistance, but they were cut down to a man, and the Pope was overtaken in his flight and captured.

Clissau (Swedo-Polish Wars).

Fought July 13, 1702, between the Swedes, 12,000 strong,

under Charles XII, and 24,000 Poles and Saxons under Frederick Augustus. The Saxons fought gallantly, but the Poles fled at the first onslaught, and in the end the Swedes gained a complete victory. Among those who fell was the Duke of Holstein, commanding the Swedish cavalry.

Clontarf (Norse Invasion of Ireland).

Fought April 24, 1014, when the Scandinavian invaders were totally routed by the Irish of Munster, Connaught, Ulster and Meath, under Brian Boru. The Norsemen are said to have lost 6,000 men. Brian Boru and his son fell in the battle.

Clusium (Conquest of Cisalpine Gaul).

Fought B.C. 225, when the Gauls utterly routed a Roman army with a loss said to have amounted to 50,000 men.

Cnidus.

Fought B.C. 394 between 120 Spartan triremes under Pisander and a largely superior Persian fleet under Pharnabazus, and Conon the Athenian. Pisander was defeated and slain, and his fleet destroyed. Persia thus reestablished her power in the Greek cities of Asia, and the maritime power of Sparta was destroyed.

Cockerel (Hundred Years' War).

Fought May, 1364, between the Navarrese under Jean de Grailli, aided by a force of English mercenaries under John Joel, and the French, 10,000 strong, under Bertrand du Guesclin. Du Guesclin, who was executing a strategic retreat, was attacked by the English, who were surrounded and overpowered, Joel falling. De Grailli came to their aid, but was also overwhelmed and made prisoner, and the Navarrese, deprived of their leaders, laid down their arms.

Colenso (Second Boer War).

Fought December 15, 1899, being the first action in Sir Redvers Buller's campaign for the relief of Ladysmith. Buller attempted to carry by a frontal attack the Boer position on the opposite side of the Tugela, and notwithstanding the gallantry of the troops, was compelled to retire, with a loss of 71 officers and 1,055 rank and file. Of this total the Irish Brigade lost about half. The Boers captured 10 guns.

Colline Gate (Civil War of Marius and Sulla).

Fought B.C. 82 between the adherents of Sulla, and the Roman democrats and Samnites under Pontius, outside the walls of Rome. The battle was obstinately contested, but, after a fight lasting throughout the night, the insurgents were routed, and 4,000 prisoners taken. This victory of the aristocratic party ended the civil war.

Colombey (Franco-German War).

Fought August 11, 1870, between the retiring French army, and the advance guard of the First German Army Corps under von Steinmetz. The French maintained most of their positions, but two of their divisions were overthrown, and Bazaine's retreat on Verdun was seriously delayed. The French lost about 7,000 ; the Germans 222 officers and 5,000 men.

Colombo (Wars of the French Revolution).

This town was captured from the Dutch in 1796, by a squadron of four British warships, and a small force of troops under Admiral Peter Rainier and Colonel Stuart.

Concha Rayada (South American War of Independence).

Fought February 1818, between the Spanish Royalists, 5,000 strong, under General Osorio, and the Chilians and Colombians under San Martin. The Spaniards gained a complete victory.

Concon (Chilian Civil War).

Fought August 21, 1891, between 10,000 Congressists under General del Canto, and 11,000 Balmacedists under General Barbosa. Aided by the fire of three warships, the Congressists, who had landed unopposed on the 20th, stormed the entrenchments of the Balmacedists, and drove them out with a loss of 1,648 killed and wounded, and 1,500 prisoners. The victors lost 869.

Condorcanqui. See Ayacucho

Constantine (Conquest of Algeria).

This fortified city in Eastern Algeria, which, under Hadji Ahmad, had held out for six years against French rule, was invested by the French, 7,000 strong, under Marshal Clausel, in the autumn of 1836. Having no breaching pieces, Clausel essayed an assault, but was repulsed with a loss of 2,000 men, and abandoned the siege. In the following year General

Damrémont sat down before Constantine October 6, with 10,000 men, and on the 12th, a breach having been effected, an assault was on the point of taking place, when Damrémont was killed. His successor, General Valée, however, took the place by storm on the following day.

Constantinople (Moslem Invasion of Europe).

This city was besieged in 668, by the Saracens under Sophian, the lieutenant of the Caliph Moawiyeh. The Moslem fleet passed the Hellespont unopposed, but their attack upon the city was met with a most determined resistance. After keeping the field from April to September, Sophian retired into winter quarters, but renewed active operations during the following and five succeeding summers, without success, until, in 675, he finally abandoned the siege, having lost in its progress over 30,000 men.

In 716, the Saracens again laid siege to the city, with 120,000 men under Moslemeh, brother of the Caliph Solyman. A fleet of 1,800 sail co-operated with the land forces, but was destroyed by the Greek fire ships, and thus obtaining the command of the sea, the citizens were relieved from all fear of famine, and repulsed all Moslemeh's assaults. After a siege of 13 months, the Saracens withdrew, after a defeat at the hands of a Bulgarian relieving army, in which they lost 22,000 men.

Constantinople (Fourth Crusade).

The city was besieged July 7, 1203, by the French and Venetian Crusaders under Count Thibaut de Champagne. After a feeble defence, it was surrendered July 18, by the Usurper, Alexius, and occupied by the Crusaders, who restored Isaac Angelus to the throne, and withdrew.

In January 1204 the Crusaders again laid siege to Constantinople, and at the end of three months, in the course of which Isaac Angelus died, and Mourzoufle assumed the purple, they stormed and pillaged the city. Baldwin was then proclaimed first Latin Emperor of the East.

On July 25, 1261, Constantinople was taken by surprise by the troops of the Greek Emperor, Michael Palæologus, under his lieutenant, Alexius Strategopulus. The Latin Emperor, Baldwin II, made no attempt at resistance, but escaped to the Venetian galleys, and the restoration of the Greek Empire was accomplished without opposition.

Constantinople.

A naval action fought February 13, 1352, between 64 Genoese galleys under Doria, and 75 Greek and Venetian galleys under Pisani. The Genoese were victorious, taking or sinking 26 galleys, and forcing Pisani to retire into the fortified harbour. The Genoese lost 13 galleys.

Constantinople (Ottoman Invasion of Europe).

On June 10, 1422, Amurath II, with 200,000 Turks, laid siege to the city, which was defended by the Greek garrison under the Emperor Manuel.

After a siege of two months, in which the Turks lost heavily in their numerous assaults, and in the defenders' sallies Amurath, was called away to Boursa by a domestic revolt, and raised the siege.

On April 6, 1453, the Turks again laid siege to Constantinople with 258,000 men under Mohammed II. · The garrison, consisting of 5,000 Greeks and 2,000 foreigners, though short of ammunition, made a gallant defence, but were overpowered by numbers in a general assault on May 25, and the city was captured. Constantine Palæologus, the last Emperor of the East, was killed by an unknown hand, in the tumult which followed the storming of the ramparts.

Copenhagen (Napoleonic Wars).

Fought April 2, 1801, between the British fleet of 20 sail of the line, besides frigates, under Admirals Hyde Parker and Nelson, and the Danish fleet of 10 line of battleships, aided by the shore batteries. Nelson attacked with 12 ships, Parker remaining in reserve, but three of Nelson's vessels running aground, he met the Danish line with 9 only. The Danes offered a strenuous resistance, and Parker hoisted the signal to retire, but Nelson put the telescope to his blind eye, and refused to see the signal. The action continued until the Danish fire was silenced. The British lost 1,200 men, and had six vessels seriously damaged. The Danes had one ship destroyed, and the rest of their fleet completely disabled. The result of this victory was the dissolution of the league of the Northern Powers.

Copenhagen (Napoleonic Wars).

The city was captured September 5, 1807, by 20,000 British troops under Lord Cathcart, after a four days' bombardment of the forts and citadel by 27 ships of the line. The Danish fleet of 18 sail of the line, which was surrendered, would otherwise, under a secret clause of the Treaty of Tilsit, have been placed at the disposal of Napoleon.

Copratus, The (Wars of Alexander's Successors).

Fought B.C. 316, between the Macedonians under Antigonus, and the Asiatics under Eumenes. Each army was about 30,000 strong, and Eumenes fell upon the Macedonians as they were crossing the Copratus, and signally defeated them, though Antigonus was able to retreat in good order.

Cordova (Moorish Empire in Spain).

Fought August 1010, between the Berbers under Sulaiman, aided by the Spaniards under Sancho, Count of Castile, and the Moors of Cordova under Almudy. Almudy marched out of Cordova to meet the Berbers, but was utterly routed, with a loss of 20,000, including most of his principal Emirs.

Corinth (Peloponnesian War).

Fought B.C. 429, between 47 Peloponnesian ships under Cnemus, and 20 Athenian triremes under Phormio. Phormio, who was blockading the Gulf of Corinth, allowed Cnemus to pass into the open sea, and when disordered by the heavy weather

F

prevailing, he attacked and completely defeated the Peloponnesians, capturing 12 ships.

Corinth (Corinthian War).

Fought B.C. 394 between 14,000 Spartans, and 26,000 Athenians, Corinthians, Thebans and Argives. The allies were defeated, losing twice as many men as their opponents, but the Spartans, in spite of their victory, were obliged to retire, leaving the Isthmus in their possession.

Corinth (American Civil War).

Fought October 3 and 4, 1862, between the Confederates under Van Dorn, and the Federals under Rosecrans. Rosecrans was strongly entrenched at Corinth, where he was attacked on the 3rd, and driven into his inner lines. The attack was renewed on the 4th, but an attempt to storm the entrenchments was repulsed, and the Federals, taking the offensive against the disordered Southerners, drove them from the field with a loss of 6,423 killed and wounded, and 2,248 prisoners. The Federals lost 2,359 killed, wounded, and missing.

Coroneia (Bœotian Wars).

Fought B.C. 447, when an Athenian army under Tolmides, which had entered Bœotia to reduce certain of the Bœotian towns which had thrown off their allegiance to Athens, was encountered and totally defeated by a largely superior force of Bœotians. Almost all the surviving Athenians were captured, and, to secure their release, Athens resigned her claims over Bœotia.

Coroneia (Corinthian War).

Fought August B.C. 394, between the Athenians, Argives, Thebans, and Corinthians, and the Spartans under Agesilaus. The Spartan right defeated the Argives, but their left fled before the Thebans, who then attacked the Spartan right, but, after a desperate struggle, were defeated. The Spartans, however, had suffered so severely that Agesilaus was compelled to evacuate Bœotia.

Corrichie (Huntly's Rebellion).

Fought 1562, between the troops of Mary, Queen of Scots, and the Scottish rebels under the Earl of Huntly. The rebels, whose forces had been greatly reduced by desertions, were totally defeated, and Huntly slain.

Corte Nuova (Guelfs and Ghibellines).

Fought 1237, between the Imperialists under Frederick II, and the Lombard Guelfs under the leadership of the Milanese. Frederick won a signal victory, capturing the *carroccio* of Milan.

Corumba (Paraguayan War).

Fought 1877, between the Paraguayans and a Brazilian army corps which was endeavouring to enter Paraguay from the north-east. The Brazilians retired in disorder, being pursued for many miles, and suffering heavy loss. The battle is remarkable for the presence in the Paraguayan army of a corps of Amazons led by Eliza Lynch.

Coruña (Peninsular War).

Fought January 16, 1809, between 14,000 British under Sir John Moore, and 20,000 French under Soult, who was endeavouring to prevent the British from embarking. The French attacks were uniformly repulsed, and the troops safely embarked, with a loss of about 800, including Sir John Moore. The French lost about 2,000.

Compedion (Wars of Alexander's Successors).

Fought B.C. 281 between the Macedonians under Lysimachus, and the Syrians under Seleucus. The two generals met in single combat, in front of their armies. and Seleucus, though 81 years of age, defeated and slew his ancient comrade in arms. The two armies then engaged, and the Syrians gained a complete victory.

Coulmiers (Franco - German War).

Fought November 9, 1870, between 20,000 Germans under Von der Tann, and a largely superior French force under General d'Aurelle de Paladines. After maintaining their position for the greater part of the day, the Germans were driven back, having lost 576 killed and wounded, 800 prisoners, an ammunition column and 2 guns. The French losses were about 1,500.

Courtrai (Flemish War).

Fought 1302, between the French under Robert d'Artois, and the Flemings under Guy de Namur. The French were utterly routed, and so great was the carnage among the French nobility and knighthood, that after the battle 4,000, some say 7,000, gilt spurs, were hung up as trophies in Courtrai cathedral. From this circumstance this battle is commonly known as the Battle of the Spurs.

Coutras (Eighth Civil War).

Fought 1587 between the Huguenots under Henry of Navarre (Henri IV) and the Catholics under the Duc de Joyeuse. The Catholic army was annihilated, Joyeuse being amongst the slain.

Covelong (Seven Years' War).

This fortress, held by a French garrison of 350, was captured by Clive in 1752, after a few days' siege. Clive had only 200 European recruits and 500 Sepoys, and had great difficulty in getting his men to face the French fire. Having, however, managed to erect a battery which commanded the place, the Governor surrendered. On the following day Clive ambushed and defeated, with a loss of 100 men, a relieving force approaching from Chingleput.

Coverypank (Seven Years' War)

Fought February 1752, between the British, 380 Europeans, and 1,300 Sepoys, under Clive, and the troops of Rajah Sahib, with 400 Frenchmen, in all about 5,000. Clive's advance guard marched into an ambush, and with difficulty held its ground against the fire of 9 guns. Meanwhile Clive passed round the enemy's position, and attacked them vigorously in the rear, whereupon they fled in panic. Most of the Frenchmen and the guns were captured.

Craonne (Allied Invasion of France).

Fought March 7, 1814, between 55,000 French under

Napoleon, and about 90,000 of the allies under Blucher. Blucher occupied a very strong position on the heights about Craonne, which was attacked and carried by Victor's and Ney's corps at the point of the bayonet. The French lost 9,000, the allies 7,000 killed and wounded.

Cravant (Hundred Years' War).

Fought July 31, 1423. A force of Armagnacs under Buchan, Constable of France, with some Scottish mercenaries under Sir John Stewart, was advancing upon Craonne, the capture of which town would secure Charles VII's communications with Champagne. They were attacked by the Burgundians and English under the Earl of Salisbury, and defeated with heavy loss. Both Buchan and Stewart were captured.

Crayford (Jutish Invasion).

Fought 456 between the Jutes under Hengest, and the Britons under Vortigern. The Britons were defeated, and driven out of Kent.

Crefeld (Seven Years' War).

Fought June 23, 1758, between 32,000 Hanoverians, Hessians and Brunswickers under Prince Ferdinand of Brunswick, and about 50,000 French under the Comte de Clermont. The French were totally defeated, with heavy loss.

Cremona (Second Gallic Invasion).

Fought B.C. 198, when the Romans defeated with heavy slaughter an invading army of Gauls under Hamilcar, a Carthaginian. Hamilcar was slain.

Cremona (Revolt of Vitellius).

Fought December 69, between the Vitellians, and the Flavians under Antonius Primus, 40,000 strong. The Vitellians, who were without a leader, having deposed their general, Cæcina, were attacked in their camp, and after a hard fight, which lasted throughout the night, were totally routed. The victors sacked and burnt Cremona.

Cremona (War of the Spanish Succession).

This city, held by a French garrison, was surprised by the Imperialists under Prince Eugene, February 1, 1702. The town was entered without the alarm being given, and many important officers, including Marshal Villeroy, were made prisoners. A portion of the garrison, however, still held out in the citadel, and made Eugene's tenure of the town precarious, and finally, on the approach of a relieving force under the Prince de Vaudemont, he was forced to withdraw his troops. The garrison lost 1,000 killed.

Cressy (Hundred Years' War).

Fought August 26, 1346, when a very inferior force of English under Edward III defeated the French under Philip VI. The battle is notable as being the first in which the English army was mainly composed of infantry, and as proving the powerlessness of mounted men against the English archers. The French losses were 11 princes, 1,200 knights, and 30,000 of lesser ranks, a total exceeding the whole English force.

Crimisus (Third Carthaginian Invasion of Sicily).

Fought June B.C. 340, between 10,000 Sicilians under Timoleon, and 70,000 Carthaginians, including the " Sacred Band " of 2,500 Carthaginian citizens of good birth, under Hamilcar and Hasdrubal. Timoleon attacked the Carthaginians while they were crossing the Crimisus, and routed and dispersed the Sacred Band before the main army had crossed. A heavy storm of rain in the faces of the Carthaginians came to the aid of the Sicilians, and after a severe struggle, they gained a signal victory, and the Carthaginians fled, leaving 10,000 dead in the field, and 15,000 prisoners. Many more were drowned in their endeavour to recross the river.

Cronion (Second Carthaginian Invasion of Sicily).

Fought B.C. 379 between the Syracusans under Dionysius, and the Carthaginians. The Syracusans were defeated, with enormous loss, and Dionysius forced to accept unfavourable terms of peace.

Cropredy Bridge (Civil War).

Fought June 29, 1644, between the Royalists under Charles I, and a detachment of the Parliamentary army under Sir William Waller. Waller crossed the Cherwell near Banbury with the object of taking the Royalists in the rear, but was repulsed with considerable loss.

Crosskeys (American Civil War).

A rearguard action, fought June 8, 1862, between 8,000 Confederates under Ewell, and about 15,000 Federals under Tremont. Ewell was given the task of holding Tremont in check, while General Jackson marched to meet the Federals under Shields, who were endeavouring to effect a junction with Tremont. The Confederates held their ground, beating back their opponents with a loss of 664 killed and wounded. After the action, Ewell crossed the river, burning the bridge behind him, and Jackson was enabled to fall upon Shields with his whole force.

Crotona.

Fought 983, between the Germans under Otho II, and the Greeks, aided by 40,000 Saracens under the Caliph of Egypt. After an obstinate engagement, Otho was totally defeated, losing many of his bravest knights.

Crotoye (Hundred Years' War).

Fought 1347, during the siege of Calais by Edward III. The French fleet attempted to relieve the town, but was defeated and driven off with heavy loss by the English fleet.

Cuaspad.

Fought December 6, 1862, between the Ecuadorians under Flores, 6,000 strong, and 4,000 Colombians under Mosquera. The Ecuadorians were utterly routed, losing 1,500 killed and wounded, 2,000 prisoners, and all their guns.

Cuddalore.

Fought June 13, 1783, when a portion of the British force under General Stewart attacked the French entrenchments in front of Cuddalore, and after hard fighting, drove the French into the town with a loss of 700 men and 13 guns. The British lost 1,013 killed and wounded.

Cuddalore.

A naval action was fought off Cuddalore June 30, 1783, between a British squadron of 17 sail under Sir Edward Hughes, and 12 French ships under Suffren. The French, as usual, declined to come to close quarters, and after a long range action, in which Hughes lost 532 men, fighting was suspended at nightfall, leaving Suffren in possession of the roads, and able to prevent the complete investment of Cuddalore.

Culloden (Rebellion of the Forty-five).

Fought April 16, 1746, between the Royal troops under the Duke of Cumberland, and the Highlanders under the Young Pretender. The rebels were completely routed by the English regulars, and in addition to heavy loss in the field, suffered terribly in the pursuit, being ruthlessly cut down by the cavalry. Cumberland's cruelty on this occasion earned for him the title of " Butcher." The Royalists lost 309 killed and wounded. This battle is sometimes called the Battle of Drummossie Moor.

Cunaxa (Expedition of Cyrus the Younger).

Fought B.C. 401 between the Persians, about 400,000 strong, under Artaxerxes, and the army of his brother Cyrus, consisting of 100,000 Orientals, with 14,000 Greek mercenaries, under Clearchus. The Greeks on the right wing drove back the Persian left, and Cyrus in the centre broke the king's bodyguard, which fled in disorder. While pursuing his brother, however, he was struck down, and his Orientals at once took to flight. The Greeks refused to surrender, and were allowed to retain their arms and march, to the coast. This expedition of Cyrus forms the subject of Xenophon's " Anabasis."

Curicta (Civil War of Cæsar and Pompey).

Fought B.C. 49, when the Cæsarian fleet under Dolabella was totally destroyed by the Pompeian fleet under Marcus Octavius. This victory cut off the Cæsarian army under Caius Antonius, which was quartered on the island of Curicta, and Antonius was forced to surrender.

Curupayti (Paraguayan War).

Fought September 22, 1866, between the troops of Brazil, Argentine and Uruguay, under General Flores, and the Paraguayans under Lopez. The allies were totally defeated, and Flores abandoned the army, returning to Montevideo.

Custozza (Seven Weeks' War).

Fought June 24, 1866, between 60,000 Austrians under the Archduke Albert, and 140,000 Italians under General La Marmora. La Marmora crossed the Mincio, and advanced against the Archduke, who was covering Verona. The Italians having to pass through a hilly country, the columns were much broken up, and as they debouched into the plain of Custozza, they were beaten in detail, and driven back by the Austrians, who gained a signal victory. The Austrians lost 4,650 killed and wounded ; the Italians, 720 killed, 3,112 wounded, and 4,315 prisoners. La Marmora was compelled to recross the Mincio.

Cuzco (Conquest of Peru).

This city was besieged 1536, by 200,000 Peruvians, and was defended by 250 Spaniards under Juan and Gonzalo Pizarro. After a siege of five months, Almagro, to whom certain of the conquered territories had been assigned by the king of Spain, arrived with his troops, and attacked and totally routed the Peruvians. He then laid siege to the place on his own account, and shortly afterwards compelled Gonzalo Pizarro to capitulate. Juan died in the course of the siege.

Cyme.

Fought B.C. 474, between the fleet of Hiero, tyrant of Syracuse, and the Etruscan fleet, which was investing the Greek colony of Cyme. The Etruscans were routed, and from this defeat dates the rapid decline of the Etruscan power.

Cynoscephalæ.

Fought July 364 B.C., between the Thebans and Thessalians under Pelopidas, and the forces of Alexander, Despot of Pheræ. Both armies made a forced march to seize the heights of Cynoscephalæ, and reached the spot almost simultaneously. The Theban cavalry drove back Alexander's horse, but lost time in the pursuit, and his infantry made good their position on the heights. However, after very hard fighting, they were dislodged, and Alexander com-

pletely routed, though **Pelopidas** fell in the battle.

Cynoscephalæ (Second Macedonian War).

Fought B.C. 197, between the Romans, 26,000 strong, under Flamininus, and the Macedonians, in about equal force under Philip. The Roman vanguard, coming unexpectedly upon the enemy, was repulsed, but Flamininus bringing up the legionaries, the battle became more equal. On the right Philip, with half his phalanx, drove back the Romans, but his left wing was utterly routed, and the victorious Roman right then turned and attacked the Macedonian right in flank and rear, and won a complete victory. The Macedonians lost 13,000 killed and wounde d The Roman losses were small. ⁊⁊

Cynossema (Peloponnesian War).

Fought 411 B.C., between 86 Peloponnesian ships under Mindarus, and 76 Athenian triremes under Thrasybulus and Thrasyllus. The Athenian centre was broken, but, in the moment of victory, Thrasybulus fell upon the Peloponnesians with the right wing, and totally routed them, while Thrasyllus on the left also drove off his adversaries, after hard fighting.

Cyssus (War with Antiochus the Great).

Fought B.C. 191 between the Roman fleet of 105 triremes under Caius Livius, and the fleet of Antiochus, numbering 70 sail, under Polyxenides. Polyxenides sailed out of Cyssus to encounter the Romans, but was defeated with a loss of

23 ships, and forced to seek refuge at Ephesus.

Cyzicus (Peloponnesian War).

Fought 410 B.C., when Alcibiades, with 86 Athenian ships, surprised the Peloponnesian Admiral Mindarus, who was besieging Cyzicus, and, after a hard fight, totally defeated him. Mindarus was slain, 60 triremes were taken or destroyed, and the Peloponnesian fleet was practically annihilated.

Cyzicus (First Mithridatic War).

Fought B.C. 88, when the army of Mithridates, who was besieging Cyzicus, was hemmed by the Romans under Lucullus, and though the latter, with inferior forces, did not venture on a pitched battle, he fought a series of minor engagements, in which he eventually destroyed the Pontic army, their losses amounting in the end to over 200,000 men.

Czarnovo (Campaign of Friedland).

Fought December 24, 1806, between the French under Napoleon, and the Russians, about 15,000 strong, under Count Tolstoy. Napoleon, with Davoust's corps, crossed the Ukra, and made a night attack upon the Russians, driving them out of Czarnovo with a loss of 1,600 and several guns. The French lost 700.

Czaslau (War of the Austrian Succession).

Fought 1742, between the Prussians under Frederic the Great, and the Austrians under Prince Charles of Lorraine. The Prussians were driven from the field, but the Austrians

abandoned the pursuit to plunder, and the king, rallying his troops, broke the Austrian main body, and defeated them with a loss of 4,000 men.

D

Daegastan.

Fought 603 between the Northumbrians under Æthelfrith, and the Picts and Scots under Aidan, King of the Scots. Æthelfrith was victorious, and extended his dominions as far as Chester.

Dalmanutha (Second Boer War).

Fought August 21 to 28, 1900, when the position of the Boers from Belfast to Machadodorp covering the Delagoa Bay Railway, and extending over a line 30 miles long, was attacked on the west by Lord Roberts, and on the south by Sir Redvers Buller. On the 28th Buller entered Machadodorp, by which time the Boers, who were under General Botha, had been driven from all their positions. Kruger at once fled to Delagoa Bay. The British loss in the four days amounted to about 500.

Damascus (Moslem Invasion of Syria).

This city was besieged by the Moslems under Khaled in 633, and was defended by a large garrison of Greeks and Romans. The city made an obstinate defence, and the defenders succeeded in sending a demand for succour to Werdan, the general of Heraclius. Werdan's approach drew Khaled away from the place, and as he was retiring he was attacked by the garrison, whom he defeated with enormous loss. He then marched against Werdan, defeated him, and returned to prosecute the siege. After a gallant defence, the city, 70 days later, was taken by storm.

Damascus (Tartar Invasion of Syria).
On January 25, 1401, Damascus was captured, through treachery, by the Tartars under Tamerlane.

Damme (Wars of Philip Augustus).
Fought April, 1213, when an English fleet of 500 vessels under the Earl of Salisbury attacked and dispersed a large fleet of French ships designed to support Philip Augustus' invasion of Flanders. The English captured 300 and burnt 100 vessels, and Philip Augustus was forced to abandon his design.

Dan-no-ura (Taira War).
Fought 1189, between the army of the Shôgun, Yoritomo, under his brothers Noriyori and Yoshitsune, and the Taira Clan under Munemori, when the Taira were routed and dispersed, This defeat broke the power of the clan, and the Minamoto became the dominant clan in Japan.

Dantzig (Thirty Years' War).
This fortress was besieged by the Swedes under Gustavus Adolphus in 1627, and was defended by a Polish garrison which successfully resisted all attempts to storm the place, until the truce of September 16, 1629. In a night attack on May 27, 1627, the King of Sweden was severely wounded, while in the autumn of the same year a sally was made from the port by the Dantzig ships, which defeated the Swedish fleet under Admiral Stjernsköld, the Admiral being killed, 1 ship captured and 1 destroyed.

Dantzig (Campaign of Friedland).
On March 19, 1807, Marshal Lefebvre, with 18,000 French, laid siege to the city, which was defended by a garrison of 14,000 Prussians, and 4,000 Russians under Marshal Kalkreuth. For complete investment it was necessary for Lefebvre to encompass a circuit of about 17 leagues, for which purpose his numbers were too few, and he made little progress. Receiving reinforcements, however, he opened his first parallel April 1, while on the 12th an important outwork was carried. On the 23rd the batteries opened fire, and on May 15 a determined effort to relieve the place was made by a force of 8,000 Russians, who were repulsed with a loss of 2,000, the French losing 400 only. From this point the city was left to its fate, and an assault was ordered for the 21st. Before this date, however, Marshal Kalkreuth signified his readiness to parley, and on May 26 the place was surrendered, the garrison being then reduced to 7,000 effectives.

Dantzig (Campaign of Leipsic).
After the Moscow retreat, General Rapp, with 30,000 French, mostly survivors of the Moscow campaign, was besieged in Dantzig, January 1813, by the allies, 30,000 in number, under the Duke of Würtemberg.

Rapp made a strenuous defence, but his works were mastered one by one, and, finding his garrison dwindling rapidly from starvation and exposure, he surrendered November 29, 1813, by which date the defenders numbered only 18,000 men.

Dargai (Tirah Campaign).

Fought October 20, 1897, when a British brigade, under General Yeatman Biggs, stormed the heights, which were held by a large force of Afridis. The actual storming was accomplished by the Gordon Highlanders, and the British loss amounted to 37 killed and 175 wounded. Colonel Mathias' speech to the Gordons, before leading them to the charge was, " Highlanders, the General says the position must be taken at all costs. The Gordons will take it."

Dazaifu (Chinese Invasion of Japan).

In 1281, Hwan Buako, the General of Kublai Khan, at the head of 100,000 Chinese, and 10,000 Koreans, endeavoured to effect a landing at Dazaifu, The Japanese, however, kept them at bay for 60 days, at the end of which time the Chinese fleet was wrecked and dispersed by a typhoon. The survivors, under Chang Pak, took refuge in the island of Takashima, where they were attacked and cut to pieces by the troops of the Daimiyo of Choshiu, under Shoni Kagasuke, only 3,000 out of the vast host making their way back to China.

Deeg (First Mahratta War).

Fought 1780 between the British, 6,000 strong under

General Fraser, and the Mahrattas under Holkar of Indore, with 14 battalions of infantry, a numerous cavalry, and 160 guns. The Mahrattas were utterly routed, leaving 87 guns on the field. The British lost 643, including General Fraser, killed.

Deeg (Second Mahratta War).

The fortress, which was held by a garrison of Holkar's troops, was besieged December 11, 1804, by the British under Lord Lake. After six days' bombardment, it was stormed on the 23rd, and the citadel captured on the following day. Over 100 guns were taken.

Delhi (First Mongol Invasion).

Fought 1297, between 200,000 Mongols under Kuttugh Khan, and 300,000 Delhi Mohammedans, with 2,700 elephants, under Ala-ud-Din. The Indian right wing, with a successful charge, broke the Mongols left, but carried the pursuit too far. Meanwhile the right of the Mongol army assailed the Indian left and drove it from the field. Kuttugh Khan, however, had lost so heavily, that he was unable to follow up his advantage, and retreated with all speed from India.

Delhi (Second Mongol Invasion).

Fought 1398, between the Mongols under Tamerlane, and the Delhi Mohammedans under Mahmud Tughlak. Tamerlane, having crossed the Jumna to reconnoitre with an escort of 700 horsemen, was attacked by Mahmud with 5,000 cavalry. Tamerlane repulsed the attack, and later, having brought his main body across the river, totally defeated Mahmud, and drove him into Delhi, which at once surrendered. The city was plundered, and Tamerlane withdrew laden with spoil.

Delhi (Second Mahratta War).

Fought September 11, 1803, between 4,500 British under General Lake, and 19,000 Mahrattas of Scindiah's army under Bourguin. The enemy occupied a strong position with the Jumna in their rear, and Lake, feigning a retreat, drew them from their lines, and then turning upon them drove them with the bayonet into the river, inflicting enormous loss upon them. The British lost 400 only.

Delhi (Second Mahratta War).

The city was invested October 7, 1804, by 20,000 Mahrattas, with 100 guns, under Jeswunt Rao Holkar, and was successfully defended for nine days by a small British garrison. At the end of this period, Holkar withdrew. So small was the garrison, that they were on constant duty on the ramparts, throughout the siege, without relief.

Delhi (Indian Mutiny).

After the outbreak at Meerut, Delhi became the rallying place of the mutineers, and on June 8, 1857, Sir Harry Barnard commenced the siege of the city. His force was too small for a complete investment, while the mutineers numbered 30,000, and could obtain continual reinforcements, and ample supplies. The garrison made constant sorties, and fighting was incessant at the outposts. On September 8 the breaching batteries opened fire, and on

the 14th the final assault was made and the city entered. It was not, however, till the 20th that the Palace was taken, and all resistance at an end. Among those who fell was John Nicholson.

Delium (Peloponnesian War),

Fought B.C. 424 between the Athenians under Hippocrates. 17,000 strong, and the Bœotians under Pagondas, 18,000 strong. The armies met on a plain before Delium, and after an obstinate encounter, in which the Thebans on the right overpowered the Athenians, while their left attack was repulsed, the appearance of a large body of cavalry on their flank alarmed the Athenians, who broke and fled. Hippocrates fell in the battle.

Delphi (Sacred War).

Fought B.C. 355, between the Phocians, 5,000 strong, under Philomelus, and the Locrians. Philomelus, who had seized Delphi, attacked the Locrians on the heights above the sacred city, and routed them with heavy loss, many being driven over the precipice.

Denain (War of the Spanish Succession).

Fought 1712, when the camp of the allies, held by 10 battalions under the Earl of Albemarle, was attacked by 130 French battalions under Marshal Villiers. Prince Eugene made an effort to relieve the Earl, but was unable to cross the Scheldt, and the allies were overwhelmed by superior numbers, only about 4,000 making good their retreat. Five generals were killed or captured.

Dennewitz (Campaign of Leipsic).

Fought September 6, 1813, between the French army of the north under Ney, and the allies under the Crown Prince of Sweden. Ney had detached Bertrand's division to mask Dennewitz, while his main body marched past the position on the road to Berlin, but Bertrand delayed so long before Dennewitz, that what was intended for a demonstration became a serious action, in which the full force of both sides was engaged. The French were defeated with a loss of 10,000 men and 43 guns.

Deorham.

Fought 577, when Ceawlin, King of Wessex, defeated the Welsh, and extended the borders of Wessex to the Bristol Channel, thus severing the Welsh nation into two parts.

Dessau (Thirty Years' War).

Fought April 15, 1626, between the German Protestants under Count von Mansfeldt, and the Imperialists, about 20,000 strong, under Wallenstein. Mansfeldt was attacking the fort of Dessau, on the Elbe, when Wallenstein, approaching under cover of the woods, fell upon his flank, and totally routed him, killing or capturing nearly three-fourths of his army.

Dettingen (War of the Austrian Succession).

Fought June 27, 1743, between the British, 40,000 strong, under George II, and 60,000 French under the Duc de Noailles. The British, who were retiring upon Hanau from Aschaffenburg, found their retreat cut off by the French, Dettingen being held by 23,000 men under de Grammont, while the main body was on the opposite bank of the Maine. De Grammont left his lines to attack the British, whereupon George II put himself at the head of his troops, and led a charge which broke the French and drove them headlong into the river. Their losses in crossing were heavy, and they left 6,000 killed and wounded on the field. This is the last occasion on which the Sovereign has led British troops in battle.

Deutschbrod (Hussite War).

Fought 1422 between the Taborite section of the Hussites under John Zisca, and the Germans under the Emperor Sigismund. Zisca was completely victorious.

Devicotta.

This fortress, held for Pertab Singh by a garrison of the Tanjore army, was captured in 1749, after a three days' bombardment, by a British force of 2,300 men under Major Lawrence. An attack upon the breach, headed by Clive, was nearly disastrous, as the Sepoys hung back, and of the Europeans engaged, only Clive and three others escaped, but Lawrence arriving opportunely with the main column, the place was stormed.

Diamond.

A faction fight, known as the battle of Diamond which took place September 21, 1795, at a village in Co. Armagh, between the Peep o' Day Boys and the Defenders. The former were victorious, killing 48 of their opponents.

Diamond Hill (Second Boer War).

Fought June 11 and 12, 1900, when General Botha, with the main Boer army of 15,000 men, strongly entrenched about 15 miles from Pretoria, was attacked by Lord Roberts with 17,000 men and 70 guns, and driven from his position. The Boer lines were so extended that three distinct actions were in progress at the same time. The British lost 25 officers and 137 men killed and wounded.

Dingaan's Day.

Fought December 16, 1838, between the Boers of the Transvaal, and the Zulus under Dingaan. The Zulus were totally routed, with heavy loss. The Boer losses were small.

Dipæa (Arcadian War).

Fought B.C. 471, between the Spartans and the Arcadian League. The Arcadians were totally defeated, and Tegea, the head of the League, shortly afterwards submitted to Sparta.

Diu.

This fortified Portuguese factory was besieged early in September, 1537, by a fleet of 76 Turkish galleys, and 7,000 soldiers under Solyman, Pasha of Egypt, acting with whom was an army of 20,000 Gujeratis under Bahadur Shah, and Khojah Zofar, an Italian renegade. The garrison of 600, under Antonio de Silveira, repulsed assault after assault, but were nearly at the end of their resources, when the false rumour of an approaching Portuguese fleet caused Solyman to withdraw.

Diu.

In 1545 Diu was again besieged by the Gujeratis, the garrison being commanded by Mascarenhas. Khojah Zofar, who led the besiegers, was killed in the course of the siege, and was succeeded by Rami Khan. The garrison, at the end of several months, was on the point of surrendering, owing to famine, when it was relieved by Juan de Castro, who signally defeated the Gujeratis, and raised the siege.

Djerbeh (Ottoman Wars).

Fought 1560, between the fleet of Solyman I, Sultan of Turkey, under Piycála Pasha, and the combined squadrons of Malta, Venice, Genoa and Florence. The Christian fleet was utterly routed, the Turks securing thereby the preponderance in the Mediterranean.

Dniester (Ottoman Wars).

Fought September 9, 1769, between the Russians under Prince Gallitzin, and the Turks under Ali Moldovani Pasha. The Turks crossed the river in the face of the Russian army, and attacked their lines with great impetuosity. After severe fighting, however, they were beaten off, and forced to withdraw from Choczim.

Dodowah (First Ashanti War).

Fought 1826, between the Ashanti army, which had invaded the Gold Coast, and the British under Colonel Purdon. The Ashantis fought bravely, but were routed with heavy loss.

Dogger Bank (Dutch Wars).

Fought August 15, 1781, between a British fleet of seven battleships and six frigates,

under Admiral Hyde Parker,
and a Dutch fleet of equal
strength under Admiral Zout-
man. After a severe engagement, the Dutch bore away,
and reached their port in safety,
the British fleet being too
crippled to pursue. The British
lost 109 killed and 362 wounded ;
the Dutch 1 ship, the *Hol-
landia,* 142 killed and 403
wounded.

Dollar (Danish Invasion).
Fought 875, when the Danish
invaders under Thorstem totally
defeated the men of Alban under
Constantine. The Danes sub-
sequently occupied Caithness,
Sutherlandshire, Ross and
Moray.

**Dolni-Dubnik (Russo-Turkish
War).**
Fought November 1, 1877,
when General Gourko, with two
divisions of the Russian guard,
dislodged the Turks from the
redoubt of Dolni-Dubnik, and
forced them to retire upon
Plevna. There was little actual
fighting, the Turks retiring
without much resistance, but
the action is important, because
the capture of the redoubt made
the investment of Plevna complete.

Dominica.
Fought April 12, 1782, between the British fleet of 36 sail
of the line, under Rodney, with
Hood second in command, and
the French fleet of 33 sail under
de Grasse. Rodney departed
from the usual tactics of a ship
to ship action, and broke the
enemy's line, gaining a complete victory, and capturing or
destroying 5 ships, while 2 more
were captured within the next

few days. The British lost
261 killed and 837 wounded.
The French losses have been
put as high as 15,000, but it is
probable that they lost about
3,000 killed and wounded, while
7,980 were taken in the captured ships. This action is also
known as the battle of the
Saints.

Domokos (Greco-Turkish War).
Fought May 17, 1879, be-
tween five Turkish divisions of
the army under Edhem Pasha,
and the Greeks under the Crown
Prince of Greece, about 40,000
strong. The Greeks held their
ground till late in the evening,
when the right was outflanked,
and forced to give ground,
though, when the action ceased,
the Turks had made no other
advance. Edhem was prepared
to renew the fight on the following day, but the Crown Prince
found that the retirement of his
right had rendered the position
untenable, and retreated during
the night. The Greeks lost 600
killed and wounded ; the Turks
about 1,800.

Donabew (First Burmah War).
Fought March 7, 1825, when
General Cotton, with about 700
troops, attacked three strong
stockades held by 12,000 Burmans under Maha Bandoola.
The smallest of the three was
carried, but Cotton's force was
too small, and it was not till the
25th that Sir Archibald Campbell arrived, and, shelling the
stockade, forced the Burmans
to evacuate the position.
Maha Bandoola was killed.

**Donauwörth (War of the Spanish
Succession).**
Fought July 2, 1704, between

the British and Imperialists under the Duke of Marlborough, and the French and Bavarians under Marshal Tallard. The Duke attacked the enemy's entrenched position at Schellenberg, in front of Donauwörth, and drove them out, forcing them to abandon the town. The victors lost 5,374 killed and wounded. The French losses are unknown, but were probably heavier.

Dormeille.

Fought 602, between the Neustrians under Clothaire II, and Austrasians and Burgundians under Theodobert and Thierry. Clothaire was defeated with great slaughter.

Dorylæum (First Crusade).

Fought July 1097, between 70,000 Crusaders under Bohemond and Raymond of Thoulouse, and 250,000 Saracens under the Sultan Soliman. The Saracens drove back Bohemond's division on their camp, which they proceeded to plunder, and, while so engaged, were attacked by Raymond and totally routed with a loss of 30,000. The Crusaders lost 4,000.

Douai (War of the Spanish Succession).

This place was besieged by the allies under Prince Eugene, April 25, 1710, and was defended by a French garrison, 8,000 strong, under General d'Albergotti. The place was obstinately defended, numerous sorties being made, but, the French army being unable to relieve it, d'Albergotti was forced to surrender June 26. The besiegers lost 8,000 killed and wounded.

Douro (Peninsular War).

Fought May 12, 1809, when 12,000 British under Wellesley (the Duke of Wellington) crossed the Douro and drove the French under Soult out of Oporto. The French numbered about 24,000, of whom 5,000 were killed, wounded or captured, mainly during the pursuit. In the action itself, the French lost 500, the British, 116.

Dover (Dutch Wars).

Fought November 29, 1652, between a Dutch fleet of 95 sail, under Van Tromp, and an English fleet of 40 ships, under Blake. The Dutch were victorious, the English fleet being much cut up, and two ships captured.

Downs, The (Dutch Wars).

Fought June 1, 2 and 3, 1666, between the English fleet under the Duke of Albemarle, and the Dutch under De Ruyter, Van Tromp and De Witt. After an obstinate fight, Albemarle, on the 3rd, retired, after setting fire to his disabled vessels, but the Dutch were too seriously crippled to pursue.

Drepanum (First Punic War).

Fought B.C. 249, during the siege of Lilybæum, between the Roman fleet of 123 galleys under Publius Claudius, and the Carthaginians under Adherbal. Claudius was defeated, losing 93 ships, 8,000 killed and 20,000 prisoners, while the victors did not lose a ship.

Dresden (Campaign of Leipsic).

Fought August 27, 1813, between 130,000 French under Napoleon, and 200,000 Russians, Prussians and Austrians, under Count Wittgenstein, Kleist, and Prince Schwartzemberg, respectively. The Emperors of Russia and Austria, and the King of Prussia, were present on the field. Napoleon, who was in possession of Dresden, made his main attack upon the Austrian left, which was separated from the centre by the ravine of Planen. This attack, which was entrusted to Murat, was completely successful, and the Austrians were driven with heavy loss into the ravine. Meanwhile, the centre and right of the allies had been attacked with equal success, and finally they were driven from the field with a loss of 10,000 killed and wounded. 15,000 prisoners, and 40 guns, The French lost about 10,000.

Dreux (First Civil War).

Fought 1562, between the Huguenots under the Prince de Condé, and the Catholics under the Constable, Montmorency. The Constable, heading a charge of the Catholic cavalry, was overthrown and captured by Coligny. The Catholics then fled, but the Huguenots, carrying the pursuit too far, were charged and routed by François de Guise, and Condé made prisoner. The victory thus rested with the Catholics.

Driefontein (Second Boer War).

Fought March 10, 1900, between the Boer Army covering Bloemfontein, under de Wet, and the British under Lord Roberts. The Boers occupied a position about seven miles in extent, which was attacked in front by Kelly-Kenny's division, and on the left flank by

that of Tucker. The Boers were driven out and the road to Bloemfontein opened, at a cost to the British of 424 killed and wounded. The Boers left over 100 dead on the field.

Dristen.

This strong post on the Danube was defended for fifty-five days in 973, by the Russians under their Duke Swatoslaus, against the Greeks under the Emperor John Zimisces. At the end of that time the Russians were forced to surrender, thus ending their invasion of Byzantine territory.

Drogheda (Great Irish Rebellion).

Siege was laid to this town, which was held by an English garrison under Sir Henry Tichborne, by the Irish rebels, under Owen Roe O'Neil, in December, 1641. The garrison held out successfully for three months, when O'Neil was compelled to raise the siege.

Drogheda (Civil War).

On September 3, 1649, siege was laid to the place by the Parliamentary army under Cromwell, the garrison of 2,500 English regulars being under Sir Arthur Aston. An assault on the 10th was repulsed, but on the 12th the town was stormed, and the garrison put to the sword. Four thousand soldiers and inhabitants, including Aston, are said to have perished.

Drumclog (Covenanters' Rising).

Fought June 11, 1679, when a party of Covenanters, under Balfour of Burleigh, defeated the royal troops, under Claverhouse.

Drummossie Moor.

See Culloden.

Dubba (Scinde Campaign).

Fought March 24, 1843, between 5,000 British troops, under Sir Charles Napier, and 20,000 Beluchis, under the Amir Shir Mohamed. The enemy was strongly posted behind a double nullah, which was carried by the infantry with great gallantry, and the Beluchis were totally defeated.

Duffindale (Kat's Rebellion).

The scene of the defeat of the rebels under Kat, by the royal troops, under the Earl of Warwick, in 1549.

Dunbar (Scottish Wars).

Fought April 27, 1296, between the English, under Edward I, and the Scots under the Earl of Athol. The Scots were defeated, with a loss of 10,000 men. This defeat led to the surrender of Balliol, and Edward was proclaimed King of Scotland.

Dunbar (Scottish Wars).

This town was besieged, 1339, by the English, under the Earl of Salisbury, and was defended by Agnes, Countess of March, known as Black Agnes of Dunbar, whose husband, the Governor, was absent at the time. So vigorous was the defence, that Salisbury was compelled to withdraw from the siege.

Dunbar (Civil War).

Fought September 3, 1650, between 14,000 Parliamentarians under Cromwell and Monk, and the Scottish Royalists, 27,000 strong, under David Leslie. Leslie left a strong position on the heights near Dunbar, to meet Cromwell, and was routed with a loss of 3,000

killed and wounded, and 10,000 prisoners. Cromwell's losses were small.

Dundalk (Scottish Invasion of Ireland).

Fought October 5, 1318, between the Scots under Edward Bruce, 3,000 in number, and the English and Irish under John de Bermingham. The Scots were totally defeated, Bruce, with about 30 of his kinghts, and over 80 men-at-arms, being killed, and the invasion came to an end.

Dundee.

See Talana Hill.

Dunes (Wars of Louis XIV).

Fought June 14, 1650, between the Spaniards, 14,000 strong, under Don John of Austria and the Great Condé, and the French in equal force under Turenne. A force landed from the English fleet commenced the attack on the Spaniards, which was vigorously supported by Turenne, and the Spaniards were totally defeated, with a loss of 4,000 killed, wounded and captured. Ten days later the town of Dunkirk capitulated.

Dunganhill (Great Irish Rebellion).

Fought August 8, 1647, between the Irish rebels, and an English force under Colonel Michael Jones. The Irish were routed with a loss of 6,000.

Dunkeld (Jacobite Rising).

Fought August 21, 1689, between the Highlanders under Colonel Cannon, and the Cameronian Regiment under Colonel Cleland. The fight took place in the town of Dunkeld, where the Cameronians held a house belonging to the Marquis of Athole. The Highlanders were unable to dislodge them, and eventually retired, Cannon being killed.

Dunsinnan.

Fought 1054, between the usurper, Macbeth, and the Anglo-Saxons under Siward, Earl of Northumberland, who was supporting Malcolm Canmore, the son of the murdered Duncan. Macbeth was defeated, losing 10,000 men, and fled to the north. The Anglo-Saxons lost 1,500.

Duplin (Baliol's Rising).

Fought August 12, 1332, between the Scottish barons, under Edward Baliol, and the forces of David, King of Scotland. Though largely outnumbered Baliol was victorious.

Düppel (Schleswig - Holstein War).

This fortress, protected by an outer chain of ten redoubts, was invested by the Prussians, 16,000 strong, under Prince Frederick Charles, and the first parallel opened, March 30, 1864. The Danish garrison numbered 22,000. On April 17, after a heavy bombardment, the Prussians were launched at the first six of the chain of redoubts, and, after a brief resistance, they were captured and the place was immediately afterwards surrendered. The Prussians lost 70 officers and 1,331 men, the Danes, including prisoners, 5,500.

Durazzo (Norman Invasion of Italy).

This fortress, which was defended by a garrison of Greeks and Macedonians under George Palæologus, was besieged by the Normans, under Robert Guiscard, July 17, 1081. On October 18, the besiegers, now reduced to 18,000, were attacked by a force of about 75,000 Greeks, under Alexius Comnenus, and after a terrible struggle, in which the Normans were almost overpowered, the victory rested with Guiscard. The Greeks lost about 6,000. On the Norman side, the Italian auxiliaries suffered heavily, but only 20 Norman knights were killed. Notwithstanding this disaster, the city still held out, and it was not till February 8, 1082, that a night surprise rendered the Normans masters of the place.

Dürrenstein (Campaign of the Danube).

Fought November 11, 1805, during Napoleon's advance on Vienna, when Mortier, with one French division, was attacked by 30,000 Russians, and would have been overwhelmed but for the timely arrival of another division. The French lost 3,000 ; the Russians about the same number.

Dwina, The (Swedo-Polish War).

Fought 1701, between 15,000 Swedes under Charles XII, and 12,000 Saxons under Marshal von Stenau. Charles, who was marching upon Riga, found the passage of the Dwina barred by von Stenau. Having the wind at his back, he set fire to a large quantity of straw, and under cover of the smoke, crossed the river unperceived. He then attacked the Saxons, who, after an obstinate engagement, were defeated and driven from the field.

Dyle (Norman Invasion of France).

Fought 896, between the Norman invaders, and the Germans under Arnulph, Emperor of Germany. The Normans were totally routed with enormous loss.

Dyrrachium (Civil War of Cæsar an d Pompey).

Fought B.C. 48, between the Cæsarians, under Julius Cæsar, and the Pompeians, under Pompey. The latter having formed an entrenched camp some distance from Dyrrachium, Cæsar interposed his army between the camp and the town. This interrupted Pompey's communications, and he, in consequence, attacked the Cæsarian lines, which he forced, at the cost of 1,000 men, and obliged Cæsar to retire.

E

Ebersberg (Campaign of Wagram).

Fought May 3, 1809, when Massena's corps stormed the bridge and castle of Ebersberg, which was held by about 30,000 Austrians under the Archduke Charles. After the bridge was captured, a terrible conflict followed in the streets of Ebersberg, and finally the Austrians were driven out, with a loss of about 3,000 killed and wounded, 4,000 prisoners and many guns. The French admit a loss of 1,700 only.

Eckmühl (Campaign of Wagram).

Fought April 22, 1809, between 90,000 French, under Napoleon, and 76,000 Austrians, under the Archduke Charles. The Austrians occupied a position on the high ground above Eckmühl, from which they were dislodged after severe fighting, but the approach of night enabled the Archduke to draw off his troops in tolerable order towards Ratisbon, with a loss of about 5,000 killed and wounded, and 3,000 prisoners. The French loss is stated at 2,500. By this victory Napoleon cut the main Austrian army in two.

Ecnomus (First Punic War).

Fought B.C. 256, between 330 Roman galleys, with crews of 100,000 men, under L. Manlius Valso, and M. Attilius Regulus, and 350 Carthaginian ships under Hanno. After a hardfought battle, in which the Romans lost 24 vessels, they defeated the Carthaginians, with a loss of 30 ships sunk and 64 captured, and drove the rest of the fleet to Carthage.

Edessa (Persian Wars).

Fought 259, between the Romans under Valerian, and the Persians under Sapor I. The Romans were totally defeated, and Valerian taken prisoner.

Edgeworth (Wars of the Roses).

Fought July 26, 1469, between the Yorkists under Pembroke, and the troops of the revolted Nevilles. The Lancastrians attacked Pembroke, whose troops were chiefly Welshmen, and, notwithstanding a stubborn resistance, defeated them with heavy loss, no less than 168

Welsh knights falling, besides rank and file. Edward IV, who was in the neighbourhood, though not present at the battle, was captured soon after.

Edgehill (Civil War).

The first battle of the Civil War, October 23, 1642, between the Royalists under Charles I, and the Parliamentarians, under Essex, each army being about 20,000 strong. The victory was claimed by both sides, but the advantage rested with the King, as the Parliamentarians failed to face Prince Rupert's cavalry, and the Royalists were not prevented from continuing their march on London.

Elandslaagte (Second Boer War).

Fought October 21, 1899, between a strong Boer force under General Koch, and 3 battalions and 5 squadrons of British troops, with 12 guns, under General French. The Boers occupied a strong position, on high ground near the Ladysmith-Dundee railway, from which they were driven by the infantry and Imperial Light Horse (dismounted) with a loss of 250 killed and wounded, and 200 prisoners, including Koch. The British lost 35 officers and 219 men.

Elands River (Second Boer War).

On August 4, 1900, a force of 400 Australians, under Colonel Hore, were surrounded by 2,500 Boers, with 6 guns. The Australians occupied an exposed kopje, with no water nearer than the river half-a-mile away. Their maxim became unserviceable, an attempt by General Carrington to relieve them failed, and so severe was the Boer fire that,

in 11 days, 1,800 shells fell within their lines. They held out, however, till August 15, when they were relieved by Lord Kitchener, having lost 75 killed and wounded, and nearly all their horses.

El Caney (Spanish-American War).

Fought July 1, 1898, when 12,000 Americans, under General Shafter, captured from the Spaniards, after heavy fighting, the strong position of El Caney and San Juan Hill, commanding Santiago de Cuba. The Spaniards made various attempts on the 2nd and 3rd to dislodge them, but without success. The American losses during the three days amounted to 115 officers and 1,570 men killed and wounded.

Elchingen (Campaign of Austerlitz).

Fought October 14, 1805, when Ney's corps, after repairing the bridge of Elchingen under fire, stormed and captured the convent and village, driving out 20,000 Austrians, and taking 3,000 prisoners and a number of guns.

Elena (Russo-Turkish War).

Fought 1877, between the Russians under Loris Melikoff, and the Turks under Muhktar Pasha, in which the former were victorious.

Elinga (Second Punic War).

Fought B.C. 206, between 74,000 Carthaginians, under Hanno, and 48,000 Romans under Scipio Africanus. The battle was fought on the open plain in front of Hanno's camp, and resulted in a complete victory for the Romans. This battle, which is also known as the battle of Silpia, ended the Carthaginian domination in Spain.

Elk Horn.
See Pea Ridge.

Ellandune.
In this battle, fought 823, the Mercians under Beorwulf, were totally routed by the West Saxons under Egbert.

Elleporus.
Fought B.C. 389, between the Sicilians, 23,000 strong, under Dionysius of Syracuse, and the Italiots, 17,000 strong, under Heloris. Dionysius attacked the Italiot vanguard, under Heloris himself, on the march, and the Italiot army, coming into action in detachments, was beaten piecemeal, and finally routed with heavy loss. The survivors, 10,000 in number, surrendered, and were allowed to go free. Heloris was slain.

El Teb (Soudan Campaigns).
Fought February 4, 1884, when a column of 3,500 Egyptian troops under Baker Pasha, marching to relieve Sinkat, was overwhelmed, and practically annihilated by 12,000 Soudanese under Osman Digna. The Egyptians lost 2,360 killed and wounded.

El Teb.
See Trinkitat.

Embata (Social War).
Fought B.C. 356, when an Athenian fleet of 120 sail, under Chares, designed to attack the Chians, with 100 galleys, in the straits between Chios and the mainland. The day proving stormy, however, his colleagues Iphicrates and Timoleon declined the enterprise as too hazardous, and Chares attacking alone, with a third of the fleet, was defeated with heavy loss.

Emesa (Expedition to Palmyra).
Fought 272, between the Romans under Aurelian, and the Palmyrenians under Zenobia. Zenobia was completely defeated, and forced to retire within the walls of Palmyra, to which Aurelian at once laid siege.

Empingham (Wells' Rebellion).
Fought March 12, 1470, when Edward IV totally routed the northern rebels, under Sir Robert Wells. The battle is called " Loose-coat Field," from the precipitate flight of the rebels, who threw off their upper garments to flee the faster.

Engen (Wars of the French Revolution).
Fought May 3, 1800, between the French, 75,000 strong, under Moreau, and 110,000 Austrians under De Kray. Moreau had crossed the Rhine on the 1st, and was advancing through the Black Forest, and the battle was in reality two distinct actions. Moreau's right, 25,000 strong, under Lecourbe, overtook the Austrian rear-guard, and drove them into and through Stokach, capturing 4,000 prisoners, and a large depot of munitions and stores. Moreau in the centre was attacked at Engen by 40,000 Austrians, under De Kray, whom he repulsed with a loss of 2,000 killed and wounded, and 5,000 prisoners. The French lost 2,000 killed and wounded.

Englefield (Danish Invasion).

Fought 871, the first of the series of battles between the West Saxons and the Danish invaders. The former, under their king, Æthelred, defeated the Danes.

Enslin.

See Graspan.

Entaw Springs (American War of Independence).

Fought September 8, 1781, between the British garrison of Charleston, under Colonel Stewart, and the Americans, under General Greene. The British were attacked and at first driven back, but rallying carried the American positions, but with a loss of 700 men, which so weakened their small force that they were unable to profit by the victory.

Entholm (Dano-Swedish Wars).

Fought June 11, 1676, between the Danish fleet, under van Tromp, and Swedes. The Swedes were defeated with very heavy loss in ships and men.

Entzheim.

See Sinzheim.

Ephesus (Ionian War).

Fought 499 B.C., between the Athenians and Ionians, under Aristagorus, and the Persians, under Artaphernes. The Greeks who were retreating to the coast after burning Sardis, were overtaken by the pursuing Persians, under the walls of Ephesus, and signally defeated. The Athenians thereupon withdrew their fleet, and took no further part in the war.

Ephesus (Gallic Invasion of Asia).

Fought B.C. 262, between the Syrians, under Antigonus, and the Gallic invaders. Antigonus was disastrously defeated.

Erbach (Wars of the French Revolution).

Fought May 15, 1800, between 15,000 French under Sainte-Suzanne, and 36,000 Austrians under de Kray. The Austrians, who had 12,000 cavalry, attacked vigorously, but the French, though driven back at certain points, were not routed, and held to their main positions for 12 hours, until the approach of St. Cyr's corps forced the Austrians to retire. Both sides lost heavily in the action.

Erisa (South American War of Independence).

Fought December, 1814, between the Spanish royalists, under Bover, 8,000 strong, and the American patriots, under Ribas. Ribas was totally defeated, and taken prisoner, and in revenge for the death of Bover, who fell in the battle, he was beheaded, and his head publicly exposed in Caraccas.

Espinosa (Peninsular War).

Fought November 10, 1808, between 18,000 French under Victor, and 30,000 Spaniards under Blake. The Spaniards were routed, and Blake's army scattered. The French lost about 1,100 men.

Essling.

See Aspern.

Etampes.

Fought 604, between the Burgundians, under Queen

Brunehilde, and the Neustrians under Clothaire II. The latter were totally defeated with heavy loss.

Ethandun (Danish Invasion).

Fought 878, between the West Saxons, under Alfred, and the Danes, under Guthrum. The Danes were totally defeated, and Alfred's victory was followed by the Peace of Wedmore, which lasted for fifteen years.

Eurymedon, The (Third Persian Invasion).

Fought B.C. 470, between the Persian fleet and army, and the Athenians and Delians, under Cimon. The Greeks were victorious both by land and sea, defeating the Persian fleet with a loss of 200 ships, and routing the land army with great slaughter. This victory secured the adhesion of the south of Asia Minor to the Athenian Confederacy.

Evesham (Barons' War).

Fought August 4, 1265, between the royalists under Prince Edward, and the Barons under Simon de Montfort. The Barons were taken by surprise, having at first mistaken Edward's army for reinforcements under young de Montfort, and were totally defeated, Simon de Montfort falling. This defeat ended the Barons' War.

Eylau (Campaign of Friedland).

Fought February 8, 1807, between 90,000 French under Napoleon, and 80,000 Russians under Bennigsen. Napoleon attacked at daybreak, all along the line, but could at first make no impression on the Russian infantry. Later in the day Davoust all but succeeded in turning the Russian left, but the opportune arrival of a Prussian corps under l'Estocq enabled the Russians to repulse him, and after a sanguinary engagement, which lasted till ten p.m., both armies retained their original positions. On the following day the Russians retired unmolested. The French lost about 30,000 ; the Russians about 20,000 killed and wounded.

F

Faenza (First Gothic War).

Fought 541, between 20,000 Roman legionaries, and the Goths under Totila, King of Italy. The Romans made no attempt to resist the onslaught of the Goths, but throwing down their arms fled ignominiously, giving the Goths an easy victory.

Fair Oaks (American Civil War).

Fought May 31, and June 1, 1862, between the Federals under General M'Clellan and the Confederates under General Johnston. M'Clellan was advancing upon Richmond, and his left wing was attacked in the afternoon of the 31st, and notwithstanding the arrival of Sumner's corp in support, was driven back for two miles. On the 1st the Federals recovered the ground they had lost, but made no further progress, and at the end of the day the Confederates, who were largely outnumbered, were permitted to retire unmolested. The Federals lost over 7,000 killed and wounded, the Confederates about 4,500, including General Johnston. This is also called the Battle of Seven Pines.

Falkirk (Scottish Wars).

Fought July 23, 1298, between the English under Edward I, and the Scots under Sir William Wallace. The Scots, who were greatly inferior in numbers, were strongly posted behind a morass, which at first greatly hampered the English attack. In the end, however, the English archers overcame the Scottish defence, and a final charge, led by the king in person, utterly routed them. Wallace escaped from the field, but was a fugitive for the rest of his life.

Falkirk (Rebellion of the Forty-five).

Fought August 17, 1746, between the rebel Highlanders, 8,000 strong, under the Young Pretender, and a force of 8,000 British troops, with 1,000 Campbells under General Hawley. The charge of the Highlanders broke the British line, and they were driven headlong from the field, with a loss of 600 killed and wounded, 700 prisoners, 7 guns, and all tents and baggage. The rebels lost 120 only.

Famagosta (Cyprus War).

This place was besieged by the Turks under Mustapha Pasha, in October, 1570, and was defended by 7,000 men, half Venetians, half Cypriotes, under Marcantonio Bragadino. The garrison held out until August 1, 1571, when it capitulated, marching out with the honours of war. After the surrender, however, Mustapha murdered in cold blood, Bragadino and four of his lieutenants.

The Turks lost 50,000 men in the course of the siege.

Fafquhar's Farm (Second Boer War).

Fought October 29, 1899, between the main Boer army, under Joubert, and the garrison of Ladysmith, under Sir George White. The Boer position covered about eight miles, and White attacked in three columns, one of which, detached to the left to hold a position at Nicholson's Nek, was overwhelmed and surrendered. The Boers meanwhile developed a strong attack against the British right, and White, having no guns capable of coping with the heavy Boer ordnance, ordered a retreat. This was effected in good order, and was greatly aided by the opportune arrival of two heavy naval guns, under Captain Hedworth Lambton. The British lost 317 killed and wounded, and 1,068 missing. The Boer losses are unknown, but were certainly small.

Farrington Bridge (Arundel's Rebellion).

Fought July 27, 1549, between a small force of Cornish rebels, and an equal number of Royal troops under Lord Russell. The rebels were defeated and driven from the field, but there was no pursuit. Each side lost about 300.

Faventia (Civil War of Marius and Sulla).

Fought B.C. 82, between the consular army of Norbanus, and the Sullans under Metellus. Norbanus attacked with his army wearied by a long march, and his force was totally broken up, only 1,000 remaining with the eagles after the battle.

Fehrbellin (Swedish Invasion of Brandenburg).

Fought June 28, 1675, between the Swedes, under Charles XI, and the Brandenburgers, 15,000 strong, under the Elector, Frederick William. The Swedes were totally defeated, and forced to evacuate Brandenburg.

Ferkeh (Soudan Campaigns).

Fought June 7, 1896, between 9,500 Egyptian troops, with a British horse battery, under Sir Herbert Kitchener, and 4,000 Mahdists under the Emir Hamada. Kitchener, by a night march, surprised the Mahdists in their camp, and after two hours' fighting, drove them out with a loss of 1,500 killed and 500 prisoners. Of 62 Emirs present in the camp, 44 fell and four were captured. The Egyptians lost 20 killed and 81 wounded.

Ferozeshah (First Sikh War).

Fought December 21, 1845, between 50,000 Sikhs, with 108 guns, under Lal Singh, and 16,700 British and native troops, under Sir Hugh Gough. An attempt was made to carry the Sikh entrenched camp by a night attack, but this was unsuccessful. When the attack was renewed at dawn, dissensions among the Sikh leaders enfeebled the resistance, and the Sikhs were defeated with a loss of about 7,000. The British losses were 694 killed, 1,721 wounded.

Ferrara (Hundred Days).

Fought April 12, 1815, when Murat, with 50,000 Italians, endeavoured to force the passage of the Po in the face of an Austrian army, under General Bianchi. He was repulsed with heavy loss, and forced to retreat southward.

Ferrybridge (Wars of the Roses).

Fought 1461, shortly before the battle of Towton, when a force of Lancastrian cavalry, under Lord Clifford, defeated the Yorkists, under Lord Fitzwalter, who was endeavouring to secure the passage of the Aire at Ferrybridge. Lord Fitzwalter was killed.

Fethanleag.

Fought 584, between the West Saxons, under Ceawlin, and the Britons under Cutha. The Britons were defeated.

Fish Creek (Riel's Second Rebellion).

Fought April 24, 1885, when General Middleton, with 400 Canadians, attempted to drive the rebels, 280 strong, from a strong position near Fish Creek. After losing 50 men, Middleton withdrew. The rebels lost 29 killed and wounded.

Fisher's Hill (American Civil War).

Fought September 21, 1864, between 40,000 Federals, under General Sheridan, and 12,000 Confederates, under General Early. The Confederates were defeated and driven from their position with a heavy loss in prisoners and 11 guns.

Fleurus (Thirty Years' War).

Fought August 29, 1622, between the Spaniards, under Spinola, and the Palatinate troops, under Count von Mansfeldt and Christian of Brunswick. The Germans were endeavouring to retreat into Holland after their defeat at Hoechst and were intercepted by the Spaniards, through whom they tried to fight their way. In this effort the infantry was almost entirely cut to pieces, but about 7,000 cavalry reached Breda with the two generals.

Fleurus.

Fought July 1, 1690, between the French, under Marshal Luxembourg, and the Germans and Dutch under the Prince of Waldeck. The French gained a signal victory, the allies being driven from the field in disorder with a loss of 14,000 killed and wounded, and 49 guns.

Fleurus (Wars of the French Revolution).

Fought June 16, 1794, between the Austrians, 80,000 strong, under the Duke of Coburg, and an equal force of French, under Jourdan. The Austrians attacked, and after a severe engagement, were repulsed and compelled to fall back in the direction of Brussels to cover that city.

Flodden (Scottish Wars).

Fought September 9, 1513, when the English, under the Earl of Surrey, attacked the Scots, under James IV, in a strong position on the hill of Flodden. The position was turned by the English left wing, under Stanley, and the Scots totally defeated with heavy losses. James and all his principal nobles fell.

Florence (German Invasion of Italy).

This city was besieged in 406, by the German invaders under Radagaisus, and was almost on the verge of starvation, when the approach of Stilicho at the head of a large Roman army, encouraged the defenders to further resistance. The besiegers, in fact, now became the besieged, for Stilicho surrounded their camp, and starved the Germans into surrender.

Flushing (Walcheren Expedition).

This town was besieged by the British under Lord Chatham and surrendered after a feeble defence, August 16, 1809.

Foksani (Ottoman Wars).

Fought July 21, 1789, between the Turks, under Yusuf Pasha, and the Russians and Austrians under Suwaroff and the Prince of Saxe-Coburg. The allies stormed the Turkish entrenched camp and drove out the Turks with a loss of 2,000 men.

Fontenoy (War of the Austrian Succession).

Fought May 11, 1745, between 50,000 British, Dutch and Austrian troops, under the Duke of Cumberland, and the French, under Marshal Saxe. The Duke endeavoured to relieve Tournay, which the French were besieging, and the British troops captured the heights on which the French were posted. The Prince of Waldeck, however, who commanded the Dutch, failed to support the Duke, and the French being reinforced, the trenches were retaken, and the British beaten back. Tournay fell shortly afterwards.

Formigny (Hundred Years' War).

Fought April 15, 1450, when the newly landed English reinforcements under Kyrielle were totally defeated, and almost annihilated, by the French under the Comte de Clermont. This defeat practically put an end to the English domination in the north of France.

Fornham St. Genevieve (Rebellion of the Princes).

Fought 1173, between the supporters of the rebel princes under Robert de Beaumont, and the forces of Henry II under the Justiciary, Richard de Lucy. The rebels were defeated.

Fornovo (Italian Wars).

Fought July 6, 1495, between 34,000 Venetians and Mantuans under Francisco de Gonzaga of Mantua, and 8,000 French and Swiss under Charles VIII. The French were attacked as they were retiring, but succeeded in repulsing the Italians at a cost of only 100 of all ranks, while the assailants lost 3,500 killed and wounded.

Fort Frontenac (Seven Years' War).

This place, held by about 110 French troops, under Noyan, was captured by Colonel Bradstreet with 3,000 Colonials, August 27, 1758. The capture was of extreme importance, as it robbed the French of the control of Lake Ontario, and severed their communications with their posts on the Ohio.

Fort St. David (Seven Years' War).

This fortress was besieged, May 14, 1758, by a French force under Lally Tollendal, and defended by a garrison of 800 British and 1,600 native troops. The defence was not energetically conducted, and, on the arrival in the roads of a French fleet under Comte d'Aché, the garrison surrendered, June 2.

Fort St. David (Seven Years' War).

A naval action was fought off this place, April 29, 1758, between 7 British ships under Admiral Pococke, and a squadron of 9 French vessels under Comte d'Aché. After a short and indecisive engagement, the French sheered off, but the British were too severely damaged in the rigging to give chase. The French lost one ship, driven ashore.

Fort William Henry (Seven Years' War).

This fort, held by 2,200 British and Colonial troops under Colonel Monro, was besieged, August 4, 1757, by Montcalm, with 6,000 French and Canadians and 1,600 Indians. Montcalm's batteries opened on the 6th, and on the 9th, having lost 300 killed and wounded, and nearly all his guns being disabled, Monro surrendered. He was to be permitted to retire unmolested to Fort Edward, but the French were unable to control their Indian allies, who attacked the unarmed column as it retired. Before order was restored, some 50 had been killed, and 400 carried off prisoners by the Indians.

Forum Terebronii (First Gothic Invasion of the Empire).

Fought 251, between the Romans under Decius, and the Goths under Cuiva. The Gothic army was drawn up in three lines, and the legionaries overthrew the two first, but, in attacking the third, they became entangled in a morass, and were utterly routed. Decius and his son were slain.

Frankenhausen (Peasants' War).

Fought May 15, 1525, between the troops of Saxony, Hesse and Brunswick, and the revolted peasants under Thomas Münzer. The peasants were utterly routed, and Münzer captured and hanged out of hand. This entirely put an end to the rising.

Frankfort - on - Oder (Thirty Years' War).

This place was taken by storm by Gustavus Adolphus, at the head of 15,000 Swedes, April 2, 1631. Schaumberg and Montecuculi, who were in the town, escaped with a portion of the cavalry, but 1,800 of the Imperialist garrison were killed, and 800 captured, with 30 standards and 18 heavy guns.

Franklin (American Civil War).

Fought June 30, 1864, between 30,000 Federals under General Schofield, and 40,000 Confederates under General Hood. Schofield occupied a strong position covering Nashville, where he was attacked by Hood, who penetrated his lines. The Federals, however, rallied, and recaptured the lost positions, and after nightfall, Schofield was enabled to cross the Harpeth in good order, and

effect a junction with General Thomas. The Confederates lost about 4,500 ; the Federals, 1,500 killed and wounded and 1,000 prisoners.

Frastenz (Suabian War).

Fought April 20, 1499, when the Swiss, under Heinrich Wolleb, attacked the Austrians who occupied a strongly entrenched position, and drove them out with a loss of 3,000 killed. Wolleb, who led the charge, was the first to fall on the Swiss side.

Fraubrunnen (Invasion of the " Guglers.")

Fought January, 1376, between the Bernese, and the " Guglers," French and English mercenaries, under Baron Ingelram von Coucy, who claimed the Canton of Aargau in right of his mother. The " Guglers " were totally routed, and compelled to retire from Switzerland.

Frauenstadt (Russo - Swedish Wars).

Fought February 12, 1706, between 10,000 Swedes under Marshal Reinschild, and 20,000 Russians and Saxons under General Schulemburg. The battle did not last a quarter of an hour, for the allies fled without making any resistance. No less than 7,000 *loaded* muskets were picked up on the battlefield.

Fredericksburg (American Civil War).

Fought December 13, 1862 between 150,000 Federals under General Burnside, and 80,000 Confederates under General Lee. The Confederates, who occupied a range of heights fringing the Massaponax River, were attacked by the Federals, whom they repulsed after hard fighting, with a loss of 13,771 killed and wounded. The Confederates lost 1,800 only, but Lee, owing to his inferior numbers, did not feel strong enough to push his victory home, and allowed Burnside to evacuate Fredericksburg unmolested.

Fredericshall (Dano-Swedish Wars).

This fortress, the strongest in Norway, was besieged by the Swedes, under Charles XII, early in December, 1718. On the 11th, as he was inspecting the advanced batteries, the king was struck by a round shot, and fell dead. The Swedes at once raised the siege.

Freteval.

Fought 1194, between the English under Richard Cœur de Lion, and the French under Philip Augustus. Richard gained a complete victory.

Fribourg (Thirty Years' War).

Fought August 3, 5 and 9, 1644, between 20,000 French under the Great Condé and Turenne, and 15,000 Bavarians under the Comte de Mercy. On the 3rd, Turenne, after a long flank march, attacked the Bavarians on the flank, while Condé assailed their front, at 5 p.m. When night fell, the Bavarians were giving way, and during the night de Mercy retired to a fresh position. Here he was attacked on the 5th, but held his ground throughout the day. The French losing twice as many men as their opponents. Three days later de Mercy found it necessary to retreat, and on the 9th he was attacked while retiring by a force of cavalry. This he repulsed, but Condé, coming up, rescued his cavalry, and drove the Bavarians headlong before him, capturing all their artillery and baggage.

Friedland (Campaign of Friedland).

Fought June 14, 1807, between 80,000 French under Napoleon, and 70,000 Russians under Bennigsen. The battle began at 3 a.m., at which time only Lannes' corps was on the field. Bennigsen at first contented himself with an artillery duel, and did not attack in force till 7 a.m., when 26,000 French were in position. These held their ground till the arrival of Napoleon, who with his fresh troops launched an attack against the Russian columns massed in a bend of the river Alle, drove large numbers of them into the river, and occupied Friedland after hard fighting. It was 10 p.m. before the Russians were finally driven from the field, having lost 15,000 killed and wounded and 10,000 prisoners. The French lost between 9,000 and 10,000. This victory was followed by the signature of the Peace of Tilsit.

Fuentes d'Onoro (Peninsular War).

Fought May 5, 1811, in the course of Masséna's attempt to relieve Almeida. Wellington, with 34,000 men, occupied a position behind Fuentes d'Oñoro, which was attacked by Masséna with 34,000 troops and 36 guns. He failed to capture the position, and finally retired, in good order. The British lost 1,200 killed and wounded, and 300 prisoners. The French losses are variously estimated, but were certainly heavier.

Fulford (Norse Invasion).
Fought 1066, between the Norsemen under Harold Hardrada, King of Norway, the English under Earls Edwin and Morcar. The English were defeated.

Furruckabad (Second Mahratta War).
Fought November 14, 1804, between a small British force under Lord Lake, and an army of 60,000 Mahrattas under Jeswunt Rao Holkar. Holkar was signally defeated with heavy loss. The British casualties were only 2 killed and 20 wounded.

Fushimi (Japanese Revolution).
Fought 1868, between the troops of Aizu and Kuwana, under the Shôgun, Yoshinobu, and the forces of Satsuma and Choshu, who gained a complete victory.

Futteypur (Indian Mutiny).
Fought July 12, 1857, between a strong force of rebels, and the British troops under Havelock, who was marching to the relief of Lucknow. The rebels were completely defeated, losing 11 guns, while not a single European in the British force was killed.

G

Gadebesk (Dano-Swedish Wars).
Fought December 20, 1712, between the Swedes, 12,000 strong, under General Steinbock, and 24,000 Danes and Saxons. The allies occupied a position protected by marshy ground, where they were attacked by the Swedes, and, after three hours' hard fighting, driven from their entrenchments with heavy loss.

Gaines' Mill.
See Seven Days' Battles.

Gangud (Russo-Swedish Wars).
Fought 1714, between the Russian fleet under Peter the Great, and the Swedish, under Admiral Ehrenskiöld. The Swedes were utterly routed and Ehrenskiöld and the whole of his squadron captured.

Garigliano (Italian Wars).
Fought November 8, 1503, between the Spaniards, 12,000 strong, under Gonsalvo de Cordova, and the French, in greatly superior force, under Francisco de Gonzaga of Mantua. Gonzaga, wishing to pass the Garigliano, had thrown a bridge over it, and proceeded to cross in face of the Spanish army. After very severe fighting, the French drove back the Spaniards, and made good the passage of the river.

Garigliano (Italian Wars).
Fought December 29, 1503, between the Spaniards, about 15,000 strong, under Gonsalvo de Cordova, and the French, slightly superior in number, under the Marquis of Saluzzo. Gonsalvo crossed the Garigliano at two points, and fell upon the French, who were retiring on Gasta. After hard fighting, in which the Chevalier Bayard bore a notable part, the French

were utterly routed, leaving 4,000 dead on the field, and all their artillery and baggage. The Spanish loss is unknown.

Garigliano (Italian Rising).

Fought October, 1850, between the Italian patriots under Cialdini, and the Neapolitans under Francis II of Naples. The patriots were victorious.

Gate Pah (Maori War).

Fought April 27, 1864, when 1,700 British soldiers and blue-jackets, under General Cameron, attacked the Maori stockade known as the Gate Pah. After a short bombardment, 600 men forced their way into the stockade, but were repulsed. On the following day it was found that the stockade had been evacuated. The British lost 14 officers, and 98 men killed and wounded. Only 30 dead and wounded Maories were found in and near the Pah.

Gaulauli (Indian Mutiny).

Fought May 22, 1858, between a British column under Sir Hugh Rose, and 20,000 rebels under Tantia Topi, the Ranee of Jhansi, and other rebel leaders. The overwhelming numbers of the rebels at first gave them the advantage, but a bayonet charge broke them, and they fled in disorder with heavy loss. This victory was followed by the recovery of Calpi.

Gaza (Alexander's Asiatic Campaigns).

This city, defended by a Persian garrison, under Batis, was besieged by Alexander the Great October, 332 B.C. Utilizing the engines he had employed against Tyre, he succeeded, after some

weeks, in breaching the walls, and, after three unsuccessful assaults, carried the city by storm, the garrison being put to the sword.

Gaza (Wars of Alexander's Successors).

Fought B.C. 312, between the Syrians and Egyptians under Seleucus and Ptolemy Soter, 25,000 strong, and an equal force of Macedonians under Demetrius Poliorcetes. The Macedonians were routed, losing 5,000 killed, 8,000 wounded, and all their treasure and baggage.

Gebora (Peninsular War).

Fought February 19, 1811, between 8,000 French, under Marshal Soult, and 12,000 Spaniards, under Mendizabal. The Spaniards were routed with a loss of 2,000 killed and wounded, 5,000 prisoners and all their guns.

Gelt, The.

Fought February, 1570, between the rebel Borderers under Leonard Dacre, and the royal troops under Lord Hunsdon The rebels were completely routed.

Gemblours (Netherlands War of Independence).

Fought January 31, 1578, between the Netherlands patriots, 20,000 strong, under General Goignies, and the Spaniards, in about equal force, under Don John of Austria. The patriots, who were retiring from Namur, were followed by Don John, who sent forward a picked force of 1,600 men, under Gonzaga and Mondragon in pursuit. They attacked the rearguard, under Philip Egmont, and dispersed it, and then, falling suddenly upon the main body, utterly routed it, with a loss, it is said, of 10,000 killed and prisoners. The Spaniards lost ten or eleven at most.

Genoa.

In 1746, the Genoese, incensed by the license of the soldiery, rose against the Austrian garrison, under General Botta, and after five days' street fighting, lasting from December 6 to 10, drove them out of the city, with a loss of 5,000 men.

Genoa (Wars of the French Revolution).

Fought March 13, 1795, between a British fleet of 14 sail of the line under Admiral Hotham, and a French fleet of 15 sail. The action lasted throughout the day, and on the following morning the French retired, leaving two line-of-battle ships in the hands of the British. The British lost 74 killed and 284 wounded.

Genoa (Napoleon's Italian Campaigns).

In April, 1800, Genoa, held by the French, under Masséna, was besieged by the Austrians under General Melas, and later in the siege under General Ott. The city had for some time been blockaded on the seaward side by the British fleet, under Lord Keith. Provisions were consequently scarce, and notwithstanding some successful sorties, Masséna was forced to capitulate, June 5, the garrison marching out without laying down their arms.

Geok Tepe (Russian Conquest of Central Asia).

This place, the stronghold of the Tekke Turcomans, defended by a garrison of 15,000, was besieged, September 9, 1878, by the Russians, under General Lomakine. After a short bombardment, an attempt was made to storm the fortress, which was repulsed with a loss of 500. The breaching guns were with difficulty saved, and the Russians retired on the following day. About 4,000 Turcomans were killed by shell fire.

In 1881, a second attempt was made by Skobeloff, with 10,000 Russians, the garrison being now nearly 30,000 strong. After a regular siege, lasting from the 8th to the 17th of January, the place was stormed, 6,500 Turcomans falling in the assault, and 8,000 in the subsequent pursuit.

Gerberoi.

Fought 1080, between the troops of William the Conqueror, and those of his son Robert, who claimed the Dukedom of Normandy, and was receiving aid from Philip I of France. Robert was defeated and made prisoner, and, obtaining his father's forgiveness, resigned his claim to the Dukedom.

Gergovia (Gallic War).

Fought B.C. 52, between the Romans under Julius Cæsar, and the Gauls under Vercingetorix. Cæsar was besieging the town, but was compelled to retreat. Before retiring, however, he delivered an assault which was repulsed by the Gauls, the Romans leaving over 700 legionaries, and 46 centurions dead on the field.

Germaghah.

Genghis Khan's first battle, fought 1193, when with 6,000 men he defeated the army of his father-in-law, Ung Khan, under Sankun, 10,000 strong, surprising them in a narrow pass, and inflicting heavy loss upon them.

Germantown (American War of Independence).

Fought October 4, 1777, between the Americans under Washington, and the British under Sir William Howe. The Americans attacked the British entrenchments, and were repulsed with heavy loss.

Gerona (Peninsular War).

This fortress, held by 3,000 Spanish regulars, under Mariano Alvarez, was besieged, June 4, 1809, by General Verdier, with 18,000 French. Though ill-provided with food, medicines, and money, and receiving but little assistance from outside, Alvarez held out gallantly till December 10, when he capitulated, and the garrison marched out with the honours of war.

Gettysburg (American Civil War).

Fought July 1, 2 and 3, 1863, between the army of the Potomac under General Meade, and the army of Virginia under General Lee. On the 1st, Meade's position in front of Gettysburg was attacked by A. P. Hills' corps, and the Federals driven in confusion into the town. On the 2nd, Meade took up a fresh position behind Gettysburg, where he repulsed all the Confederate attacks, though at a heavy cost. On the 3rd, Meade succeeded in driving back the Confederate left, but Lee's main attack succeeded in driving the Federals from the ridge. They rallied and retook it, but had lost too heavily to assume the offensive. Lee again offered battle on the 4th, but the Federals declined it, and Lee retired unmolested, having lost about 20,000 men in the three days. The Federal losses were about the same.

Gherain.

Fought August 2, 1763, between the army of Mir Cossim, the deposed Nawab of Bengal, and the British under Major Adams. A severe engagement, lasting four hours, ended in a signal victory for the British.

Ghoaine (First Afghan War).

Fought August 30, 1842, between General Nott's force, on its march from Kandahar to Ghuzni, and the Afghans, under Shems-ud-din, Governor of Ghuzni. The Afghans were totally defeated, losing all their guns, tents and baggage.

Ghuzni (First Afghan War).

This fortress, garrisoned by 3,000 Afghans, under Haidar Khan, was captured, January 21, 1839, by the British. The besiegers having no breaching guns, it was found necessary to blow in the main gate, and the place was then stormed, at a cost of 18 officers and 162 rank and file, killed and wounded. The garrison lost 500 killed.

Gibbel Rutts (Irish Rebellion).

Fought May 26, 1798, when the regulars, under Sir James Duff, attacked the camp of the

H

rebels on the Curragh, and dispersed them at the point of the bayonet, with a loss of 350 killed.

Gibraltar (War of the Spanish Succession).

This fortress was captured, July 24, 1704, by a combined British and Dutch fleet, under Sir George Rooke, from the Spaniards under the Marquis de Salinas. The resistance of the garrison lasted 2 days only, during which the allies lost 12 officers and 276 men killed and wounded.

Gibraltar.

From 1779 to 1783, Gibraltar sustained a siege at the hands of a combined French and Spanish force, who, though provided with powerful floating batteries, were unable to make any impression on the defences. In the course of the siege, the garrison, under General Elliot, were several times reinforced and revictualled by British fleets, which ran the gauntlet of the blockade.

Gihon, The.

Fought 1362, between the Getes under their Khan, and the Tartars under Tamerlane. The Tartars were defeated, and the Getes marched upon Samarcand, but sickness robbed them of nearly all their horses, and they were forced to retire.

Gingi (Mogul Invasion of the Deccan).

This place was besieged by the Moguls in 1689, and was defended by Rajah Ram. The siege was carried on in desultory fashion, first by Zulfikar Khan, then by Kambaksh, son of Aurungzebe, and then again by Zulfikar Khan. After three years had been wasted, Aurungzebe took command in person, and after conniving at the escape of Rajah Ram, carried the place by storm.

Gislikon (War of the Sonderbund).

Fought November 23, 1847, when the Federals, under General Dufour, attacked the troops of the Sonderbund, under Colonel Salis-Soglio, strongly posted at Gislikon, near Lake Zug, and drove them from their position. The losses were very small. On the following day the Federals entered Lucerne, and the Civil War, which had lasted 20 days only, came to an end.

Gitschin (Seven Weeks' War).

Fought June 29 and 30, 1866, between the Prussians, 16,000 strong, under Prince Frederick Charles, and the Austrians and Saxons, 30,000 strong, under Count Clam Gallas. The Austrians were defeated, and driven from all their positions with a loss of 3,000 killed and wounded, and 7,000 prisoners.

Gladsmuir.

See Prestonpans.

Glen Fruin.

Fought 1604, between the royal troops under the Duke of Argyll, and the Macgregors and other clans, when the Highlanders gained a complete victory.

Glenlivet (Huntly's Rebellion).

Fought October 4, 1594, between the troops of James VI, 10,000 strong, under the Earl of Argyll, and the rebel Earls of Errol and Huntly. Though inferior in numbers, the rebels gained a complete victory, driving off the royal troops with a loss of 500 men.

Glen Malone.
Fought 1580, between the English settlers under Lord Grey de Wilton, and the Irish septs. The English suffered a serious defeat, among the slain being Sir Peter Carew.

Glenmarreston.
Fought 638, when the Scots under Donald Bree, King of Dalriada, utterly routed the invading Angles.

Glorious First of June.
See Ushant.

Goits (Italian Rising).
Fought May 30, 1848, between the Piedmontese under Charles Albert of Savoy, and the Austrians under General Radetsky. The Austrians were completely defeated, and Radetsky compelled to take refuge behind the line of the Adige.

Golden Rock (Seven Years' War).
Fought August 7, 1753, between 1,500 British under Major Lawrence, together with 5,000 Tanjore troops under Monakji, and a detachment of French and Mysoris, forming part of the army besieging Trichinopoly. The Golden Rock was taken by assault, and the enemy driven off in confusion, but the victory would have been more decisive had the Tanjore horse pursued with more vigour.

Goodwins, The (Dutch Wars).
Fought July 1, 1666, between a British fleet of 60 sail, under the Duke of Albemarle, and a Dutch fleet of 71 sail-of-the-line, and 30 smaller vessels. under van Tromp and de Ruyter, The action lasted two days, and was desperately contested, but the Dutch being reinforced in the morning of the 3rd, Albemarle bore away. On the 4th, having been joined by Prince Rupert's squadron, he renewed the attack, but without success. The English lost 10 ships, while most of the others were disabled. The killed and wounded amounted to 1,700, while 2,000 were taken prisoners.

Goraria (Indian Mutiny).
Fought November 23 and 24, 1857, between a British column, about 3,000 strong, under Brigadier Stuart, and a body of 5,000 rebels. The mutineers occupied a strong position, and the British were unable to dislodge them on the 23rd. On the following day the attack was renewed, and the rebels were driven out and dispersed, with a loss of over 1,500.

Gorni-Dubnik (Russo-Turkish War).
Fought October 24, 1877, between the 2nd Division of the Russian Guard, under General Gourko, and the Turks, who were holding the redoubt of Gorni-Dubnik, under Achmet Hefzi Pasha. After very heavy fighting, the Russians succeeded in dislodging their opponents, with a loss of 1,500 killed and wounded, and 53 officers and 2,250 men captured, including the Pasha. The Russians lost 3,300 killed and wounded, including 116 officers of the Guards.

Gorodeczno (Campaign of Moscow).

Fought August 12, 1812, between 36,000 French and Austrians, under General Reynier and the Prince of Schwartzemberg, and the Russians, in equal force, under General Tormazoff. The Russians were defeated and driven from their positions, with a loss of 4,000 men. The French and Austrians lost about 2,000.

Goa.

In 1511, Goa, held by a Portuguese garrison, under Albuquerque, was invested by Kumal Khan, General of the Rajah of Bijapore, at the head of 60,000 men. After a siege of 20 days Albuquerque found his communication with his fleet threatened, and withdrew the garrison. In the same year, however, having collected a force of 1,500 men with 23 ships at Cananore, he attacked Goa, and at once forced an entrance. After severe fighting in the streets, the Deccanis fled in confusion to the mainland, with a loss of 6,000. The Portuguese lost 50 only.

Goa.

This fort, which was held by a Portuguese garrison of 700, under the Viceroy, Luis de Ataida, was attacked by Ali Adil Shah, Rajah of Bijapore, with 135,000 men and 350 guns, in 1570. Aided by the civilians, and 1,300 monks, the garrison made so strenuous a defence, that the Rajah was beaten off, after losing 12,000 men.

Grampians, The (Roman Invasion of Scotland).

Fought 84, probably on the Moor of Ardoch, between the Romans under Agricola, and the Caledonians, 30,000 strong, under Galgacus. The Caledonians attacked with great bravery, but were beaten by the superiority of the Roman discipline, and retired with a loss of 10,000 men. The Romans also lost heavily.

Granada (Moorish Empire in Spain).

Fought 1319, when a Spanish army, under the Regents Pedro and John of Castile, appeared under the walls of Granada. A sortie of 5,000 picked Moors, under Said Othman took place, and the Christians were utterly routed, both the Regents being slain.

Granada (War of Granada).

On April 26, 1491, Ferdinand the Catholic, with an army of 50,000 Spaniards, sat down before Granada, the last stronghold of the Moors in Spain. The siege was carried on in somewhat desultory fashion, and in the early days one serious sortie was made by the inhabitants and garrison, who were, however, defeated, with a loss of 2,000 killed. The city held out until November 25, when Abdallah, the last king of Granada, capitulated.

Grandella (Italian Wars).

Fought 1266, between the troops of the Two Sicilies, under Manfred, son of the Emperor Frederick II, and the French, under Charles of Anjou. Manfred was defeated, and fell in the battle, Charles seizing the crown of the double kingdom.

Grandson (Burgundian Wars).

Fought March 2, 1476, between the Swiss, 18,000 strong, and the Burgundians, numbering 36,000, under Charles the Bold. Charles endeavoured to entice the Swiss into the plain, and to that end ordered a retreat. He was followed by the Swiss, and his rearguard being attacked, was seized with panic, and fled, and in the end Charles was completely defeated and his camp captured.

Granicus, The (Alexander's Asiatic Campaigns).
Fought May, 334 B.C., between 35,000 Macedonians, under Alexander the Great, and 40,000 Persians and Greek mercenaries, under Memnon of Rhodes, and various Persian satraps. Alexander crossed the Granicus in the face of the Persian army, leading the way himself at the head of the heavy cavalry, and having dispersed the Persian light horse, he brought up the phalanx, which fell upon and routed the Greek mercenaries. The Persians lost heavily, while the Macedonians' loss was very slight.

Grant's Hill (Seven Years' War).
Fought September 14, 1758, when Major Grant, with 800 Highlanders, and Provincials, attacked a body of Indians in the French service near Fort Duquesne. He was repulsed, and in turn attacked by the garrison of the Fort, 3,000 strong, under M. de Ligneris. Grant was totally defeated, losing 273 in killed, wounded and prisoners, and was himself captured.

Graspan (Second Boer War).
Fought November 25, 1899, between Lord Methuen's divi-

sion, with a naval brigade, 400 strong, and a Boer commando of about 2,500 men. The Boers occupied a strong position, the key of which, a high kopje, was attacked in front and flank, and carried, with a loss of 9 officers and 185 men. The marines, who numbered 200, lost 3 officers and 86 men of this total. The Boers lost about 100. This is also called the battle of Enslin.

Gravelines.
Fought July 13, 1538, between 8,500 French and Germans, under Marshal de Thermes, and about 10,000 Spanish, Germans and Flemings, under Count Egmont. De Thermes' right rested on the sea, and a cavalry charge, headed by Egmont, broke his line, after severe hand-to-hand fighting, and the French fled in confusion, leaving 1,500 dead on the field, while as many more were driven into the sea, and drowned. Large numbers were cut down in the pursuit, and de Thermes was captured.

Gravelotte (Franco-German War).
Fought August 18, 1870, between the French, under Bazaine, and the combined German army under the supreme command of William of Prussia. The battle was most hotly contested, but while the French held their ground in the neighbourhood of Gravelotte, the Germans turned their right flank at St. Privat, and they were eventually obliged to abandon all their positions, and retire into Metz, where they were subsequently blockaded. The German losses amounted to 899 officers and 19,260 men killed

and wounded. The French losses were somewhat less. This battle is also known as the battle of St. Privat.

Great Meadows (Seven Years' War).

Fought July 3, 1752, between 350 Virginians, under Washington, and 700 French, under Coulon de Villiers. The Virginians occupied a square log enclosure, known as Fort Necessity, where they resisted the French attack for nine hours, till lack of ammunition forced Washington to surrender. The Virginians lost 60 killed and wounded ; the French considerably less.

Grenada (American War of Independence).

Fought July 3, 1779, between a British fleet of 24 sail, under Admiral Byron, and a French fleet of 20 sail-of-the-line, and 10 frigates, under the Comte d'Estaing. Admiral Byron attacked the French with a view of recapturing Grenada, but was unsuccefssul, though he inflicted upon them a loss of 1,200 killed and 1,500 wounded. The British lost 183 killed and 346 wounded.

Grangam (Russo-Swedish Wars).

Fought 1721, between the Swedes, and the Russian fleet under Admiral Golitshin. The Swedes were completely defeated, losing four line-of-battle ships captured.

Grochow (Second Polish Rising).

Fought February 25, 1831, between the Poles, 90,000 strong under Prince Michael Radziwill, and 120,000 Russians, under General Dubitsch. After a sanguinary

engagement, the Russians were defeated, with a loss of 10,000 killed and wounded. The Poles lost about 5,000.

Gross-Beeren (Campaign of Leipsic).

Fought August 23, 1813, between the French army of the north, under Oudinot, and the allies, 80,000 strong, under the Crown Prince of Sweden, who was covering the road to Berlin. Regnier, whose corps formed the centre of Oudinot's army, captured Gross-Beeren, which was retaken by the Prussians under von Bulow, and again recovered by Fournier's and Guilleminot's divisions, but Oudinot was not sufficiently strong to press his advantage, and retired with a loss of 1,500 men, and 8 guns.

Gross-Jägersdorf (Seven Years' War).

Fought August 30, 1757, between 28,000 Prussians, under Marshal Lehwaldt, and a largely superior force of Russians, under General Apraxine. The Prussians were defeated, but Apraxine failed to follow up his victory, and recrossed the frontier.

Grozka (Ottoman Wars).

Fought 1739, between the Austrians, under Count Neipperg, and the Turks, under the Grand Vizier. The Austrians were defeated, with heavy loss.

Grunnervaldt.

Fought 1404, between the Poles, under Vladislas IV, and the Teutonic Knights, under their Grand Master. The Poles gained a complete victory, and it is said that 50,000 knights perished, though it is more than doubtful whether their whole army amounted to so many.

Guadeloupe (Wars of the French Revolution).

This island was taken by a British force under Sir John Jervis, July 3, 1794, with a loss of 3 officers and 33 men killed and wounded. It was recaptured by the French, on December 10, of the same year.

Guad-el-Ras (Moroccan War).

Fought March 23, 1860, when 25,000 Spaniards, under Marshal O'Donnell, routed a large force of Moors, entrenched in a very strong position behind the Guad-el-Ras. This victory ended the war.

Guastalla (War of the Polish Succession).

Fought September 19, 1734, between the Imperialists, under the Prince of Würtemberg, and the French, under Marshal de Coligny. The Imperialists were defeated with a loss of about 4,000, including the Prince of Würtemberg. The French losses were about the same.

Gubat.

See Abu Klea.

Guildford Court House (American War of Independence).

Fought March 16, 1781, between the British, under Lord Cornwallis, and a largely superior force of Americans, under General Greene. The Americans occupied a strongly entrenched position in and round Guildford, and the battle consisted of a series of independent actions, in which the British were uniformly successful, driving out the Americans with heavy casualties, and the loss of all their guns and ammunition. The British lost 548 killed and wounded, but the victory served little purpose, as Lord Cornwallis was too weak to pursue his advantage.

Guinegate.

Fought August 16, 1513, when a body of French cavalry, who aimed at relieving Terouënne, which was besieged by the English, under Henry VIII, and the Imperialists, under Maximilian I, were put to flight by the allies without striking a blow. The French fled so precipitately that the action was dubbed the Battle of the Spurs.

Gujerat (Second Sikh War).

Fought February 22, 1849, between the British, 25,000 strong, under Lord Gough, and 50,000 Sikhs, under Shir Singh. The British artillery, numbering 84 pieces, broke the Sikh lines, and after resisting for over two hours, they fled, and were practically annihilated in the pursuit. Fifty-three guns were taken. The British lost only 92 killed and 682 wounded.

Gunzburg (Campaign of the Danube).

Fought October 9, 1805, when Ney's corps carried the three bridges over the Danube, at or near this town, driving off the Austians with a loss of 300 killed and wounded, and 1,000 prisoners.

Gwalior (First Mahratta War).

This strong fortress was captured from the Mahrattas, August 3, 1780, by a British force of about 2,000 men, mostly sepoys, under Captain Popham. The wall was scaled by two companies of sepoys, under Captain Bruce, supported by 20 Europeans, and followed by two battalions. The garrison was completely surprised, and an entrance effected without opposition, whereupon the place was surrendered to the assailants, who had not lost a man.

Gwalior (Indian Mutiny).

Fought June 17, 18 and 19, 1858, between a British column under Sir Hugh Rose, and a large body of rebels, led by the Ranee of Jhansi in person. On the 17th the mutineers were driven out of the cantonments with heavy loss, while on the following days the important positions in the town were captured in succession, until by the evening of the 19th, the British were in undisputed possession of Gwalior. The Ranee was known to be amongst the slain, though her body was never found.

H.

Haarlem (Netherlands War of Independence).

This city was invested by the Spaniards, 30,000 strong, under Don Francisco de Toledo, December 11, 1572. It was held by a garrison of 4,000, under Ripperda, including a corps of Amazons, led by a widow named Kenau Hasselaer. The batteries opened on the 18th, and on the 21st an assault was repulsed, the assailants losing 400, the garrison three or four only. A second assault, on January 31, 1573, was also repulsed, while a brilliant sortie,

on March 25, captured a large and welcome convoy of provisions. On May 28, however, the patriot flotilla of 150 vessels under Martin Brand, on the lake, was defeated by 100 Spanish ships, under Count Bossu. From this point the reduction of the city by famine was inevitable, and the place was surrendered, July 12, 1573. The garrison, reduced to 1,800, was massacred, with the exception of 600 Germans, and altogether 2,300 persons perished after the capitulation. The Spaniards lost 12,000 men in the course of the siege.

Hadranum.

Fought B.C. 344, between Timoleon, the deliverer of Sicily, with 2,000 followers, and Hiketas, Tyrant of Leontini, with 10,000 men. The two had been summoned to the assistance of the rival factions in Hadranum, and Hiketas, who arrived first, was resting his men under the walls, when he was surprised by Timoleon, and totally routed. This was Timoleon's first exploit, and Hadranum became his headquarters.

Hadrianople (War of the Two Empires).

Fought July 3, 323, between Constantine, Emperor of the West, with 120,000 troops, and Licinius, Emperor of the East, with 165,000. Licinius, by the skilful manœuvring of Constantine, was enticed from his entrenched camp into the open plain, and his raw levies being powerless against the Western veterans, he was totally defeated. It is said that 34,000 perished in the battle.

Hadrianople (Second Gothic Invasion of the East).

Fought August 9, 378, between the Romans, under the Emperor Valens, and the Goths, under Fritigern. The Roman cavalry fled from the field, and the legionaries were surrounded and ridden down by the overwhelming masses of the Gothic horse. Two thirds of the legionaries, and 39 great officers and tribunes perished. Valens was carried off the field wounded, but the hut in which he was lying was fired, and he perished in the flames.

Hahozaki (Tartar Invasion of Japan).

Fought 1274, between the troops of the province of Kiushiu and the Tartars forming the expedition, despatched by Kublai Khan, under Lin Fok Heng. After severe fighting, in which the Japanese suffered heavily, Lin was severely wounded, and withdrew to his ships. A heavy gale destroyed a large number of the Tartar and Korean vessels, and finally the remnant of the invading force made good its escape.

Haliartus.

Fought B.C. 395, when Lysander, at the head of a Spartan force, without waiting as had been arranged to effect a junction with Pausanius, attacked the town of Haliartus. The Haliartians, seeing from the battlements that a body of Thebans was approaching, made a sortie, and the Spartans, attacked simultaneously in front and rear, were routed, and Lysander slain.

Halidon Hill (Scottish Wars).

Fought 1383, in the course of an attempt by Archibald Douglas, the Regent, to relieve Berwick, which was besieged by Edward III. The Scots were powerless against the English archers, and were defeated with a loss of 30,000, including the Regent, and four Earls. This defeat resulted in the submission of Scotland, and Edward placed Balliol upon the throne.

Halieis.

Fought B.C. 459, between the Athenians, and the combined forces of Corinth and Epidamnus. The Athenians were victorious.

Hallue (Franco-German War).

Fought December 23 and 24, 1870, between 40,000 French, under General Faidherbe, and 22,500 Germans, under Manteuffel. The French lost heavily in the village lying in front of their position, but the Germans were unable to carry the entrenchments on the heights. After their attack had been repulsed, the French assumed the offensive, but with no decisive result. The Germans lost 927 killed and wounded ; the French over 1,000, besides 1,300 prisoners.

Hampton Roads (American Civil War).

Fought March 8 and 9, 1862, between the Confederate armoured frigate, *Merrimac*, and 5 gunboats, under Captain Buchanan, and 5 Federal warships, under Captain Marston. On the 8th, the *Merrimac* destroyed two Federal vessels, and drove one ashore, but on the 9th, the

Federals were reinforced by the arrival of the turret-ship *Monitor*, and after an indecisive action, the *Merrimac* drew off. In the two days, the Confederates lost only 10 killed and wounded, but the Federal losses were far heavier, the *Cumberland* alone losing 150 out of a crew of 400.

Hanau (Campaign of Leipsic).

Fought October 30 and 31, 1813, between 80,000 French, the survivors of Leipsic, under Napoleon, and 45,000 Austrians and Bavarians, under General Wrede, who had occupied a position at Hanau, barring Napoleon's retreat to France. On the 30th, Napoleon attacked Wrede's left, which was astride of the road, and driving it back continued his retreat with the main body, leaving three divisions, under Marmont, to secure his rearguard. On the 31st, the rearguard, under Mortier, attacked Hanau, and Wrede being dangerously wounded, his successor, Fresnel, drew off, leaving the road clear. The French lost 6,000, the allies 10,000 men in the two days.

Hardenberg (Netherlands War of Independence).

Fought June 15, 1580, between the Dutch Patriots, under Count Philip Hohenlo, and the Royalists, under Martin Schenck, Fatigued by a long march, the Patriots were no match for Schenck's fresh troops, and after an hour's fighting, were broken and almost annihilated.

Harlaw.

Fought July 24, 1411, between the rebel Highlanders, under Donald, Lord of the Isles,

and the Lowland Scots, under the Earl of Mar, together with the town militia of Aberdeen, led by their Provost. After a most sanguinary battle, the Lowlanders were utterly routed. Among the slain were the Provost, many knights, 500 men-at-arms, and the majority of the burghers forming the militia. The Highlanders lost 500 only.

Harper's Ferry (American Civil War).

Fought September 16, 1862, when the Confederates, three divisions, under General " Stonewall " Jackson surrounded the Federal garrison of Harper's Ferry, 11,000 strong, with 73 guns, and forced them to surrender.

Hashin (Soudan Campaigns).

Fought March 20, 1885, when 8,000 British troops, under General Graham, defeated a detachment of Osman Digna's army, inflicting upon them a loss of about 1,000 killed. The British lost 48 killed and wounded.

Haslach (Campaign of the Danube).

Fought October 11, 1805, when General Dupont, with 6,000 French, marching upon Ulm, was suddenly confronted with an army of Austrians, 60,000 strong, strongly posted on the Michelberg. Dupont at once seized and entrenched the village of Hanau, which he held until dark against 25,000 Austrians, under the Archduke Ferdinand. After nightfall he withdrew, carrying off 4,000 prisoners.

Hastenbech (Seven Years' War).

Fought July 26, 1757, between 50,000 Hanoverians and others, under the Duke of Cumberland, and 80,000 French, under Marshal d'Estrées. The Duke, who had taken post on the Weser, to protect Hanover, was overpowered by d'Estrées, and driven back to Slade, on the Elbe, with a loss of several hundred men. This defeat was followed by the signature of the Convention of Closter-Seven.

Hastings (Norman Conquest).

Fought October 14, 1066, a fortnight after the landing of William the Conqueror. The English, under Harold, fought entirely on the defensive, at first with success, but were at last lured from their position by a feigned flight of the Normans, and were then totally routed. Harold was among the fallen. This battle is also known as the Battle of Senlac.

Hatvan (Hungarian Rising).

Fought April 2, 1849, when the Austrians, 15,000 strong under Marshal Schlick, attacked the 7th Hungarian corps, of about equal strength, and after a severe engagement, were totally defeated.

Havana (War of the Austrian Succession).

Fought October 12, 1748, between a British squadron of seven ships, under Admiral Knowles, and a Spanish squadron of equal strength. The action was fought with little determination, and though the British captured one ship, the ·result was far from decisive. The Spaniards lost 298, the British 179 killed and wounded.

Havana (Seven Years' War).

In June, 1762, the Earl of Clanwilliam, with 11,000 British troops, supported by a squadron, under Admiral Pococke, laid siege to Havana. Moro Castle, the key of the defences, was taken by storm, and after a siege of two months and eight days the city was captured.

Heathfield.

Fought 633, between the Mercians, under Penda, and the Northumbrians, under Edwin. The latter were defeated and Edwin slain.

Heavenfield.

Fought 634, between the Anglo-Saxons, under the Bretwalda, Oswald of Northumbria, and the Britons, under Cadwallon. The Britons were totally routed.

Hedgeley Moor (Wars of the Roses).

Fought April 25, 1464, between the Lancastrians, under Margaret of Anjou and Sir Ralph Percy, and the Yorkists, under Lord Montague. The Lancastrians were totally defeated, Percy falling in the battle.

Heiliger-Zee (Netherlands War of Independence).

Fought May 23, 1568, between the "'Beggars," under Louis of Nassau, and 5,000 veteran Spaniards, under Aremberg. Louis occupied a very strong position on a wooded height, near the monastery of the Holy Lion, his front being protected by a morass crossed by a narrow causeway. The Spanish infantry traversed this to the attack, but were repulsed, and Count Aremberg, leading a charge of horse, in the hope of restoring the day, fell mortally wounded. Upon this the Spaniards broke and fled, having suffered a loss of 1,600 men.

Heilsberg (Campaign of Friedland).

Fought June 10, 1807, between 30,000 French, under Marshal Soult, and 80,000 Russians, under General Bennigsen. The Russians occupied the heights on both sides of the Alle, and the plains below, being in greater force on the left bank. The French attacked and drove the Russians into the entrenchments, but could make no further progress, and night put an end to an obstinate but inconclusive conflict, in which the Russians lost about 10,000, the French, 8,000 killed and wounded.

Hekitai-Kan (Invasion of Korea).

Fought 1595, between the Japanese, under Kobayagawa Takakage, and the Chinese, under Li Chin. The Chinese were utterly routed, Li's army being almost annihilated, and he himself escaping with difficulty from the field.

Heligoland (Napoleonic Wars).

This island was captured, August 31, 1807, from the Danes, by a small British squadron, under Admiral Thomas Russell.

Heliopolis (French Invasion of Egypt).

Fought March 20, 1800, between 10,000 French, under Kléber, and about 70,000 Turks, under Ibrahim Bey. The Turks were utterly routed, with a loss of several thousand men, while the French only lost about 300 killed and wounded.

Hellespont (War of the Two Empires).

Fought 323, between the fleet of Constantine the Great, consisting of 200 small galleys, under Crispus, and that of Licinius, numbering 350 sail, under Amandus. After two days' hard fighting, Crispus forced the passage of the Hellespont, and totally routed the Eastern fleet, with a loss of 130 ships and 5,000 men.

Helorus.

Fought B.C. 492, between Hippocrates, Tyrant of Gela, and the Syracusans, The Syracusans were totally routed, and were so weakened by this defeat, that Syracuse fell an easy prey to Gelon, Hippocrates' successor, in the following year.

Helsingborg (Dano - Spanish Wars).

Fought 1710, between 20,000 Swedes, of whom 12,000 were raw recruits, under General Steinbock, and the Danish invading army. The Swedes won a signal victory, and the invaders were compelled to take refuge under the walls of Helsingborg, and a few days later to embark for Denmark. Besides killed, they left 4,000 wounded prisoners in the hands of the Swedes.

Hemushagu (Invasion of Korea).

Fought 1595, between the Japanese, under Konishi Yukinaga, and the Chinese, under Li Chin. The Japanese were defeated, and forced to retire upon the capital.

Hengestesdun (Danish Invasion).

Fought 835, when the men of Wessex, under Egbert, totally defeated the Danes and Cornish Britons.

Hennersdorf (War of the Austrian Succession).

Fought November, 1745, between 60,000 Prussians, under Frederick the Great, and 40,000 Austrians and Saxons, under Prince Charles of Lorraine. Frederick surprised Prince Charles on the march, and utterly routed his vanguard, comprised of Saxons, with enormous loss. The Austrians were compelled in consequence to retire into Bohemia.

Heraclea (Pyrrhus' Invasion of Italy).

Fought B.C. 280, between the Epirots, 30,000 strong, under Pyrrhus, and about 35,000 Romans, under P. Laverius Lævinus. The Romans crossed the Siris in the face of the enemy, when they were attacked by Pyrrhus, and after a furious conflict, were at last broken by his elephants, and fled in disorder, losing about 7,000 men. The Epirots lost 4,000.

Heraclea.

Fought 313, between the Illyrians, under Licinius, afterwards Emperor of the East, and the troops of the reigning Emperor Maximinus. Licinius was marching with 30,000 men to the relief of Heraclea, when he was attacked by Maximinus, with 70,000. Licinius was at first driven back by weight of numbers, but his skill, and the steadiness of his troops, enabled him to rally, and eventually Maximinus was defeated with heavy loss.

Herat (Tartar Invasion of Afghanistan).

This city was captured, 1220, by 20,000 Tartars, under Sudah Bahadur. The Governor, Emin Malek, was entirely unprepared to stand a siege, and surrendered when the Tartars appeared before the walls. Having meanwhile been retaken by a *coup-de-main*, by Shems-ed-din, who held it as an independent chieftain, Herat was again besieged by the Mongols, under Tuli Khan, in 1221. After a brief, but resolute resistance, during which Shems-ed-din fell, the inhabitants opened the gates to the besiegers, and the garrison was put to the sword.

Herat (Perso-Afghan Wars).

On November 22, 1837, Mohamed, Shah of Persia, laid siege to the city, which was held by an Afghan garrison, under Yar Mohamed. After a somewhat desultory siege, an attempt was made to storm the place, June 24, 1838, when the Persians were repulsed with a loss of 1,700 men. From this time a tacit armistice existed till September 9, when the Shah withdrew his army.

Herdonea (Second Punic War).

Fought B.C. 210, when the Carthaginians, under Hannibal, defeated, and practically destroyed an army of 25,000 Romans, under Cnæus Fulvius. Fulvius was among the slain.

Héricourt (Burgundian Wars).

Fought November 13, 1474, between the Swiss, 18,000 strong, and the Burgundians,

10,000 in number. The Burgundians were totally defeated, the town of Héricourt taken.

Hermanstadt (Ottoman Wars).

Fought 1442, and notable as being the first appearance of John Huniades in arms against the Turks. With an army of Hungarians he totally defeated Mejid Bey, who was besieging Hermanstadt, inflicting on the Turks a loss of 20,000 men, and relieving the place. The Hungarians lost 3,000.

Hernani (First Carlist War).

Fought August 29, 1836, between the British legion, under General Evans, and the Carlists. Evans was defeated.

Hernani (First Carlist War).

Fought March 15 and 16, 1837, between the British legion, and a small contingent of Cristinos, under General Evans, and about 17,000 Carlists, under Don Sebastian, strongly posted on the Hernani road. On the 15th, Evans attacked the Carlists on the Venta heights, and after five hours' fighting occupied the position. On the 16th, when the conflict was resumed, the Carlists retired into Hernani, but reinforcements arriving, they took the offensive, and forced Evans to retreat.

Herrera (First Carlist War).

Fought August 23, 1837, between the Carlists, under Don Carlos, with General Moreno in actual command, and the Cristinos, under General Buerens. Don Carlos, who was marching upon Madrid, attacked Buerens before he could effect a junction with Espartero, and severely defeated him, the Cristinos losing 50 officers, and 2,600 men killed, wounded and missing. Don Carlos, after this victory, advanced to within twelve miles of Madrid, when the appearance of Espartero, at the head of 20,000 troops, obliged him to retire.

Herrings, The (Hundred Years' War).

Fought at Roncray-St.-Denis, February 12, 1429. Sir John Fastolfe was in charge of a convoy of salt fish for the English army before Orleans, and hearing of the approach of a French force, under the Bastard of Orleans, intrenched himself at Roncray. Here the French attacked him, and were repulsed with heavy loss. the Bastard being severely wounded.

Hexham (Wars of the Roses).

Fought May 15, 1464, when the Yorkists, under Montague, surprised the Lancastrians, under Somerset, in their camp at Linnels, near Hexham. The Lancastrians were practically in a trap, and had no option but to surrender. Somerset and many other important leaders were taken, and promptly executed. This success secured Edward IV on the throne.

Himera (First Carthaginian Invasion of Sicily).

Fought 480 B.C., between the Syracusans and Agrigentines, 557,000 strong, under Gelon, Tyrant of Syracuse, and the Carthaginians, said to number 300,000, under Hamilcar. The Carthaginians were totally routed, and Hamilcar slain.

Himera (Second Carthaginian Invasion of Sicily).

This place was besieged by the Carthaginians, under Hannibal, B.C. 409. A first assault was repulsed, and Diocles arriving in the harbour with 25 ships, rescued half the inhabitants. Three days later he returned for the remainder, but too late, for before he could reach the harbour the breach was stormed. The town was sacked, and 3,000 prisoners were sacrificed to appease the shade of Hamilcar, who had fallen in the battle of 480.

Hippo (Invasion of the Vandals).

Siege was laid to this city in May, 430, by the Vandals, under Genseric. It was defended by Boniface, Count of Africa, who having command of the sea, was able to keep the city well provisioned, and after fourteen months Genseric retired. Among those who died during the siege was St. Augustine.

Hochkirchen (Seven Years' War).

Fought October 14, 1758, between the Prussians, under Frederick the Great, and the Austrians, under Count Daun. Frederick, who was encamped on the heights of Hochkirchen, was surprised in the early morning by the Austrians, who broke into his camp and seized his artillery. He succeeded, however, in forming up his troops, and descending into the plain, made good his retreat to Bautzen. The Prussians lost 9,000 men, including the Prince of Brunswick and Marshal Keith, all their tents and baggage, and 101 guns. The Austrians lost 8,000 killed and wounded.

Hochstett (Wars of the French Revolution).

Fought June 19, 1800, between 70,000 French, under Moreau, and about 80,000 Austrians, under de Kray. Moreau crossed the Danube with the object of cutting off the Austrians from their base, and forcing them to evacuate Ulm. In a battle which lasted 18 hours, he succeeded in establishing himself upon the left bank, and making Ulm untenable. The French took 5,000 prisoners and 20 guns, but the losses on both sides in killed and wounded were small for the numbers engaged.

Hoechst (Thirty Years' War).

Fought June 10, 1622, between 20,000 Palatinate troops, under Christian of Brunswick, and 33,000 Imperialists, under Tilly. Christian having failed to join forces with Mansfeldt, was in retreat, and was engaged in holding a bridge over the Main. While thus employed he was overtaken by Tilly, and though a village covering the bridge was held gallantly for five hours, he was at last overpowered, losing about 12,000 in killed, wounded and prisoners. The Imperialist loss was comparatively small.

Hogland (Russo-Swedish Wars).

Fought 1789, between the Russian fleet, under Admiral Greig, and the Swedes, under the Duke of Sudermanland. Each side lost a ship, but strategically the affair was a Russian victory, for the Swedes were compelled to seek the protection of the forts of Sveaborg.

Hohenfriedberg (War of the Austrian Succession).

Fought June 3, 1745, between the Austrians and Saxons, under Charles of Lorraine, and the Prussians, under Frederick the Great. The Saxons, who were encamped at Strigau, were attacked in the early morning, and defeated before the Austrians could come to their aid. Frederick then turned upon the Austrians, and routed them, after desperate fighting. The Austrians and Saxons lost 4,000 killed and wounded, 7,000 prisoners, including 4 generals, and 66 guns. The Prussians lost 2,000.

Hohenlinden (Wars of the French Revolution).

Fought December 3, 1800, between the French, 60,000 strong, under Moreau, and 70,000 Austrians, under the Archduke John. Moreau occupied the small clearing of Hohenlinden, and the surrounding forest, while the Austrian army marched by five distinct routes to rendezvous at Hohenlinden. The Archduke's attack on the village was repulsed, and meanwhile Moreau had fallen upon his advancing columns at various points, and after severe fighting defeated them. The Austrians lost 7,000 killed and wounded, 12,000 prisoners and 87 guns.

Hollabrunn (Campaign of the Danube).

A rearguard action to protect the retreat of the main Russian army, under Kutusoff, November 16, 1805, between 7,000 Russians, under Prince Bagration, and the French, under Lannes. Bagration did not retire until he had lost half his force.

Homildon Hill (Scottish Wars).

Fought September, 1402, when the Percies lay in wait for a Scottish force, under Murdach Stewart, and Archibald, Earl of Douglas, who were returning from a foray into England. The Scots were totally routed, losing Stewart, 4 Scottish peers, and 80 gentlemen of rank.

Honain.

Fought 629, between 12,000 Moslems, under Mohammed, and a force of pagan Arabs, 4,000 strong. The Moslems were lured into the valley of Honain, and were assailed by slingers and archers from the surrounding heights. They were, however, rallied by the Prophet, and totally routed the Pagans, who submitted to the rule of Mohammed.

Hondschook (Wars of the French Revolution).

Fought September, 1793, between the Austrians, under Freytag, and the French, under Houchard. The Austrians occupied a strong position from which they were driven in disorder, and with heavy loss As a consequence of this victory, the siege of Dunkirk was raised.

Hooghly, The.

Fought November 24, 1759, between three British ships, under Commodore Wilson, and a Dutch squadron of seven sail. After two hours' fighting, the Dutch were completely defeated, and all their ships captured. Meanwhile a force of 700 Europeans and 800 Sepoys landed from the Dutch fleet, was defeated with heavy loss by 330 British troops and 800 Sepoys, under Colonel Forde.

Huesca (Mohammedan Empire in Spain).

Fought 1105, when the Moors, under Ali attacked the Spaniards, who, under Alfonso VI of Castile, were besieging Huesca. Ali was utterly routed, losing 10,000 killed in the battle.

Huesca (First Carlist War).

Fought May 23, 1837, between 20,000 Carlists, under Don Carlos and Don Sebastian, and 12,000 Cristinos and British under General Irribarreu. The British legion behaved unsteadily and the Cristinos were driven from the field, though the pursuit was checked by a brilliant cavalry charge, in which Irribarreu fell. The Cristinos lost over 1,000 killed and wounded, of which number the British legion lost 277.

Humaita (Paraguayan War).

Fought May, 1866, between the Paraguayans, under Lopez, and the Argentinians, under Mitre. Mitre attacked the Paraguayan entrenchments, but was repulsed with heavy loss.

Humaita (Paraguayan War).

Fought February, 1868, between the Paraguayan batteries, and a flotilla of Brazilian gunboats, endeavouring to force the passage. Their attempt was a complete failure, and the whole flotilla was sunk.

Humaita (Paraguayan War).

Fought September, 1868, between the Paraguayans, under Lopez, and the allied armies of Brazil, Argentina and Uruguay. The allies largely outnumbered Lopez's forces, and forced him to abandon his entrenchments at Humaita, and retire to Tebienari.

Humblebeck (Dano-Swedish Wars).

Fought 1700, when Charles XII, with a small force of Swedes, landed in face of the Danish army, which was strongly entrenched close the shore, and drove them headlong from their position with heavy loss.

Hydaspes, The (Alexander's Campaigns in Asia).

Fought B.C. 327, between 65,000 Macedonians and 70,000 Asiatics, under Alexander the Great, and the army of the Indian king Porus, numbering 30,000 infantry, with 200 elephants and 300 war chariots. Alexander crossed the river a few miles above Porus' entrenchments, and utterly routed him, with a loss of 12,000 killed and 9,000 prisoners, including Porus himself. The Macedonians lost 1,000 only.

Hyderabad (Conquest of Scinde).

Fought March 24, 1843, between 6,000 British troops, under Sir Charles Napier, and 20,000 Beluchis, under Shir Mohammed. The latter was strongly entrenched behind the Fullali, but the Beluchis, being thrown into disorder by a heavy artillery fire, were overthrown by a charge of cavalry on their exposed flank, and a frontal attack by the 22nd Regiment. This defeat put an end to the resistance of the Scinde Emirs.

I

Hysiæ.

Fought, approximately, 668 B.C., between the Spartans and the Argives. The former were totally defeated, and Argos was left in undisputed possession of the supremacy of the Peloponnesus.

I.

Ichinotani (Taira War).

Fought 1189, between the troops of the Shogun Minamoto-no-Yoritomo, under his brothers Norigoris and Yoshitsune, and the forces of the Taira clan. The Taira were signally defeated.

Iclistavisus (Germanic Wars).

Fought 16, between 8 Roman legions, under Germanicus, and the Germans, under Arminius. The Germans attacked the Romans in the open plain, but failed against the superior discipline of the legionaries, and were routed with enormous loss. Arminius with difficulty cut his way out of the press and escaped.

Immac (Revolt of Elagabalus).

Fought June 7, 218, between the Syrian legions, under Elagabalus, and the Imperial troops and Pretorians, under the Emperor Macrinus. The Pretorians, by their superior valour and discipline, broke the legions opposed, and the victory would have been theirs, but at the crisis of the fight, Macrinus fled, and this so discouraged his troops, that in the end they were totally defeated.

Imola (Napoleon's Italian Campaigns).

Fought February 3, 1797, when 8,000 French and Italians, under Victor, defeated the Papal troops, 7,000 strong, under General Colli. Victor took the Papal army in the rear, and routed them with a loss of a few hundred only, as no stand was made.

Indus, The (Tartar Invasion of Kharismia).

Fought B.C. 1221, between 300,000 Tartars, under Genghis Khan, and the army of Jellalladin, Sultan of Kharismia, 30,000 strong. Jellalladin fought with his back to the river, and after an obstinate conflict, in which he inflicted heavy loss on his assailants, was driven across the Indus, having lost 19,000 men killed and drowned. The Tartars lost 20,000.

Ingavi.

Fought November 18, 1841, between the Bolivians, under Ballivian, 3,800 strong, and the Peruvians, 5,200 strong, under Gamarra. The Peruvians were utterly routed, and their army dispersed, Gamarra being among the killed.

Ingogo (First Boer War).

Fought February 8, 1881 when a small British column, consisting of 5 companies of infantry, 4 guns, and a small mounted force, attacked the Boer position, and were repulsed with a loss of 139 killed and wounded. The Boers admitted a loss of 14 only.

Inhlobane Mountain (Zulu War).

Fought March 28, 1879, when a British force of 1,300 men, under Colonels Buller and Russell, attacked a strong Zulu kraal, and after severe fighting, were repulsed with considerable loss.

Inkerman (Crimean War).

Fought November 5, 1854, when 50,000 Russians, under Prince Mentschikoff, attacked the British position at Inkerman, held by about 8,000 troops. There was a dense fog, and the battle was chiefly a series of detached hand-to-hand combats some of the most serious fighting being round the Sandbag Battery, where the Russians lost 1,200 killed. At 10 o'clock, the French arrived on the scene, and the Russians were soon in full retreat, having suffered very heavy loss.

Inverlochy (Civil War).

Fought February 2, 1645, when Montrose, with 1,500 Royalist Highlanders, defeated 3,000 Campbells and Lowland Covenanters, with a loss of 1,700 men. Argyle left the command of his forces to Campbell of Auchinbrech, taking refuge in a vessel on Loch Linnhe. This defeat broke the power of the Campbells in the Highlands for many years.

nverkeithing (Scottish Wars).

Fought 1317, between the English invaders, and the Scots, under the Earl of Fife. The first onslaught of the English drove the Scots from their positions, but they were rallied by William Sinclair, Bishop of Dunkeld, and forced the English to retire to their ships.

Inverary (Scottish Wars).

Fought 1510, between the Scots, under Robert Bruce, and the English, under Sir John Mowbray, with whom was a small force of Scottish sympathisers with the English claims, under the Earl of Buchan. The English were totally defeated and driven from the field with heavy loss.

Ipsus (Wars of Alexander's Successors).

Fought B.C. 302, between the Syrians, 32,000 strong, under Seleucus, and the Macedonians, 30,000 in number, under Antigonus. Seleucus utterly routed the Macedonians, Antigonus being among the slain. Demetrius Poliorcetes, who now took command, only succeeded in rallying 8,000 men, after fleeing for 200 miles.

Irun (First Carlist War).

This fortress was captured, May 18, 1837, by 10,000 Cristinos and British, under General Evans. Evans appeared before the place at noon, and summoned it to surrender. On the Carlists refusing, an assault was ordered ; by 11 p.m. the fortress was taken, with very small loss to the assailants.

Isandhlwana (Zulu War).

Fought January 22, 1879, when six companies of the 24th Regiment, with two guns and a small force of Natal volunteers, under Colonel Durnford, were overwhelmed and massacred by the Zulus, under Matyana. Of the regulars, 26 officers and 600 men were killed, in addition to 24 officers, and a large number of men in the Colonial force.

Isara, The (Third Gallic Invasion).

Fought August 8, 121 B.C., between the Arverni and Allobroges, under Betuitdus, and the

Romans, under Q. Fabius Maximus. The Gauls were totally defeated, and a bridge breaking down under the press of the fugitives, they suffered enormous loss.

Isaszcq (Hungarian Rising).

Fought April 6, 1849, between the Hungarians, 42,000 strong, under Görgey, and the Croats, under Jellachich. The Hungarian First Corps, under Klapka, was put to flight, but the rest stood their ground, and repulsed the Croat attack. Both armies bivouacked for the night on the ground they held, but early on the following morning Jellachich retired, the Hungarians thus being entitled to claim a victory.

Isle de France (Napoleonic Wars).

This island, now known as Mauritius, was captured from the French, December 3, 1810, by a fleet of 19 ships, under Admiral Bertie, convoying a number of transports, carrying 10,000 troops, under General Abercromby. The British lost 167 killed wounded and missing. Seven frigates and ten sloops were taken, as well as 21 French and 3 captured British merchantmen.

Isly (Abd-el-Kader's Rebellion).

Fought August 14, 1844, between 8,000 French, under Marshal Bugeaud, and 45,000 Algerines, chiefly cavalry, under Abd-el-Kader. The French infantry repulsed all the charges of the Algerine Horse, and aided by the artillery, inflicted heavy loss upon them; when sufficiently shaken, a charge of the French cavalry completed the rout, and the Algerines fled,

leaving 1,500 dead on the field. Abd-el-Kader was captured.

Ismail (Ottoman Wars).

This fortress was taken by assault by the Russians, under Suwaroff, December 22, 1790. The Russians lost enormous numbers in the storm, and in revenge they massacred the garrison and inhabitants without mercy.

Issus. (Alexander's Asiatic Campaigns).

Fought B.C. 333, between 35,000 Macedonians, under Alexander the Great, and a vast horde of Asiatics, with 30,000 Greek mercenaries, under Darius, King of Persia. The Persians were drawn up on the right bank of the Pinarus, which crosses the plain of Issus. Alexander, led his heavy cavalry to the attack on the left, crossing the river, and routing the Persian cavalry. The phalanx in the centre was opposed to the Greek mercenaries, and after heavy fighting, the Macedonians made good their footing on the right bank. Alexander meanwhile led his squadrons against the bodyguard of Darius, who fled from the field, followed by the whole of the Asiatics, and the victory was complete.

Issus (Ottoman Wars).

Fought 1488, between the Turks, under Bajazet II, and the Egyptians, under the Sultan of Egypt. The Turks were defeated.

Itabitsu.

Fought October, 740, between, the Japanese rebels, under Hirotsuke, 13,000 strong, and the troops of the Emperor Shommu under Ono-no-Atsuma. The Imperial troops, who were only 8,000 in number, attacked the rebels as they were crossing the river, and routed them with heavy loss. Hirotsuke was killed.

Ivry (Eighth Civil War).

Fought March 14, 1590, between the Huguenots, under Henri IV, and the Catholics, under the Duc de Mayenne. Henri gained a complete victory, and marched forward to invest Paris.

J.

Jalula (Moslem Invasion of Persia).

Fought 637, between the Moslems, under Said, and the Persians, under Yezdegerd. Yezdegerd fled from the field, and his troops discouraged, were totally routed with heavy loss.

Jamaica.

This island was captured from the Spaniards, May, 1655 by a combined English naval and military force, under Admiral Penn and General Venables.

Jarnac (Third Civil War).

Fought March 13, 1569, between the Catholics, under the Marshal de Tavannes, and the Huguenots, under the Prince de Condé. The brunt of the action was borne by the Huguenot cavalry, who were overpowered by the Catholics, and Condé slain.

Jassy (Ottoman Wars).

Fought September 20, 1620, between the Poles under Grati-

ani, and the Turks, under Osman II. The Poles were completely defeated.

Jellalabad (First Afghan War).

This fortress was besieged by the Afghans, under Mohammed Akbar Khan, March 11, 1842, after the destruction of General Elphinstone's force in the Khoord Cabul pass. It was defended by a small British garrison, under General Sale. Akbar led his whole army to the assault, but was gallantly repulsed, and then sat down to besiege the place in form. An attempt to relieve it by Brigadier Wyld, in January, 1843, failed, Wyld being defeated in the Khyber Pass by the Khyberis. The garrison meanwhile made several successful sorties, and on April 7, drove Akbar Khan out of his entrenchments, with a loss of all his guns, and many men, forcing him to raise the siege. All chance of a renewal of the investment was ended by the arrival on the 18th, of a strong relieving force, under General Pollock.

Jemappes (Wars of the French Revolution).

Fought November 6, 1792, between the Austrians, under the Archduke Albert, and the French, under Dumouriez. The Austrians occupied a very strong position on the heights above Jemappes, from which they were driven with heavy loss, the French gaining a signal victory.

Jena (Campaign of Jena).

This name is generally given to the two battles fought October 14, 1806, by the two wings of the French army under Napoleon, at Auerstadt and Jena. At Auerstadt the Prussian left, 70,000 strong, under the Duke of Brunswick, was encountered by the French right, under Davoust, with slightly inferior numbers, and after very severe fighting, were defeated, the Duke of Brunswick being killed. Napoleon, on the left, with 100,000 men, attacked the Prince of Hohenlohe with 70,000 Prussians, and after a sternly fought engagement, drove him from the field, The two defeated armies, retiring by converging routes upon Weimar, the retreat became a rout, and Napoleon's pursuing cavalry caused them further heavy losses. The Prussians in the two actions lost 22,000 killed and wounded, 18,000 prisoners and 300 guns. Twenty generals were killed, wounded or captured. The French lost 11,000 killed and wounded, 7,000 of whom fell at Auerstadt.

Jersey.
Fought 1550, when an English squadron, under Sir William Winter, attacked a French fleet, which was besieging St. Heliers. The French were completely routed, losing 1,000 killed and wounded, and the siege was raised.

Jerusalem (Jewish War).
This city was besieged by Titus, with 60,000 Romans, in March, 70 A.D. It was defended with the utmost heroism by the Jews, who were led by the Zealot faction. At the end of six weeks Titus gained possession of the suburb of Bezetha, and then by hard fighting, captured position after position, until on Sep-

tember 8, the resistance of the defenders was finally overcome. Josephus says that 1,100,000 persons perished in the siege, but this is doubtless an exaggeration. The Romans after the capture sold 97,000 into slavery.

Jerusalem (Moslem Invasion of Syria).
Early in 637 Jerusalem was besieged by the Moslems, at first, under Abu Obeidah, and later by the Khalif Omar. After a defence of four months, during which scarcely a day passed without a sortie or an assault, the city was surrendered by the Patriarch Sophronius.

Jerusalem (First Crusade).
The Crusaders, under Godefroi de Bouillon, laid siege to the city, June 7, 1099, and on July 15, it was taken by assault, and for three days was the scene of a promiscuous massacre, in which 70,000 Moslems perished.

Jerusalem.
On October 2, 1187, the Holy City was besieged by the Saracens, under Saladin, and after a siege lasting fourteen days, in the course of which several determined sorties were repulsed, the Moslems forced an entrance, and Guy de Lusignan, the last King of Jerusalem, surrendered. The Christians were given forty days to evacuate the city.

Jhansi (Indian Mutiny).
This place, which fell into the hands of the mutineers in June, 1857, was recaptured by Sir Hugh Rose, who invested it in March, 1858, and carried the city by assault, April 2.

Jidballi (Somali Expedition).

Fought January 10, 1904, between the Somalis, 5,000 strong, and a small British and native force, under Sir Charles Egerton. The Somalis' camp was attacked, and after a brisk action they were driven out and pursued by the cavalry for twelve miles, losing 1,000 killed in the fight and pursuit. The British losses were very small.

Jiron.

Fought February 28, 1829, between the Peruvians, under Lamar, and the Colombians, under Sucre. The battle was indecisive, both sides claiming the victory, and it was followed by the signature of peace, September 23.

Jitgurh (Gurkha War).

Fought January 14, 1815, between 4,500 British troops, under General Wood, and 1,200 Gurkhas, occupying a strong stockade. The British were led unexpectedly into the zone of fire by a treacherous guide, and though Wood fought his way to a position from which he could have carried the stockade, he retired, having suffered considerable loss, just when the Gurkhas were about to abandon their works.

Jotapata (Jewish War).

This place was besieged by Vespasian, with 60,000 Romans, December, 67, and was defended by the Jewish army under Josephus. The fortress held out for 47 days, when it was stormed and sacked. Josephus gave himself up to Vespasian.

Jugdulluck (First Afghan War).

At this place the remnant of General Elphinstone's army made their last stand, January 12, 1842, against the Afghans and Ghilzais. Of the few who escaped the massacre at this point, only one, Dr. Brydon, succeeded in reaching Jellalabad.

Julian's Defeat by the Persians (Persian Wars).

Fought June 28, 363, between the Romans, under Julian, and the Persians, under Sapor II. Julian had advanced against Ctesiphon, the Persian capital, but finding himself too weak to attack it, was retreating along the left bank of the Tigris. In the course of the retreat he was attacked by the Persians, and worsted in an action unimportant in itself, but resulting in the death of Julian, who was mortally wounded in the skirmish. The election of Jovian as Emperor was followed by a peace which restored to Sapor almost all the Roman conquests in Persia.

Junin (South American War of Independence).

Fought 1824, between the Spanish Royalists, under General Cauterac, and the Colombian Patriots, under Sucre. The Spaniards were completely defeated.

K.

Kaiping (Chino-Japanese War).

Fought January 10, 1895, when a Chinese force in a strongly entrenched position was attacked and driven out by a Japanese brigade under General Nogi. The fighting lasted three hours, the Chinese showing more steadiness than usual, and inflicting on the assailants a loss of 300 killed and wounded.

Kagoshima (Satsuma Rebellion).

On August 18, 1876, the rebels, who were closely besieged in their lines at Enotake, succeeded in passing through the Imperial troops, and making a forced march, under Saigo Takamori, seized the city of Kagoshima. They were quickly followed by the Imperial army, under Prince Taruhito, and an engagement followed which lasted for ten days, at the end of which time the insurgents were driven out and retired to Shirogama, both sides having suffered heavy loss.

Kagul (Ottoman Wars).

Fought August 3, 1770, between 17,000 Russians, under Roumiantsoff, and 150,000 Turks, under Halil Pasha. The Russian rear was threatened by a force of 80,000 Tartars, under the Khan of Crim Tartary, but Roumiantsoff boldly attacked the Turkish lines, and after severe fighting drove the Turks out of their entrenchments in headlong flight, capturing all their artillery and baggage.

Kalisch (Russo-Swedish War).

Fought 1706, between 10,000 Swedes, under General Meyerfeld, and 30,000 Russians and Poles, under Prince Mentschikoff. The Swedes were defeated with considerable loss.

Kalunga (Gurkha War).

This place was attacked by the British under General Gillespie, in October, 1814, and was defended by the Gurkhas

under Bulbuddur Singh. An unsuccessful assault cost the besiegers 260 officers and men, and after waiting a month for the arrival of heavy guns, a breach was made, and a general assault ordered. This also failed, 680 men being killed and wounded. The fortress was then shelled for three days, at the end of which time the survivors of the garrison, 70 only out of 600, made their escape, and the place was captured.

Kalpi (Indian Mutiny).

This town, which had fallen into the hands of the mutineers, was besieged by Sir Hugh Rose, May 19, 1858. The garrison made two ineffectual sorties, in which they were repulsed with heavy loss, and on the 23rd the town was entered without further resistance, the mutineers having fled.

Kamarut (First Burmah War).

Fought July 8, 1824, when a small British force, under Sir Archibald Campbell, stormed a series of stockades held by 10,000 Burmans, under Tuamba Wangyee. The Burmans left 800 dead on the field, including their leader.

Kambula (Zulu War).

Fought March 29, 1879, when Colonel Wood, with 2,000 British and native auxiliaries, was attacked in his lager by three Zulu impi. The Zulus were repulsed with very heavy loss, and pursued for seven miles. The British lost 81 killed and wounded. The defeat practically broke Cetewayo's power.

Kandahar (Tartar Invasion of Afghanistan).

This city was besieged by the Tartars, under Tuli Khan, in 1221. The Tartars possessed themselves of the city, and were investing the citadel, when Jellalladin, Sultan of Kharismia, fell upon them with a large force and cut them to pieces.

Kandahar.

Siege was laid to Kandahar in March, 1545, by the Moguls, under Humayun. The place, which was defended by an Afghan garrison under Mirza Askari, held out for five months, when, weakened by famine and desertion, the garrison was forced to surrender.

Kandahar (Perso-Afghan Wars).

In the autumn of 1648 the Persians, under Abbas II, laid siege to the city, which was defended by a Mogul garrison. An attempt to relieve it was made by Aurungzebe, but he arrived to find it already in the hands of the Persians. He in turn laid siege to it, but was unsuccessful, and after four months was compelled to retire. Subsequent attempts to recapture the city were made by Said Ullah, the Vizier, and Dara Sheko, the eldest son of Shah Jehan, but without success.

Kandahar.

Fought July 29, 1834, when Shah Sujah, the expelled Amir of Afghanistan, attempted to take the city. His successor, Dost Mahomed, and Kohandil Khan sallied forth at the head of their troops, and totally defeated Shah Sujah, dispersing his followers.

Kandahar (Second Afghan War).

Fought September 1, 1880, between the British, under Lord Roberts, and the Afghans, under Ayub Khan, immediately after the completion of the famous march from Kabul. Ayub was completely defeated, with a loss of 2,000 men, and his army dispersed. The British losses were only 248 killed and wounded

Kapolna (Hungarian Rising).

Fought February 26 and 27, 1849, between four Hungarian divisions, under Dembinski, and the Austrians, under Windischgrätz, of whom only Schlick's corps, 15,000 strong, was seriously engaged. The Hungarians held their own on the 26th, but on the evening of the 27th Schlick captured the key of the position at Kapolna, whereupon the Hungarians retired, though unpursued.

Kappel (Second War of Kappel).

Fought October 10, 1531, between the army of the Swiss Catholic Cantons, 8,000 strong, and 1,300 Zurichers, under George Göldli, reinforced later in the day by a similar number under Rudolf Lavater. Göldli attacked in defiance of orders, and was totally defeated, among those who fell being Zwingli.

Kara Burur (Ottoman Wars).

Fought August 11, 1791, when the Russian fleet, under Admiral Ouschakoff, totally defeated the Turks after a sanguinary engagement.

Karamuran.

Fought during the winter of 1225, between 300,000 Tartars under Genghiz Khan, and

500,000 Turks, Chinese and others under Shidasker of Tangat. Shidasker was totally routed, with a loss, it is said, of 300,000 men.

Karaku (Tartar Invasion of Kharismia).

Fought 1218, between the Tartars, 700,000 strong, under Genghiz Khan, and 400,000 Kharismians under the Sultan Mehemed. At nightfall the battle was undecided, and the armies withdrew to their camps, but Mehemet, who had lost 140,000, refused to renew the conflict on the following day, and Genghiz Khan, having suffered too severely to attack his entrenchments, withdrew.

Karee (Second Boer War).

Fought March 29, 1900, when a Boer force holding a line of hills about eighteen miles north of Bloemfontein were driven from their entrenchments by a British division under General Tucker. The British lost 10 officers and 172 men killed and wounded.

Kargaula (Cossack Rising).

Fought 1774, between the insurgent Cossacks of the Don, under Ikkelman Pugatcheff, and the Russians, under Prince Gallitzin. The insurgents were routed with great slaughter, and Pugatcheff fled to the mountains.

Kars (Crimean War).

This fortress, held by a Turkish garrison under General Williams, was besieged by the Russians in the course of the Crimean war. The place was most gallantly defended but was finally forced by famine to capitulate, November, 1855.

Kars (Russo-Turkish War).

This fortress, garrisoned by 24,000 Turks under Hussein Pasha, was stormed by the Russians under Loris Melikoff on the night of November 17, 1877. The attacking force was led by Lazareff, and after severe fighting captured all the eastern forts. Hussein then endeavoured to cut his way through to the west, but the bulk of his force was driven back, and only he and a few of his officers succeeded in the attempt. The Russians lost 2,273, killed and wounded; the Turks 2,500 killed, 4,500 wounded, 17,000 prisoners, and 303 guns.

Kashgal (Soudan Campaigns).

On November 3, 1883, an Egyptian force, 11,000 strong, under Hicks Pasha, with several British officers, was led by a treacherous guide into a defile, where they were attacked by the Mahdists, and after fighting for three days, were massacred almost to a man.

Kassassin (Arabi's Rebellion).

Fought August 28, 1882, between the British, under General Graham, and the Egyptians, under Arabi Pasha. Arabi attacked the British position, Graham remaining on the defensive throughout the day, but towards evening he launched his heavy cavalry, under Sir Baker Russell, against the enemy, who broke and fled. The British losses were only 11 killed and 68 wounded.

Katzbach (Campaign of Leipsic).

Fought August 22, 1813, between 130,000 French, under Napoleon, and 100,000 Prussians, under Blucher. Blucher, who had on the previous day retired behind the Haynau, was pressed hard by Napoleon, and driven across the Katzbach, with considerable loss.

Katzbach (Campaign of Leipsic).

Fought August 26, 1813, between the French, under Macdonald, and the Prussians, under Blucher. Macdonald crossed the Katzbach, and while waiting for his left wing and cavalry under Souham, was attacked by Blucher, and driven back. As Macdonald was retiring Souham appeared on the field, but before he could deploy he was attacked and routed with great slaughter, while the centre under Lauriston also suffered severely in recrossing the river. The French lost 15,000 killed and wounded, and over 100 guns.

Kazan (Cossack Rising).

Fought 1774, between the rebel Cossacks, under Pugatcheff, and the Russians, under General Michelson. The Cossacks were utterly routed.

Kemendine (First Burmah War).

Fought June 10, 1824, when 3,000 British troops, under Sir Archibald Campbell, stormed a series of stockades, occupied by a large force of Burmans, and drove out the defenders with heavy loss.

Keresztes (Ottoman Wars).

Fought October 24 to 26, 1596, between the Turks, under Mohammed III, and the Imperialists and Transylvanians, under the Archduke Maximilian and Prince Sigismund of Transylvania. The battle at first went badly for the Turks, and Mohammed would have fled but for the remonstrances of the Grand Vizier. In the end, however, they gained the upper hand, and the Archduke was totally defeated.

Kharisme (Tartar Invasion of Kharismia).

This city, the capital of Kharismia, was besieged by the Tartars under the three sons of Genghiz Khan, in the summer of 1220. It was most obstinately defended for a period of seven months by the inhabitants, under Himartekin, but in February the Tartars mastered the place, massacring 100,000 persons.

Khartoum (Soudan Campaign).

This city, defended by an Egyptian garrison under General Gordon, was invested by the Mahdi in the early part of 1884, and, after a gallant defence, was stormed January 26, 1885. The forerunners of the relieving force, consisting of the river gunboats under Lord Charles Beresford, arrived off the city on the 28th, two days too late, and after a brief engagement with the Mahdist batteries, returned down the river.

Khelat (First Afghan War).

This place, which was defended by a garrison of Beluchis, under Mehrab Khan, was captured by a British force, 1,000 strong, under General Willshire, November 13, 1839. The defenders lost 400 killed, including their leader and 2,000 prisoners. The British lost 37 killed and 107 wounded.

Khojah Pass (First Afghan War).

Fought March 28, 1842, when General England, in an endeavour to relieve General Nott in Kandahar, marched into the pass with 500 men only, without waiting for the rest of his brigade, and was defeated by the Afghans with a loss of 100 killed and wounded, and compelled to retire to Quettah.

Khoord Kabul Pass (First Afghan War).

While passing through this defile, the British force, under General Elphinstone, retreating on Jellalabad, was attacked by the Afghans, January 8, 1842, and lost 3,000, including followers.

Killiecrankie (Jacobite Rising).

Fought July 27, 1689, between 4,500 Royal troops, under General Mackay, and 2,500 Highland Jacobites, under Dundee. Dundee allowed Mackay to enter the plain below the pass of Killiecrankie, and then descending from the heights, fell upon and utterly routed the Royalists, with a loss of over 2,000 killed and 500 prisoners. The Jacobites lost about 900, but amongst them was Dundee. Mackay on reaching Stirling had only 400 men with the colours.

Kilsyth (Civil War).

Fought August 15, 1645, between the Royalists, under Montrose, and the Covenanters, under Baillie. The Royalists won a signal victory, Baillie's infantry, 6,000 in number, being cut down almost to a man.

Kimberley (Second Boer War).

This town, defended by a garrison of 4,000 (including armed townsmen) under Colonel Kekewich, was besieged October 15, 1899, by the Boers, under Commandant Wessels, and later under General Cronje. It withstood a severe and continuous bombardment till February 15, 1900, when it was relieved by a force of cavalry, 5,000 strong, under General French. The losses of the garrison during the siege amounted to 18 officers and 163 men.

Kin-chau. *See* Naushan.

Kineyri (Second Sikh War).

Fought June 18, 1848, between 8,000 Bhawalpuris, under Futteh Mohammed Khan, aided by 3,000 Sikh irregulars, under Lieutenant Edwardes, and the Sikhs, 8,000 strong, under Rung Ram. The Bhawalpuris were repulsed in an attack on the Sikh positions, but the arrival of Lieutenant Edwardes' guns turned the scale, and at a second attempt the entrenchments were stormed and captured, with a loss to the victors of 300 men. The Sikhs lost 500 killed in the action, and many more during their flight to Multan.

Kinloss (Danish Invasion of Scotland).

Fought 1009, between the Danes under Sweyn of Denmark, and the Scots, under Malcolm II. The Danes were besieging Nairne, and Malcolm attempting to raise the siege, they attacked and defeated him after hard fighting, in which Malcolm was wounded.

Kinnesaw Mountain (American Civil War).

Fought June 27, 1864, between 90,000 Federals, under General Sherman, and 50,000 Confederates, under General Johnston. Sherman attacked Johnston in a strong position and was repulsed with a loss of about 3,000, the Confederates losing 500 only.

Kinsale (O'Neil's Rebellion).

This town, which had been seized in September, 1601, by 5,000 Spaniards, under Juan d'Aguila, sent to support the rebels, was besieged by the Royal troops, under Lord Mountjoy and the Earl of Thomond. On December 23 an attempt by Sir Hugh O'Neil to relieve the place was defeated, whereupon d'Aguila surrendered and was permitted to ship for Spain.

Kiöge (Dano-Swedish Wars).

Fought July, 1677, between the Danish fleet, under Admiral Juel, and the Swedes, under Admiral Horn. The Swedes suffered a disastrous defeat, losing eleven ships of the line sunk or captured.

Kirbekan (Soudan Campaigns).

Fought February 10, 1885, when the British, about 1,000 strong, under General Earle, stormed the heights of Kirbekan, which were held by a strong Mahdist force, and totally routed them, with heavy loss. The British lost 60, among whom was General Earle, killed.

Kirch-Denkern (Seven Years' War).

Fought July 16, 1761, between the Prussians, under Prince Ferdinand, and the French, under Soubise and the Duc de Broglie. The French attacked the strong Prussian position in and around Kirch-Denkern, and after severe fighting were repulsed with a loss of 4,000 killed and wounded.

Kirkee (Third Mahratta War).

Fought November 5, 1817, between the Mahrattas under Bajee Rao, and a British force of one European and three native regiments, under Colonel Burr. On moving out of his entrenchments, the flanks of Burr's force were attacked by the Mahratta horse, but their charge was repulsed, and the British advancing drove off the enemy with a loss of over 500. The British loss was 75 killed and wounded.

Kiso (Taira War).

Fought September, 1180, between the adherents of the Minamoto clan, under Yoshinaka, and the troops of Taira-no-Kiyomori. The Taira men attacked the position of Yoshinaka at Kiso, but were defeated and driven from the field with heavy loss.

Kissingen (Seven Weeks' War).

Fought July 10, 1866, between the Prussians, under General Falkenstein, and the Bavarians, under General Zoller. The Bavarians were defeated and driven out of Kissingen with heavy loss.

Kiu-lien-cheng (Russo-Japanese War).

Fought May 1, 1904, between 40,000 Japanese, under Marshal Kuroki, and the Russians, about 30,000 strong, under General

Sassulitch. After four days of skirmishing, the Japanese crossed the Yalu, April 30, and on the following day attacked the Russian position at Kiu-lien-Cheng, driving out the defenders with a loss of 4,000 killed and wounded, 30 officers and 500 men prisoners, and 48 guns. The Japanese lost 898 killed and wounded.

Kizil-Tepe (Russo-Turkish War).

Fought June 25, 1877, between the Russians, under General Loris Melikoff, and the Turks, in superior numbers, under Mahktar Pasha. The Russians were defeated, and forced to raise the siege of Kars.

Klausenburg (Ottoman Wars).

Fought May, 1660, between the Turks, under the Grand Vizier, Mahomet Köprili, and the Transylvanians, under the Voivode, George Ragotski II. The Turks gained a complete victory, Ragotski being mortally wounded.

Klonchino.

Fought July 4, 1610, between the Russians, under Choniski, aided by a contingent of 5,000 Swedes, under James de la Gardie, and the Poles, under Sigismund III. The Russians were totally defeated, and, as a result, the usurper, Basil Choniski, was deposed.

Koeniggratz (Seven Weeks' War).

Fought July 3, 1866, between 200,000 Austrians, with 600 guns, under Marshal Benedek, and the Prussian armies of Prince Frederick Charles and the Crown Prince, together about equal to the Austrians in number. The Austrians, who occupied a very strong position, were attacked in the early morning by Prince Frederick Charles, who, however, made little impression upon them, and it was not till the arrival of the Crown Prince on their right flank at 2 p.m. that any advantage was obtained. Then, however, the Prussians succeeded in piercing the Austrian lines, and seized the key of the position, after which further resistance being hopeless, the Austrians retired, with a loss of 20,000 killed and wounded, 20,000 prisoners, and 174 guns. The Prussians lost 10,000.

Koenigswartha (Campaign of Leipzig).

Fought May 19, 1813, when General Peyri's Italian division, about 8,000 strong, was attacked and defeated by 15,000 Russians, under Barclay de Tolly, with a loss of 2,000 killed and wounded. The opportune arrival of the cavalry of Ney's corps saved the division from destruction.

Kojende (Tartar Invasion of Kharismia).

This fortress was besieged in 1219, by the Tartars, under Tuchi Khan, and defended by a Kharismian garrison, under Timar Malek. After an obstinate resistance, Timar, finding he could hold out no longer, embarked with his officers and his best troops, and sailed down the Jaxartes, pursued by the Tartars, whom, however, after heavy fighting, he succeeded in escaping. The city surrendered the day after Timar's departure.

Kokein (First Burmah War).

Fought December 12, 1824, when 1,800 British troops, under Sir Archibald Campbell, stormed and captured two large stockades, garrisoned by about 20,000 Burmans, under Maka Bandula.

Kolin (Seven Years' War).

Fought June 18, 1757, between 34,000 Prussians, under Frederick the Great, and 54,000 Austrians, under Marshal Daun. Daun occupied the heights between Kolin and Chotzewitz, where he was attacked by Frederick, who had nearly succeeded in turning his right flank when the Prussian right broke and fled. The Prussian cavalry charged gallantly six times, but could make no impression on the Austrian defence, and Frederick was beaten back with a loss of 14,000 men and 43 guns. The Austrians lost 9,000.

Komatsu (Nine Years' War).

Fought September 5, 1062, between the Japanese rebels, under Sadatoki, and the Imperial troops, under Yoriyoshi. Sadatoki, who was besieged in his camp, made a vigorous sortie at the head of 8,000 men, but after a severe conflict was repulsed. The fighting was renewed on subsequent days, and on the 16th Sadatoki was slain, and the rebellion came to an end.

Komorn (Hungarian Rising).

An action fought by Görgey, April 26, 1849, for the relief of Komorn, which was besieged by the Austrians. In the early morning two Hungarian corps, under Klapka and Damjanics, surprised the Austrian entrenched camp, taking 6 guns and 200 prisoners. The Austrians retired, though not energetically pursued, and the fortress was relieved.

Koniah (Mehemet Ali's First Rebellion).

Fought 1831, between the Turks, under Reschid Pasha, and the Egyptians and Syrians, under Ibrahim Pasha. After a severe engagement, the Turks were totally defeated, and fled in disorder. Reschid was severely wounded, and captured.

Kornspruit. *See* Sanna's Post.

Korygaom (Third Mahratta War).

Fought January 1, 1818, when a small British force of under 1,000 men, chiefly native troops, under Captain Staunton, was attacked by 25,000 Mahrattas, under the Peshwa, Baji Rao. The British held their ground gallantly all day, and the approach during the night of large reinforcements under General Smith determined the Peshwa to retreat, with a loss of 600. The British lost 275, including 5 out of 8 British officers.

Kossova (Ottoman Wars).

Fought June 15, 1389, between the Turks, under Murad I, and the combined army of the Servians, Bosnians, and Albanians, under Lazar, Despot of Servia. The Turks gained a signal victory, though Murad was mortally wounded in the battle. This success secured the Turkish domination over Servia and the neighbouring states.

Kossova (Ottoman Wars).

Fought October 17, 1747, and two following days, between the Hungarians and Wallachians, 80,000 strong, under John Hunniades, and a vastly superior Turkish army, under Murad II. The Hungarians left their entrenchments to attack the Turks, and throughout the day the battle was evenly contested. On the 18th, however, the Wallachians deserted to the Turks, and the Hungarians, assailed in front and rear, were hard pressed, while on the 19th they were unable to maintain their position, and were forced to retire, defeated, with a loss of 17,000 killed and wounded. The Turks are said to have lost 40,000 men in the three days.

Kotah (Indian Mutiny).

This place, which had been seized by the rebellious troops of the Rajah of Kotah, 5,000 in number, was besieged by General Roberts, March 22, 1858. The Rajah, who held the citadel, joined forces with the British, and after a short bombardment the town was stormed, March 30.

Kotzim (Ottoman Wars).

Fought September 22, 1622, between the Poles, 60,000 strong, under Chodkiewicz, and the Turks, 300,000 in number, under Osman II. Chodkiewicz, old and worn out by fatigue, was forced to retire to his tent in the middle of the battle, and on his death-bed handed over the command to Labomirski, by whom the Turks were totally routed, with a loss of 30,000 men.

Kotzim (Ottoman Wars).

Fought November 11, 1673, between 40,000 Poles and Lithuanians, under John Sobieski, and 80,000 Turks, under Hussein Pasha. The Turks occupied a strongly entrenched position, which was stormed by the Poles, and the Turks driven into the river, losing over 40,000 killed. In consequence of this signal victory, Kotzim capitulated, and Caplan Pasha, who was approaching with a large army, recrossed the frontier.

Krakovicz (Ottoman Wars).

On January 17, 1475, 40,000 Moldavian peasants, aided by 7,000 Hungarian and Polish regulars, under Stephen of Moldavia, fell upon Suleiman Pasha, with 100,000 Turks, in an untenable position near Lake Krakovicz, and totally defeated them, driving them into the lake. Very few of the Turks escaped death, either by the sword or by drowning.

Krasnaoi (Moscow Campaign).

Fought November 17, 1812, when the Russians, 50,000 strong, under Kutusoff, after a series of combats on the two preceding days, during which they had inflicted heavy losses on the retreating French army, were defeated by the corps of Davoust and the Young Guard. The French losses amounted to 5,000 killed and wounded, and about 8,000 missing.

Kringellen (Dano-Swedish Wars).

Fought August 29, 1612, when a force of Scots in the Danish service, under Colonel George Sinclair, were ambushed in the mountains by the Norwegians, and massacred, notwithstanding a strenuous resistance. Only two of the Scots succeeded in escaping.

Kronia (Ottoman Wars).

Fought 1738, between the Imperialists under Counts Wallis and Neipperg, and the Turks. The latter were defeated, but at very heavy cost, and the Imperial army was so weakened that it was unable to prevent the Turks capturing Semendaia, Orsova, and other important fortresses.

Krotzka (Ottoman Wars).

Fought July 23, 1739, between 56,000 Austrians, under Count Wallis, and over 100,000 Turks, under El Hadj Mohammed Pasha. The Austrian vanguard was attacked by the Turks when approaching Kotzin and driven back, but the main body withstood the Turkish onslaught from 5 a.m. to sunset, when Wallis retired, with a loss of 5,700 killed and 4,500 wounded, including 9 generals. The Turkish loss is unknown, but was very heavy.

Kulevtcha (Ottoman Wars).

Fought 1829, between the Russians, under General Diebitsch, and 40,000 Turks, under Reschid Pasha. The Russians were lying in wait for Reschid in the Kalevtcha defile, and after a severe struggle, totally routed the Turks, with a loss of 5,000 killed and wounded, and all their guns. The Pasha himself escaped with difficulty.

Kulm (Campaign of Leipsic).

Fought August 29 and 30, 1813, between the French, under Vandamme, and the Austrians, and Russians, with a small force of Prussians, under the Prince of Schwartzenberg, who were retreating after their defeat at Dresden. To check the pursuit they occupied Kulm, from which they were driven by Vandamme on the 29th. On the 30th, however, not having received his expected reinforcements, Vandamme was compelled to remain on the defensive, and being attacked in front by the Austrians and Russians, and in the rear by the Prussians, he was totally routed, with a loss of 6,000 killed, 7,000 prisoners, and 48 guns, being himself wounded and captured. The allies lost about 5,000.

Kumai.

Fought February, 1355, between the troops of the Emperor Gomarakami, under Yoshinori, and the rebel Japanese, under Moronoshi and Tokiushi. The rebels were defeated, and Moronoshi severely wounded.

Kumamoto (Satsuma Rebellion).

The castle in this town was besieged February 22, 1876, by the Satsuma rebels, 15,000 strong, under Saigo. The place was gallantly defended by the garrison under General Tani Tateki, though many Samurai deserted to the rebels, and strenuous efforts were made by the Imperial army under Prince Taruhito to come to its relief. In the course of March Saigo was attacked in the rear by a force under General Kuroda, but still maintained the siege, and it was not till April 14, when the garrison was on the verge of starvation, that Kuroda, bringing up every available man, succeeded in driving off the rebels and raising the siege.

K

Kunersdorf (Seven Years' War).

Fought August 12, 1759, between 40,000 Prussians, under Frederick the Great, and 80,000 Austrians and Russians, under Generals Landon and Soltykoff. Frederick first attacked the Russians in flank, driving them out of their entrenchments, and capturing 180 guns. Then, against the advice of Seidlitz, he attacked the Austrian position on the left of the allies, and, though deserted by the Russians, the Austrians held their ground, and, bringing all their artillery to bear on the Prussians at close quarters, totally routed them, with a loss of 20,000 men. The allies lost 24,000.

Kunobitza (Ottoman Wars).

Fought 1443, between the Turks, under Amurath II, and the Hungarians, under John Hunniades. The Turks were utterly routed, and in consequence Amurath concluded with them a ten years' truce.

Kurdlah.

Fought March 11, 1795, between the army of the Mahratta Confederacy, under the Peshwa, Madhao Rao II, and Hari Pant, and the forces of the Nizam of Hyderabad. The troops of the Nizam gained an advantage in the fight, but the Nizam being persuaded to leave the field, his troops followed him, and were soon in headlong flight. The Nizam was captured a few days later.

L.

La Belle Famille. *See* Niagara.

Lade (Ionian War).

Fought B.C. 494, between a Persian fleet of 600 sail, which was blockading Miletus under Artaphernes, and 353 Lesbian, Chian and Samian ships, which attempted to raise the siege. The Samians, bribed by the Persians, deserted at the beginning of the action, with the exception of 11 vessels, and the Greeks were totally defeated, with heavy loss. The Chians made a specially gallant fight.

Lade.

Fought B.C. 201, between the Rhodian fleet, under Theophiliscus, and the Macedonians, under Heraclides. The Macedonians had rather the better of the encounter, though both sides claimed the victory.

Ladysmith (Second Boer War).

Sir George White, with about 12,000 troops, was shut up in Ladysmith by the invading army, under General Joubert, November 2, 1899. The Boers, who were well provided with heavy guns, contented themselves in the main with a continuous bombardment. On January 6, 1900, however, a picked force, under Commandant de Villiers, supported by several thousand Boer marksmen posted on the heights, made attempt to force the British lines at Waggon Hill and Caesar's Camp. The battle lasted throughout the day, and more than once the defenders were very hard pressed, but they held their ground till nightfall, when the Boers withdrew, having lost about 800 men. From this date the Boers again contented themselves with bombarding the town, until it was finally relieved by Sir Redvers Buller, February 27. In addition to deaths by disease, the garrison lost during the siege 89 officers and 805 men, more than half of whom fell in the battle of January 6.

La Favorita (Napoleon's Italian Campaigns).

Fought January 16, 1797, between the French, under Napoleon, and the Austrians, under Provera. Provera moved upon Mantua to succour the beleaguered garrison, and was aided by a sortie in force. Napoleon, making a forced march from the field of Rivoli, fell upon Provera and totally routed him, while the sortie was repulsed by the French besieging force at the point of the bayonet. Provera surrendered, with 5,000 men.

La Fère Champenoise (Allied Invasion of France).

Fought March 25, 1814, between Marmont's and Mortier's corps, 30,000 strong, and the allied army marching on Paris. The French were defeated and forced to retire, with a loss of about 5,000 men and many guns. This was the last action fought in the north before the first abdication of Napoleon.

Lagos (War of the Revolution).

Fought June 17, 1693, when a squadron of 23 Dutch and English ships, under Sir George Rooke, was attacked by a French fleet of 71 sail, whilst convoying 400 merchantmen to the Mediterranean. The French destroyed 90 merchant ships, and one English and two Dutch warships. The skilful manœuvring of Rooke, however, saved the rest of the convoy from destruction.

La Hogue (War of the Revolution).

Fought May 19 and 20, 1692, between a combined Dutch and English fleet of 96 sail, under Admirals Russell and Allemande, and a French fleet of 64 sail of the line and 47 smaller vessels, under de Tourville. After heavy loss on both sides, the French fleet was dispersed, with a loss of three ships. On the 22nd Admiral Rooke destroyed 16 sail of the line and a number of transports.

Lahore (First Tartar Invasion of India).

Fought 1296, between the Mongols, 100,000 strong, under Amir Daood, and the army of Ala-ud-Din, King of Delhi, under his brother, Alaf Khan. The Mongols were routed, with a loss of 12,000 men.

Lake Erie (Second American War).

Fought September 10, 1813, between the English flotilla of six schooners, under Commodore Barclay, and a largely superior American squadron, under Commodore Perry. The whole British flotilla was destroyed, with a loss of 134 killed and wounded. The Americans lost 27 killed and 96 wounded.

Lake George (Seven Years' War).

Fought September 8, 1755, between 1,500 French and Indians, under Baron Dieskau, and 2,500 New England militia, under Colonel William Johnson.

A small force sent by Johnson to the relief of Fort Lyman was ambushed by the French and driven back to camp, but Dieskau pursuing, was repulsed in his attack upon the camp, with a loss of about 400. Dieskau himself was wounded and captured. The loss of the New England men during the day was 216 killed and 96 wounded, most of whom fell in the ambush

Lake Kerguel (Tartar Invasion of Russia).

Fought July, 1391, between 300,000 Russians, under Tokatmich, and an equal force of Tartars, under Tamerlane. The battle began at daybreak, and by mid-day the Russians were utterly routed, and fled in disorder, leaving their camp in the hands of Tamerlane.

Lake Regillus.

Fought 497, the first authentic date in the history of Rome. The details handed down, however, belong to the domain of legend rather than to that of history. According to the chroniclers, this was the last attempt of the Tarquinian family to recover the throne of Rome. They were, however, totally routed by the Romans, under Aulus Postumius, and all the sons of Tarquinius, and his son-in-law, Mamilius, were slain in the battle. The legend avers that the Romans, when victory was trembling in the balance, found at their head two young men on white horses, whom they claimed to be Castor and Pollux.

Lake Vadimon (Gallic Invasion of Italy).

Fought B.C. 283, between the Romans, under P. Cornelius Dolabella, and the Gauls and their Etruscan allies. Dolabella attacked the Etruscans as they were crossing the Tiber close to the lake, and destroyed the flower of their army. He then fell upon the Gauls, whom he also defeated with heavy loss, with the result that in the following year they made peace and withdrew from Italy.

Landau (War of the Spanish Succession).

This fortress, held by a French garrison under M. de Melac, was besieged by the Imperialists, under Prince Louis of Baden, June 19, 1702. The garrison made a gallant defence, but was forced to surrender, September 10. The Comte de Soissons, elder brother of Prince Eugene, fell during the siege.

Landen. *See* Neerwinde.

Landskrone (Dano - Swedish Wars).

Fought July 14, 1676, between the Swedes, under Charles XI, and the Danes, under Christian V, in which the Danes suffered a serious defeat.

Langensalza (Seven Weeks' War).

Fought June 27, 1866, between 12,000 Prussians, under General Flics, and the Hanoverians, in about equal strength, under George, King of Hanover. The Prussians attacked the Hanoverian position, and after severe fighting were repulsed with a loss of about 1,400 killed and wounded, and 900 prisoners. The Hanoverians lost 1,392. The victory, however, was fruitless, as the Prussians in the neighbourhood were in overwhelming numbers, and the King was compelled to surrender on the 29th. This is the last appearance of Hanover in history as an independent state.

Langport (Civil War).

Fought July 10, 1645, between the Parliamentarians, under Fairfax, and the Royalists, under Lord Goring. The Royalists were routed, and driven by Cromwell's horse nearly into Bridgwater, with a loss of 300 killed and 1,400 prisoners.

Lang's Nek (First Boer War).

Fought January 28, 1881, when a British column, 1,100 strong, under General Colley, attacked the Boers in a strong position at Lang's Nek. The British were repulsed with a loss of 198 killed and wounded. The Boers lost 14 killed and 27 wounded.

Langside.

Fought May 13, 1568, when the army of Mary Queen of Scots, 6,000 strong, was defeated and dispersed by the forces of the Regent, Murray. The Queen's troops were broken by a cavalry charge, in which they lost 300, while only one man of the victorious horse was killed, and fled in confusion from the field. Mary escaped to England.

Lannoy (Netherlands War of Independence).

Fought January, 1567, between 3,000 Flemish Protestants, under Pierre Cornaille, and a small force of the Duchess of Parma's troops, under Novicarmes. The Flemings, mostly half-armed peasants, were cut to pieces by the Spaniards, 2,600 being killed in one hour's fighting.

Lansdown (Civil War).

Fought July 5, 1643, between the Royalists, under Sir Ralph Hopton, and the Parliamentarians, under Waller, who was endeavouring to prevent Hopton's advance upon Bath. The Royalists stormed Waller's entrenchments and forced him to retreat, though at a heavy cost to themselves.

Laon (Allied Invasion of France).

This fortress, held by the allies under Blucher, was attacked May 9, 1814, by the French under Ney and Marmont. Ney seized two of the suburbs, but Marmont, failing to support him as promised, he could not make good his footing. During the night the allies attacked and routed Marmont, and on the 10th Ney, after hard fighting, was forced to yield the ground he had gained. The French lost about 6,000 men ; the allies 5,000.

La Paz.

Fought January, 1865, between the partizans of General Belza and those of Colonel Melgarejo, each of whom had proclaimed himself Provisional President of Bolivia. Belza's forces were totally defeated, and himself slain.

La Placilla (Chilian Civil War).

Fought August 28, 1891, between 10,000 Congressists, under General Del Canto, and 14,000 Balmacedists, under General Barbosa. The latter were routed with a loss of 3,363 killed and wounded, including

Barbosa, while thousands laid down their arms on the field. The Congressists, who lost 1,609, at once occupied Valparaiso, and a few days late Balmaceda committed suicide.

La Puebla (Franco-Mexican War).

Fought May 5, 1862, between the French, 7,500 strong, under General Lorencez, and about 12,000 Mexicans, under General Zaragoça. The French endeavoured to carry the ridge of the Cerro de Guadalupe, commanding the town, but were repulsed by General Negreti, with 1,200 men, losing 456 killed and wounded, and forced to retire from La Puebla. The Mexicans lost 215 only.

La Puebla (Franco-Mexican War).

On May 4, 1863, the French army, 25,000 strong, under General Forey, laid siege to La Puebla, which was held by a Mexican garrison under General Ortega. Forey's force was too small for a complete investment, and he began operations against the Fort of San Xavier. On the 29th this post was taken by storm, the French losing 230, the defenders 600 men. From this point the French obtained foothold in the town, and then proceeded to capture the houses block by block. So determined was the resistance, however, that their progress was very slow, and by April 7 they had made next to no advance, though they had lost a further 600 men. Later in the month an attack on the Convent of Santa Cruz was re-

pulsed with a loss of 480. On May 8 a relieving force of 10,500 men, under General Comonfort, was defeated by a small French column under Bazaine, losing 8 guns and 1,000 prisoners, and from this point further resistance was useless. Ortega, therefore, after a most gallant defence, surrendered with 1,455 officers and 11,000 men, May 17, 1863.

Larcay (Chilian Revolution).

Fought December, 1829, between the Federalists, or Government Party, under General Zastera, and the Pelucones, or Unitarians, under General Prieto. The Pelucones gained a signal victory, following which they drove out the Government and abrogated the constitution of 1828.

Largs (Norse Invasion of Scotland).

Fought October 2, 1263, between the Norsemen, under Haco, and the Scots. The Norse fleet of 160 ships was driven ashore off Largs by a violent storm, and many of them wrecked, and Haco landed a force to protect the shipwrecked crews. This force was attacked by the Scots and utterly routed, and Haco was forced to withdraw, and abandon the project of invasion. The only name on the Scottish side which has come down to us as taking part in the battle is that of Sir Pierce Curry.

Larissa (Third Macedonia War).

Fought 171 B.C., between the Romans, 40,000 strong, under P. Licinius Crassus, and 43,000 Macedonians, under Perseus. The Romans were defeated with a loss of 2,200 killed and 600 prisoners.

Larissus, The (Wars of the Achæan League).

Fought B.C. 209, between the Achæans, under Philopœmen, and the Ætolians and Eleans. The allies were defeated and cut to pieces, the Elean general being among the slain.

La Rochelle (Hundred Years' War).

Fought June 22, 1372, when an English fleet, under the Earl of Pembroke, intended for the relief of La Rochelle, was intercepted by a greatly superior Spanish fleet, under Don Ambrosio Bercenegra, and after very hard fighting was entirely destroyed or captured.

La Rochelle (Huguenot Rebellion).

This fortress, the principal Huguenot stronghold in France, was besieged by the Royal troops, under Richelieu, in 1627. The garrison, under the mayor, Guiton, made a gallant defence, but the assassination of Buckingham prevented the arrival of the promised English succours, and the town surrendered, after holding out for fourteen months.

La Rothière (Allied Campaign in France).

Fought February 1, 1814, between 32,000 French, under Napoleon, and 100,000 Prussiansians, Russians, and Würtembergers, under Blucher. Napoleon held a strong position, where he was attacked by Blucher, whom he succeeded in holding at bay till late in the afternoon, when Bucher captured the village of La Rothière. Napoleon with the Young Guard retook the village, and the battle ended with the French in possession of the field. The French lost 5,000, the allies about 8,000, and Napoleon was enabled to continue his retirement without molestation.

Las Navas de Tolosa (Moorish Empire in Spain).

Fought July 10, 1212, between a huge army of Moors, said by the chroniclers to have amounted to 600,000, under Mohammed al Nasin, and the allied armies of the Kings of Castile, Leon, Aragon, Navarre, and Portugal. The Moors were utterly routed, very few of their enormous host escaping from the field.

Las Salinas (Conquest of Peru).

Fought April 20, 1538, between the forces of Francisco Pizarro and those of Almagro. The latter were totally routed, and Almagro captured and executed.

Laswari (Second Mahratta War).

Fought November 1, 1803, between the British, 10,000 strong, under General Lake, and Scindhia's army, consisting of 9,000 infantry and 5,000 cavalry. Scindhia's veteran infantry made a most gallant defence, standing their ground until 7,000 had fallen, when the survivors laid down their arms. The cavalry also suffered heavily. The British loss amounted to about 800. Seventy-two guns and a large quantity of ammunition and stores were captured.

Laupen (Burgundian Wars).

Fought June 21, 1339, between 5,000 Swiss of Berne and the Forest Cantons, under Rudolf von Erlach, and 15,000 Burgundians, under the Counts of Kiburg and Nidau. Despite their superior numbers, the Burgundians were unable to withstand the charge of the Swiss, and were utterly routed and forced to raise the siege of Laupen.

Lautulæ (Second Samnite War).

Fought B.C. 316, between the Samnites, under Pontius, and the Romans, under Q. Fabius Maximus. The Romans were defeated with great slaughter.

Lawfeldt (War of the Austrian Succession).

Fought July 2, 1747, between the allied Austrians and British, under the Duke of Cumberland, and the French, under Marshal Saxe. The village of Lawfeldt was thrice carried by the French and thrice recaptured, but about noon the British centre was driven in, and defeat was imminent, when a cavalry charge, headed by Sir John Ligonier, saved the day, and enabled the Duke to retire in good order. The allies lost 5,620 killed and wounded, the French about 10,000.

Le Bourget (Franco-German War).

A determined sortie by the French from Paris, October 27, 1870, in which they carried the village of Le Bourget. They held their ground there until October 30, when they were driven out by the Prussian Guard Corps, leaving 1,200 prisoners in the hands of the Germans, who lost 34 officers and 344 men.

Leck, The (Thirty Years' War).

Fought April 5, 1632, between 26,000 Swedes and German Protestants, under Gustavus Adolphus, and 20,000 Imperialists, under Count Tilly. Gustavus had prepared a bridge to cross the river, and immediately after daybreak his engineers commenced to fix it, the Swedish artillery meanwhile keeping the Imperialists in check. In the artillery duel Tilly was mortally wounded, and his troops retired, leaving the Swedes to effect the passage unmolested.

L'Ecluse (Hundred Years' War).

Fought 1340, when the English fleet surprised the French in a narrow channel, and totally routed them, with a loss of 90 ships and 30,000 men.

Leghorn.

Fought off Leghorn March 31, 1653, when six English ships, under Commodore Appleton, were destroyed by a Dutch fleet of 16 sail, under Admiral Van Gelen. Only a sloop escaped the destruction. Van Gelen was mortally wounded during the action.

Legnano (Wars of the Lombard League).

Fought May 29, 1176, between the Lombard League, aided by Venice and the Pope, and the Imperialists, under Frederick Barbarossa. Frederick was utterly routed, and fled from Italy in disguise.

Leipsic (Thirty Years' War).

Fought September 7, 1631, between 20,000 Swedes and an

equal force of Saxons, under Gustavus Adolphus and John George, Elector of Saxony, and 44,000 Imperialists, under Tilly. The Imperialist right totally routed the Saxons, who fled from the field, headed by the Elector. Meanwhile, the Swedes had completely defeated the left of the Imperialists, under Pappenheim, and repulsed the centre under Tilly, and on the return of the right from pursuing the Saxons, they were attacked by the Swedish left, and driven from the field, only four regiments holding their ground in a wood until nightfall. The Imperialists lost 8,000 killed and wounded and 5,000 prisoners ; the allies 2,700, of whom only 700 were Swedes. Gustavus captured the whole of Tilly's artillery, and his victory was the salvation of the Protestant cause, which was trembling in the balance.

Leipsic (Campaign of Leipsic).

Fought October 16, 17, and 18, 1813, between the French, under Napoleon, and the forces of the Great Coalition. Napoleon, who held Leipsic with 155,000 men, was faced by 160,000 Austrians and Russians, under the Prince of Schwartzemberg, and 60,000 Prussians, under Blucher. On the 16th Schwartzemberg attacked, being faced by Napoleon with 115,000 men, and, after an obstinate engagement, which lasted till nightfall, the French had gained a little ground. At the same time Blucher attacked Marmont, who, with 24,000 men, held his own throughout the day. The French lost 27,000 ; the allies

about 35,000. Both sides receiving reinforcements during the night, Napoleon on the morning of the 17th was at the head of 150,000 troops, while the allies numbered nearly 300,000, including the Swedes under Bernadotte. Little was done on the 17th, but on the 18th Napoleon moved out to drive back the allies, and leave a road of retreat open. He was repulsed at all points, and driven back into Leipsic, whence during the night of the 18th to 19th, the French retired by the only serviceable bridge. The corps under Poniatowski left to cover the retreat was almost annihilated, and Poniatowski killed. The French lost in the three days over 60,000 men, while the losses of the allies were also enormous.

Leitskau (Campaign of Leipsic).

Fought August 27, 1813, between 5,000 French, under General Girard, and a Prussian division, under General Hirschberg, aided by some Cossacks, under Czernitcheff. Girard was defeated, losing heavily in killed and wounded, besides 1,500 prisoners and 6 guns.

Le Mans (Franco-German War).

Fought January 10, 11, and 12, between the Germans, 50,000 strong, under Prince Frederick Charles, and the French, numbering about 150,000, under General Chanzy. The French army was completely routed, and the whole force so completely demoralised as to be no longer an effective fighting unit. The Germans took 20,000 prisoners, 17 guns, and great quantities of war material, at a cost to themselves of 200 officers and 3,200 men.

Lens (Thirty Years' War).

Fought August 20, 1648, between the French, 14,000 strong, under Condé, and the Austrians, in somewhat superior force, under the Archduke Leopold. Condé feigned a retreat, to draw the enemy from their lines, and then turning upon them, decisively defeated them, with a loss of 4,000 killed, 6,000 prisoners, and all their baggage and artillery.

Leontini.

This city, the stronghold of the National party in Sicily, held by a garrison of Syracusans and Roman deserters, was stormed and sacked, B.C. 211, by three Roman legions under M. Marcellus. Two thousand Roman deserters captured in the place were put to the sword. Hippocrates succeeded in escaping.

Lepanto (Cyprus War).

Fought October 17, 1571, betwen a fleet of 250 Spanish and Venetian ships, under Don John of Austria, and a Turkish fleet of 270 sail, under Piale, the Capitan Pasha. The Turkish left wing, under the Dey of Algiers, met with some success, but the centre and right were almost destroyed, the Turks losing 200 vessels, and, it is said, 30,000 men. Piale was killed. The Dey of Algiers succeeded in extricating the majority of his ships. The allies lost between 4,000 and 5,000 men, including 15 Venetian captains.

Lerida (Thirty Years' War).

Fought September, 1642, between the Spaniards, under Leganez, and the French, under Lamothe-Houdancourt. The Spanish army was defeated, and this victory, in conjunction with the fall of Perpignan, gave the French possession of Roussillon.

Lerida (Thirty Years' War).

This city, held by a garrison of 4,000 Spaniards, under Don Jorge Britt, was besieged by the French, under the Great Condé, May 12, 1647. The defence was vigorous, the garrison making constant sorties, and about the middle of June the appearance of a large Spanish army at Fraga forced Condé either to deliver an assault or to raise the siege. He chose the second alternative and withdrew his troops June 17.

Lesno (Russo-Swedish War).

A series of actions, fought 1709 between 40,000 Russians, under Peter the Great, and 15,000 Swedes, under General Levenhaupt, who was escorting a convoy of 8,000 waggons to the army of Charles XII. The battle lasted over five days, at the end of which time the remnant of the Swedes, though defeated, were permitted to retire in good order, but without their convoy. The Swedes lost in this series of actions two-thirds of their numbers. The Russians lost 10,000 men.

Leucopetra (Wars of the Achæan League).

Fought 146 B.C., between a Roman Consular Army, under Lucius Mummius, and the forces of the Achæan League, under Diacus. The Greeks, who were only half as strong as their opponents, were routed, and all resistance came to an end, the Greek cities, one after another, opening their gates to the Romans.

Leuctra (Bœotian War).

Fought July, 371 B.C., between 11,000 Spartans, under Cleombrotus, and 6,000 Thebans, under Epaminondas. The principal fighting took place on the Theban left, where Epaminondas had massed his best troops, and after a fierce encounter the Spartans were driven back, leaving 1,000 dead, including Cleombrotus, on the field. As a result of this defeat, the Spartans evacuated Bœotia.

Leuthen (Seven Years' War).

Fought December 5, 1757, between 33,000 Prussians, under Frederick the Great, and 90,000 Austrians, under Prince Charles of Lorraine and Count Daun. Frederick made a feigned attack on the Austrian right wing, and then under cover of the ground withdrew the major part of his force, and strongly attacked the Austrian left, which was driven back and finally overthrown by a charge of cavalry. The Austrians lost 7,000 killed and wounded, 20,000 prisoners, including three generals, and 134 guns. The Prussians lost 5,000 killed and wounded. In consequence of this victory, Breslau surrendered to Frederick, with over 18,000 troops, on December 10.

Lewes (Barons' War).

Fought May 14, 1264, between the Barons, under Simon de Montfort, and the Royalists, under Henry III and Prince Edward. The king was completely defeated, and the two parties signed an agreement, known as the Mise of Lewes, to submit the points in dispute to arbitration.

Lexington (American War of Independence).

Fought April 19, 1775, between the Royal troops, under General Gage, and the Americans. After a brief engagement the Americans were defeated, and retired. The losses on both sides were very small.

Lexington (American Civil War).

This place was invested September 18, 1861, by the Confederates, 8,000 strong, under General Price, who having cut off their supplies, forced the garrison of 3,500, under Colonel Mulligan, to surrender, September 20. The Confederates lost 100 men only.

Leyden (Netherlands War of Independence).

This city was invested May 26, 1574, by 8,000 Walloons and Germans under Valdez, who in the course of a few days had erected 62 batteries round the place. There was no garrison, with the exception of a few " freebooters " and a burgher guard, under Jan van der Does. The Prince of Orange, in order to save the city, determined to open the dykes, and on August 3 the gates at Schiedam and Rotterdam were opened, and the dykes broken along the course of the Yssel. Meanwhile the citizens had come to an end of their bread, but by strenuous efforts the fleet under Admiral Boisot succeeded in throwing relief into the city at the beginning of October. By this time the city was on the verge of starvation, and 8,000 of the inhabitants had perished of pestilence. The Spaniards, however, had been driven from work after work, and on October 3 the last of their redoubts was mastered, and Valdez was forced to raise the siege.

Lignitz (Seven Years' War).

Fought August 15, 1760. Frederick the Great with 30,000 Prussians was posted near Lignitz, and expecting to be attacked by the Austrians, 90,000 strong, under Count Daun, commenced a retreat towards Parchwitz, and took up a position which, according to Daun's plan was to have been occupied by Landon's corps. Landon, quite unconscious of the presence of the Prussians, marched into the middle of Frederick's lines, and was utterly routed, with a loss of 4,000 killed and wounded, 6,000 prisoners and 82 guns.

Ligny (Hundred Days).

Fought June 16, 1815, between 84,000 Prussians under Blucher and 60,000 French under Napoleon. The French attacked Blucher's position, and met with a stout resistance, especially at the village of Ligny, but by sundown the Prussians had exhausted their last resources, and Napoleon, bringing up the Guard, and a division of heavy cavalry, drove them from their positions, with a loss of about 12,000. The French lost 8,000 killed and wounded.

Lille (War of the Spanish Succession).

This city was besieged August 12, 1708, by the Imperialists, under Prince Eugene, and was defended by a French garrison, under M. de Bouflers, which after repulsing several determined assaults, surrendered October 25. The besiegers lost in the course of the siege 3,632. The French lost about 7,000.

Lilybæum (First Punic War).

This fortress was besieged B.C. 250, by the Romans, under C. Attilius and L. Manlius, and was defended by a Carthaginian garrison, 10,000 strong, under Himilcon. The Romans invested the place both by sea and land, but the superior seamanship of the Carthaginians enabled them from time to time to throw succour into the place. The first line of the defences was soon carried but the Romans were then confronted with a second rampart, equally strong, and the siege was begun anew. In 249 P. Claudiûs took over the command, but a defeat of the Roman fleet at Drepanum gave the Carthaginians complete command of the sea, and though the Romans continued to blockade the fortress on the land side, it held out till 241. After the naval battle of Ægusæ Carthage sued for peace.

Lincoln, Fair of.

Fought in the streets of Lincoln, 1217, between the Royal troops, under the Earl of Pembroke, and the adherents of the Dauphin Louis, under the Comte de la Perche. The Royalists were victorious, and the French leader was killed.

Lindley (Second Boer War).

At this place a force of 500 yeomanry, under Colonel Spragge, after holding out for four days against a largely superior Boer force, surrendered May 27, 1900.

Linkoping.

Fought 1598, between the Poles, under Sigismund III, King of Poland and Sweden, and the Swedes, under Charles the Regent. The Poles were surprised and totally defeated, with a loss of 20,000 men, the Swedes losing, it is said, only 240. This victory was shortly followed by the dethronement of Sigismund and the accession of Charles as King of Sweden.

Liparæan Islands (First Punic War).

The scene of a naval battle, B.C. 257, in which the Roman fleet, under the Consul, C. Attilius, completely defeated the Carthaginians.

Lippe (Germanic Wars).

Fought B.C. 11 between the Romans, under Drusus, and the Sicambri, Suevi and Cherusii. The Romans were largely outnumbered and surrounded, and so certain were the Germans of victory, that they had already apportioned the spoil among the various tribes. Drusus, however, attacked the barbarians vigorously, and totally routed them with very heavy loss.

Lissa (Seven Weeks' War).

The only naval action between ironclads in European waters, fought July 20, 1866, between the Austrian fleet of 7 armoured ships and some obsolete wooden vessels, under Admiral Tegethoff, and the Italian fleet of 10 armour-clads, under Admiral Persano. Tegethoff attacked in wedge formation, with his flagship as the apex, and broke the line of the Italian fleet, which was steaming, line ahead, across his bows. He rammed and sank the Italian flagship, and the rest of the action was a melée in which the Italians were defeated and driven off, with a loss of 3 ships and over 1,000 men. This defeat forced the Italians to raise the siege of Lissa.

Little Big Horn (Sioux Rising).

On June 25, 1876, General Custer, with the 7th United States Cavalry, 700 strong, attacked the village of the Sioux chief, Sitting Bull. He divided his force into three columns, one of which, led by himself, marched into an ambush, and was massacred to a man. The other two columns were vigourously attacked by the Sioux, and forced to retire. The cavalry lost on this occasion 265 killed.

Lodi, Bridge of (Napoleon's Italian Campaigns).

Fought May 10, 1796, during Napoleon's pursuit of the retiring Austro - Sardinian army, under Beaulieu. The bridge over the Adda was defended by the Austrian rear-guard, with some 20 guns, commanding passage. Napoleon sent a force of cavalry round by a ford to take the defenders in rear, and then rushed the bridge, the stormers being led by Berthier and Masséna, while Napoleon himself was in the thick of the fighting. The French loss is said not to have exceeded 400, while the Austrians lost in the action and subsequent pursuit, 2,000 killed and wounded, 1,000 prisoners, and 20 guns.

Loftcha (Russo-Turkish War).

Fought September 3, 1877, between 20,000 Russians, under Prince Imeretinsky, and 15,000 Turks, under Adil Pasha. The actual attack on the Turkish positions was made by Skobeleff, at first with 5,000, and afterwards with 9,000 men, and the Turks were driven out of Loftcha with a loss of 5,200 killed. The Russians lost 1,500 killed and wounded.

Loigny - Pouprey (Franco - German War).

Fought December 1, 1870, between the Germans, 34,000 strong, under the Grand Duke of Mecklenburg, and about 90,000 French, forming the army of the Loire, under General d'Aurelle de Paladines. The Germans gained a signal victory, completely breaking the aggressive power of the Army of the Loire. The French lost 18,000 killed and wounded and 9 guns, the Germans 4,200.

Loja (War of Granada).

Fought July 4, 1482, between the Spaniards, under Ferdinand the Catholic, and the Moors, under Ali Atar. The King, who was besieging Loja, was encamped on the heights of Almohacen, but finding the position insecure, decided upon a retreat. As he was retiring he was vigorously attacked by the garrison, and though, after very heavy fighting, he succeeded in withdrawing in good order, he lost most of his baggage and artillery.

Lonato. See Castiglione.

Londonderry (War of the Revolution).

This town in which the Ulster Protestants, to the number of about 30,000, had taken refuge, was besieged by James II, April 19, 1689. It was defended by about 7,000 armed citizens, under Major Henry Baker, and held out until July 30, when Colonel Kirke succeeded in forcing the boom at the head of Lough Foyle and reprovisioning the town. The besiegers then withdrew, having lost 5,000 men during the siege. The garrison was reduced to 4,000. Among those who died during the siege was Major Baker.

Loose Coat Field. See Empingham.

Loudon Hill (Scottish Wars).

Fought 1306, between the Scots, under Robert Bruce, and the English, under the Regent Pembroke. Bruce met the attack of the English cavalry with a line of spearmen, which they were unable to break, and they were driven off with heavy loss. Pembroke thereupon withdrew his army and returned to England.

Louisburg (War of the Austrian Succession).

This place, the strongest fortress in America, was captured June 16, 1745, by a force of New Englanders, under Pepperel, aided by a naval force under Commodore Warren.

Louisburg (Seven Years' War).

Louisburg, having been re stored to the French, was invested June 3, 1758, by a force of 11,600 British troops, under General Amherst, and a fleet of of 41 ships of war, under Admiral Boscawen. It was defended by 3,800 French regulars, besides Indians and armed citizens, under the Chevalier de Drucour, while in the harbour were 12 ships of war, with crews numbering 3,000 men. Owing to heavy weather no siege guns were landed till the 18th, but by July 20 a practicable breach had been effected, whereupon the garrison surrendered. During the siege the defenders lost 1,200 men killed or died of disease, while the prisoners numbered 5,637, and 239 guns and mortars were taken. Wolfe, who commanded a brigade, specially distinguished himself.

Löwenberg (Campaign of Leipsic).

Fought August 21, 1813, between 130,000 French, under Napoleon, and 80,000 Prussians, under Blucher. Blucher being vigorously attacked, retired behind the Haynau without offering any serious resistance to the French advance. The Prussians lost 2,000 killed and wounded.

Lowositz (Seven Years' War).

Fought October 1, 1756, between 24,000 Prussians, under Frederick the Great, and a somewhat superior force of Austrians, under Marshal Brown. Brown was marching to relieve the Saxons penned up in Pirna, when he was attacked by the Prussians, who, after hard fighting, forced him to retire. Each side lost about 3,000, but the victory was of great importance to Frederick, as it led to the surrender at Pirna of 17,000 Saxons and 80 guns.

Lunceña (War of Granada).

Fought April, 1483, when the Moors, under Abdullah and Ali Atar, who were besieging Lucena, were attacked by a Spanish relieving force under the Comte de Cabra. The Moorish infantry fled, and Ali Atar, heading a charge of cavalry in a gallant attempt to retrieve the day, was slain, whereupon his following broke and fled, pursued by the Christians to the banks of the Xenil, where the majority were cut to pieces.

Lucknow (Indian Mutiny).

On the approach of the rebel Sepoy army, July 1, 1857, the garrison and residents took refuge in the Residency, which had been prepared to stand a siege. On September 19, 1857, a force of 3,179 British troops, under Havelock and Outram, left Cawnpore to relieve the garrison. On the 23rd they encountered and defeated a force of 12,000 rebels at the Alumbagh, capturing 5 guns. On the 25th they forced the Charbagh bridge, and captured the Secunderbagh, and the main body, after prolonged street fighting, reached the Residency, the rearguard with the wounded getting in on the 26th. The loss during the operations amounted to 535, while the garrison up to this time had lost 483 killed and wounded. Outram now took command

and the garrison held out until November 19, when it was relieved, after very heavy fighting, by a column under Sir Colin-Campbell, and the whole force withdrawn. On March 1, 1858, the recovery of the city from the rebels commenced by the capture of the Alumbagh, and was completed on the 21st, when the mutineers were finally driven from the place. During the interval the various fortresses and palaces held by the rebels were successively carried by assault, the fighting in many cases being exceedingly severe.

Lugdunum. *See* Lyons.

Luncarty (Danish Invasions of Scotland).

Fought 980, between the Scots, under Kenneth III, and the Danish corsairs, who had landed on the Tay to attack Dunkeld. After a furious hand-to-hand fight the Danes were defeated and driven to their ships.

Lunden (Dano-Swedish Wars).

Fought 1676, between the Swedes, under Charles XI, and the Danes, under Christian V. Both sides claimed the victory, but the advantage rested with the Swedes, for Christian had to fall back upon Copenhagen, while Charles forced the Danes to raise the siege of Malmoe.

Lundy's Lane (Second American War).

Fought July 25, 1814, between 5,000 Americans, under General Jacob Brown, and 3,000 British, under Sir George Drummond. Drummound occupied high ground on each side of Lundy's Lane, where he was attacked by the Americans. The fighting lasted till far into the night, when a final assault was repulsed, and the Americans retired to Chippewa with a loss of 858. The British lost 878.

Lutter (Thirty Years' War).

Fought August 27, 1626, between the Imperialists, under Tilly, and the Danes and Germans, under Christian IV of Denmark. The allies were retreating before Tilly, who came up with them in an open plain near the Castle of Lutter, where the King had taken up a strong position. Tilly attacked, and notwithstanding Christian's personal gallantry, his infantry was overwhelmed, while the German cavalry refused to take any part in the fight. The Danes left 4,000 dead on the field, and Tilly captured 2,000 prisoners, 22 guns and 60 standards. The King with difficulty cut his way through the enemy's horse, and escaped.

Lützen (Thirty Years' War).

Fought November 16, 1632, between 20,000 Swedes, under Gustavus Adolphus, and 30,000 Imperialists, under Wallenstein. The Swedes attacked with success on their right, but their left was driven back by Pappenheim, and Gustavus, hurrying off to rally them fell mortally wounded. The fall of their king, however, did not dishearten the Swedes, and a fresh charge, in which Pappenheim was killed, gave them a complete victory. A dense fog, however, came on, which enabled Wallenstein to effect an orderly retreat, though he left all his guns on the field.

Lützen (Campaign of Leipsic).

Fought May 2, 1813, between the French, 70,000 strong, under Napoleon, and the Russians and Prussians, 65,000 strong, under Wittgenstein and Blucher. The King of Prussia and the Russian Emperor were present on the field. Napoleon held five villages in front of Lützen, round which the battle centred. They were taken and re-taken several times during the day, but at 8 p.m., in spite of the remonstrances of Blucher, the two sovereigns ordered a retreat, and the honours of the day rested with the French. The allies lost about 20,000 ; the French about 18,000.

Luzzara (War of the Spanish Succession).

Fought August 15, 1702, between the French, 35,000 strong, under the Duc d'Anjou, and 25,000 Imperialists, under Prince Eugene. The Prince attacked the French in their entrenchments in front of Luzzara, and after a stubborn resistance, drove them out with a loss of about 4,000 men. The Imperialists lost 27,000 killed and wounded.

Lynn Haven Bay.

Fought September 5, 1781, between a British fleet of 19 ships of the line and 7 frigates, under Admiral Thomas Graves, and a French fleet of 25 line of battle ships. Admiral Graves attacked the French as they were lying in Lynn Haven Bay, but was unsuccessful, and drew off after two hours' hard fighting, with a loss of 79 killed and 230 wounded. The French lost 22 officers and 200 men killed and wounded.

Lyons.

Fought 197 between the legions of Britain, under Clodius Albinus, and the legions of Pannonia, under Severus, both generals having been proclaimed Emperor by their respective troops on the death of Pertinax. Albinus was defeated and slain.

M.

Macalo (Italian Wars).

Fought October 11, 1427, when the Venetians, under Carmagnola, in a strong position near Macalo, were attacked by the Milanese, under Malatesta. The Venetians repulsed the attack, and assuming the offensive, surrounded Malatesta, and compelled him to surrender with his whole force, numbering about 10,000 men.

Madonna dell' Oleno (War of the Austrian Succession).

Fought September 30, 1744, between the French and Spaniards, under Prince Louis de Conti and Don Philip of Spain, and the Imperialists, under the King of Sardinia. With a view of relieving Cuneo, which the allies were besieging, the King attacked their lines, and though he was defeated in the battle, he gained his object, for Conti was compelled by lack of supplies to raise the siege, October 22, having suffered heavy losses from famine, flood and battle.

Madras.

This city was invested by the French under Labourdonnais,

L

with 9 ships and about 3,700 troops, mostly Europeans, September 14, 1746. It was defended by a garrison of 200, and after a week's bombardment, surrendered September 25. The garrison lost 5 men only ; the French not a single man.

Madras (Seven Years' War).

On December 16, 1758, Madras was invested by Lally-Tollendal with 2,000 European and 4,000 native troops. The garrison consisted of 4,000 men, more than half of whom were Sepoys, under Colonel Laurence. After a bombardment lasting from January 2, 1759, to February 16, Lally-Tollendal was on the point of ordering an assault, when the arrival of the British fleet caused him to raise the siege and retire. The garrison lost during the siege 1,341 killed and wounded. The French losses amounted to 700 Europeans, besides Sepoys.

Madeira (Napoleonic Wars).

This island was occupied without bloodshed by a combined naval and military force, under Admiral Sir A. J. Cochrane and General Bowyer, December 26, 1807.

Maestricht (Netherlands War of Independence).

This city, the German Gate of the Netherlands, was besieged by the Spaniards, under Prince Alexander of Parma, March 12, 1579. It was held by a garrison of 1,000 troops and 1,200 armed burghers, under Melchior, while the besiegers numbered 20,000. Two unsuccessful assaults were made April 8, which cost the Spaniards 670 officers and 4,000

men, but finally the place was taken by surprise, and a massacre followed, in which 6,000 of the inhabitants perished.

Mafeking (Second Boer War).

This small township, entirely destitute of regular defences, was invested October, 1899, by a force of 5,000 Boers under General Cronje, and defended by a garrison of about 700 irregulars and armed townsmen, under Colonel Baden-Powell. Later in the siege Cronje withdrew a large part of his force, leaving about 2,000 under Snyman to prosecute the siege. Though the bombardment was continuous, only one resolute attempt was made to penetrate the defences ; when on May 12, 1900, 300 Boers, under Sarel Eloff, succeeded in getting within the lines, but were surrounded and forced to surrender. On May 17, the place was relieved by a cavalry column under Colonel Mahon. The garrison lost 273, the Boers about 1,000, in the course of the siege.

Magdeburg (Thirty Years' War).

This city, held by a small Swedish garrison, under Falkenberg, was besieged by the Imperialists, under Tilly, March, 1631. After a desultory bombardment, Tilly was forced by the approach of Gustavus Adolphus either to raise the siege or to attempt a storm. Choosing the latter course, an assault was delivered, under Pappenberg, and after two hours' severe fighting, in the course of which Falkenberg fell, the garrison was overpowered. The victory was sullied by an infamous massacre of the unarmed inhabitants, thousands of whom perished at the hands of the Croats and Walloons.

Magenta (Franco-Austrian War).

Fought June 4, 1859, between the 2nd French Corps d'Armée, under Macmahon, and the main Austrian army, under Marshal Giulay, about 100,000 strong. Macmahon attacked the Austrian position, and, after hard fighting, drove them out of Magenta, and totally defeated them with a loss of about 6,000 killed and wounded. The French lost 4,400.

Magersfontein (Second Boer War).

Fought December 11, 1899, between 9,000 Boers, under General Cronje, and Lord Methuen's division, with the addition of the Highland Brigade. Cronje's position was exceedingly strong, and an attempt to turn it by a flank march undertaken at night led to a disaster to the Highland brigade, who came under a heavy fire before they were extended, and lost 57 officers and over 700 men, including their brigadier, General Wauchope. Eventually the attacking force was withdrawn, without having made any impression on the Boer position. The total British losses were 68 officers and 1,011 men. The Boers admitted a loss of 320, but it was probably considerably heavier.

Magnesia (War with Antiochus the Great).

Fought B.C. 190, between Antiochus the Great, with 80,000 troops, and the Romans, 40,000 strong, under Cnæus Domitius. Antiochus, leading the right wing, drove back the Roman left and penetrated to their camp, which he nearly succeeded in capturing. His left wing, however, was routed, and his elephants becoming unmanageable, broke the ranks of the phalanx, whereupon his whole army fled in confusion, with a loss, it is said, of 50,000 killed. The Romans lost 300 only.

Maharajpur (Gwalior War).

Fought December 29, 1843, between the British, 14,000 strong, with 40 guns, under Sir Hugh Gough, and the troops of Bhagerat Rao Scindhia, 18,000 strong, with 100 guns. The Mahrattas occupied a strong position at Maharajpur, the exact locality of their lines being unknown to Sir Hugh, until his troops came under fire. The British at once charged and carried the batteries, and finally routed the Gwalior infantry at a cost of 787 killed and wounded. The Mahrattas lost 3,000 killed and wounded, and 56 guns.

Maharajpur (Indian Mutiny).

Fought July 16, 1857, between 5,000 rebels, under the Nana Sahib, and the British relieving force, under Havelock. The Nana was entrenched across the Grand Trunk Road, and his position being too strong for a frontal attack, Havelock turned his left flank. After severe fighting the rebels were defeated, though Havelock was left with only 800 Europeans available for further service. On the following day Cawnpore was re-occupied.

Mahidpur (Third Mahratta War).

Fought December 21, 1817, between the British, under Sir Thomas Hislop, and the army of Holkar of Indore. The Mahrattas, with 70 guns, were strongly posted behind the Sipra, which Sir Thomas crossed in the face of a heavy fire, and completely defeated them. The British lost 778 killed and wounded, the Mahrattas about 3,000.

Maida (Napoleonic Wars).

Fought July 4, 1806, between the British expeditionary force in Calabria, 5,000 strong, under Sir John Stuart, and the French, in equal strength, under General Reynier. The British charged with the bayonet, and the French, though veterans, failing to withstand the onslaught, broke and fled, losing very heavily in the pursuit.

Maidan (First Afghan War).

Fought September 14, 1842, between the British, under General Nott, and 12,000 Afghans, under Shems-ud-din, who occupied the heights commanding the road to Kabul. Nott attacked and carried the Afghan position, the Afghans being driven off with heavy loss.

Maiwand (Second Afghan War).

Fought July 27, 1880, between a small British force, with 6 guns, under General Burrows, and the Afghan army, under Ayub Khan. A Bombay native regiment was broken by a Ghazi rush, and although the 66th Regiment fought magnificently, the British were routed, with a loss of 32 officers and 939 men killed, and 17 officers and 151

men wounded. The survivors escaped with difficulty to Kandahar.

Main, The (Germanic War).

Fought B.C. 9, when the Romans, under Drusus, attacked and totally routed the Marcomanni, driving them to the eastward and occupying their territory.

Majorca (Napoleonic Wars).

This island was captured from the Spaniards in 1706, by a small British force under Sir John Leake.

Majuba (First Boer War).

Fought February 27, 1881, when a British column, 647 strong, under Sir George Colley, posted on the summit of Majuba Hill, was attacked and driven off by the Boers under General Joubert. A strong party of young Boers stormed the hill while the fire of the defenders was kept down by a picked body of marksmen, and the British were driven from their position with heavy loss, especially during the retirement down the hillside. The casualties amounted to 223 killed and wounded, Sir George Colley being killed, and 50 prisoners. The Boer losses were very small. After this disaster an armistice was agreed to, and peace soon afterwards concluded.

Malacca.

This city, which was defended by 30,000 Malays, under the Sultan Mohammed, was captured by Albuquerque, with 19 ships and 1,400 Portuguese regulars, after a very feeble defence, in 1513.

Malaga (War of Granada).

This city, defended by a Moorish garrison, under Hamet Zeli, was besieged by the Spaniards, 60,000 strong, under Ferdinand the Catholic, April 17, 1487. After an obstinate resistance, lasting for four months, the garrison was forced to surrender, and Ferdinand and Isabella entered the city August 18th. The inhabitants were sold into slavery.

Malaga (War of the Spanish Succession).

Fought August 13, 1704, between the combined British and Dutch fleets, consisting of 45 sail of the line, under Sir George Rooke, and the French fleet of 53 line-of-battle-ships, under the Comte de Thoulouse. The French admiral was endeavouring to effect a junction with the Spanish fleet, which was engaged in the siege of Gibraltar, and was brought to action by Sir George Rooke off Malaga. The fighting was severe, and though no ships were lost on either side, the British gained an important strategic victory as the junction of the two hostile fleets was prevented. The British lost 6 officers and 687 men killed, and 18 officers and 1,645 men wounded. The French lost 191 officers and 3,048 men killed and wounded.

Malakand Pass (Chitral Campaign).

Fought April 3, 1895, when the British expedition, under General Low, 15,000 strong. forced the pass, which was held by about 12,000 tribesmen, with a loss of 8 officers and 61 men killed and wounded. The Chitralis lost about 500.

Malakoff (Crimean War).

This fort, forming an important part of the southern defences of Sebastopol, was stormed by 30,000 French, under General Pelissier, September 8, 1855. The Russians being taken by surprise, made but a feeble resistance.

Malavilly (Third Mysore War).

Fought March 20, 1799, when the camp of the British force, under Lord Harris, marching on Seringapatam, was attacked in force by Tippu Sahib. The enemy was thrown into confusion by a charge of cavalry, under General Floyd, and retired with a loss of about 1,000, The British losses were trifling.

Maldon (Danish Invasion).

Fought 991, between the Anglo-Saxons, under Brihtnoth, and the Danes, under Olaf Triggvason and Guthmund. The Anglo-Saxons were completely defeated and Brithnoth slain.

Malegnano (Franco-Austrian War).

Fought June 8, 1859, between three French divisions, under Marshal Baraguay d'Hilliers, and the Austrians, in about equal force. After three hours' hard fighting, the Austrians were defeated and driven out of Malegnano, with heavy loss, including 1,000 prisoners. The French lost 850 killed and wounded.

Mahnate. *See* Varese.

Malo-Jaroslawetz (Moscow Campaign).

Fought October 24, 1812, between 24,000 Russians, under General Doctoroff, and a portion of Eugène Beauharnais' corps, 15,000 strong, under General Delzons. After a sanguinary engagement, in which Malo-Jaroslawetz was taken and retaken seven times, the action ended in a drawn battle, but the strategical success lay with the Russians, who obliged Napoleon to abandon the southerly line of retreat he had projected. The French lost 5,000, including General Delzons killed, the Russians about 6,000.

Malplaquet (War of the Spanish Succession).

Fought September 11, 1709, between the British and Imperialists, under Marlborough and Prince Eugene, and the French, under Marshal Villars. Villars offered battle with the object of relieving Mons, which the allies were besieging, but while they were waiting for reinforcement from Tournay, he was enabled to entrench himself strongly on the ground he had chosen. After desperate fighting, however, the French position was carried from end to end, and they were driven out with a loss of 17,000 killed and wounded. The allies lost, according to most accounts, about 8,000, though some contemporaries assert that their losses were even heavier than those of the French.

Malta (Ottoman Wars).

This place was besieged May 19, 1565, by 30,000 Turks, under Mustapha Pasha, aided by a fleet of 185 sail, under Piale, the Capitan Pasha. It was defended by the Knights of Malta, under their Grand-Master Lavalette, and though St. Elmo was taken, Valetta held out against numerous assaults until September 11, when Mustapha raised the siege. The garrison lost 5,000 men, the Turks 20,000.

Malta (Wars of the French Revolution).

The town of Valetta and the island of Malta were captured from the French September 5, 1800, by a combined British naval and military force, under Captain George Martin, R.N., and Major-General Pigott. Two line-of-battle-ships and three frigates were seized in the harbour.

Malvern Hill. *See* Seven Days' Battles).

Mandonia.

Fought B.C. 338, between the Italian Greeks, under Archidamus, King of Sparta, and the Lucanians. The Greeks were defeated, and Archidamus slain.

Mangalore (First Mysore War).

This place was besieged June 20, 1783, by Tippu Sahib with his whole army, and was defended by a small British garrison, under Colonel Campbell. On the conclusion of peace between France and England, the French officer assisting Tippu withdrew, and on August 2 an armistice was arranged, during which the garrison was to receive regular supplies. This article was evaded, and the defenders half starved, and after some delay Tippu renewed the siege. No attempt, however, was made to relieve the place, and after a gallant defence, Campbell surrendered January 26, 1763.

Manilla (American-Spanish War)

Fought May 1, 1898, between the American squadron of 6 ships, under Admiral Dewey, and 11 Spanish vessels, chiefly small, and unarmoured. The Spanish fleet was totally destroyed, the Americans suffering no loss.

Mansfield (American Civil War).

Fought April 8, 1864, between 20,000 Federals, under General Banks, and about 8,000 Confederates, under General Taylor. Banks, while marching through a difficult country, was attacked by Taylor, and utterly routed, at a cost to the assailants of less than a thousand men. Besides heavy losses in killed and wounded, the Federals lost 3,500 prisoners, 22 guns, and 220 waggons of stores and ammunition.

Mantineia (Peloponnesian War).

Fought B.C. 418, between 10,000 Spartans and Tegeans, under Agis, and an equal force of Athenians, under Laches and Nicostratus. The Spartan left was completely routed, but the Athenian centre and left failed to withstand the Spartan attack, and but for the defeat of Agis' left wing, would have been surrounded and captured. In the end the Spartans gained a signal victory. Larches and Nicostratus both fell in the action.

Mantineia (Bœotian War).

Fought B.C. 362, between the Bœotians, under Epaminondas, and the combined forces of Athens, Sparta, and Mantineia. Epaminondas attacked strongly with his left, holding back his right in reserve, and after the driving back of the Mantineians, routed the Spartans in the centre. The Athenians were hardly engaged, but the Bœotian victory was complete. In the pursuit Epaminondas, fell and the loss of the great leader so disheartened the Bœotians that they did not further press their victory.

Mantineia (Wars of the Achæan League).

Fought B.C. 208, between the Achæans, under Philopœmen, and the Spartans, under Machanidas. The Achæans drove the Spartans into a ravine in great disorder, and routed them with a loss of 4,000 killed, amongst whom was Machanidas.

Mantua (Napoleon's Italian Campaigns).

This city was invested by Napoleon June 4, 1796, and was defended by 14,000 Austrians, under General Canto d'Irles. The siege was vigorously prosecuted, but the approach of Wurmser with a large Austrian army forced Napoleon to concentrate his forces, and he raised the siege July 31, After a brief campaign, which resulted in the dispersal of Wurmser's army, that general, with the remnant of his forces, was shut up in the city, which was again closely invested September 19. Wurmser held out till his provisions were exhausted, when, on February 2, 1797, he surrendered, with 20,000 men, of whom only 10,000 were fit for service. It is computed that 27,000 perished during the siege.

Maogamalcha (Persian Wars).

This fortress, defended by a Persian garrison, and considered impregnable, was besieged by the Romans under the Emperor Julian in 363. A mine was carried from the trenches under the ramparts, and three cohorts broke through into the streets, whereupon the garrison deserted the ramparts and the besiegers entered. The place was sacked, and afterwards razed to the ground.

Marathon (Second Persian Invasion).

Fought September 490 B.C., between the Athenians and Platæans, 10,000 and 1,000 strong respectively, under Miltiades, and the army of Darius Hystaspes, about 100,000 in number, under Datis. Being greatly outnumbered, Miltiades altered the usual arrangement of the Greek line, so as to extend his wings across the whole width of the valley in which the battle was fought, and thus escape being outflanked. To effect this he was forced to weaken his centre, which was repulsed, but both his wings drove back the invaders, and then fell upon and routed the victorious Persian centre. The Persians fled in confusion to their ships, which they succeeded in launching, and escaped with a loss of 6,400. The Athenians lost 192 only.

Marcianopolis (Gothic Invasion of Thrace).

Fought 376, between the Romans, under Lupicinus, and the Goths, under Fritigern. The Romans were totally defeated, but stood their ground to the last, and were cut to pieces almost to a man. Lupicinus fled as soon as the ultimate success of the Goths became apparent.

Mardis (War of the Two Empires).

Fought 315, shortly after the battle of Cibalis, between Constantine, Emperor of the West, and Licinius, Emperor of the East. Constantine moved a body of 5,000 men round his opponent's flank, and attacked him simultaneously in front and rear. The Illyrian veterans formed a double front, and held their ground, though with heavy loss, till nightfall, when Licinius, having lost thousands of his best troops, drew off his army towards the mountains of Macedonia. The consequence of this defeat was the acquisition by Constantine of Pannonia, Dalmatia, Dacia, Macedonia and Greece.

Marengo (Napoleon's Italian Campaigns).

Fought June 14, 1800, between 30,000 French, under Napoleon, and 40,000 Austrians, under Melas. The Austrians attacked, and drove back in disorder the first line under Victor, and, following up their success, a serious defeat for Napoleon seemed inevitable, when the arrival of the reserve corps under Desaix turned the scale. Under cover of his attack, the broken divisions reformed, and the Austrians were finally repulsed at all points, and fled in disorder. Desaix was killed at the head of his troops.

Margus.

Fought May, 285, between the legions of the Emperor Carinus and those of Diocletian, who had been raised to the purple by his soldiers. The troops of Diocletian, wasted by the Persian War, were all but overpowered by the fresher legions of Carinus, but the defection during the battle of one of his generals turned the scale, and Carinus himself being killed by an officer whom he had wronged, Diocletian gained a complete victory.

Maria Zell (Campaign of the Danube).

Fought November 8, 1805, during the French advance on Vienna, between Davoust's corps, and the Austrian corps, under General von Meerfeld. The Austrians were defeated and driven off in disorder, leaving 4,000 prisoners in the hands of the French.

Mariendahl (Thirty Years' War).

Fought May 2, 1645, between the French, under Turenne, and the Imperialists, under Merci. Turenne, who had 3,000 infantry and 8 regiments of horse, was surprised in his camp by Merci at 2 a.m., and being placed between two fires, was compelled to beat a disastrous retreat, with the loss of almost all his infantry, 1,200 cavalry, and all his artillery and baggage.

Marignano (Italian Wars).

Fought September 13 and 14, 1575, between 50,000 French, under Francis I, and about 40,000 Swiss mercenaries. The Swiss attacked the French camp, and forcing the lines, fought till midnight without decisive result. On the morning of the 14th the battle was renewed, and the Swiss were on the point of success, when the arrival of a small force of Venetians obliged them to withdraw. The French lost 6,000 men, and the Swiss losses were very heavy, including 1,200 who perished in the flames of a village they were defending after the repulse of the attack. Marshal Trivulzio, who commanded a wing of the French army, called the action the "Battle of Giants."

Marosch, The (Conquest of Dacia).

Fought 101, between the Dacians, under Decebalus, and the Romans, under Trajan. The Dacians were utterly routed, and driven across the river with heavy loss.

Marseglia (Wars of Louis XIV).

Fought October 4, 1693, between the French, under Marshal de Catinat, and the Austrians, Spanish, and English, under the Duke of Savoy. The allies, who were inferior in numbers, were attacked by the French, and, after severe fighting, driven across the Po with a loss of about 6,000. The Duke of Schomberg and Lord Warwick were taken prisoners. The loss of the French was slightly less.

Mars-la-Tour (Franco-German War).

Fought August 18, 1870, between the French, under Marshal Bazaine, and the 3rd and

10th German Army corps, under Von Alvensleben. The Germans, though at times very hard pressed, succeeded in holding their ground, and prevented the French breaking through to the westward. The battle is chiefly remarkable for the desperate charges of the German cavalry, and especially of Von Bredow's brigade, against the French infantry, under cover of which the shattered German infantry was enabled to reform. The losses were about equal, amounting to about 16,000 killed and wounded on each side. The action is also known as the Battle of Vionville.

Marston Moor (Civil War).

Fought July 2, 1644, between 18,000 Royalists, under Prince Rupert, and 27,000 Parliamentarians, under Manchester, Leven and Fairfax. For the first time in the war, Rupert's cavalry was repulsed by Cromwell's Ironsides, and though the right wing under Fairfax was broken, the left and centre were victorious, and the Royalists were totally defeated, with a loss of 4,000. This victory gave the Parliament complete control of the north.

Martinesti (Ottoman Wars).

Fought September 23, 1789, between the Austrians and Russians, 27,000 strong, under the Prince of Coburg and Suwaroff, and the Turks, 80,000 strong, under Osman Pasha. The allies stormed the Turkish entrenchments, and drove out the defenders, of whom 7,000 were killed and wounded, while 8,000 were drowned in crossing the Rymna. The victors lost 617 killed and wounded.

Martinique (Wars of the French Revolution).

This island was captured from the French in 1794, by a combined naval and military force under Sir John Jervis and Sir George Grey, with a loss to the victors of 6 officers and 37 men killed and wounded.

Martinique (Napoleonic Wars).

Having been restored to France at the Peace of Amiens, Martinique was again taken by the British, February 24, 1809, the force engaged being under Admiral Sir A. J. Cochrane, and Lieut.-General Beckwith.

Maserfield.

Fought 642, between the Northumbrians, under Oswald, and the Mercians, under Penda. The latter were defeated, and Penda slain.

Masulipatam (Seven Years' War).

This fortress, held by a French garrison, under Conflans, was besieged by the British, about 2,500 strong, under Colonel Forde, in March, 1759. After a fortnight's bombardment the place was taken by storm, the resistance being very feeble, and Conflans surrendered with his whole force, which considerably outnumbered the assailants. One hundred and twenty guns were taken in the fortress.

Matchevitz (First Polish Insurrection).

Fought October 10, 1794, between the Russians, under Baron de Fersen, and the Poles, under Kosciusko. The Poles, after hard fighting, were totally defeated, leaving 6,000 dead upon the field, while Kosciusko was severely wounded.

Matchin (Ottoman Wars).

Fought July 10, 1791, between the Turks, under Yussuf Pasha, and the Russians, under Prince Repnin. The left and centre of the Turkish army held its ground manfully, and the victory was long in doubt, but a brilliant charge of the Russian left, under General Kutusoff, drove back the Turks who were defeated with heavy loss.

Maxen (Seven Years' War).

Fought November 21, 1759, between the Austrians, under Marshal Daun, and the Prussians, under General Finck. Daun surrounded Finck's position, and after comparatively little fighting compelled him to surrender with over 15,000 men, including 17 generals. Seventeen guns were captured. The casualties on both sides were very small.

Maya (Peninsula War).

Fought July 25, 1813, between a British division, under General Stewart, and the French divisions of d'Armagnac, Abbé and Maransin. The French, at a cost of 1,500 men, forced the pass of Maya, driving back the British with a loss of 1,400 men and 4 guns.

Maypo (South American War of Independence).

Fought April 5, 1818, between the Chilian Patriots, 9,000 strong, under San Martin, and 6,000 Spanish Royalists, under General Osorio. The Spaniards were totally defeated with a loss of 1,000 killed and 2,350 prisoners, the Chilians losing over 1,000 killed and wounded. The result of the battle was the establishment of the independence of Chili.

Medellin (Peninsular War).

Fought March 28, 1809, between the French, under Marshal Victor, and 30,000 Spaniards, under Cuesta. The Spaniards soon gave way, and were mercilessly sabred in the pursuit by the French cavalry, losing, it is said, 18,000 killed and wounded. The French lost 300 only.

Medina (Mohammed's War with the Koreish).

Siege was laid to this town in 625 by 10,000 Koreish, under Abu Sophian. It was defended by Mohammed with 3,000 Moslems, and during the space of 20 days several half-hearted assaults were easily repulsed. At the end of this time Abu Sophian withdrew, and the Koreish made no further attempt to interfere with the progress of Mohammedanism.

Medola (Napoleon's Italian Campaigns).

Fought August 5, 1796, between the French, 23,000 strong, under Napoleon, and 25,000 Austrians, under Wurmser. The Austrians were totally defeated, and driven back to Roveredo, with a loss of 2,000 killed and wounded, 1,000 prisoners and 20 guns. Prior to this defeat Wurmser had succeeded in revictualling Mantua, but at very heavy cost, the Austrian losses during the three days' fighting, from the 3rd to the 5th, amounting to 20,000 men and 60 guns.

Meeanee (Scinde Campaign).

Fought February 17, 1843, between 2,800 British and native troops, under Sir Charles Napier, and about 20,000 Beluchis, under the Amirs of Scinde. The infantry were at one time almost overpowered by the overwhelming numbers of the enemy, who attacked with great bravery, but they were rescued by a charge of the 9th Bengal cavalry, who broke up the assailants, and in the end the Beluchis were routed with a loss of 5,000 men and several guns. The British lost 256 killed and wounded.

Meerut (First Mongol Invasion of India).

This place was besieged in 1398 by the Tartars, under Tamerlane. It was considered impregnable, and Tamerlane commenced mining operations, but these methods were too slow for his followers, who by means of scaling ladders carried the fortress by storm, and massacred all the inhabitants. Tamerlane afterwards completed his mines and destroyed all the defences.

Megaletaphrus (First Messenian War).

Fought 740 B.C., between the Messenians, under Aristomenes, and the Spartans. The Messenians were surrounded and cut to pieces, Aristomenes escaping with a few followers.

Megalopolis.

Fought B.C. 331, in the attempt of the Spartans, aided by the Arcadians, Achæans and Eleians, to shake off the Macedonian yoke, during Alexander's absence in Asia The allies, under Agis, King of Sparta, were besieging Megalopolis, which had declined to join the league, when they were attacked by the Macedonians, under Antipater, and completely routed, Agis falling in the battle.

Megalopolis (Wars of the Achæan League).

Fought B.C. 226, between the Spartans, under Cleomenes, and the forces of the Achæan League, under Aratus. The Achæans early gained an advantage, and the Spartans fled, pursued by the light troops. These, however, being unsupported, the Spartans turned and routed them, and then overwhelmed the Achæan hoplites in their turn with enormous slaughter.

Melanthias (Sclavonian Invasion).

Fought 559, between the Imperial troops, under Belisarius, and the Sclavonians and Bulgarians, under Zabergan, Prince of Bulgaria. The barbarians assailed the Roman lines, but were easily repulsed, and so precipitate was their flight that only about 500 fell. This was Belisarius' last victory, and it was closely followed by his disgrace and death.

Meldorp.

Fought 1500, between the Danes, 30,000 strong, under John of Denmark, and the inhabitants of the province of Dithmarsh, which John designed to bring again under Danish rule, after two centuries of virtual independence. The advancing Danes delivered an assault against a small fortified outpost, but were repulsed, and driven in confusion into the surrounding marshes, where over 11,000 perished.

Melitene (Persian Wars).

Fought 578, between the Imperial troops, under Tiberius, and the Persians, under Chosroes. After a somewhat indecisive battle, at the end of which each side had held its ground, Chosroes, owing to his heavy losses, found it necessary to retire during the night. The battle was, however, signalised by an exploit of a Scythian chief, in command of the Roman left wing, who at the head of his cavalry charged through the Persian ranks, plundered the royal tent, and then cut his way out through the opposing hosts.

Memphis (Athenian Expedition to Egypt).

This city was captured B.C. 459 by an Athenian fleet of 200 ships, which sailed up the Nile to the assistance of Inaros, who had raised the standard of revolt against Persia. The citadel, however, held out until B.C. 456, when a Persian army, under Megabyzus defeated the Athenians and drove them out of Memphis.

Memphis (Moslem Conquest of Egypt).

In 638, Amron, lieutenant of the Caliph Omar, with 8,000 Moslems, invested the city, and after a siege of seven months, in the course of which the besiegers were nearly overwhelmed by the rising of the Nile, the place was taken by assault. On the site of the Moslem encampment were laid the foundations of Old Cairo.

Memphis (American Civil War).

A river action fought June 6, 1862, between 8 Confederate armed vessels, under Commodore Montgomery, and 10 Federal gunboats, under Commodore Davis. Only one of the Confederate vessels escaped destruction, and Memphis fell.

Mensourah (Fifth Crusade).

Fought 1249, between the French, under Louis IX, and the Moslems. The town of Mensourah was seized by the Comte d'Artois, but being surrounded, he and the knights with him were killed. The king meanwhile had seized the Saracen camp, but was unable to hold his ground, and was driven back to Damietta. In the course of his retreat, however, he was surrounded and taken prisoner by the Saracens, with his whole army.

Mentana (Garibaldian Rising).

Fought November 3, 1867, between 10,000 Garibaldians, under Garibaldi, and the French and Papal troops, 5,000 strong, under General Kanzler. Garibaldi was totally defeated, a result largely due to the brilliant work of 1,500 Papal Zouaves, who drove them out of position after position. The Garibaldians lost 1,100 killed and wounded, and 1,000 prisoners. The allies' losses were only 182 killed and wounded, of which the Papal troops lost 144.

Merida (Moorish Empire in Spain).

This place was besieged in 712 by 18,000 Moors, under Musa.

After a defeat in the open plain before the city, the Spaniards made a long and obstinate defence, which cost the besiegers many lives, but in the end they were forced by famine to surrender.

Merseburg.

Fought 934 between the Germans, under Henry the Fowler, and the Hungarian invaders. The Hungarians were completely defeated, with heavy loss, and withdrew from Germany, which they did not again invade for twenty years.

Merta (Mogul Invasion of the Deccan).

This strong fortress, belonging to the Rajput Rajah of Malwar, was besieged, 1561, by Sharf-ud-Din Hussein, one of the generals of Akbar, the Great Mogul. The place held out gallantly for several months, but was then forced by famine to capitulate. One of the Malwar chiefs, however, refused all terms, and cut his way out at the head of 500 men, of whom 250 fell in the enterprise.

Merton (Danish Invasion).

Fought 871, between the West Saxons, under Alfred, and the Danish invaders. After a severe engagement the Danes were victorious.

Messina.

Fought October 2, 1284, between the Sicilian and Catalan fleet, under the Grand Admiral, Roger de Lauria, and the French fleet, under Charles of Anjou. The Sicilians, who largely outnumbered the French, totally defeated them, burning or destroying practically the whole of their fleet. Charles of Anjou was captured, and henceforth made no further attempt to reestablish his authority in Sicily.

Messina. *See* Cape Passaro.

Metauras (Second Punic War).

Fought 207 B.C., between 50,000 Romans, under Claudius Nero and Marcus Livius, and the Carthaginians, in rather smaller force, under Hasdrubal. The Carthaginians were surprised at early dawn as they were endeavouring to find a ford in the Metaurus, and being vigorously attacked, were totally routed, Hasdrubal being slain. The completeness of the victory was due to Nero, who being in command of the right wing, where the ground prevented his getting to close quarters, and seeing the Roman left hard pressed by Hasdrubal's best troops, led the major part of his force round the Roman rear, and fell upon Hasdrubal's right, routing him utterly.

Methuen (Scottish Wars).

Fought June 19, 1306, when a small Scottish force, under Robert Bruce, was attacked and defeated by the English in superior force.

Metz (Franco-German War).

This fortress was invested by the Germans after the defeat of Bazaine at Gravelotte in August 18, 1870, and after several fruitless attempts to break through the German lines had been repulsed, Bazaine surrendered to Prince Frederick Charles on October 26, with 3 marshals, 6,000 officers, and 173,000 men.

The Germans took 56 eagles, 622 field guns, 72 mitrailleuses, 876 pieces of fortress artillery, and about 300,000 rifles.

Mexico (Conquest of Mexico).

Fought June 20, 1520, when the Spaniards, under Cortez, who were evacuating Mexico during the night, were attacked by the Aztecs, and suffered heavy loss. The Spaniards called this event the " Noche Triste."

Michelberg (Campaign of the Danube).

Fought October 16, 1805. Ney's corps stormed the heights of the Michelberg at the same time that Lannes carried the Frauenberg, driving the Austrians back into Ulm, where on the 17th General Mack capitulated with 30,000 men.

Middelburg (Netherlands War of Independence).

This fortress, the last stronghold in Walcheren to hold out for the Spanish king, was besieged by the Patriots in the winter of 1593. It was defended by a garrison under Colonel Mondragon, who in spite of a gallant resistance and numerous attempts to relieve him, was forced by famine to surrender, February 18, 1594.

Milazzo (Unification of Italy).

Fought July 18, 1860, between the Italian Volunteers, under Garibaldi, and the Neapolitans, under General Bosco. The Neapolitans occupied a strongly entrenched position, which Garibaldi succeeded in turning, the Neapolitans, after a severe struggle, being totally defeated and driven out.

Miletopolis (First Mithridatic War).

Fought B.C. 86, between the Romans, under Flavius Fimbria, and the Pontic troops, under Mithridates. The Romans gained a complete victory.

Millesimo (Napoleon's Italian Campaigns).

Fought April 13, 1796, when the divisions of Augereau, Masséna and La Harpe attacked the Austrians, strongly entrenched, under General Colli, and after severe fighting, drove them back, thus cutting Colli's communications with General Beaulieu, the Austrian Commander-in-Chief. The Austro-Sardinians lost about 6,000 men and 30 guns, and all effective co-operation between the two wings was at an end. Also called the Battle of Monte Lezino

Mill Springs (American Civil War).

Fought January 19, 1862, between the Federals, about 9,000 strong, under General Thomas, and 8,000 Confederates, under General Crittenden. The Confederates attacked, and at first drove back the Federals, who began the action with 5,000 men only, but reinforcements arriving, Thomas repulsed the assailants with considerable loss, capturing 12 guns. The Federals lost 246 only. This was the first considerable defeat suffered by the Confederates in the war.

Minden (Seven Years' War).

Fought August 1, 1759, between the French, 64,000 strong, under the Marquis de Contades, and the Hanoverians, British and Prussians, 54,000 strong, under Ferdinand of Brunswick. Ferdinand detached a force of 10,000 men to threaten de Contades' rear, and then, attacking strongly, broke the first line of the French. But for the failure of the allies' cavalry to advance, the French would have been routed. As it was, they were able to rally, and effect an orderly retreat, though with a loss of 7,086 killed, wounded and prisoners, 43 guns and 17 standards. The allies lost 2,762, fully a half of this number being in the ranks of the six English regiments present, who bore the brunt of the battle.

Minorca (Seven Years' War).

This place, garrisoned by 2,800 British troops, under General Blakeney, was invested by the French, under the Duc de Richelieu, May, 1756. On May 20, a British squadron of 15 line-of-battle-ships and 3 sloops, under Admiral Byng, attacked Richelieu's blockading squadron of 12 sail of the line and 5 frigates, with the object of throwing succours into the place. The attack, however, was conducted with so little resolution and resource, that Byng failed in his object, and allowed the French ships to escape him. Blakeney was shortly afterwards forced to surrender, and Byng was tried by court-martial, condemned and shot.

Minorca.

Having been restored to England by the Treaty of Paris in 1762, Minorca was again recaptured in 1781, by a force of 12,000 French and Spaniards, the garrison, under General Murray, being only 700 strong. Murray made a sturdy defence but was forced to surrender.

Miohosaki.

Fought September, 764, between the Japanese rebels, under Oshikatsa, and the Imperial troops, under Saiki-no-Sanya. The rebels were totally routed, and Oshikatsa and his son slain.

Miraflores (Peruvio-Chilian War).

Fought January 15, 1881, between the Chilians, under General Baquedano, and the Peruvians, under General Caceres. The Pervuians were totally defeated, losing 3,000 killed and wounded, while the victors lost 500 killed and 1,625 wounded. Following up their victory, the Chilians occupied Lima on the 17th, and the war came to an end.

Missionary Ridge. *See* Chattanooga.

Missolonghi (Greek War of Independence).

This place was besieged in 1821 by a force of 11,000 Turks, under Omar Brionis Pasha, and was defended by a small Greek garrison, under Mavrocordatos. The little garrison made so gallant a defence, that at the end of two months Omar was forced to raise the siege. On April 27, 1825, the town was again besieged by the Turks and was again most obstinately defended by the garrison and inhabitants. So little progress was made that it was found necessary to call for the aid of the Egyptian army, under Ibrahim, son of Mehemet Ali. It was not, however, till three months after his arrival before the place that it was finally taken by storm, April 22, 1826, having held out for all but a year.

Mita Caban.

Fought 1362, between the Tartars, under Tamerlane, and the Getes, under the Khan Elias. The Getes were routed with heavy loss.

Miyako.

Fought June, 1353, between the revolted Moronoshi, and the troops of the Emperor of the South, Gomurakami, under Yoshinori. Moronoshi gained a complete victory, and Yoshinori and the Emperor fled into the Eastern provinces.

Miyako.

Fought December 30, 1391, between the troops of the provinces of Idzumo and Idzumi, under Mitsuyaki, and those of the Emperor of the South, Gokameyama. A series of engagements took place in and around Miyako, and in the end Mitsuyaki was driven off with heavy loss, among the killed being the Daimio of Idzumi.

Modder River (Second Boer War).

Fought November 28, 1899, between a Boer force, about 9,000 strong, under General Cronje, and the British, under Lord Methuen. Cronje held a strong position on both banks of the river, which was not accurately known to Lord Methuen, who was marching to the Modder. His columns came under fire about 7 a.m., and the action lasted till evening, when a turning movement enabled him to drive Cronje from his entrenchments. The British losses were 24 officers and 461 men killed and wounded, those of the Boers being about the same.

Mohacz (Ottoman Wars).

Fought August 29, 1526, between 30,000 Hungarians, under King Lewis, and Tomore, Bishop of Kolocz, and over 100,000 Turks, with 300 guns, under Solyman the Magnificent. The Hungarians made a heroic resistance against overwhelming numbers, but were finally routed, leaving 22,000 dead on the field, including the king, 7 bishops, 28 magnates, and over 500 nobles. This disaster placed Hungary at the mercy of Solyman, and was quickly followed by the fall of Buda-Pesth.

Mohacz (Ottoman Wars).

On the battlefield where 160 years previously Solyman had gained so decisive a victory, the Austrians and Hungarians signally defeated the Turks, under Mohammed IV, in 1687. In consequence of this disaster, following upon a long series of reverses, Mohammed was deposed by the discontented solidery.

Mohilev (Moscow Campaign).

Fought July 23, 1812, between 28,000 French, under Davoust, and 60,000 Russians, under Prince Bagration. Bagration attacked Davoust in a strong position, which counterbalanced the great disparity of numbers, and the Russians were repulsed with a loss of about 4,000. The French lost barely 1,000.

M

Mohrungen (Campaign of Friedland).

Fought January 25, 1807, between 10,000 French, under Bernadotte, and 14,000 Russians, under General Marhof. The French were defeated with a loss of about 1,000 killed and wounded.

Molino del Rey (Peninsular War).

Fought December 21, 1808, between 26,000 French, under General St. Cyr, and the Spaniards, about equal in strength, under Reding. The Spaniards were routed with a loss of 10,000 killed, wounded and prisoners, and 50 guns, at very slight cost to the victors.

Molwitz (War of the Austrian Succession).

Fought April 8, 1741, between the Prussians, 30,000 strong, under Frederick the Great, and the Austrians, under Marshal Neuperg. Frederick surprised the Austrian general, and, after severe fighting, drove him from his entrenchments, with a loss of about 5,000 killed, wounded and prisoners. The Prussians lost 2,500.

Monarda (Moorish Insurrection).

Fought March 18, 1501, between the Spaniards, under the Count di Cifuentes and Alonso de Aguilar, and the insurgent Moors. The Spaniards were largely outnumbered, and were overpowered by the rebels, suffering a disastrous defeat. De Aguilar was killed, fighting to the end.

Monongahela (Seven Years' War).

Fought July 9, 1755, between 900 French and Indians, under Contrecœur, and about 1,400 British and Virginians, under Braddock. The English were attacked shortly after crossing the river, and though the officers and the Virginians fought gallantly, the troops, ignorant of Indian warfare, gave way to panic, and after three hours' fighting, were driven across the Monongahela, with a loss of 877 killed and wounded. Of 86 officers, 63 fell, including Braddock, who was mortally wounded. The French lost 16 only ; their Indian allies somewhat more heavily.

Mons-en-Puelle (Flemish War).

Fought 1304, between the French, under Philip IV, and the Flemings. The Flemings were unable to withstand the charge of the French cavalry, and broke and fled, leaving 6,000 dead on the field.

Montcontour (Third Civil War).

Fought October 3, 1569, between the Huguenots, under Henri le Béarnais, and the Catholics, under the Duc d'Anjou and Marshal de Tavannes. The Huguenots occupied an untenable position, and at the end of half an hour were utterly routed, and almost exterminated, some 700 only remaining with the colours after the battle.

Monte Aperto (Guelfs and Ghibellines).

Fought September 4, 1260, between the Florentine Guelfs, and the Ghibellines, who had been driven from the city, under Manfred of Sicily. The Guelfs were totally routed, and the victors took possession of Florence, and re-established their rule.

Montebello (Napoleon's Italian Campaigns).

Fought June 9, 1800, between the French, under Napoleon, and the Austrians, under General Ott. Napoleon, being ignoran of the fall of Genoa, was marching to the relief of that city, when his advanced guard, under Lannes, was attacked by Ott, who was endeavouring to effect a junction with Melas. Lannes held his ground until reinforcements arrived, when he assumed the offensive, and drove the Austrians from the field with heavy loss, capturing 5,000 prisoners.

Montebello (Franco - Austrian War).

Fought May 20, 1859, between the Austrians, under General Stadion, and about 7,000 French, under General Forey. The Austrians were defeated and driven back to Stradella, with a loss of 2,000 killed and wounded, and 200 prisoners.

Monte Caseros (Urquiza's Rising).

Fought February 3, 1852, between the Argentine Government troops, under President Rosas, the leader of the Gaucho party, 25,000 strong, and 20,000 insurgents, under Urquiza. Rosas was totally defeated, and compelled to fly to England, thus ending the long domination of the Gauchos in the Argentine Republic.

Monte Lezino. *See* Millesimo.

Montenotte (Napoleon's Italian Campagns).

Fought April 10 and 11, 1796,

when d'Argentian, with the central division of the Austro-Sardinian army, attacked the French position at Montenotte, held by Cervoni's division. Cervoni was driven back, but the key to the position was held throughout the day by Tampon, with 1,500 men, and on the 12th d'Argentian found himself outflanked by Augereau and Masséna, and was compelled to fall back, with a loss of 1,000 killed, 2,000 prisoners, and some guns. This was Napoleon's first victory.

Montereau (Allied Campaign in France).

Fought February 18, 1814, between the rearguard of the French army, under Napoleon, and the Würtembergers, under Prince Eugène of Würtemberg. Eugène attacked Napoleon's position, but was repulsed with a loss of about 2,000 killed and wounded and 4,000 prisoners.

Monterey (Americo - Mexican War).

This town in southern California was captured from the Mexicans, September 23, 1846, by the Americans, under General Taylor, and this success was followed by the occupation of the whole of Northern Mexico by the American army.

Montevideo (Napoleonic Wars).

This city was taken by assault February 3, 1807, by 3,000 British troops, under Sir Samuel Auchmuty. The capture was preceded by an action outside the town, in which the Rifle corps, now the Rifle Brigade, especially distinguished itself. The British losses amounted to about 600.

Montevideo (Uruguayan War of Independence).

This city was besieged February 16, 1843, by the Argentine troops, under Oribe, and was defended by the Uruguayans, and a number of foreign residents, amongst others Garibaldi, under General Paz. In the course of the siege, Garibaldi, at the head of 160 Italians, made a sortie, in which he held his own for a whole day against 12,000 Argentines, and eventually effected a retreat in good order. The intervention of France and England eventually forced Oribe to raise the siege, November, 1845.

Montevideo (Uruguayan War of Independence).

Fought October 8, 1851, between the combined forces of Uruguay, Brazil and Paraguay, under Urquiza, and the Argentines, under Oribe. The Argentines were besieging Montevideo, and Oribe was hemmed in in his lines by the allies, and forced to capitualte.

Montevideo.

Fought August, 1863, between the Colorados, or Liberal party, of Uruguay, under General Venancio Flores, and the, Blancos, under General Medina. The Blancos were victorious.

Montfaucon (Norman Invasion of France).

Fought 887, between the French, under Eudes, and the Norman invaders. The latter were totally defeated, losing 19,000 men in the battle, and were forced to retire from before the walls of Paris, which they were besieging.

Montiel.

Fought 1369, between the French, under Bertrand du Guesclin, and the Spaniards, under Pedro II of Castile. Pedro was routed and taken prisoner, and Henry of Trastamare placed on the throne of Castile.

Montlhéry (War of the Public Good).

Fought 1465, between the forces of the Ligue du Bien Public, under the Comte de Charolais, and the Royal troops, under Louis XI. Louis was totally defeated, after a sanguinary engagement, and driven from the field.

Montmirail. See Champ Aubert.

Montmorenci (Seven Years' War).

Fought July 31, 1759, during the siege of Quebec, when Wolfe, with 5,000 men, attacked the entrenched camp of the French, which was defended by 12,000 men under Montcalm. As the British were landing, 13 companies of grenadiers advanced to the attack without waiting for the main body. They were repulsed with heavy loss, which so weakened Wolfe that he decided not to press the attack further. The British loss amounted to 443, almost the whole of which fell upon the grenadiers. The French losses were very small.

Montreal (Seven Years' War).

This city was surrendered to the British, under General Amherst, by Vaudreuil, Governor-General of Canada, September 8, 1760. One of the conditions of the surrender was that the whole of the French army in Canada and its dependencies must lay down their arms. Canada thus became a part of the British dominions.

Mont Valérien. See Buzenval.

Moodkee (First Sikh War).

Fought December 18, 1845, between the British, 12,000 strong, with 42 guns, under Sir Hugh Gough, and the Sikhs, 30,000 strong, with 40 guns, under Taj Singh. Gough, at the end of a long march, was surprised by the Sikhs, and his force thrown into some confusion, but he succeeded in rallying them, and finally drove the Sikhs from the field, capturing 17 guns. The British loss was 872 killed and wounded, among the former being Generals M'Caskill and Sir Robert Sale.

Mook (Netherlands War of Independence).

Fought April 14, 1574, between the Dutch Patriots, 8,000 strong, under Count Louis of Nassau, and 5,000 Spaniards, under Don Sancho d'Avila. The village of Mook was held by the Dutch infantry, who were driven out by the Spaniards, and totally routed, with a loss of at least 4,000. Among the slain were the Counts Louis and Henry of Nassau.

Morat (Burgundian Wars).

Fought June 22, 1746, between the Burgundians, 35,000 strong, under Charles the Bold, and 24,000 Swiss, under Hans Waldmann. After a few hours' hard fighting the Burgundians were driven into the plain, where the Swiss utterly routed them, no less than 8,000 falling. The Swiss chroniclers aver that the victors only lost 500 killed.

Morawa (Ottoman Wars).

Fought November 3, 1443, between the Hungarians, under John Hunniades, with 12,000 horse and 20,000 foot, and a greatly superior Turkish army, under Amurath II. The Turks were defeated, with a loss of 2,000 killed and 4,000 prisoners. This battle is also called the Battle of Nissa.

Morazzone (Italian Rising).

Fought 1848 between 1,500 Garibaldian volunteers, under Garibaldi, and 5,000 Austrians, under General d'Aspre. After a resistance lasting eleven hours, Garibaldi, hopelessly out-numbered, withrdew his force from the town, and executed a masterly retreat to Arona.

Morella (First Carlist War).

This fortress, the last stronghold of the Carlists, was besieged by Espartero, with 20,000 Cristinos, May 23, 1840. It was defended by a garrison of 4,000 veterans, under Cabrera, who on the 30th attempted to break through the besiegers' lines. His plan, however, had been betrayed, and he was met and driven back, whereupon the place surrendered. Cabrera, however, with a portion of the garrison, made a second and this time a successful attempt to cut his way out.

Morgarten (First Swiss-Austrian War).

Fought November 16, 1315. The men of Schwyz, 1,400 in number, took post in the Pass of Morgarten, and lay in wait for the Archduke Leopold, who, with 15,000 Austrians, was marching into Schwyz. Having disordered the Austrian ranks by rolling down boulders upon them, the Swiss then fell upon them with their halberds, and totally routed them, with a loss of 1,500 killed.

Morshedabad.

Fought July 24, 1763, between the troops of Mir Cossim, the deposed Nawab of Bengal, and a British force of 750 Europeans and a large body of native troops, under Major Adams. The British stormed Cossim's entrenchments, driving out his army in confusion, and followed up their victory by the occupation of Morshedabad, without further opposition.

Mortara (Italian Rising).

Fought March 21, 1849, between the Piedmontese, under the Duke of Savoy (Victor Emmanuel) and General Darando, and the main Austrian army, under Radetsky. No steps had been taken by the Piedmontese to render Mortara defensible, and little guard was kept, with the result that they were surprised by Radetsky, and driven out of the town in confusion, with a loss of 500 killed and wounded, 2,000 prisoners and 5 guns. The Austrians lost 300 only.

Mortimer's Cross (Wars of the Roses).

Fought February 2, 1461, when Edward, Duke of York, defeated the Lancastrians, under the Earls of Pembroke and Wiltshire, and drove them back into Wales, thus preventing a concentration of the Lancastrian forces.

Mortlack (Danish Invasion of Scotland).

Fought 1010, between the Danes, under Sweyn, and the Scots, under Malcolm II. After a long and obstinate engagement the Danes were totally defeated, and forced to flee to their ships. A victory for them on this occasion would probably have given them a permanent lodgment in Scotland, as Malcolm had his last available man in the field.

Mortmant (Allied Invasion of France).

Fought February 17, 1814, between the Russian advanceguard, under the Count de Pahlen, and the French rearguard, under Victor. The Russians were repulsed with a loss of 3,000 killed and wounded, and 11 guns.

Möskirch (Wars of the French Revolution).

Fought May 5, 1800, between 50,000 French, under Moreau, and 60,000 Austrians, under de Kray. The French advanceguard, under Lecourbe, approaching Möskirch found the heights strongly held by the Austrians, and attempted to carry them, but without success. The arrival of the main body, however, turned the scale, and the Austrians were obliged to abandon all their positions, with a loss of about 5,000 men. The French lost about 3,500.

Moskowa. *See* Borodino.

Motya.

This city, the chief stronghold of the Carthaginians in Sicily, was besieged by Dionysius of

Syracuse, with 83,000 men, B.C. 398. Having built a mole to connect the mainland and the island on which Motya stood, he erected thereon his new engines of war, the catapults, used for the first time in this siege. He also built large moving towers to enable him to cope with the lofty defences of the place, and by these devices succeeded in effecting an entrance. Every house, however, was in itself a small fortress, and after days of street fighting, which cost the assailants a heavy price, the city was still unsubdued. At last by a night surprise he mastered the quarter which still held out, and the inhabitants were massacred or sold as slaves.

Mount Gaurus (First Samnite War).

Fought B.C. 342, between the Romans, under Valerius Corvus, and the Samnites. The Romans won a signal victory.

Mount Lactarius (Second Gothic War).

Fought March 553, between the troops of the Emperor Justinian, under Narses, and the Goths, under Teias. the last Gothic king of Italy. The Romans gained a signal victory, and Teias was slain, the Goths thereupon accepting the rule of Justinian.

Mount Panium.

Fought B.C. 198, between the Syrians, under Antiochus the Great, and the Greeks and Egyptians, under Scopas. Scopas was routed, and Antiochus took possession of all the territory held by Egypt in Asia, up to the frontier of Egypt proper.

Mount Seleucus (Revolt of Magnentius).

Fought August 10, 353, between the rebels, under Magnentius, and the Imperial legions, under Constantius. Constantius forced the passage of the Cottian Alps, and defeated Magnentius in a sanguinary battle, which dispersed his army and finally broke his power, Gaul and Italy being thus again brought under the Imperial sway.

Mount Tabor (French Invasion of Egypt).

Fought April 15, 1799, when Napoleon defeated and dispersed the Syrian army raised to create a diversion in favour of the beleaguered garrison of Acre. Kleber's division bore the brunt of the fighting.

Mount Taurus (Moslem Invasion of Asia Minor).

Fought 804, between the Moslems, under Harroun-al-Raschid, and the Greeks, under the Emperor Nicephorus I. The Greeks were totally defeated, with a loss of 40,000 men, and Nicephorus, wounded in three places, with difficulty escaped from the field.

Mount Tifata (Civil War of Marius and Sulla).

Fought B.C. 83, when the legions of Sulla defeated the army of the Consul, Norbanus, with heavy loss, and drove them to take refuge in Capua.

Mouscron (Wars of the French Revolution).

Fought 1794, between the French, under Moreau and Souham, and the Austrians, under General Clarifait. The French were victorious.

Mühlberg (Wars of Charles V).

Fought April 24, 1547, between the German Protestants, 9,000 strong, under the Elector Frederick of Saxony and the Landgrave of Hesse, and the Imperial army, together with 3,500 Papal troops, 13,000 in all, under Charles V. The Protestants were totally defeated, and their two leaders taken prisoners. The Imperialists lost 50 only.

Mühldorf.

Fought 1322, between the Imperial troops, under the Emperor Louis the Bavarian, and the German malcontents, under Frederick, Duke of Austria. Louis won a signal victory, and put an end to the resistance to his rule.

Mühlhausen (Gallic War).

Fought B.C. 58, between the Romans, 36,000 strong, under Julius Cæsar, and the Sequani, under Ariovistus. The Romans occupied two camps, one of which was held successfully by two legions against a determined attack of the Gauls. The attack having been repulsed, Cæsar united his forces, and led them against the Sequani, whom he totally routed with enormous loss.

Mukwanpur (Gurkha War).

Fought February 27, 1816, when a village, forming part of Sir David Ochterlony's position, was attacked by 2,000 Gurkhas. The village was defended by three companies of Sepoys and 40 men of the 87th Regiment, and the defenders were hard pressed, but the arrival of reinforcements enabled them after severe fighting to beat off the assailants with very heavy loss.

Multan (Second Sikh War).

This fortress, defended by the Sikhs, under Mulraj, was besieged by Lieutenant Edwardes with about 1,200 men in July, 1848. After an ineffectual bombardment, the siege was raised September 22, but was renewed December 27 by General Whish, with 17,000 men and 64 guns. After a heavy bombardment the place was stormed January 2, 1849, and on the 22nd of the same month Mulraj surrendered the citadel. The British loss during the siege was 210 killed and 910 wounded.

Münchengrätz (Seven Weeks' War).

Fought June 28, 1866, between the advance-guard of Prince Frederick Charles' army, and the Austrians, under Count Clam-Gallas. The Austrians were defeated with a loss of about 300 killed and wounded, and 1,000 prisoners. The Prussian losses were very small.

Munda (Civil War of Cæsar and Pompey).

Fought March 17, B.C. 45, between the Pompeians, under Cnæus Pompeius, and the Cæsareans, under Julius Cæsar. The Pompeians were totally defeated, losing 30,000 men, including Labienus and Varro, while the Cæsareans lost 1,000 only. Cnæus Pompey was wounded. This defeat put an end to the resistance of the Pompeian faction in Spain, and the action is further notable as being Cæsar's last battle.

Muret (Albigensian Crusade).

Fought 1213, between the Catholics, under Simon de Montfort, and the Albigenses, under the Count of Thoulouse, aided by Pedro II of Aragon. The Albigenses were routed, and this defeat put an end to their organized resistance. Pedro fell in the battle.

Murfreesboro (American Civil War).

Fought December 31, 1862, between 35,000 Confederates, under General Bragg, and 40,000 Federals, under General Rosecrans. Bragg attacked and drove back the Federal right, but the centre and left held their ground, and prevented the defeat degenerating into a rout. Both sides lost heavily, but the Confederates captured a large number of prisoners and over 20 guns. On the following day the Federal right retook the ground it had lost on the 31st, and at the end of the day both armies occupied their original positions. Early on January 2, however, Bragg retired in good order. Each side lost about 8,000, killed, wounded and missing, in the two days' fighting.

Mursa (Revolt of Magnentius).

Fought September 28, 351, between the usurper Magnentius, with 100,000 troops, and the Emperor Constantius, with 80,000. The battle was severely contested, but finally the legions of Magnentius were driven from the field with a loss of 24,000 ; that of the victors amounting to 30,000.

Musa Bagh (Indian Mutiny).

Fought March 19, 1858, when a British force, under Sir James Outram, totally routed a body of mutineers, 7,000 strong, under Huzrat Mahul, Begum of Oude, which was holding the Musa Bagh, a fortified palace in the outskirts of Lucknow.

Muta (Moslem Invasion of Syria).

Fought 629, between the Moslems, under Zaid, and the troops of the Emperor Heraclius. Zaid was slain, and so successively were Jaafar and Abdallah, who followed him in the command, but the banner of the prophet was then raised by Khaled, who succeeded in repulsing the onslaught of the Imperial troops, and on the following day led the Moslems undefeated from the field. This is the first battle between the Mohammedan Arabs and a foreign enemy.

Muthal, The (Jugurthine War).

Fought B.C. 108, between the Numidians, under Jugurtha, and the Romans, under Metellus Numidicus. The Numidians were strongly posted on the heights above the river, but were driven out by the legionaries with heavy loss. Jugurtha did not again face the Romans in the field, contenting himself with a guerilla warfare.

Mutina (Mark Antony's First Rebellion).

Fought April 16, 43 B.C., between the adherents of Antony, and three Consular armies, under Hirtius, Octavius, and Vibius Pansa. Antony, who was besieging Mutina, was attacked simultaneously by the three armies. That of Pansa was routed, and Pansa slain but Octavius and Hirtius gained some small success. Antony, however, was undefeated, and continued the siege. On the 27th Octavius and Hirtius made a combined attack on his lines, and succeeded in forcing their way through into the town, though Hirtius fell in the action.

Mycale (Third Persian Invasion).

Fought August, 479 B.C., between the Greeks, under Leotychides the Spartan, and a large Persian army. The Greeks effected a landing near Cape Mycale, and drove the Persians back upon their entrenchments, which they then carried by storm, whereupon the Persian auxiliaries fled. The fugitives were slaughtered in detail by the revolted Ionians, and the whole army destroyed.

Mylæ (First Punic War).

Fought B.C. 260, when the Roman fleet, under Caius Duilius, defeated the Carthaginians, under Hannibal, with loss of 50 ships, 3,000 killed and 7,000 prisoners. Duilius had introduced the boarding bridge, which was lowered on to the deck of the opposing galley, and this gave full scope to the superior powers of the Romans in hand-to-hand fighting.

Mylex (Civil War of Cæsar and Pompey).

Fought B.C. 36, between the Pompeian fleet, under Sextus Pompeius, and the fleet of the Triumvirs, under Agrippa. The Pompeians were defeated.

Myonnesus (War with Antiochus the Great).

Fought B.C. 190, between the Roman fleet, under Caius Livius, and the fleet of Antiochus, under Polyxenides, who had an advantage of nine ships. He was, however, defeated by the superior seamanship of the Romans, with a loss of 42 vessels.

Mytilene (Peloponnesian War).

This city, which had revolted against Athens, was invested in the autumn of 428 B.C. by the Athenians, under Paches, with 1,000 hoplites and a fleet of triremes. A feeble attempt at relief by a Peloponnesian squadron, under Alcidas, was unsuccessful, and in May, 427, the city surrendered, and all the male inhabitants were condemned to death. In the end, however, only the leaders of the revolt were executed.

Mytilene (Peloponnesian War).

A naval action fought B.C. 406, between 140 Peloponnesian vessels, under Callicratidas, and 70 Athenian triremes, under Conon. Conon was defeated, with the loss of 30 ships, the rest of his fleet being driven into Mytilene, where it was blockaded.

N

Nachod (Seven Weeks' War).

Fought June 27, 1866, between the 5th Prussian Corps, under General Steinmetz, and the Austrians, under General Ramming. The Austrian cavalry, which was considerably superior in number, was defeated by the Prussian Uhlans, and the action resulted in the retreat of the Austrians, with a considerable loss in killed and wounded. The Prussians, who lost 900, captured 2,000 prisoners and 5 guns.

Næfels (War of Kiburg).

Fought April 9, 1388, between 6,000 Austrians, under Tockenburg, and 500 men of Glarus with a few Schwyzers. The Swiss were driven from their first position behind the " Letzi" at the entrance to the valley, but, retiring to the heights of the Rauhberg, disordered the advancing columns by rolling boulders upon them, and, then attacking, utterly routed them. The Austrians lost 80 knights and 2,000 soldiers.

Nagy-Sarló (Hungarian Rising).

Fought April 19, 1849, between the Hungarians, 25,000 strong, under Görgey, and the Austrians, who endeavoured to prevent Görgey constructing bridges over the Gran. The Austrians were signally defeated, and the river successfully bridged.

Naissus (Gothic Invasion of the East).

Fought 269 between the Imperial troops, under the Emperor Claudius Gothicus, and the invading Goths. The Romans were hard pressed, when the Gothic lines were attacked in the rear by a force of 5,000 men, which Claudius had concealed for this purpose in the neighbouring mountains, and being thrown into confusion, were totally routed. Fifty thousand men are said to have fallen in the battle.

Najara. *See* Navarrete.

Nanshan (Russo-Japanese War).

Fought May 26, 1904, between three Japanese divisions, under General Oku, and a Russian division, with a large force of artillery, under General Stoessel. The Russians occupied a very strongly entrenched position on the heights of Nanshan. After an artillery preparation, the Japanese attempted to storm the heights, eight successive attacks failing before the concentrated fire of the Russian guns, though the last survivors of the assailants got within 30 yards of the trenches. The infantry were then retired, and after a further bombardment, aided by the Japanese fleet in Kiuchau Bay, the whole force attacked simultaneously, and, penetrating the defences on the Russian left, drove them from their positions with heavy loss, the defenders leaving 500 dead on the field. The Japanese lost 4,304 killed, wounded and missing. Seventy-eight guns were taken, and the Russians penned up in Port Arthur.

Narva (Russo-Swedish War).

Fought November 30, 1700, between 8,000 Swedes, under Charles XII, and 80,000 Russians, under General Dolgorouky, The Russians were besieging Narva, and after driving in two large bodies who occupied advanced positions, Charles boldly attacked their entrenched camp. After a brief cannonade, the Swedes stormed the trenches, and though the Russian artillerymen stood to their guns, after three hours' hard fighting, the defenders were driven out in disorder having lost 18,000 in the trenches, while many more fell in the fight. The Swedes lost 600 only.

Naseby (Civil War).

Fought June 14, 1645, between 14,000 Parliamentarians, under Fairfax, and 7,500 Royalists, under Charles I, with Prince Rupert in actual command. Rupert's first charge broke the Parliamentary left wing, but, as usual, the pursuit was carried too far, and before the cavalry returned, Cromwell on the right had turned the scale, and the battle was over. The Royalist infantry, overwhelmed by superior numbers, was almost annihilated, 5,000 prisoners, and all the artillery and munitions of war being captured.

Nashville (American Civil War).

Fought December 15 and 16, 1863, between 50,000 Federals, under General Thomas, and 40,000 Confederates, under General Hood. Thomas attacked the left of Hood's lines before Nashville, and after hard fighting, in which Hood lost 1,200 prisoners and 16 guns, the Confederates withdrew during the night to a position a few miles in the rear. Here they were again attacked on the 16th, and, though at first holding their ground, were in the end driven from the field in confufusion, with heavy loss in killed and wounded, besides 4,460 prisoners and 54 guns.

Naulachus (Civil War of Cæsar and Pompey).

Fought September 3, B.C. 36, between the Pompeian fleet of 300 ships, under Sextus Pompeius, and the fleet of the Triumvirs, of equal strength, under Agrippa. The action was severely contested, but in the end Agrippa was victorious, and Pompeius fled with 17 vessels only.

Naupactus (Peloponnesian War).

Fought 429 B.C. between 20 Athenian ships, under Phormio, and 77 Peloponnesian ships, under Cnemas. The Athenians were entrapped by Cnemas at the entrance to the Bay of Naupactus, and 9 of his vessels driven ashore. The remaining 11 fled towards Naupactus, closely pursued by the Peloponnesians, when the rearmost of the flying Athenians suddenly turned, and rammed the leading ship of Cnemas' squadron. The pursuers hesitated, and the rest of the Athenians then returned, and gained a complete victory, taking 6 ships, and recovering 8 of the 9 which had run ashore.

Navarino (Greek War of Independence).

Fought October 20, 1827, when the allied fleets of Great Britain, France and Russia under Codrington, de Rigny, and Heiden respectively, and numbering in all 24 ships, annihilated the Turkish and Egyptian fleets, 60 vessels being entirely destroyed, and the remainder driven ashore. The allies lost 272 in killed and wounded ; the Turks over 4,000. This battle is noteworthy as being the last general action fought under the old conditions between wooden sailing ships.

Navarrete (Hundred Years' War).

Fought April 3, 1367, between 24,000 English, under Edward the Black Prince, and 60,000 French and Spaniards, under Bertrand du Guesclin and Henry de Trastamare. The English, mainly owing to the skill of their archers, completely defeated their opponents, with heavy loss, du Guesclin being made prisoner. This battle is also known as the Battle of Najara.

Naxos.

Fought September, 376 B.C., between 80 Athenian triremes, under Chabrias, and 60 Spartan ships, under Pollio, who was endeavouring to waylay the Athenian grain ships from the Euxine. Pollio was totally defeated, with a loss of 49 triremes.

Nechtan's Mere.

Fought May 20, 685, between the Picts, under Brude, and the Northumbrians, under Ecgfrith. The latter was defeated, and the Picts by their victory freed themselves from the Northumbrian domination.

Neerwinde (War of the Revolution).

Fought July 19, 1693, between the English, under William III, and the French in superior force, under Marshal Luxemberg. The French attacked the English entrenchments, and were at first repulsed, but after eight hours' hard fighting, they succeeded in driving them back all along the line, though owing largely to the personal bravery of the King, the retirement was in good order. This victory which cost the French 10,000 men, was a barren one, for William's retreat was unmolested, and he was almost at once in a condition to renew the conflict. This is also called the Battle of Landen.

Neerwinde (Wars of the French Revolution).

Fought March 18, 1793, between the French, under Dumouriez, and the Austrians, under the Prince of Coburg. The Austrians won a signal victory, and in consequence of his defeat Dumouriez was compelled to evacuate Belgium.

Negapatam.

Fought 1746, off the Coromandel coast between a British squadron of 6 ships, under Captain Peyton, and 9 French ships, under Labourdonnais. The fight was conducted almost entirely at long range, and was indecisive, but after the action Peyton sheered off and made for Trincomalee, thus practically admitting defeat, though the French had in fact suffered the heavier loss.

Negapatam.

Siege was laid to this place October 21, 1781, by a British force, 4,000 strong, under Colonel Braithwaite. The garrison, partly Dutch and partly Mysore troops, though 8,000 in number, did not wait for a bombardment, but surrendered November 3.

Negapatam.

A naval action was fought off this place in 1782 between a British squadron, under Sir Edward Hughes, and a French squadron, under Suffren. The opposing forces were of about equal strength, and the action was indecisive, but the French designs on Negapatam were frustrated, and Suffren drew off to the southward.

Nehavend (Moslem Invasion of Persia).

Fought A.D. 637 between the Moslems, under Said, the lieutenant of the Caliph Omar, and a Persian army, 150,000 strong. The Persians were utterly routed, this being the last stand made against the conquering Moslems.

Neon (Sacred War).

Fought B.C. 354, between the Phocians and certain mercenary troops, 10,000 in all, under Philomelus, and the Thebans and Locrians. The Phocians were totally defeated, and Philomelus, driven fighting and covered with wounds to the edge of a precipice, preferred death to surrender, and sprang over the cliff.

Neuwied (Wars of the French Revolution).

Fought April 18, 1797, between the French, 80,000 strong, under Hoche, and the Austrians, under Werneck. Hoche won a signal victory, driving the Austrians beyond the Lahn, with a loss of 8,000 men and 80 guns.

Neville's Cross (Scottish Wars).

Fought October 17, 1346, between the Scottish invading army, under David II, and the northern levies, under Henry Percy and Ralph Neville. The Scots were completely routed, with a loss of 15,000 men, and David and many of his nobles captured.

Newburn (Scottish Wars).

Fought August 28, 1640, between 4,500 English, under Lord Conway, and the Scottish army, 22,500 strong, under Leslie. Conway endeavoured to hold the ford of Newburn, near Newcastle, but his raw levies, after a cannonade of three hours, fled in confusion. Conway was consequently obliged to evacuate Newcastle, which was occupied by the Scots. The losses on both sides were small.

Newbury (Civil War).

Fought September 20, 1643, between the Royalists, under Charles I, and the Parliamentarians, under Essex. The object of Charles was to stop Essex's march on London, and though his troops held their ground throughout the day, he could not be said to have gained a victory, as during the night he felt himself obliged to abandon his position.

A second indecisive battle was fought at Newbury, October 27, 1644, when the Royalists, under Charles I, again sustained throughout the day, without giving ground, the attacks of the Parliamentary army, under Waller, Manchester, and others, but, as on the previous occasion, retired during the night.

Newmarket (American Civil War).

Fought May 13, 1864, between 15,000 Federals, under Sigel, and 3,500 Confederates, under Breckenridge. The Confederates, by a rapid flank movement, fell upon Sigel's force while on the march, and drove them to seek shelter in a wood behind their artillery. The guns were then most gallantly attacked and taken by 250 boys, pupils of the Lexington Military School, who lost 80 of their number in the charge. Sigel retired, having lost very heavily in men, and leaving 6 guns in the enemy's hands.

New Orleans (Second American War).

This city, held by a garrison of 12,000 Americans, under General Jackson, was attacked December, 1814, by a British force of 6,000 men, under General Keane, aided by the fleet. On the 13th the American warships, lying in the Mississippi, were captured by a boat attack, and by the 21st the whole of the troops were disembarked. After a few skirmishes, Sir Edward Pakenham, arrived and took command on the 25th, and on January 1, 1815, a determined attack was made upon the American position. This failed, and owing to difficulties as to supplies, the British retired. On the 7th a final assault took place, but the assailants were again repulsed, with a loss of 1,500, including Pakenham, and the expedition then withdrew. At the time of the action peace had already been concluded, though of course neither party was aware of the fact.

New Orleans (American Civil War).

On April 16, 1862, the Federal fleet of 30 armed steamers and 21 mortar vessels, under Commodore Farragut, began the attack on this city by the bombardment of Fort Jackson.

After this fort and Fort Mary had been shelled with little intermission until the 25th, Faragut forced the passage, and anchoring off the Levée of New Orleans, the city at once surrendered. The forts, however, still held out, but a mutiny broke out in Fort Jackson, and on the 28th they surrendered to Commodore Porter.

New Ross (Irish Rebellion).

Fought June 5, 1799, between 30,000 rebels, under Father Roche and Bagenal Harvey, and about 1,400 regulars, under General Johnstone. The rebels attacked the troops posted in New Ross, and penetrated into the centre of the town, but were then driven back with the bayonet, and totally routed, with a loss of 2,600 killed.

Newtown Butler (War of the Revolution).

Fought August 2, 1689, between 5,000 Catholics, under Maccarthy, and 3,000 Protestants, under Colonel Wolseley, in defence of Enniskillen. The Catholics were totally routed, and fled in disorder, losing 1,500 in the action, and 500 drowned in Lough Erne.

Niagara (Seven Years' War)

This fort was besieged in June, 1759, by 2,500 British, with 900 Indians, under General Prideaux, the garrison consisting of 600 French, under Captain Pouchot. Prideaux was killed by the premature explosion of a shell, and Sir William Johnson succeeded to the command. On July 24, when the garrison were almost *in extremis*, an attempt to relieve the fort was made by 1,300 French and Indians, under Ligneris, but he was repulsed by Johnson with considerable loss, at La Belle Famille, and Pouchot at once surrendered.

Nicæa (First Crusade).

This city was besieged by the Crusaders, under Godefroi de Bouillon, May 14, 1097. The Saracens were greatly aided in the defence by the possession of Lake Ascanius, but with great labour the crusaders transported boats from the sea to the lake, and thus completed the investment of the place. Two determined attempts to relieve it were made by the Sultan Soliman, but both were repulsed, and Nicæa surrendered June 20.

Nicholson's Nek. *See* Farquhar's Farm.

Nicopolis (Third Mithridatic War).

Fought B.C. 66, between the Romans, under Pompey, and the army of Mithridates. The Romans had occupied the heights in front of the retreating Asiatics, and Mithridates encamped under their position. In the night the Romans attacked him in his camp, and utterly routed him. This was the last battle fought by Mithridates against the legions of Rome.

Nicopolis.

Fought B.C. 47, when Domitius Calvinus, with one Roman legion and a contingent of Pontic and other Asiatic troops, encountered the Bosporans, under Pharnaces. Calvinus'

Asiatic troops fled at the first onset, and he was completely defeated, only the steadiness of the Romans saving him from disaster.

Nicopolis (Ottoman Wars).

Fought September 28, 1395, between 10,000 French and 50,000 Hungarians, under the Duc de Nevers and Sigismund of Hungary, and the Turkish army of Bajazet I. The French charged the Turkish lines, without waiting for the Hungarians, and penetrated the two first lines, killing 1,500 Turks, but they were then overpowered by the Janissaries in the third line and 3,000 killed, while all the survivors were captured. Bajazet then turned upon the Hungarians, who fled without striking a blow. Bajazet massacred all his prisoners, excepting 25 nobles.

Nicopolis (Russo-Turkish War).

This place was captured July 16, 1877, by the 9th Russian Army Corps, under General Krudener, after two days' bombardment, when the garrison of 7,000 Turks surrendered. The Russians lost 1,300 killed and wounded.

Nieuport (Netherlands War of Independence).

Fought July 2, 1600, between the Dutch, under Maurice of Orange, and the Spaniards, under the Archduke Albert of Austria. Prince Maurice was surprised by the Archduke in a very critical position, but succeeded in holding his own, and after a long and evenly-contested engagement, ultimately defeated the Spaniards with heavy loss.

Nikko (Japanese Revolution).

Fought 1868, between the adherents of the Shogun, under Otori Keisuke, and the Imperial army, under Saigo Takamori. The rebels were defeated, and fled to the castle of Wakamatsu.

Nile (French Invasion of Egypt).

Fought August 1, 1798, Admiral Brueys, with 13 ships of the line and 4 frigates, was anchored in Aboukir Bay. Nelson, with 13 line-of-battle-ships and one 50-gun ship, penetrated with half his squadron between the French line and the shore, while his remaining ships engaged them on the outside. Thus caught between two fires, the French were utterly routed, only two of their vessels escaping capture or destruction. Admiral Brueys was killed, and his ship L'Orient blown up. This battle is also known as the Battle of Aboukir.

Nineveh (Persian Wars).

Fought December 1, 627, between the Imperial troops, under the Emperor Heraclius. and the Persians, under Rhazates, the general of Chosroes II. The Persians stood their ground manfully throughout the day and far into the night, and were almost annihilated before the surviving remnant retreated in good order to their camp. The Romans also lost heavily, but the victory opened the way to the royal city of Destigerd, which fell into the hands of Heraclius, and peace was made the following year.

Niquitas (South American War of Independence).

Fought 1813, when the Colom-bian Patriots, under Bolivar, completely defeated the Spanish Royalists.

Nisib (Mehemet Ali's Second Rebellion).

Fought June 23, 1839, between 30,000 Turks, under Hafiz Pasha, and Mehemet Ali's Syro-Egyptian army, under his son Ibrahim. Ibrahim was far the stronger in artillery, and his fire so shattered the Turks, that when he finally advanced his infantry, they made no stand, but turned and fled. Von Moltke, as a captain in the Turkish service, was under fire in this action for the first time.

Nisibis (Persian Wars).

This fortress, known as the Bulwark of the East, was thrice besieged in 338, 346 and 350 by Sapor II, King of Persia. In the two former years he was compelled to retire after a siege of 60 and 80 days respectively, In 350 the city was defended by a garrison under Lucilianus, and Sapor, finding the ordinary methods unavailing, diverted the course of the Mygdonius, and by building dams formed a large lake, upon which he placed a fleet of armed vessels, and attacked the city almost from the level of the ramparts. Under pressure of the water a portion of the wall gave way, and the Persians at once delivered an assault, but were repulsed ; and by the following day the garrison had rebuilt the wall. At the end of about three months, Sapor, having lost 20,000 men, raised the siege.

Nissa.

A naval action, fought at the

mouth of the Nissa in 1064, between the Danish fleet, under Sweyn II, and the Norwegians under Harold Hardrada. Sweyn was totally defeated, and his fleet destroyed, he himself escaping with difficulty to Zealand.

Nissa. *See* **Morawa.**

Nive (Peninsular War).
Fought December 13, 1813, between 35,000 French, under Soult, and 14,000 British and Portuguese, under Wellington. Having crossed the Nive on the 10th, Wellington took up a strong position on the heights near the village of St. Pierre. Here he was attacked by Soult, but repulsed him, and occupied the French position in front of the Adour. The French losses in this battle and the combats which preceded it, amounted to 10,000 men. The British lost 5,019 killed and wounded.

Nivelle (Peninsular War).
Fought November 10, 1813, when the French, under Soult, were driven from a very strong position by the British, under Wellington, and forced to retire behind the Nivelle. The French lost 4,265, including about 1,200 prisoners, 51 guns, and all their field magazines. The British lost 2,694 killed and wounded.

Nordlingen (Thirty Years' War).
Fought September 6, 1634, between 40,000 Imperialists, under Ferdinand of Hungary, and a numerically inferior force of Germans and Swedes, under the Duke of Weimar and Count Horn. The action was fought to relieve Nordlingen, which Ferdinand was besieging, and

resulted in the total defeat of the allies, who lost 12,000 killed, 6,000 prisoners, including Horn, and 80 guns.

Nordlingen (Wars of Louis XIV).
Fought August 3, 1645, between 17,000 French under Condé, and 14,000 Imperialists, under Mercy. The French attacked the village of Allersheim, where the Imperialists were strongly entrenched, and after very severe fighting, the left under Turenne succeeded in expelling them, with a loss of 6,000 killed, wounded and prisoners, and almost all their guns. General Mercy was killed. The French loss amounted to about 4,000.

Noisseville (Franco - German War).
A sortie of the French, under Bazaine, from Metz, August 31, 1870, in the endeavour to break through the investing line of the Germans, under Prince Frederick Charles. The French had some slight success at first, and maintained the ground they had won during the day, but on September 1, their further efforts to advance were fruitless, and they were driven back into Metz with a loss of 145 officers and 3,379 men. The Germans lost 126 officers and 2,850 men.

Northallerton. *See* **Standard.**

Northampton (Wars of the Roses).
Fought July 10, 1460, between the Lancastrians, under Henry VI, and the Yorkists, under the Earl of Warwick. The king's entrenchments were betrayed by Lord Grey de

Ruthyn, and the Lancastrians were defeated with a loss of 300 killed, including Buckingham, Shrewsbury, Egremont, and other prominent men. The King was made prisoner.

North Foreland (Dutch Wars).

Fought July 25, 1666, between the English fleet, under the Duke of Albemarle and Prince Rupert, and the Dutch, under Van Tromp and de Ruyter. The English gained a complete victory, capturing or burning 20 ships. The Dutch had 4,000 men killed or drowned.

Notion (Peloponnesian War).

Fought B.C. 407 between the Peloponnesian fleet, under Lysander, and the Athenian fleet of Alcibiades, which was lying at Notion. Alcibiades was not present during the action, which was the result of a surprise, and the Athenians were defeated with a loss of 15 ships

Nova Carthago (Second Punic War).

This city, defended by a small Carthaginian garrison, under Mago, was stormed by 27,500 Romans, under Scipio, B.C. 209.

Novara (Italian Wars).

Fought June 6, 1515, between 10,000 French, under La Tremouille, and 13,000 Swiss. The French camp was surprised by the Swiss, who, after hard fighting, totally routed the French with a loss of 6,000 men. The Swiss losses were also heavy.

Novara (Italian Rising).

Fought March 23, 1849, between 50,000 Piedmontese, under Chrzanowski, and three Austrian army corps, under Radetsky. After hard fighting, the Piedmontese were completely defeated and driven from the field in disorder.

Novi (Wars of the French Revolution).

Fought August 15, 1799, between the French, under Joubert, and the Russians and Austrians, under Suwaroff. Early in the action Joubert fell, Moreau succeeding to the command. The result was disastrous to the French, who were defeated with a loss of 7,000 killed and wounded, 3,000 prisoners, and 37 guns, The allies lost 6,000 killed and wounded and 1,200 prisoners.

Nujufghur (Indian Mutiny).

Fought August 24, 1857, between 6,000 rebels, under Mohammed Bukht Khan, and a small British force, under John Nicholson. The rebels were defeated, at small cost, with a loss of over 800 men and all their guns.

Numantia (Lusitanian War).

This city, defended by the inhabitants under Megaravicus, was besieged B.C. 142 by a Roman consular army. In the course of 141 the Romans were twice defeated under the walls, and though negotiations for a surrender were entered into in the following year, they were not concluded, and in 139 the new Roman commander, Popilius Lænas, refused to ratify the terms. Shortly afterwards he was again defeated by the Numantians, as was his successor Mancius in 137. It was not till the arrival of Scipio Æmilianus in 134 that the lengthy resistance of the inhabitants was at last overcome, and fifteen months after he took command the city fell, in the autumn of 133 B.C.

O

Oberstein.

Fought 1533, between the Poles, under Tarnowski, and the Wallachians, under Bogdan. The Wallachians were signally defeated, with heavy loss.

Obligado (Uruguayan War of Independence).

Fought November, 1845, between the Argentine fleet, under Oribe, and the combined French and British squardons. The allies were victorious, and Oribe was forced to raise the siege of Montevideo, while the waters of the Parana were opened to the shipping of all nations.

Ocaña (Peninsular War).

In this action, at which Joseph Buonaparte was present, Soult, with 30,000 French, defeated 53,000 Spaniards, under Areizaga, with a loss of 5,000 killed and wounded, 26,000 prisoners, including 3 generals, 45 guns, and all their baggage and transport. The French only lost 1,700 men.

Ocean Pond (American Civil War).

Fought February 20, 1864, between 5,000 Confederates, under General Finnegan, and 6,000 Federals, under General Seymour. The Confederates occupied a strong position, protected by swamps and forests, near Lake City, where they were attacked by Seymour, whom they defeated with a loss of 1,200 men and 5 guns. The Confederates loss amounted to 700.

Ockley (Danish Invasion).

Fought 851, between the Danes, and the West Saxons, under Ethelwulf. The Danes were completely defeated.

Oczakov (Ottoman Wars).

This fortress, defended by 10,000 Turks and Bosnians, was besieged 1737, by the Russians, under Count Münnich, and after the magazine had been blown up was stormed by the besiegers, and the garrison cut to pieces. In 1788 the place was again besieged by the Russians, under Potemkin, and after a strenuous resistance of six months, was taken by storm, December 17. In the massacre which followed, 40,000 of the garrison and inhabitants were put to the sword.

Odawara (Hojo Rebellion).

The castle of Odawara, the last stronghold of the Hojo family, was besieged by the Japanese Imperial troops, under Hideyoshi. The castle held out for over three months, but at last finding that they could hope for no support from without, the garrison surrendered, and the power of the Hojo family came to an end.

Œnophyta.

Fought B.C. 457, between the Athenians, under Myronides, and the Thebans and other Bœotian states. The Bœotians were totally defeated, and were in consequence compelled to acknowledge the headship of

Athens, and to contribute men to her armies.

Ofen (Hungarian Rising).

This fortress, held by an Austrian garrison, under General Hentzi, was besieged by the Hungarians, under Görgey, May 4, 1849. After an unsuccessful assault, a siege in due form was commenced, and several further assaults having also failed, the place was finally taken by storm on the 21st. General Hentzi was mortally wounded.

Ohud (Mohammed's War with the Koreish).

Fought 623, between 950 Moslems, under Mohammed, and 3,000 Koreish of Mecca, under Abu Sophian. The latter were victorious, 70 Moslems being slain, and the Prophet himself wounded, but Abu Sophian did not feel himself strong enough to follow up his victory by an attack upon Medina.

Olmedo.

Fought 1467, between the Spanish adherents of the Infante Alfonso, a claimant to the throne, under the Archbishop of Toledo, and the Royal troops, under Henry of Castile. After an action which began late in the afternoon, and lasted for three hours, without any very decisive result, the Archbishop, who was considerably inferior in numbers, withdrew his troops, leaving Henry in possession of the field.

Olmütz (Seven Years' War).

This place was besieged by Frederick the Great, May, 1758. Having insufficient troops to completely invest the place,

Frederick's task was a difficult one, and Marshal Daun was able to keep communications open, and supply the town with provisions. After a siege of seven weeks, the Austrians captured a convoy of 4,000 waggons, under the escort of Landon, destined for the Prussian army, and Frederick was forced by this loss to raise the siege, and retire.

Olpæ (Peloponnesian War).

Fought 426 B.C., between a small Athenian force, under Demosthenes, and a force of Ambraciots, with 3,000 Spartan hoplites, under Eurylochus. Demosthenes gained a complete victory, by means of an ambuscade, and Eurylochus was slain.

Oltenitza (Crimean War).

Fought 1853, when a Turkish army, superior in numbers, under Omar Pasha, totally defeated the Russian army which had invaded the Danubian Principalities.

Omdurman (Soudan Campaigns).

Fought September 2, 1898, between the British and Egyptians, 23,000 strong, under Sir Herbert Kitchener, and 50,000 Dervishes, under the Khalifa. The Dervishes attacked the British zareba, and were repulsed with heavy loss. Kitchener then advanced, to drive the enemy before him into Omdurman, and capture the place. In the course of the operation, however, the Egyptian Brigade on the British right, under General Macdonald, became isolated, and was attacked in front by the centre of the Dervish army, while his flank and rear were threatened by the Dervish left, which had not previously been engaged. The position was critical, but through the extreme steadiness of the Soudanese, who changed front under heavy fire, the attack was repulsed. The British and Egyptian losses were 500 killed and wounded. The Dervishes lost about 15,000.

Onao (Indian Mutiny).

Fought July 28, 1857, between Havelock's relieving force, 1,500 strong, and the rebels, who occupied a strong position near Onao, so protected on the flanks that a frontal attack was necessary. This was successful, and after the town had been passed, a further attack by the mutineers was repulsed, with a loss of 300 men and 15 guns.

Onessant.

Fought July 27, 1778, between 30 British ships of the line, under Admiral Keppel, and a French squadron of equal force, under the Comte d'Estaing. After a fight which lasted throughout the day, the two fleets drew off to repair damages, neither side having lost a ship.

Oondwa Nullah.

Fought September, 1763, when 3,000 British and native troops, under Major Adams, carried by storm the entrenchments and the fort held by Mir Cossim's army of 60,000 men with 100 guns. Mir Cossim fled and his army was entirely dispersed.

Ooscata.

Fought August 23, 1768, when the camp of the Mahratta contingent, under Morari Rao, forming a part of Colonel Donald Campbell's column, was attacked by a detachment of Hyder Ali's army. The Mahrattas repulsed the Mysore cavalry with a loss of about 300, at a cost to themselves of 18 only.

Opequan (American Civil War).

Fought September 19, 1864, between 13,000 Confederates, under General Early, and 45,000 Federals, under General Sheridan. Success at first inclined to the side of the Southerners, but their left wing was broken by a charge of 7,000 cavalry, under Custer, and the Confederates were completely routed and fled in confusion.

Oporto (Peninsular War).

Fought March 28, 1809, when the French, under Soult, completely defeated the Portuguese under Lima and Pareiras, outside the city of Oporto. Soult followed up his success by storming Oporto, with horrible slaughter, it being computed that 10,000 of the inhabitants perished. The French lost 500 only.

Oran (Ximenes' Expedition to Morocco).

Fought May 17, 1509, between the Moors and the Spaniards, under Navarro. The Spaniards, late in the evening, attacked and drove off the Moors from a strong position on the heights above the city. They then stormed the city itself, escalading the walls by placing their pikes in the crevices of the stones. The Moors lost in the battle and the storm 4,000 killed and about 8,000 prisoners, while the losses of the victors were very small.

Orchomenus (First Mithridatic War).

Fought B.C. 85, between the Pontic army, under Archelaus, and the Romans, under Sulla. The Asiatic cavalry attacked and drove back the Roman line, but Sulla himself rallied his troops, and led them in a charge which totally routed the enemy with heavy loss.

Ordovici, The.

Fought A.D. 50, between the Romans, under Ostorius Scapula, and the Britons, under Caractacus. The Britons occupied the slope of a hill, where they were attacked by the Romans and totally routed. Caractacus fled to the Brigantes, by whom he was surrendered, and sent a captive to Rome.

Orleans (Hundred Years' War).

This city was besieged by the English, under the Regent, the Duke of Bedford, in October, 1428. In April, 1429, a French force, 7,000 strong, under Dunois and Joan of Arc, succeeded in entering, it having been found impossible to invest the place completely. After various successful attacks on the batteries erected by the besiegers, Joan, on the 6th and 7th of May, led the garrison to victory against the English lines, and on the 8th Bedford was compelled to raise the siege.

Orthez (Peninsular War).

Fought February 27, 1814, between the British under Wellington, and the French, under Soult. The French were driven out of Orthez and across the Luy de Béarn, with a loss of 4,000 killed and wounded, and 6 guns.

Oruro.

Fought 1862, between the Bolivian Government troops, under the President, General Acha, and the rebels, under General Perez, who had proclaimed himself President. Perez was utterly routed.

Ostend (Netherlands War of Independence).

This place was besieged, July 5, 1601, by the Spaniards, under the Archduke Albert. The town made a most remarkable defence, holding out for more than three years, but Spinola having taken command of the besiegers, it was finally captured, September 14, 1604, by which time scarcely a house in the town was left standing. The Spaniards lost 70,000 men in the course of the siege.

Ostia (Italian Wars).

This place, held by a French garrison, under Menaldo Guerri, was besieged in 1500 by the Spaniards, under Gonsalvo de Cordova. After five days' bombardment, an attack was made upon the town on the opposite side by a small party of Spaniards resident in Rome, under Garcilasso de la Vega. Thus between two fires, Guerri surrendered.

Ostrolenka (Crimean War).

Fought 1853, between the Turks, under Omar Pasha, and the Russian army which had invaded the Danubian Principalities. The Turks, who were considerably superior in numbers, gained a complete victory.

Ostrowno (Campaign of Moscow).

Fought July 25 and 26, 1812, between the French corps of Ney and Prince Eugène, with Murat's cavalry, and the Russian corps of Count Osterman and General Konownitzyn. The Russians were defeated and driven back on both days, with a loss of 3,000 killed and wounded, 800 prisoners and 8 guns. The French loss was about the same.

Oswego (Seven Years' War).

This place, held by a garrison of 1,400 Provincial troops, under Colonel Mercer, was besieged by the French, under Montcalm, August 11, 1756. After a bombardment of 3 days, in the course of which Mercer was killed, the place surrendered. The losses on both sides were very small.

Otrar (Tartar Invasion of Kharismia).

This city was besieged, 1219, by 200,000 Mongols, under Oktai and Zagatai, sons of Genghiz Khan, and defended by a garrison of 60,000, under Gazer Khan. The place was entered after a four months' siege, by which time the garrison was reduced to 20,000 men, but with this remnant Gazer Khan held out in the citadel for another month.

Otterburn (Scottish Wars).

Fought August 19, 1388, between 9,000 English, under Henry Percy (Hotspur) and a greatly inferior force of Scots, under Earls Douglas and Murray. Hotspur attacked the Scottish entrenchments, and was totally defeated, with a loss of about 2,000. The battle is celebrated in the old ballad of "Chevy Chace."

Otumba (Conquest of Mexico).

Fought July 8, 1520, between 200 Spaniards, with some thousands of Tlascalan auxiliaries, under Cortes, and a force of about 200,000 Aztecs. The Spaniards, wearied by a long march on their retreat from Mexico, were intercepted by the Aztecs, and after many hours' fighting, were on the verge of defeat, when a charge of a few cavaliers, headed by Cortes, into the very heart of the Aztec army, so discouraged them that they fled in disorder. It is said that 20,000 Aztecs fell.

Oudenarde (War of the Spanish Succession).

Fought July 11, 1708, between 80,000 British and Imperialists, under Marlborough and Prince Eugene, and 100,000 French, under the Duke of Burgundy and Marshal Vendôme. The French, who were besieging Oudenarde, raised the siege on the advance of the allies, and marched to meet them, but were totally defeated with a loss of 3,000 killed, 7,000 prisoners, and 10 guns. The allies lost 2,000.

P

Paardeberg (Second Boer War).

Fought February 18, 1900, between 5,000 Boers, under Cronje, and the British, numbering 4 Infantry Brigades, with 4 batteries, under Lord Kitchener. Cronje had taken refuge in the bed of the Tugela river, and an attempt was made to dislodge him. The absence of cover for the attacking force, however, rendered this impossible, but he was surrounded, and on the arrival of Lord Roberts, subjected to a sustained artillery fire, which lasted until he surrendered on the 27th. The British losses during the operations amounted to 98 officers and 1,437 men, of whom 1,100 fell in the battle of the 18th. The prisoners taken numbered 3,000 Transvaalers and 1,100 Free Staters, with 6 guns.

Pabon.

Fought September 17, 1861, between the troops of Buenos Ayres, under Mitre, aided by an Italian legion, under Piloni, and the army of the Argentine Confederation, under Urquiza. The latter were defeated.

Pagahar (First Burmah War).

The only occasion during the war when the Burmans met the British in the open. In 1825 Sir Archibald Campbell, with 1,300 men, encountered 15,000 Burmans, under Zay - ya - Thayan but the battle was almost a bloodless one, for the Burmans failed to make any stand, their general being the first to flee.

Pagasæan Gulf (Sacred War).

Fought B.C. 352, between the Phocians, under Onomarchus, and the Macedonians, under Philip. Philip's infantry was about equal in numbers to that of the Phocians, but he was far superior in cavalry, and in the end the Phocians were completely defeated, with the loss of a third of their number. Onomarchus was slain.

Palais Gallien (War of the Fronde).

Fought September 5, 1649, between the Royal troops, 8,000 strong, under the Marshal de la Meilleraic, and 7,000 Bordelais, under the Ducs de Bouillon and de la Rochefoucauld. The Bordelais successfully repulsed four or five assaults, but by nightfall were driven from their entrenchments into the city, with a loss of about 120. The assailants lost over 1,000 killed and wounded.

Palermo (Italian Rising).

Fought May 26 and 27, 1848, when Garibaldi, with 750 of his "Thousand Volunteers," and about 3,000 Sicilian "Picciotti," succeeded in surprising one of the gates of Palermo, which was garrisoned by 18,000 Neapolitans, under General Lanza. The "Picciotti" fled at the first shot, but Garibaldi penetrated into the city, where, being joined by the citizens, he erected barricades, and after some severe fighting, in which the Neapolitans suffered heavily, General Lanza surrendered. The last of the Neapolitan troops were withdrawn on June 20.

Palestrina (Italian Rising).

Fought May 9, 1849, between 4,000 Italian Patriots, under Garibaldi, and 7,000 Neapolitans, under King Ferdinand. After three hours' fighting, the Neapolitans were totally routed. Garibaldi was wounded in the action.

Palestro (Unification of Italy).

Fought May 30, 1859, between the Sardinians, under

General Cialdini, and the Austrians, under General Stadion. The Austrians attacked the Sardinians while they were crossing the Sesia, but were repulsed, and Cialdini effected the passage successfully and drove the Austrians out of Palestro with considerable loss.

Palmyra (Expedition to Palmyra).

This city was besieged by the Romans, under Aurelian, after the defeat of Zenobia at Emesa in 272. An obstinate defence was made by the Queen, but Aurelian being reinforced by Probus early in 273, Zenobia fled from the city and the place was captured. Zenobia failed to escape, and was brought into Aurelian's camp. During his return march, Aurelian learnt that the citizens had risen, and massacred the Governor and the garrison he had left in the place. He thereupon retraced his steps, and destroyed the city, sparing neither young nor old.

Palo Alto (Americo - Mexican War).

Fought May 8, 1846, between the Americans, under General Taylor, and the Mexicans, under Arista. The Mexicans were completely routed, at very small cost to the victors.

Panama (Raids of the Buccaneers).

On December 16, 1670, Morgan the Buccaneer sailed from Hispaniola with 37 ships and about 2,000 men to plunder this town. Having captured the castle of San Lorenzo, at the mouth of the Chagre, an exploit which cost the assailants 170 out of 400 men engaged, while two-thirds of the garrison were killed, Morgan started to cross the Isthmus, at the head of 1,200 men, January 18, 1671. The garrison of Panama, 2,400 strong, met him outside the city, and were defeated with heavy loss, the Buccaneers losing 600 men. Morgan then sacked the place, and on February 24, withdrew with 175 mule loads of plunder, and 600 prisoners.

Panama (Raids of the Buccaneers).

Fought April 23, 1680, between the Buccaneers, with three ships, under John Coxon, and three Spanish vessels. The Spaniards were defeated, after a hard fight in which two Spanish vessels were captured by boarding. The Spanish commander was killed. The Buccaneers then entered the Bay, and captured six vessels lying in the roads.

Pandosia.

Fought 331 B.C., between the Italian Greeks, under Alexander of Epirus, and the Lucanians. During the battle Alexander was stabbed by a Lucanian exile serving in the Greek army, and the Greeks were in the end defeated.

Pandu Naddi (Indian Mutiny).

Fought July 15, 1857, between a British relieving force, under Havelock, and the mutineers who were opposing his advance to Cawnpore. By a forced march in the heat of the day, Havelock succeeded in seizing the bridge over the

Pandu Naddi, which the mutineers were engaged in mining, thus securing an open road to Cawnpore. The rebels were driven off after a short engagement.

Pandu Naddi (Indian Mutiny).

Fought November 26, 1857, between 1,400 British, under General Windham, and the advance guard of the mutineers and the Gwalior contingent, under the Nana Sahib. The rebels were posted beyond the river, and the British crossing the dry bed, drove them from their entrenchments, capturing 3 guns. Windham, then finding himself close to the main body of mutineers, retired towards Cawnpore.

Panipat (Third Mongol Invasion).

Fought April 20, 1526, between the Delhi Mohammedans, 10,000 strong, with 100 elephants, under Ibrahim, and the Mongols, about 2,000 picked men, under Baber, the first of the Great Moguls. Ibrahim was totally defeated, being himself among the slain. The battle marked the end of the Afghan dynasty of Delhi, and the commencement of the Mogul Empire.

Panipat.

Fought November 5, 1536, between Akbar, the Great Mogul, with about 20,000 troops, and the forces of the revolted Hindu Rajahs, 100,000 strong, under Hemu. The Hindus attacked, and the onslaught of the elephants being repulsed, their ranks were thrown into disorder, and the Moguls gained a complete victory. Hemu was wounded and captured. By this victory Akbar recovered Delhi, which had fallen into the hands of the rebels.

Panipat.

Fought 1759, between the Mahrattas, 85,000 strong, under Sedashao Rao Bhao, cousin of the Peshwa, and the Duranis, numbering, with Hindu allies, about 90,000. The Bhao attacked, and dispersed Ahmed's Indian troops, but on the Duranis coming into action, the Mahrattas were broken and utterly routed, with enormous loss. The Bhao, and the son of the Peshwa were among the slain.

Panormus (First Punic War).

Fought B.C. 250, between 25,000 Romans, under L. Cæcilius Metellus, and the Carthaginian army in Sicily, under Hasdrubal. Hasdrubal offered battle in front of Panormus, and Metellus sent out his light troops to engage him. They ran back into the town before a charge of the elephants, which, following closely, were driven into the ditch surrounding the place, where many were killed. Meanwhile Metellus sallied out with his legionaries, and taking Hasdrubal in flank completely routed him. The whole of the Carthaginian elephants in Sicily were killed or captured in this battle.

Parætakene Mountains (Wars of Alexander's Successors).

Fought 316 B.C., between the Macedonians, 30,000 strong, under Antigonus, and an equal force of Asiatics, under Eumenes,

Eumenes attacked the Macedonian camp, and after a severe engagement, in which the Asiatics held the advantage, Antigonus, by successful manœuvring, withdrew his army without serious loss, leaving Eumenes a barren victory.

Parana (Paraguayan War).

Fought 1866, between the Paraguayans, under Lopez, and the Brazilians, under Porto Alegre. Lopez was victorious.

Paris (Allied Invasion of France).

On March 30, 1814, Paris, which was defended only by 20,000 regulars and National Guard, under Marmont, was attacked by the Grand Army of the allies, under Schwartzemberg. Three columns assaulted the French positions at Vincennes, Belleville and Montmartre, while a fourth attacked the extreme left of the French line in order to turn the heights of Montmartre. The two first positions were carried, and Montmartre turned, whereupon Joseph having fled, Marmont surrendered. The French lost over 4,000 men ; the allies about 8,000.

Paris (Franco-German War).

Paris was invested by the main German army, under the King of Prussia and von Moltke, September 19, 1870, The garrison, under the command of General Trochu, made a gallant defence, many serious sorties taking place, but the Germans gradually mastered the outer defences, and finally, being much straitened by famine, the city surrendered January 28, 1871.

Parkany (Ottoman Wars).

Fought August, 1663, between 200,000 Turks, under the Grand Vizier, Achmet Köprili Pasha, and the Hungarians, in far smaller force, under Count Forgacz. The Hungarians were defeated, and driven into Neuhäusel, which town, after a valiant resistance of six weeks, capitulated September 24.

Parma (War of the Polish Succession).

Fought June 29, 1734, between the French, under Marshal de Coigny, and the Imperialists, 60,000 strong, under General de Mercy. The Imperialists were defeated with a loss of 6,000, including de Mercy. The French loss was almost as heavy.

Paso de la Patria (Paraguayan War).

Fought 1866, between the Paraguayans, under Lopez, and the Brazilians, under Porto Alegre. The Paraguayans gained a signal victory.

Patay (Hundred Years' War).

Fought June 18, 1429, between the French, under Joan of Arc and the Duc d'Alençon, and the English, under Talbot and Sir John Fastolfe. The English were retiring after the siege of Orleans, and their advanced guard under Talbot, being attacked by the French, was seized with a panic, and refusing to meet the charge of the French cavalry, broke and fled. The main body, under Fastolfe, however, maintained its formation, and made good its retreat to Etampes. Talbot was made prisoner.

Patila (Tartar Invasion of Persia).

Fought 1394, between the Tartars, under Tamerlane, and the Persians, under Shah Mansur. The Persians vigorously attacked the Tartar centre, and Tamerlane was nearly overwhelmed, but rallying his troops he led a charge which restored the battle, and gained a complete victory. The complete subjugation of Persia followed.

Pavia (Invasion of the Alemanni).

Fought 271, between the Romans, under Aurelian, and the German invaders. Aurelian gained a signal victory, and the Alemanni recrossed the frontier.

Pavia (Lombard Conquest of Italy).

This city was besieged in 568 by the Lombards, under Alboin, and after a gallant defence, lasting over three years, was at last subdued, rather by famine than by force of arms, and surrendered to the besiegers. Pavia then became the capital of the Lombard kingdom of Italy.

Pavia (Italian Wars).

Fought May 22, 1431, on the Ticino, near Pavia, between 85 Venetian galleys, under Nicolas Trevisani, and a somewhat superior number of galleys in the pay of the Milanese. The Venetians were defeated, with a loss of 70 galleys and 3,000 men.

Pavia (Wars of Charles V).

Fought February 25, 1525, between the French, under Francis I, and the Imperialists, under Lannoy. Francis, who was besieging Pavia, awaited the attack of the Imperialists on his lines, and his artillery wrought great havoc in their ranks, then, charging at the head of his cavalry, he was repulsed by Lannoy's infantry, and the Swiss mercenaries being taken in flank, and thrown into disorder, the battle was lost. Francis was captured. This is the occasion on which he wrote to his mother, " Rien ne m'est demouré, excepté l'honneur et la vie qui est sauve."

Peach Tree Creek (American Civil War).

Fought July 22, 1864, in the course of the operations round Atlanta, between the Federals, under General Sherman, and the Confederates, under General Hood. Hood attacked the Federal position, and drove off their left wing, capturing 13 guns and some prisoners ; being reinforced, however, the Federals rallied, and recovered the lost ground. The Confederates, however, claimed the victory. The Federals lost 3,722, including General McPherson. The Confederate losses were about the same.

Pea Ridge (American Civil War).

Fought March 7 and 8, 1862, between 16,000 Confederates, under General von Dorn, and the Federals, in equal force, under General Curtis. On the 7th the Confederates drove back the Federal right wing, and nearly succeeded in cutting their communications, though they lost General M'Culloch in the course of the action. On the 8th the Federals drove back the Southerners, and recovered the ground they had lost, the battle ending without decisive result. The losses on each side were about 1,000. This is also called the Battle of Gek Horn.

Peiwar Kotal (Second Afghan War).

Fought December 2, 1878, between a British force, 3,200 strong, under Sir Frederick Roberts, with 13 guns, and about 18,000 Afghans, with 11 guns, strongly posted in the Kotal. By an able, but difficult turning movement, the pass was crossed, and the Afghans completely defeated, with heavy loss, all their guns being captured. The British lost 20 killed and 78 wounded.

Peking (Tartar Invasion of China).

This city was besieged by the Tartars, under Genghiz Khan, in 1210, and after a long and obsintate defence, which so exhausted the besiegers that Genghiz Khan is said to have decimated his men in order to feed the rest, the city was taken by stratagem.

Pelekanon (Ottoman Conquest of Asia Minor).

Fought 1329, between the Turks, under Orkhan, and the forces of Andronicus the Younger, Emperor of the East. The Imperialists were defeated. This is the first occasion in which the Byzantines met the Ottoman invaders in battle.

Pelischat (Russo-Turkish War).

Fought August 30, 1877, when the Turks, 25,000 strong, with 50 guns, made a sortie from Plevna, and attacked the Russian lines in front of Poradim. The Russians, 20,000 strong, under General Zotoff, succeeded in repulsing all the Turkish attacks, with a loss of about 3,000 killed and wounded. The Russians lost 1,000.

Pelusium (Persian Conquest of Egypt).

Fought 525 B.C., between the Persians, under Cambyses, and the Egyptians, under Psammeticus. The Egyptians were totally defeated, and this victory was followed by the complete subjugation of Egypt, which became a Persian satrapy.

Pelusium (War of Alexander's Successors).

Fought B.C. 321, between the Macedonians, under the Regent, Perdiccas, and the Egyptians, under Ptolemy Lagus. Perdiccas attacked the fortress, but was driven off with heavy loss, including 1,000 drowned in the Nile.

Peña Cerrada (First Carlist War).

This fortress, held by a Carlist garrison, under Gergue, was captured by Espartero with 19,000 Cristinos, June 21, 1838. After shelling the place for 7 hours, Espartero attacked the Carlists, who held the heights outside the town, and dispersed them, capturing 600 prisoners, and all their guns. The remainder of the garrison then abandoned the place.

Penobscot Bay (American War of Independence).

Fought July 14, 1779, when a British squadron of 10 ships, under Sir George Collier, completely destroyed an American squadron of 24 ships, and captured the 3,000 men who formed their crews.

Pen Selwood (Danish Invasion).
Fought 1016, between the English, under Edmund Ironside, and the Danes, under Knut, shortly after Edmund's election as King by the Witanegemot. This was the first of the series of engagements between the two rivals, which ended with the Peace of Olney.

Pered (Hungarian Rising).
Fought June 21, 1849, between the Hungarians, 16,000 strong, under Görgey, and the Austrians and Russians, under Prince Windischgrätz. The allies attacked the Hungarian position, and after severe fighting, drove them out, with a loss of about 3,000.

Perembacum (First Mysore War).
Fought September 10, 1780, when a Mysore force, 11,000 strong, under Tippu Sahib, surrounded and cut to pieces a detachment of Sir Hector Monro's army, 3,700 in number, under Colonel Baillie. Only a few, including Baillie himself, escaped the massacre.

Perisabor (Persian Wars).
This fortress, defended by an Assyrian and Persian garrison, was captured, May, 363, by the Romans, under Julian. The fortress was dismantled and the town destroyed.

Perpignan.
This fortress was besieged by the French, 11,000 strong, under the Seigneur du Lude, at the end of 1474, and was defended by a Spanish garrison. The Spanish army could not succeed in relieving the place, and after holding out with great gallantry until March 14, 1475, the garrison, reduced to 400 men, surrendered, and were allowed to march out with the honours of war. The capture of Perpignan gave France possession of Rousillon.

Perryville (American Civil War).
Fought October 8, 1862, between 45,000 Federals, under General Buell, and a somewhat smaller Confederate army, under General Bragg. The Confederates attacked, and drove back the Federals, but no decisive result was arrived at, and during the night Bragg withdrew, having inflicted a loss of 4,000 on the enemy, and captured an artillery train. The Confederates lost about 2,500 killed and wounded.

Persepolis (Wars of Alexander's Successors).
Fought B.C. 316, between the Macedonians, 31,000 strong, with 65 elephants, under Antigonus, and 42,000 Asiatics, with 114 elephants, under Eumenes. At the first onslaught, Antigonus' infantry was overwhelmed, but his cavalry retrieved the day, and seizing the enemy's camp, threw Eumenes' phalanx into confusion. Upon this the Macedonian infantry rallied, and gained a complete victory, Eumenes being captured.

Peshawar (Second Mohammedan Invasion of India).
Fought 1001, between 10,000 Afghans, under Sultan Mahmud of Ghuzni, and 42,000 Punjabis, with 300 elephants, under the Rajah Jaipal of Lahore. The Rajah was totally defeated, and captured with 15 of his principal chiefs.

Petersburg (American Civil War).

Fought June 15 to 18, 1864, forming an episode in the Federal attack on Richmond. General Beauregard, with 8,000 men, was charged with the defence of Petersburg, and at the same time had to contain General Butler at Bermuda Hundred. His entrenchments before Petersburg were attacked on the 15th by General Smith, and a portion of the first line carried. On the 16th Beauregard withdrew the force masking Bermuda Hundred, and concentrated his troops in front of Petersburg, but after holding out till the afternoon, a panic seized the defenders, and they were driven from the first line. Beauregard, however, rallied them, and retook the entrenchments. During the night he withdrew to a second and stronger line of defences, and on the 17th and 18th repulsed, with terrible slaughter, all the efforts of the Federals to carry it.

Petersburg (American Civil War).

On June 30, 1864, a mine was exploded under the Confederate defences in front of Petersburg, and an attempt was made by the Federals to carry the entrenchments during the confusion that ensued. The Confederates, however, stood their ground, repulsing all attacks with heavy loss, and of the Federals who succeeded in entering the breastworks, 5,000 were killed or captured. Both the generals commanding, Lee and Grant, were present during the action.

Peterwaradin (Ottoman Wars).

Fought August 5, 1716, when Prince Eugene, with 80,000 Imperialists, mostly veterans from the Flanders campaign, signally defeated 150,000 Turks under Darnad Ali Pasha. The Turks lost 30,000 killed, 50 standards and 250 guns. The Imperialists lost about 3,000.

Petra (Persian Wars).

This strong fortress, garrisoned by 1,500 Persians, was besieged by the Romans, 8,000 strong, under Dagisteus, in 549. After a series of unsuccessful assaults the Romans succeeded in bringing down a large portion of the outer wall by mining. By this time the garrison was reduced to 400, but Dagisteus, delaying to storm the fortress, the Persians succeeded in throwing in reinforcements, which brought the garrison up to 3,000. Meanwhile all the breaches had been repaired, and the Romans had to undertake a second siege. At last a breach was effected, and after very severe fighting the besiegers effected a lodgement. Of the defenders 700 fell in the second siege, and 1,070 in the storm, while of 700 prisoners, only 18 were unwounded. Five hundred retreated to the citadel, and held out to the last, perishing in the flames when it was fired by the Romans.

Pharsalus (Civil War of Cæsar and Pompey).

Fought August 9, B.C. 48, between the Pompeians, 60,000 strong, under Pompey, and Cæsareans, 25,000 strong, under Cæsar. The Pompeian cavalry drove back that of Cæsar, but following in pursuit, were thrown into confusion by the legion aries, whereupon they turned and fled from the field ; the infantry followed and the battle became a rout, in which 15,000 Pompeians, and only 200 Cæsareans fell. After the battle, 20,000 Pompeians surrendered.

Pharsalus (Greco-Turkish War).

Fought May 6, 1897, when Edhem Pasha, with three Turkish divisions, drove the Greeks from their entrenchments in front of Pharsalus, at a cost of about 230 killed and wounded. The Greek loss was not very heavy.

Philiphaugh (Civil War).

Fought September 13, 1645, when 4,000 Lowland horse, under David Leslie, surprised and cut to pieces Montrose's force of Highlanders, encamped near Selkirk. Montrose escaped with a few followers.

Philippi (Rebellion of Brutus).

Fought B.C. 42, between the Republicans, under Brutus and Cassius, 100,000 strong, and the army of the Triumvirs, about equal in numbers, under Octavius and Mark Antony. Brutus on the right repulsed the legions of Octavius, and penetrated into his camp. Cassius, however, was overthrown by Antony, and would have been overwhelmed but for the arrival of aid from the successful right wing. The action was renewed on the second day, when the Triumvirs were completely victorious, and the Republican army dispersed. Brutus committed suicide on the field of battle.

Philippopolis ¡First Gothic Invasion of the Empire).

This city was besieged, 251,

by the Goths, under Cniva, and after a gallant defence, and the defeat of an attempt by Decius to relieve it, was stormed and sacked. It is said that 100,000 of the garrison and inhabitants perished in the siege and subsequent massacre.

Philippopolis (Russo-Turkish War).

Fought February 17, 1878, between the Russians, under General Gourko, and the Turks, under Fuad and Shakir Pashas. The Turks made a stubborn defence of the approaches to Philippopolis, but were overpowered by superior numbers, and forced to retreat with a loss of 5,000 killed and wounded, 2,000 prisoners, and 114 guns. The Russians lost 1,300.

Philipsburg (War of the Polish Succession).

This fortress, held by the Imperialists, was besieged 1734, by the French, under the Duke of Berwick. The Duke was killed by a cannon ball while visiting the trenches, but the place fell soon afterwards, notwithstanding the efforts of Prince Eugene to relieve it.

Pieter's Hill (Second Boer War).

The scene of the severest fighting in the course of Sir Redvers Buller's final and successful attempt to relieve Ladysmith. The operations commenced by the capture of Hlangwane, on February 19, 1900, which gave the British command of the Tugela, which was crossed on the 21st. On the 22nd a steady advance was made up to the line of Pieter's Hill, which was attacked by the Irish Brigade,

O

under General Hart, on the 23rd. At a cost of nearly half their numbers, they succeeded in establishing themselves under cover, close to the Boer trenches, but could not dislodge the defenders. It was not till the 27th, when Buller had turned the Boer left, that a general assault was successful, and the Boers evacuated the position. The British losses during the operations were 1,896 killed and wounded.

Pingyang (Chino-Japanese War).

Fought September 15, 1894, between the Japanese, 14,000 strong, under General Nodzu, and 12,000 Chinese, entrenched in a strong position. After severe fighting the Chinese were driven from their entrenchments with heavy loss. The Japanese lost 650 killed and wounded.

Pinkie Cleugh (Scottish Wars).

Fought September, 1547, between the Scots, under the Earl of Huntly, and the English, under the Protector Somerset. The Scots crossed the Esk, and attacked the English lines, at first with success, but they were thrown into confusion by a charge of cavalry, and in the end fled from the field with heavy loss.

Pirot (Servo-Bulgarian War).

Fought November 26 and 27, 1885, between 40,000 Servians, under King Milan, and 45,000 Bulgarians, under Prince Alexander. After some desultory fighting, the Bulgarians seized the town of Pirot in the course of the afternoon. At dawn on the 27th, the Servians, by a surprise attack, recovered Pirot, which was later retaken by the Bulgarians, though the Servians continued to hold a position to the south of the town till nightfall. Early next morning an armistice was concluded. The Bulgarians lost 2,500, the Servians 2,000 killed and wounded.

Pittsburg Landing. See Shiloh.

Placentia (Invasion of the Alemanni).

Fought 271, between the Romans, under Aurelian, and the invading Alemanni. The barbarians attacked the Romans in the dusk of evening, after a long and fatiguing march, and threw them into disorder, but they were rallied by the Emperor, and after severe fighting, succeeded in beating off their assailants.

Plains of Abraham (Seven Years' War).

Fought September 13, 1759, when Wolfe, who was lying on shipboard in the St. Lawrence above Quebec, with 4,000 troops, effected a landing secretly in the night of the 12th to the 13th, and took up unperceived a strong position on the Plains of Abraham. Next morning he was attacked by Montcalm, with about equal numbers, but notwithstanding the most desperate efforts, the French were unable to carry the position, and were driven back into Quebec with a loss of about 1,500. Both Wolfe and Montcalm fell mortally wounded. The British loss amounted to 664 killed and wounded. The French immediately afterwards evacuated Quebec.

Plassy (Seven Years' War).

Fought 1757, between the British, 3,000 strong, with 8 guns, under Clive, and the army of Surabjah Daulah, Nawab of Bengal, aided by a small force of Frenchmen. Clive was encamped in a grove of mangotrees, where he was attacked by the Nawab. He beat off the attack, and then stormed the Nawab's lines, totally routing his army, which fled in panic, with a loss of about 500. The British lost 72 only.

Plataea (Third Persian Invasion).

Fought B.C. 479, between the Greeks, about 100,000 strong, under Pausanias the Spartan, and 300,000 Persians, with 50,000 Greek auxiliaries, under Mardonius. The Persians fought bravely, but were overborne by the superior discipline and heavier armour of the Greeks, and Mardonius falling, a panic ensued, and they fled to their entrenched camp. This was stormed by the Athenians, and no quarter was given, with the result, it is said, that with the exception of a body of 40,000 which left the field early in the battle, only 3,000 Persians escaped.

Plataea (Peloponnesian War).

In 429 B.C., this city, held by a garrison of 400 Plataeans and 80 Athenians, was besieged by the Spartans, under Archidamus. All the useless mouths were sent out of the place, only 110 women being retained to bake bread. The garrison repulsed numerous assaults, and the siege soon resolved itself into a blockade, but provisions becoming scarce, an attempt was made to break through the enemy's lines, which half the garrison succeeded in doing, with the loss of one man. The remainder held out till 427, when being on the verge of starvation, they surrendered. The survivors were tried for having deserted Bœotia for Athens, at the outbreak of the war, and 200 Plataeans, and 25 Athenians were put to death.

Plescow (Russo-Swedish Wars).

This fortress was besieged by the Swedes, under Gustavus Adolphus, August 20, 1615, and defended by a Russian garrison. It is notable as marking a departure from the established practice of surrounding a besieged city with walls of circumvallation. For these Gustavus substituted a series of entrenched camps, communications between which were maintained by strong patrolling forces. Little progress was made, owing to a delay in the arrival of the Swedish breaching guns, and through the mediation of England, negotiations were opened with Russia, and the siege raised, October 14, 1615.

Plevna (Russo-Turkish War).

Four battles were fought in the course of the siege of Plevna, the first three being attacks on the Russian defences, and the fourth, Osman Pasha's final attempt to cut his way through the besieger's lines.

On July 20, 1877, the advance guard of Krüdener's corps, 6,500 strong, under Schilder-Schuldener, attacked the defences to the north and east of Plevna. The Russians advanced with impetuosity, and carried some of the advanced trenches, driving the defenders back to the outskirts of the town, but their heavy loss, and a failure of ammunition compelled a retreat, and the Turks rallying, drove them from the positions they had captured, and pursued them for some distance. The Russians lost two-thirds of their officers, and nearly 2,000 men.

The second battle took place, July 30, when General Krüdener, with 30,000 Russians in two divisions, assailed the Turkish redoubts to the north and east of the town. Schakofsky had command of the latter attack, Krüdener himself leading the assault on the Gravitza redoubt on the north. Krüdener was absolutely unsuccessful. Schakofsky by 5.30 p.m. was in possession of two of the eastern redoubts, but before nightfall these were retaken by the Turks, and the Russians retired, defeated all along the line. Their losses amounted to 169 officers and 7,136 men, of whom 2,400 were left dead on the field. On the 11th and 12th of September, the investing army, 95,000 strong, under the Grand Duke Michael, attacked Plevna on three sides, Osman Pasha having now 30,000 men under his command. On the 11th an attack on the Omar Tabrija redoubt was repulsed with a loss to the Russians of 6,000 men. The attack on the Gravitza redoubts resulted in the capture of the " Bloody Battery," which the Russians held till the end of the siege. On the south-west, Skobeleff captured two of the six inner redoubts which protected

that angle of the fortress. On the 12th, the attack on the second Gravitza redoubt was repulsed, and the two redoubts captured by Skobeleff were retaken, after a terrible struggle, The losses in the two days' fighting amounted to 20,600 including 2,000 prisoners, on the Russian side, on that of the Turks to 5,000, Of these, 8,000 Russians, and 4,000 Turks fell in Skobeleff's attack.

On December 10, Osman Pasha, at the head of 25,000 Turks, accompanied by 9,000 convalescents and wounded in carts, attempted to cut his way through the Russian army, now 100,000 strong, under the King of Roumania, with Todleben as Chief of the Staff. The attempt was made on the east of Plevna, and was directed against the Imperial Grenadiers, under General Ganetzki. Having successfully crossed the Vid, Osman charged down upon the Russians, on a line two miles in length, and carried the first line of entrenchments. Todleben, however, hurried up reinforcements, and the Turks were in turn attacked, and driven back in confusion across the river, Osman being severely wounded. Here they made their last stand, but were overpowered, and driven into Plevna, which before evening capitulated, after a defence lasting 143 days. In this engagement, the Turks lost 5,000, and the Russians 2,000 killed and wounded.

Podhaic.

Fought 1667, between 10,000 Poles, under John Sobieski, and 80,000 Cossacks and Tartars

who were besieging Kaminiec.
The Cossacks were totally routed
and forced to evacuate Poland.

Podol (Seven Weeks' War).

Fought June 26, 1866, be-
tween the advance-guard of
Prince Frederick Charles' army,
and the Austrians, under General
Clam-Gallas. The Austrians
were defeated and driven out
of Podol, after severe fighting,
in which they lost heavily. The
Prussians took 500 prisoners.

**Poitiers (Gothic Invasion of
France).**

Fought 507, between the
Franks, under Clovis, and the
Visigoths, under Alaric II.
Clovis and Alaric met in single
combat, and Alaric was slain,
following which the Goths were
utterly routed. By this decisive
victory, the province of Aquitaine was added to the Frankish
dominions.

Poitiers (Hundred Years' War).

Fought September 19, 1356,
between 8,000 English, under
Edward the Black Prince, and
80,000 French, under King
John of France. The English
occupied a strong position behind lanes and vineyards, in
which their archers were posted.
The French cavalry, charging
up the lanes, were thrown into
confusion by the bowmen, and
were then taken in flank by the
English knights and men-at-
arms, who completely routed
them, with a loss of 8,000 killed,
and numerous prisoners, including the King, The English
losses were very small.

Pola (War of Chiozza).

Fought 1380, when Doria,
with 22 Genoese galleys, offered

battle to the Venetian fleet,
under Pisani, which was lying
at Pola. Pisani sallied out with
20 galleys, and captured the
Genoese flag-ship, Doria being
killed. The Genoese, however,
rallied, drove Pisani back, and
defeated him with a loss of
2,000 killed, and 15 galleys and
1,900 men captured.

**Pollentia (First Gothic Invasion
of Italy).**

Fought March 29, 403, be-
tween the Goths, under Alaric,
and the Romans, under Stilicho.
Stilicho attacked the Gothic
camp while they were celebrat-
ing the festival of Easter, and
owing to the surprise, the charge
of the Roman cavalry threw
them into confusion. They
were, however, soon rallied by
Alaric, and the Romans driven
off with heavy loss, but Stilicho
advancing at the head of the
legionaries, forced his way into
the camp, and drove out the
Goths with enormous slaughter.
Alaric's wife was among the
captives.

Pollicore (First Mysore War).

Fought August 27, 1781, between 11,000 British, under Sir
Eyre Coote and the Mysoris,
80,000 strong, under Haidar Ali.
Coote seized the village of Pollicore, turning Haidar's flank
and forcing him to retreat, after
an action lasting eight hours.
The British lost 421 killed and
wounded, the Mysoris about
2,000.

Polonka (Russo-Polish Wars).

Fought 1667, between the
Russian invaders, and the Poles,
under Czarnięcki. The Russians were totally routed, a
defeat which was largely in-

strumental in bringing about the signature of peace in the same year.

Polotsk (Moscow Campaign).
Fought August 18, 1812, between 33,000 French and Bavarians, under General Saint Cyr, and 30,000 Russians, under Count Wittgenstein. The Russians were taken by surprise, and after an action which lasted two hours only, were driven back with a loss of 3,000 killed, 1,500 prisoners and 14 guns. The French lost a little over 1,000 killed and wounded.

Polotsk (Moscow Campaign).
Fought October 18, 1812, when General Saint-Cyr, with 30,000 French and Bavarians, was attacked and defeated by the Russians, in slightly superior force, under Count Wittgenstein, and forced to evacuate Polotsk.

Ponani (First Mysore War).
Fought November 19, 1780, when a force of British and native troops, about 2,500 strong, under Colonel Macleod, entrenched near Ponani, were attacked before daybreak by a strong force of Mysoris, under Tippu Sahib. The Mysoris were repulsed at the point of the bayonet, with a loss of 1,100. The British loss was 87 only.

Pondicherry.
This place was invested by the British, under Admiral Boscawen, with a fleet of 30 sail, and a land force of 6,000 men, August 30, 1748, and was defended by a French garrison of 4,800, under Dupleix. The siege was grossly mismanaged, and in October Boscawen was forced to withdraw, having lost by sickness or in action nearly a third of his land force. The French lost 250 only during the siege.

Pondicherry (Seven Years' War).
In August, 1760, Colonel Coote, with about 8,000 British and native troops, invested this place, which was held by a French garrison, 3,000 strong, under Lally-Tollendal. Coote was almost immediately superseded by Colonel Monson, but the latter having been wounded, Coote resumed the command. Fire was not opened from the breaching batteries till December 8th, and on the 31st a terrific hurricane wrecked all the land batteries, and drove ashore six ships of the blockading squadron. On January 10, 1761, however, fire was reopened, and the town surrendered on the 15th.

Pondicherry.
Having been surrendered to the French by the Peace of Paris, Pondicherry was again besieged by a British force, under Sir Hector Monro, in conjunction with a squadron of ships, under Sir Edward Vernon, August 8, 1778. It was gallantly defended by the French, under M. Bellecombe, until the middle of October, when after a month's bombardment the place surrendered.

Pondicherry.
A naval action was fought off Pondicherry, August 10, 1778, during the third siege, when a French squadron of 5 ships, under M. Tronjolly, issued from the roads, and offered battle to the 5 ships of Sir Edward

Vernon. The French were worsted, and driven back to their anchorage.

Pondicherry.

A second naval action off this place was fought June 20, 1783, between a British squadron of 18 ships of the line, and 12 frigates, under Sir Edward Hughes, and a French squadron, under de Suffren. The battle was undecided, the British ships suffering considerably in masts and rigging, and being unable to chase when de Suffren sheered off. The British loss was 520 killed and wounded.

Pontevert (Gallic War).

Fought 57 B.C., between 50,000 Romans, under Cæsar, and the Suevi, 300,000 strong, under Galba. The Suevi attacked the Roman entrenched camp, but were repulsed with very heavy loss and their army dispersed.

Pont Valain (Hundred Years' War).

Fought 1370, between the French, under du Guesclin, and the English, under Sir Thomas Granson. The French surprised the English camp, but the English rallied, and a severe conflict followed, in which the French attack was at first repulsed. A flank movement of the French, however, threw the English into disorder, and they were defeated with a loss of nearly 10,000 in killed, wounded and prisoners, among the latter being Sir Thomas Granson.

Poonah (Second Mahratta War).

Fought October 25, 1802, between the forces of Jeswunt Rao, and the united armies of the Peshwa and Sindhia of Gwalior. After an evenly contested action, Jeswunt Rao got the upper hand, and gained a complete victory, Sindhia fleeing from the field, leaving behind him all his guns and baggage.

Port Arthur (Chino - Japanese War).

This place, held by a Chinese garrison of 9,000 men, was attacked and stormed by the Japanese, after a short bombardment. The Chinese made but a feeble resistance, the assailants losing only 270 killed and wounded.

Port Arthur (Russo - Japanese War).

Fought February 8, 1904, between a Japanese fleet of 16 warships, under Vice-Admiral Togo, and the Russian fleet of 6 battleships and 10 cruisers, under Vice-Admiral Stark, lying at anchor off Port Arthur. The Japanese attacked with torpedo boats, and succeeded in seriously damaging 2 battleships and a cruiser, which were beached at the mouth of the harbour. They then opened a bombardment, in which they injured a third battleship and four more cruisers sustaining no damage to their own ships. The Russians lost 56 killed and wounded, the Japanese, 58, chiefly in the torpedo boats.

On April 13, the Japanese torpedo flotilla attacked the Russian squadron, under Makaroff. The battleship Petropavlovsk was torpedoed and sunk, Makaroff and 700 officers and men being drowned. The battleship Pobieda, and a destroyer were also torpedoed, but managed to reach the harbour. The Japanese suffered no material loss.

After numerous only partially successful attempts to block the fairway, the Japanese, on May 2, sent in a fleet of merchant steamers, accompanied by the torpedo flotilla. Of these, eight succeeded in reaching the outer harbour, and two of them broke the boom guarding the inner harbour, and were blown up by their commanders in the fairway. Several others were sunk near the harbour entrance. Of the 179 officers and men forming the crews of the merchant steamers, only 42 were rescued by the Japanese, though a few survivors fell into the hands of the Russians. This is one of the most daring exploits in the history of naval warfare.

Porte St. Antoine (Wars of the Fronde).

Fought July 2, 1652, between the Royal troops, under Turenne, and 5,000 insurgents, under Condé. Condé occupied a position round the gate, protected by barricades and fortified houses, where he was attacked by Turenne. The barricades were taken and retaken several times, but at last, after heavy fighting, Condé abandoned all idea of penetrating into Paris, and retired. His losses were heavy, especially in officers, among the severely wounded being the Duc de Nemurs, and the Duc de la Rochefoucauld.

Port Hudson (American Civil War).

This fortress was invested, May 25, 1863, by five Federal divisions, under General Banks, and defended by 6,000 Confederates, under General Gardner. An assault on the 27th was repulsed, and a regular siege commenced. After a second unsuccessful assault, on June 14, the garrison, having no hope of relief, surrendered, July 9, having lost 800 men during the siege. The losses of the besiegers were far heavier, the two unsuccessful assaults showing a heavy list of casualties.

Portland (Dutch Wars).

Fought February 18, 1653, between an English fleet of about 70 sail, under Blake, Deane and Monk, and a Dutch fleet of 73 ships, convoying 300 merchantmen, under Van Tromp, de Ruyter and Evetzen. In the early part of the engagement, which was very severely contested, three English ships were carried by the board, and that portion of the fleet which had come into action was nearly overwhelmed. At this crisis, however, the rest of the English ships engaged, the battle was restored, and the captured ships retaken. On the 19th the battle was renewed off the Isle of Wight, 5 Dutch ships being captured or destroyed. On the 20th the Dutch sheered off defeated, having lost during the three days' fighting, 11 men-of-war, 60 merchant ships, 1,500 killed and wounded and 700 prisoners. The English losses were also heavy.

Porto Bello (Raids of the Buccaneers).

This Spanish-American fortress was captured in 1665 by

460 Buccaneers, under Morgan. The walls were scaled, and the town sacked, unheard-of cruelties being perpetrated by the Filibusters.

Porto Bello (War of the Austrian Succession).

This place was captured from the Spaniards, November 21, 1740, by a British fleet of 6 ships, under Admiral Vernon. The British loss was trifling.

Porto Novo (First Mysore War).

Fought July 1, 1781, between 8,500 British troops, under Sir Eyre Coote, and about 65,000 Mysoris, under Hyder Ali. Hyder occupied a strongly entrenched camp, blocking the British advance upon Cuddalore. Here he was attacked by Coote, and after a day's hard fighting the position was stormed, and Hyder forced to retreat. The British lost 306 only, while the Mysoris are computed to have lost 10,000.

Porto Praya Bay.

Fought April 16, 1781, when Commodore Johnstone, in command of a British squadron of 5 ships of the line and 5 frigates, repulsed a determined attack of a French squadron of 11 sail, under de Suffren. The loss in the British squadron amounted to 36 killed and 147 wounded.

Port Republic (American Civil War).

Fought June 9, 1862, between the Federals, 12,000 strong, under General Shields, and an equal force of Confederates, under General Jackson. The Federals were completely defeated, a portion of their army being driven from the field in disorder and with heavy loss.

Potidæa.

This city was besieged by a force of about 3,000 Athenians, B.C. 432, and was defended by a small garrison of Corinthians, under Aristæus. The town held out until the winter of 429, when the garrison surrendered, and were permitted to go free.

Potosi. (South-American War of Independence).

Fought April, 1825, between, the Bolivians, under Bolivar, and the Spanish Royalists, under Olaneta. The Spaniards were completely defeated.

Prague (Thirty Years' War).

Fought November 8, 1620, when the Imperialists, under Maximilian of Bavaria and Count Tilly, drove 22,000 Bohemians, under Frederick of Bohemia, up to the walls of Prague, and signally defeated them, with a loss of 5,000 men and all their artillery. Frederick was obliged to take refuge in the city, and soon afterwards capitulated. The battle only lasted an hour, and the Imperialists lost no more than 300 men.

Prague (Seven Years' War).

Fought May 6, 1757, between 70,000 Austrians, under Charles of Lorraine, and 60,000 Prussians, under Frederick the Great. The Austrians occupied a very strong position on the Moldau, which was attacked and carried by Frederick, Charles being driven back into Prague with a loss of 8,000 killed and wounded and 9,000 prisoners. Marshal Braun was among the killed. The Prussians lost 13,000, including Marshal Schwerin.

Prairie Grove (American Civil War).

A sanguinary but indecisive action, fought December 7, 1862, between the Confederates, under General Hindman, and the Federals, under General Herron. The losses were about equal.

Preston (Civil War).

Fought August 17, 1648, when Langdale, with 4,000 Royalists, was deserted by the main body of the Scottish invading army, and left to face the attack of about 8,000 Parliamentarians under Cromwell, The Royalists fought desperately for four hours, but were overpowered, and the whole force killed or captured.

Preston (Rebellion of the Fifteen).

Fought November 12, 1715, between 4,000 Jacobites, under General Forster, and a small force of Royal troops, chiefly dragoons, under General Wills. The Jacobites had barricaded the approaches to the town, and held their ground throughout the day, but reinforcements arriving, Wills was able to invest the place completely ; and early on the morning of the 14th Forster surrendered, Many of the rebels having left the town on the night of the 12th, the prisoners numbered 1,468. The Jacobite loss in killed and wounded was 42, that of the Royalists about 200.

Prestonpans (Rebellion of the Forty-five).

Fought September 21, 1745, between 2,300 Royal troops, under Sir John Cope, and a slightly superior force of Jacobites, under the Young Pretender. Cope's infantry failed to stand up against the charge of the Highlanders, and fled in confusion, losing heavily in killed and wounded, and 1,600 prisoners, including 70 officers. The Highlanders lost about 140 killed and wounded. This action is also known as the Battle of Gladsmuir.

Primolano (Napoleon's Italian Campaigns).

Fought September 7, 1796, when Napoleon surprised and totally routed the vanguard of Wurmser's army. The Austrians lost over 4,000 killed, wounded and prisoners.

Princeton (American War of Independence).

Fought 1776 between the Americans, under Washington, and the British, under General Gage. The British were defeated, and this victory enabled Washington to regain possession of New Jersey.

Pruth, The (Ottoman Wars).

Fought August 2, 1770, when the Russians, under General Romanzoff, stormed the triple entrenchments held by the main Turkish army, 120,000 strong, under Halil Bey, and drove out the Turks with a loss of 20,000 killed and wounded.

Puente (South American War of Independence).

Fought February 16, 1816, between the Colombian Patriots, under Lorrices, aud the Spanish Royalists, under Morillo. The

Royalists gained a complete victory.

Puente de la Reyna (Second Carlist War).

Fought October 6, 1872, between 50,000 Carlists, under Ollo, and about 9,000 Republicans, under Moriones. The Republicans were defeated after hard fighting, and were at last driven in disorder from the field by a bayonet charge. The Carlists lost 113 only ; the losses of the Republicans were far heavier.

Pultowa (Russo-Swedish Wars).

Fought July 8, 1709, between the Swedes, 24,000 strong, under Charles XII, and the Russians, 70,000 in number, under Peter the Great. After some successes early in the battle the Swedes were overwhelmed by the Czar's great superiority in artillery, and were defeated with a loss of 9,000 killed and wounded and 6,000 prisoners. Charles with difficulty made his escape from the field by swimming the Borysthenes.

Pultusk (Russo-Swedish Wars).

Fought 1703, between 10,000 Swedes, under Charles XII, and an equal force of Saxons, under Marshal von Stenau. The Saxons made practically no resistance, but fled from the field, losing only 600 killed and 1,000 prisoners.

Pultusk Campaign of Friedland).

Fought December 26, 1806, between 43,000 Russians, under Bennigsen, and 18,000 French, under Lannes. Lannes endeavoured to pierce the Russian left and cut them off from the town, but he did not succeed in getting through, and in this part of the field the action was indecisive. On the left the French did little more than hold their own, but the Russians retired during the night, having lost 3,000 killed and wounded, 2,000 prisoners, and a large number of guns. The French admitted a loss of 1,500 only, but this is probably an understatement, Russian accounts estimating the French losses at 8,000.

Puna (Raids of the Buccaneers).

On April 27, 1687, three Buccaneering vessels, under Captain Davis, engaged two Spanish men-of-war off Puna. The action was entirely one of long-range firing, and lasted till May 3, when the Spanish commander withdrew his ships. In the seven days only three or four Buccaneers were wounded.

Punniar (Gwalior Campaign).

Fought December 29, 1843, between the left wing of Sir Hugh Gough's army, under General Grey, and a force of 12,000 Mahrattas, with 40 guns. The Mahrattas were totally routed.

Pydna (Third Macedonian War).

Fought June 22, 168 B.C., between the Romans, under Æmilius Paulus, and the Macedonians, under Perseus. The Macedonian phalanx attacked the Roman line, and drove them back on their camp, but becoming disordered by the uneven ground, was broken by the legionaries and cut to pieces. The result was a total defeat of the Macedonians, with a loss of 20,000 killed and 11,000 prisoners. The phalanx here fought its last fight and perished to a man.

Pyramids (French Invasion of Egypt).

Fought July 21, 1798, when the Mameluke army, under Murad Bey, endeavoured to arrest Napoleon's march on Cairo. The Mameluke infantry, numbering about 20,000, took no part in the fight, but their cavalry, perhaps at that time the finest in the world, charged the French squares with the utmost gallantry. They were, however, repulsed time after time, with great slaughter, and were eventually driven into the Nile, where the shattered remnants escaped by swimming.

Pyrenees (Peninsular War).

The engagements fought between Wellington's lieutenants and Soult's army, which was endeavouring to relieve San Sebastian, are known as the Battles of the Pyrenees. They include the fighting from July 25 to August 2, 1813, and specially the actions of Roncesvalles, Maya, Santarem and Buenzas. The British loss in these battles amounted to 7,300, while the French lost fully double that number.

Pylos and Sphacteria (Peloponnesian War).

The promontory of Pylos, which is separated by a narrow channel from the island of Sphacteria, was seized and fortified by an Athenian force under Demosthenes, B.C. 425. Here he was besieged by the Spartans under Thrasymelidas, with a land force and a fleet of 43 ships, the crews of which occupied Sphacteria. Demosthenes repulsed an attack on Pylos, and Eurymedon, arriving with 50 Athenian vessels, defeated the Spartan fleet, and blockaded Sphacteria. After a protracted siege, the arrival of reinforcements, under Cleon, enabled the Athenians to land 14,000 men in the island, and the garrison, reduced from 420 to 292, surrendered.

Q

Quatre Bras (Hundred Days).

Fought June 16, 1815, between the advance guard of the British army, under Wellington, and the left wing of the French army, 16,000 strong, under Ney. Napoleon's object was to prevent the junction of the British and the Prussians, and Ney's orders were to drive back the British, while Napoleon, with his main body, engaged the Prussians. Ney attacked at 3 p.m., but the British held their own till evening, when Ney, not receiving the reinforcements he expected, began to fall back. Wellington then attacked vigorously all along the line, retaking all the positions occupied by the French during the day.

Quebec (Seven Years' War).

This city was besieged June, 1759, by 9,000 British troops, under General Wolfe, assisted by a fleet of 22 ships of war, under Admiral Holmes. The place was defended by about 16,000 French, under Montcalm. Wolfe was too weak numerically for an investment, and his object was to draw Montcalm into an engagement. On July 31 he was defeated in an attack on Montcalm's lines outside the city, but on September 13, having landed above Quebec, he met and defeated the French, who evacuated the place on the 17th .

After defeating General Murray, April 27, 1760, the Chevalier de Levis laid siege to Quebec, with about 8,000 French and Canadians. The garrison consisted of no more than 2,500 effectives, but owing to the superiority of their artillery, Levis was unable to make any impression on the defences. On May 15 a small British squadron anchored off the city, and on the following day attacked and destroyed the French ships carrying de Levis' supplies and reserve of ammunition, whereupon he hastily raised the siege, leaving behind him 40 siege guns and all his sick and wounded.

Queenston Heights (Second American War).
Fought October 13, 1812, between 4,000 British (chiefly Canadian volunteers), under General Brock, and about 5,000 Americans, under Van Reusselaer. The Americans attacked the British position on Queenston Heights, and after very severe fighting, were totally defeated. The exact losses are unknown, but the British took 1,000 prisoners, and the American column was practically annihilated.

Quiberon Bay (Seven Years' War).
Fought November 20, 1759, between the British fleet, 23 sail of the line and 10 frigates, under Hawke, and 21 French line-of-battleships and 3 frigates, under Conflans. The action was fought in a heavy gale on a lee shore, and resulted in the French being driven to take refuge in Quiberon Bay, with a loss of 2 ships sunk and 2 captured. Notwithstanding the gale, Hawke followed up his advantage, and standing in, succeeded in capturing or destroying all but four of the ships which had taken refuge in the bay, though in so doing he lost two of his own ships, which were driven ashore and wrecked. The British lost in the action only 1 officer and 270 men killed and wounded.

Quipuaypan (Conquest of Peru).
Fought 1532, between the rival Peruvian chiefs, Atahualpa and Huascar. Huascar was totally routed, and taken prisoner.

Quistello (War of the Polish Succession).
Fought July, 1734, between the Imperialists, under Prince Eugene, and the French, under the Duc de Broglie. Prince Eugene gained a signal victory.

R

Raab (Campaign of Wagram).
Fought June 14, 1809, between 44,000 French, under Eugene Beauharnais, and about 40,000 Austrians, under the Archduke John. The French attacked the Austrian position, and driving them successively from the villages of Kismegyer and Szabadhegy, totally de-

feated them. Under cover of night, however, the Archduke was able to make an orderly retirement, with a loss of about 3,000 killed and wounded and 2,500 prisoners. The French lost something over 2,000.

Radcot Bridge.

Fought 1387, between the troops of Richard II, under De Vere, Duke of Ireland, and the forces of the Lords Appellant, under the Earl of Derby (Henry IV). De Vere and his troops fled almost without striking a blow, and the King was thus left entirely in the power of the Barons.

Ragatz (Armagnac War).

Fought March, 1446, between the Austrians and the Swiss Confederation. The Swiss gained a brilliant victory, which was followed by peace with Austria and the Armagnacs.

Rajahmundry (Seven Years' War).

Fought December 9, 1758, between 2,500 British troops, under Colonel Forde, in conjunction with about 5,000 native levies, and the French, 6,500 strong, under Conflans. The native troops did little on either side, but Forde's 500 Europeans routed Conflans' Frenchmen, and the latter fled with considerable loss.

Rakersberg (Ottoman Wars).

Fought 1416, between 20,000 Turks, under Ahmed Bey, and 12,000 Austrians and others, under Duke Ernest of Styria. Duke Ernest marched to the relief of Rakersberg, which the Turks were besieging, and drove

them from the field utterly routed. It is said that the Turkish losses amounted to more than the whole Christian army. Ahmed Bey was among the slain.

Ramillies (Seven Years' War).

Fought May 23, 1706, between the British and Imperialists, under Marlborough and Prince Eugene, about 80,000 strong, and the French, in equal force, under Marshal Villeroy. The allies drove the French out of Ramillies, their resistance on the whole being unworthy of them, and in the end they were disastrously defeated with heavy loss, 5,000 being killed and wounded, while 6,000 prisoners and 50 guns were taken. The allies lost less than 3,000.

Ramla.

Fought 1177, between the Saracens, under Saladin, and the Christians of Jerusalem, under Renaud de Châtillon. The Christians won a complete victory.

Ramnugger (Second Sikh War).

Fought November, 1849, when Lord Gough attempted to dislodge Shir Singh, who with about 35,000 Sikhs, had occupied a position behind the Chenab opposite Ramnugger. The attempt was made by a brigade under General Campbell, with a cavalry force under General Cureton, and failed owing to the unexpected strength of the Sikh artillery, which was well posted and served. General Cureton was killed.

Raphia.

Fought B.C. 223, between the Egyptians, under Ptolemy Philopator, and the Syrians, under Antiochus the Great. Antiochus at first held the advantage, but pressing too far in the pursuit, was overpowered and totally routed. The Syrians lost 14,000 killed and 4,000 prisoners.

Rastadt (Wars of the French Revolution).

Fought 1796, between the French, under Moreau, and the Austrians, under the Archduke Charles. After a severe engagement Moreau succeeded in seizing the heights held by the Austrians, and forced Charles to retreat to the Danube.

Raszyn (Campaign of Wagram).

Fought April 19, 1809, between 30,000 Austrians, under the Archduke Ferdinand, and about 20,000 French and Poles, under Poniatowski. The Archduke was marching on Warsaw when Poniatowski, to whom the defence of that city had been entrusted, came out to meet him, and after a stubborn fight in the woods and marshes round Raszyn, was driven back upon Warsaw, with a loss of 2,000 killed and wounded. A few days later he surrendered the city to the Austrians to save it from a bombardment.

Rathenow (Swedish Invasion of Brandenburg).

Fought June 25, 1675, between the Brandenburgers, 15,000 strong, under the Elector Frederick William, and the Swedes, under Charles XI. The Swedes, wearied by a long march, were surprised by the Elector in their camp, and suffered a serious reverse.

Rathmines (Civil War).

Fought August 2, 1649, between the Royalists, under Ormonde, and the Parliamentary garrison of Dublin, under Colonel Jones. Ormonde having ordered a night attack upon Dublin, the Parliamentarians made a sortie, and driving back the assaulting column, attacked the main body of the Royalists in their camp, totally routing them, with a loss of 4,000 killed and wounded and 2,000 prisoners. All Ormonde's artillery was captured.

Ravenna.

Fought 729 between the troops of Leo the Iconoclast, and a force of Italians, raised by Pope Gregory II, in defence of image worship. After a severe struggle, the Greeks were routed, and in their flight to their ships were slaughtered by thousands. It is said that the waters of the Po were so infected with blood, that for six years the inhabitants of Ravenna would not eat any fish caught in that river.

Ravenna (War of the Holy League).

Fought 1512, between the troops of the Holy League, and the French, under Gaston de Foix. The French gained a signal victory, but Gaston de Foix fell in the moment of his triumph, pierced with sixteen wounds.

Reading (Danish Invasion).

Fought 871, between the Danish invaders, and the West Saxons, under Æthelred and Alfred. The West Saxons, after a stubborn resistance, were defeated and driven from the field with great slaughter.

Rebec (Wars of Charles V).

Fought 1524, between the Imperialists, under Constable de Bourbon, and the French, under Bonnivet. The French were totally defeated, with heavy loss, among those who fell being the Chevalier de Bayard.

Redan (Crimean War).

This fort, forming part of the southern defences of Sebastopol, was attacked by the British Second and Light Divisions, September 8, 1855. The ramparts were stormed, but the assailants were unable to make good their footing, and were eventually repulsed with heavy loss. The fall of the Malakoff, however, rendered the southern side of Sebastopol untenable, and the Russians retired during the night. The British losses amounted to 2,184 killed and wounded.

Reddersberg (Second Boer War).

Fought April 3, 1900, when 5 companies of British infantry were surrounded by a force of Boers, with 5 guns, and after holding out for twenty-four hours, were compelled by want of water to surrender, having lost 4 officers and 43 men killed and wounded. The prisoners numbered 405.

Reims (Allied Invasion of France).

Fought March 13, 1814, when Napoleon, with 30,000 French, surprised and routed 13,000 Prussians and Russians, under Saint-Priest, with a loss of 6,000 killed, wounded and prisoners. The French lost a few hundreds only.

Revel (Russo-Swedish Wars).

This port was attacked in the spring of 1790 by the Swedish fleet, under the Duke of Sudermanland. The Russian batteries, however, aided by the fleet under Admiral Chitchagoff, drove them off with considerable loss.

Revolax (Finland War).

Fought April 27, 1808, when General Klingspoor, with about 8,000 Swedes, surprised an isolated Russian column of about 4,000 men, under General Bonlatoff. The Russians were surrounded, and tried to cut their way through, but failed, less than 1,000 succeeding in escaping from the trap. General Bonlatoff fell fighting to the last.

Rhé.

St. Martin, the capital of this island, was besieged by the English, under the Duke of Buckingham, from July 17 to October 29, 1627. An assault on October 27 was repulsed, and the landing of the Duke of Schomberg, with 6,000 French, on the island, made the English lines untenable, whereupon Buckingham raised the siege. While returning to his ships Buckingham was attacked by the French, and suffered considerably. The English losses during the operations amounted to about 4,000 men.

Rheinfeldt (Thirty Years' War).

Fought 1638, between the Protestant Germans, under Duke Bernard of Saxe Weimar, and the Imperialists, under Jean de Wert. The Duke was besieging Rheinfeldt, when he was attacked by de Wert, and forced to raise the siege and retire. After retreating, however, a short distance only, unpursued, he suddenly retraced his steps, and taking the Imperialists by surprise, inflicted upon them a severe defeat, dispersing their army and capturing de Wert. In this action fell the veteran Duc de Rohan.

Rhodes (Ottoman Wars).

This place, defended by the Knights, under their Grand Master, Pierre d'Aubusson, was besieged May 23, 1480, by a Turkish army, under Meshid Pasha, aided by a fleet of 160 ships. The siege lasted three months, and was raised after the failure of the second assault, the Turks having by that time lost 10,500 killed and wounded.

A second and successful siege was begun July 28, 1522, by Solyman the Magnificent. The Knights, under Villiers de L'Isle Adam, held out until December 21, repulsing numerous attacks, but at last, worn by famine, they were compelled to surrender. The Turks are stated to have lost by disease and battle over 100,000 men. This siege is notable as being the first in which the Turks used explosive bombs.

Riachuelo (Paraguayan War).

Fought June 11, 1865, between the fleets of Paraguay and Brazil. After a sanguinary engagement the advantage rested with the Brazilians.

Richmond (American Civil War).

Fought August 30, 1862, between the Confederates, about 6,000 strong, under General Kirby Smith, and 8,000 Fede-

rals, under General Manson. The Federals were routed and driven headlong into Richmond, where 5,000 prisoners, 9 guns and 10,000 stand of arms were captured. The Confederate losses were slight.

Richmond (American Civil War).

In the neighbourhood of this place were fought the final actions of the war, when Lee, with the army of Virginia, endeavoured to break through the ring of Grant's troops by which he was surrounded, and being everywhere repulsed, was compelled to surrender March 8, 1865, on which date he had but 10,000 effectives under his command.

Rich Mountain (American Civil War).

Fought July 12, 1861, between 15,000 Federals, under General McClellan, and 6,000 Confederates, under General Garnett. The Federals stormed the heights of Rich Mountain and Laurel Hill, and drove the Southerners from their positions, with a loss of about 1,000, including prisoners. During the pursuit on the following day, General Garnett was killed in a cavalry skirmish.

Rietfontein (Second Boer War).

Fought October 24, 1899, between 4,000 British, under Sir George White, and the Free Staters, who were advancing to interrupt the retreat of Colonel Yule from Dundee. The enemy occupied a range of hills about seven miles from Ladysmith, where they were attacked by White. After an indecisive

P

action the British retired to Ladysmith, with a loss of 111 killed and wounded, but the object aimed at was attained, for the Boers were prevented from interfering with Colonel Yule's march.

Rieti (Neapolitan Rising).

Fought March 21, 1821, between 12,000 Neapolitans, under General Pepe, and the Austrian invading army, 80,000 strong, As long as he was opposing only the advance guard, Pepe made a most resolute resistance, but on their being reinforced from the main body, the Neapolitans were overpowered by superior numbers, and finally driven in confusion from the field. Two days' later the Austrians entered Naples, and reinstated Ferdinand on the throne.

Riga (Thirty Years' War).

This place was invested by the Swedes, under Gustavus Adolphus, in the early part of August, 1621, and was defended by a garrison of 300 Poles. A resolute defence was made, and several determined assaults repulsed, but a large breach having having been effected by September 11, the garrison, now reduced to a handful, had no option but to surrender, and the town was entered by the Swedes, September 15, 1621.

Rimnitz (Ottoman Wars).

Fought September 22, 1789, when 25,000 Austrians and Russians, under the Duke of Coburg and Suwaroff, routed an army of 90,000 Turks, under the Grand Vizier. The Turkish losses were enormous, the whole army being killed, captured, or dispersed.

Rinya (Ottoman Wars).

Fought July 21, 1556, between 40,000 Turks, under Ali Pasha, and a comparatively small force of Austrians and Hungarians, under Thomas Nadasdy. The Turks were defeated with heavy loss, the Christians losing 300 men only.

Rio Seco (Peninsular War).

Fought July 14, 1808, when Marshal Bessières, with about 14,000 French, defeated 26,000 Spaniards, under Cuesta. The Spaniards lost about 6,000, while the French loss was only 370 killed and wounded. Following upon this victory, Joseph entered Madrid.

Rivoli (Napoleon's Italian Campaigns).

Fought January 14, 1797, when the Austrians, with five divisions, under Alvinzi, attacked Napoleon's position on the heights of Rivoli. The position proved too strong to be carried, and Napoleon's superb handling of his troops resulted in the total defeat of the assailants. The fifth Austrian division, which had not taken part in the frontal attack, appeared in the rear of the French position after the battle was over, and being forced by overwhelming numbers, laid down its arms. Masséna, who had specially distinguished himself, took his title from this battle when later ennobled by Napoleon.

Roanoke Island (American Civil War).

This island, which commanded the entrance to Albemarle Sound, North Carolina, and which was defended by

1,800 Confederates, under General Wise, was attacked February 7, 1862, by three brigades of Federals, under General Burnside, aided by 26 gunboats. On the 8th the Federals landed, overpowered the garrison, and occupied the island, losing 235 killed and wounded. The Confederates lost 91 killed and wounded. Of 7 Confederate gunboats employed in the defence, 5 were captured or destroyed.

Rocoux (War of the Austrian Succession).

Fought 1747, between the French, under Maurice de Saxe, and the Imperialists, under Charles of Lorraine. The French won a signal victory, as the result of which they occupied Brabant.

Rocroi (Thirty Years' War).

Fought May 19, 1643, between the French, 22,000 strong, under the Great Condé, and 27,000 Spaniards, under Don Francisco de Melo. The battle was sternly contested, and at first went against the French, their left wing being repulsed, and the centre shaken. Want of cavalry, however, prevented Melo pressing home his advantage, and the French, rallying, broke the Spanish line, and severely defeated them. The Spaniards lost 9,000 killed, and 6,000 prisoners in the infantry alone. The French only admitted a loss of 2,000, but it was doubtless considerably heavier.

Roliça (Peninsular War).

Fought August 17, 1808, when Wellington, with 14,000 British and Portuguese, of whom only 4,000 came into action, attacked the French, 3,000 strong, under Laborde, and after a half-hearted resistance drove them from their position, with a loss of 500 men. The allies lost about 400.

Rome (First Invasion of the Gauls).

The first siege of Rome by the Gauls, under Brennus, took place B.C. 387. No attempt was made to defend the city, which was seized and burnt by the barbarians, the greater part of the population fleeing to Veii and other neighbouring cities. The Capitol, however, was held by the leading Patrician families, and it is said withstood a siege of six months, when Brennus accepted a heavy ransom and withdrew his army.

Rome (Second Gothic Invasion of Italy).

The city was besieged in 408 by the Goths, under Alaric, and after being brought to the verge of starvation and losing many thousands from famine, the Romans capitulated, but retained their freedom on payment of a heavy ransom, whereupon Alaric retired northward in 409. In the course of the year, however, Alaric seized Ostia, the port of Rome, and summoned the city to surrender. In the absence of the Emperor Honorius, the populace forced the authorities to yield ; and Alaric, after deposing Honorius, and bestowing the purple on Attalus, withdrew his troops. In 410, during the month of August, Alaric for the third time appeared before the walls, and on the night of the 24th the Salarian gate was opened to the besiegers by some sympathisers within the city, and Rome was given over to pillage and massacre, in which thousands perished.

Rome (Ricimer's Rebellion).

The rebel Count Ricimer, with a large army of Burgundians, Suevi and other barbarians, laid siege to Rome in 472, and after a defence of three months the besiegers entered the city by storming the Bridge of Hadrian, and sacked it.

Rome (First Gothic War).

In March, 537, the city was besieged by the Goths, under Vitiges, and defended by Belisarius. After a determined resistance, during which a vigorous assault was repulsed, and several successful sorties made, with heavy loss to the besiegers, Vitiges in March, 538, was compelled to raise the siege.

Rome (Second Gothic War).

In May, 546, Totila, King of Italy, at the head of an army of Goths, laid siege to Rome, which was defended by a garrison of 3,000, under Bassas. An attempt to relieve it by Belisarius was on the point of success, but Bassas failed to cooperate with the relieving force, and Belisarius was forced to retire, whereupon the city surrendered, December 17, 546.

It was recovered by Belisarius in the following February, but was again besieged by Totila in 549. On this occasion it was defended by a garrison of 3,000 troops, under Demetrius, who, aided by the inhabitants, made a gallant resistance, but the Gate of St. Paul was opened to the besiegers by some Isaurian sympathisers within the walls, and Totila thus made himself master of the last Italian city excepting Ravenna, which had resisted his victorious army.

In 552, after the defeat of Totila at Tagina, Rome was invested by the Imperial army, under Narses, who, after a brief siege, stormed the defences, and finally delivered the city from the Gothic domination.

Rome.

In the course of dispute with Pope Gregory VII, who had refused to recognize him as emperor, Henry III of Germany laid siege to Rome in 1082. After two interruptions to the siege, the city was finally surrendered to him by the Roman nobles, March, 1084. Gregory was deposed, and the anti-Pope Clement III set upon the pontifical throne, Henry at the same time assuming the Imperial purple.

Rome (Wars of Charles V).

The city was taken by storm May 9, 1527, by the Imperialists under the Constable de Bourbon, who fell in the assault. A massacre followed, in which 8,000 of the inhabitants perished. The Pope retired to the Castle of St. Angelo, where he held out until November 26, when a treaty between him and Charles V put an end to the conflict.

Rome (Italian Rising).

After the proclamation of a Roman republic by Garibaldi and his adherents in 1848, a French army, under General Oudinot, was sent to restore the papal rule. On April 30, 1849, the French, 7,000 strong, attacked the Porta San Pancrazio, where they were encountered by the Republicans, under Garibaldi, and repulsed, with a loss of 300 killed and wounded and 500 prisoners. The Garibaldians lost 100.

On June 3 of the same year the French, under Oudinot, 20,000 strong, made a night attack upon the Garibaldians, who brought up about 8,000 men to oppose them. The Garibaldians were repulsed, with a loss of over 2,000, including 200 officers. Oudinot then laid siege to the city, which, after a terrible bombardment, surrendered July 2, 1849.

Romerswael (Netherlands War of Independence).

Fought January 29, 1574, between the " Beggars of the Sea," under Admiral Boisot, and a Spanish fleet of 75 ships, under Julian Romero. The " Beggars " grappled the enemy's ships in a narrow estuary, and after a very severe encounter, in which the Spaniards lost 15 vessels and 1,200 men, Romero retreated to Bergenop-Zoom.

Roncesvalles.

Fought 778 between the Franks, under Charlemagne, and the Basques and Gascons, under Loup II. The army of Charlemagne, retreating from Spain, was caught in the defile of Roncesvalles, in the Pyrenees, and the rearguard was totally annihilated, among those who fell being the famous Paladin, Roland.

Roncesvalles (Peninsular War).

One of the actions known as the " Battles of the Pyrenees," fought July 25, 1813. Soult, at the head of Clauset's division, attacked the British, consisting of three brigades, under General Byng, but was unable to carry their position, and after severe fighting was repulsed with a loss of 400. The British lost 181 killed and wounded.

Rorke's Drift (Zulu War).

On the night of January 22, 1879, after the disaster of Isandhlwana, this outpost, held by a company of the 24th Regiment and details, in all 139 men, under Lieutenants Bromhead and Chard, R.E., was attacked by a force of Zulus, estimated at 4,000. After a most heroic defence, in which many acts of heroism were performed, especially in the removal of the sick from the hospital, which was fired by the Zulus, the assailants were beaten off, leaving over 400 dead on the field. The little garrison lost 25 killed and wounded. Eight Victoria Crosses and nine Distinguished Conduct medals were awarded for this affair.

Rosbach (Seven Years' War).

Fought November 5, 1757, between 80,000 French and Austrians, under Marshal Soubise, and 30,000 Prussians, under Frederick the Great. Frederick, who occupied the heights of Rosbach, was attacked by the allies. The Prussian cavalry, however, under Seidlitz, charged down upon the Austrians, and threw them into disorder and the infantry falling upon the broken columns utterly routed them, with a loss of 4,000 killed and wounded, 7,000 prisoners, including 11 generals and 63 guns. The Prussians lost 3,000 only.

Rosbecque.

Fought 1382 between 50,000 Flemings, under Philip van Arteveldt, and the French, under Charles VI. The Flemings at first drove back the French, but were overwhelmed by the charges of the French cavalry on their flanks, and were in the end utterly routed. Thousands fell in the action and subsequent pursuit, amongst them van Arteveldt.

Rostock (Dano-Swedish Wars).

Fought June, 1677, between the Danish fleet, under Admiral Juel, and the Swedes, under Admiral Horn. The Swedes were completely defeated.

Rotto Freddo (War of the Austrian Succession).

Fought July, 1746, when the rearguard of the retreating French army, under Marshal Maillebois, was attacked by the Austrians, under Prince Lichtenstein, and after a gallant resistance defeated with heavy loss. In consequence of this defeat the French garrison of Placentia, 4,000 strong, surrendered to the Imperialists.

Rouen (Hundred Years' War).

This city was besieged 1418, by the English, under Henry V. After a gallant defence the garrison surrendered January 15, 1419, the city paying a ransom of 300,000 crowns.

Roundway Down (Civil War).

Fought July 13, 1643, when the Parliamentarians, under Waller and Hazlerigg, attacked the Royalists, under Prince Maurice, who was advancing to the relief of Devizes. The Parliamentarians were totally defeated, their attack on Prince Maurice being repulsed, while at the same time they were taken in the rear by a sortie from the town. Of 1,800 infantry, 600 were killed and the rest taken prisoners.

Roncray — St. — Denis. *See* Herrings.

Roveredo (Napoleon's Italian Campaigns).

Fought September 4, 1796, between 25,000 Austrians, under Davidowich, and the main body of Napoleon's army. Napoleon attacked the Austrian entrenched position, and in spite of a determined defence, carried it, driving the enemy out of Roveredo with heavy loss, including 7,000 prisoners and 15 guns. This victory enabled Masséna to occupy Trent, and the remnants of the Austrian army were driven headlong into the Tyrol.

Rowton Heath (Civil War).

Fought September 24, 1645, when a body of Royalist cavalry, under Sir Marmaduke Langdale, which was endeavouring to prevent the investment of Chester, was attacked by the Parliamentary horse, under Colonel Poyntz. The first attack was repulsed with loss, but Poyntz receiving infantry support, rallied his troops, and drove the Royalists from the field, with a loss of 300 killed and wounded and 1,000 prisoners.

Roseburgh (Scottish Wars).

This town, defended by an English garrison, was besieged by the Scots, under James II of Scotland, in 1460, and after a stubborn defence was captured and destroyed. This is the first occasion on which artillery was used by the Scots. During the siege the Scottish king was killed by the bursting of a gun of large calibre, August 3, 1460.

Rullion Green (Covenanters' Rising).

Fought November, 1666, between the Covenanters, under Colonel Wallace, and the Royal troops, under General Dalziel. The Covenanters were defeated.

Rumersheim (War of the Spanish Succession).

Fought August 26, 1709, between the French, under Marshal Villiers, and the Imperialists, under Count Mercy. Mercy was defeated and driven out of Alsace.

Ruspina (Civil War of Cæsar and Pompey).

Fought January 3, 46 B.C., between Julius Cæsar, with three legions, and a force of Pompeians, composed entirely of cavalry and archers, under Labienus. Cæsar's troops were surrounded, but behaving with extreme steadiness, were able to retire to Ruspina in good order, though with very heavy loss.

Rynemants (Netherlands War of Independence).

Fought August 1, 1578, between the Dutch Patriots,

20,000 strong, under Count Bossu and François de la Noue, and the Spaniards, numbering about 30,000, under Don John of Austria. Don John crossed the Demer, and attacked Bossu in his entrenchments. He was however repulsed, after severe fighting, and retired, leaving 1,000 dead on the field. He offered battle in the open on the following morning, but Bossu declined to leave his lines, and Don John was indisposed to renew the attack, and fell back upon Namur.

S

Saalfeld (Campaign of Jena).

Fought October 10, 1806, between 7,000 Prussians, under Prince Louis of Prussia, and a division of Lannes' corps, under the Marshal himself. The Prussian infantry was broken and driven under the walls of Saalfield, whereupon the prince put himself at the head of his cavalry, and charged the advancing French. The charge was repulsed, and the Prince refusing to surrender was cut down and killed. The Prussians lost in this action 400 killed and wounded, 1,000 prisoners, and 20 guns.

Sabugal (Peninsular War).

Fought April 3, 1811, between three British divisions, under Wellington, and the French, consisting of Reynier's corps. Reynier held the salient angle of the French position on the Coa, and was driven back after less than an hour's fighting, with a loss of about 1,500. The British lost 200 only.

Sacile (Napoleon's Wars).

Fought April 16, 1809, between 45,000 Austrians, under the Archduke John, and 36,000 French and Italians, under Eugène Beauharnais, Regent of Italy. After hard fighting, in which little generalship was shown on either side, a flank movement of the Austrians, which menaced the French line of retreat, forced Eugène to retire, victory thus resting with the Austrians. The losses were about equal on the two sides.

Sacripontus (Civil War of Marius and Sulla).

Fought B.C. 82, between the legions of Sulla and the army of the younger Marius, 40,000 strong. Sulla's veterans were too steady for the newer levies of Marius, and the latter was routed, with the loss of more than half his army killed or captured. After this victory Sulla occupied Rome.

Sadowa. *See* Koeniggratz.

Sadulapur (Second Sikh War).

Fought December 3, 1848. After the failure of his frontal attack on the Sikh position at Ramnugger in November, Lord Gough despatched a force under Sir Joseph Thackwell, to cross the Chenab and turn the Sikh left. An indecisive action followed, which Lord Gough claimed as a victory, but though the Sikhs retired, it was slowly, and only to take up a fresh position, which Thackwell did not consider himself strong enough to attack.

Sagunto (Peninsular War).

This fortress, held by a Spanish garrison, was besieged by the French, 22,000 strong, under Soult, September 23, 1811. Built on the heights above Murviedro, the place was accessible on one side only, and an attempt to escalade this was repulsed September 28. A regular siege was then commenced, and a second unsuccessful assault was made on October 18. On the 25th General Blake, with 30,000 Spaniards, made an attempt to relieve the place, but was defeated with a loss of 1,000 killed and wounded and 4,000 prisoners. the victory costing the French about 800 men. On the following day the garrison surrendered.

St. Alban's (Wars of the Roses).

Two engagements were fought here in the course of the war. On May 22, 1455, 2,000 Lancastrians, under Henry VI, posted in the town, were attacked by 3,000 Yorkists, under the Duke of York. The Duke pierced the Lancastrian centre, and drove them out of St. Alban's with heavy loss, among those who were killed being the Earls of Somerset and Northumberland.

The second battle took place February 17, 1461, when the army of Margaret of Anjou, led by Somerset, Exeter, and others, attacked the Yorkists, under Warwick, Warwick withdrew his main body, leaving his left unsupported to withstand the Lancastrian attacks, and these troops, after a feeble resistance, broke and fled. Henry VI, who was a prisoner in Warwick's camp, escaped and rejoined the Queen, and a rapid advance on

London would probably have led to his reinstatement. Warwick, however, took such prompt measures as to render the Lancastrian victory practically fruitless.

St. Aubin du Cormier.

Fought 1487, between the Royal troops, under La Tremouille, and the forces of the rebel Princes, under Marshal de Rieux. The rebels were totally defeated, and a large number of nobles made prisoners, including the Duc d'Orléans and the Prince of Orange.

St. Charles (French-Canadian Rising).

Fought 1837, between the Loyalists, under Colonel Wetherall, and the Canadian rebels. The latter were defeated.

St. Denis (Second Civil War).

Fought November 10, 1567, between the Catholics, under the Constable Montmorenci, and the Huguenots, under the Prince de Condé. Victory rested with the Catholics, but at the cost of the Constable, who was killed, and the battle had no decisive effect upon the course of the war.

St. Denis (French - Canadian Rising).

Fought 1837, between the Canadian rebels, and a force of British and Canadian troops, under Colonel Gore. The rebels were victorious, but the results of their victory were unimportant.

Ste Croix (Napoleonic Wars).

This island, held by a small Danish garrison, was captured by a British naval and military force, under Admiral Sir A. J.

Cochrane and General Bowyer, December 25, 1807, but little resistance being offered.

St. Eustache (French-Canadian Rising).

Fought 1837, between the rebels, under Girod, and the Government troops, under Sir John Colborne. The rebels were completely defeated, and the rebellion was suppressed.

Ste Foy (Seven Years' War).

Fought April 27, 1760, between 3,000 British troops, under General Murray, and 8,000 French, under the Chevalier de Lévis, who was approaching from Montreal, with the object of recapturing Quebec. Murray marched out to attack Lévis, but was defeated and driven back into Quebec with a loss of over a third of his force. The French lost about 800.

St. George (Ottoman Wars).

This place, the capital of the island of Cephalonia, was besieged in October, 1500, by the Spaniards and Venetians, under Gonsalvo de Cordova and Pesaro. The garrison consisted of 400 Turks only, but being veteran soldiers they made a most gallant defence ; but at the end of two months the place was stormed from two quarters simultaneously, and the survivors of the garrison, some 80 only, laid down their arms.

St. Gothard (Ottoman Wars).

Fought August 1, 1664, between 100,000 Turks, under Achmet Köpriali Pasha, and 60,000 French and Germans, under Montecucculi, who occupied a strong position behind the Raab. On the Turks advancing to the attack, a young Turk rode out, and challenged a Christian to single combat. The challenge was accepted by the Chevalier de Lorraine, who killed his adversary. The Turks then assaulted Montecucculi's entrenchment, but could make no impression, and after hard fighting were beaten off with a loss of 8,000 killed.

St. Jacob an der Mirs (Armagnac War).

Fought September, 1444, between 30,000 Armagnacs, under the Dauphin, and 1,300 Confederate Swiss. The Swiss being hard pressed, occupied the hospital of St. Jacob an der Mirs, where they maintained the unequal fight until the last man had fallen. The Armagnacs, however, had lost 2,000 killed, and the Dauphin felt compelled to abandon the invasion of Switzerland.

St. Kitts (Dutch Wars).

Fought May 10, 1667, when Sir John Harman, commanding an English squadron of 12 frigates, fell in with a combined Dutch and French fleet of 22 sail, under Commodore Kruysen and M. de la Barre, off St. Kitts. Notwithstanding his inferiority, Harman boldly attacked, and gained a signal victory, burning 5 and sinking several more of the enemy's vessels. The allies took refuge in the harbour of St. Kitts, and Sir John, following them in, destroyed the rest of their fleet, at a cost of 80 men only.

St. Lucia (Wars of the French Revolution).

This island was captured from the French, April 4, 1794,

by a British squadron, under Sir John Jervis.

St. Mary's Clyst (Arundel's Rebellion).

Fought August 4, 1549, when Lord Russell, marching with the Royal army to the relief of Exeter, was attacked by 6,000 rebels, detached from the besieging force. The rebels were defeated with a loss of 1,000 killed, and Arundel was forced to raise the siege of Exeter.

St. Privat. See Gravelotte.

St. Quentin.

Fought August 10, 1557, between 22,000 French and Germans, under the Constable Montmorenci, and about 5,000 Spanish and Flemish cavalry of the Duke of Savoy's army, under Count Egmont, supported by a small force of infantry. The French, in attempting to throw reinforcements into St. Quentin, were entrapped in a narrow pass, and were utterly routed, with a loss of 15,000 killed, wounded and captured, and all but two of their guns. The Spaniards only lost 50 men.

St. Quentin (Franco - German War).

Fought January 19, 1871, between the French, 40,000 strong, under General Faidherbe, and 33,000 Germans, under Von Göben. The French were decisively defeated, with a loss of 3,500 killed and wounded, 9,000 prisoners, and 6 guns. The Germans lost 96 officers and 2,304 men.

St. Thomas (Napoleonic Wars).

This island was captured from the Danes, December 21, 1807, by a combined British naval and military force, under

Admiral Sir A. J. Cochrane and General Bowyer.

Saints, The. *See* Dominica.

Salado. (Moorish Empire in Spain).
Fought 1344, between the Portuguese and Castilians, under Alfonso IV of Portugal and Alfonso XI of Castile, and the Moors, under Abu Hamed, Emir of Morocco. The Christians won a signal victory, and Alfonso so distinguished himself in the battle as to earn the title of the " Brave."

Salamanca (Peninsular War).
Fought July 22, 1812, when Wellington, with 46,000 British and Spanish troops, encountered 42,000 French, under Marmont. The battle was forced on by Marmont, who was endeavouring to interrupt Wellington's retreat, but the Marshal was severely wounded early in the day, and the conduct of the action was in the hands of General Bonnet. The result was a signal victory for the British, the French losing 12,500 killed, wounded and prisoners, and 12 guns. The British and Spanish loss a-mounted to about 6,000. These figures include the skirmishes of the days preceding the battle, during which the armies were in touch.

Salamanca (Mexican Liberal Rising).
Fought March 10, 1858, between the Government troops, under Miramon, and the Liberals, under Doblado. Doblado's raw levies could not face Miramon's trained troops, and were utterly routed.

Salamis (Third Persian Invasion).
Fought 480 B.C. between the Greek fleet of 370 sail, under Themistocles, and the Persian fleet, of over 1,000 galleys. The Greeks at first hesitated to attack in face of the overwhelming numbers of the Persian ships, but an Athenian trireme, commanded by Aminias, dashed in, and being followed by the rest of the Athenians and the Æginetans in good order, the Persians were, after a hard struggle, totally defeated, with the loss of more than half their fleet. Xerxes and his army witnessed the rout from the shores of Salamis.

Salamis (Wars of Alexander's Successors).
Fought B.C. 307, between the Macedonian fleet, under Demetrius Poliorcetes, and the Egyptians, under Ptolemy Soter. The Egyptians were routed, with the loss of 100 ships captured and the rest sunk, and 30,000 prisoners.

Salankemen (Ottoman Wars).
Fought August 19, 1691, between 100,000 Turks, under the Grand Vizier, Mustapha Köpriali Pasha, and 45,000 Imperialists, under the Margrave Louis. The Turks were signally defeated and Köpriali slain.

Salano (Moorish Empire in Spain).
Fought 1340 between the Spaniards, under Alfonso XI of Castile, and the Moors, under Abu 'l Hasan of Granada. The Moors, who were besieging Tarifa, were attacked by the Spaniards, who utterly routed them and relieved the town.

Abu 'l Hamed fled to Africa, and Alfonso was enabled to recover Algeciras.

Saldanha Bay (Wars of the French Revolution).

Fought August 17, 1796, when Sir Keith Elphinstone, with a British squadron, entered the bay, and after capturing a Dutch ship of war lying in the harbour, landed a force, to which the garrison surrendered after a brief resistance.

Salo. *See* Castiglione.

Samarcand (Tartar Invasion of Kharismia).

This place, which was defended by a garrison of 110,000 Turks and Kharismians, under the Governor, Alub Khan, was besieged by the Tartars, under Genghiz Khan, in June, 1220. The garrison harassed the Tartars by numerous sorties, and little progress was made with the siege, but some of the inhabitants, hoping to save the city from pillage, opened the gates to the besiegers. After heroic efforts 'to defend the city against the overwhelming hordes of the enemy, Alub Khan put himself at the head of 1,000 picked horsemen and cut his way out. The survivors of the garrison, now reduced to 30,000, were put to the sword.

Samaghar (Rebellion of Aurung-zebe).

Fought June, 1658, between the army of the Great Mogul, Shah Jehan, under Dara, and the forces of his rebellious sons, Aurungzebe and Marad. Dara was totally defeated, and his army dispersed, and three days later the rebels occupied Agra, where Shah Jehan was imprisoned and Aurungzebe seized the crown.

Sampford Courtney (Arundel's Rebellion).

The final engagement with the rebels, fought August 17, 1549, when Arundel was defeated by the Royal troops, under Lord Russell, with a loss of 700 killed and many prisoners, including most of the ringleaders in the rising.

San Giovanni (Wars of the French Revolution).

Fought June 17, 1799, between the French, under Macdonald, and the Russians, under Suwaroff. After three days' hard fighting, the French were forced to retreat, having suffered a loss of 6,000 killed and wounded and 9,000 prisoners. The Russian losses were about 6,000.

San Isidoro (Paraguay War).

Fought April, 1870, between the Paraguayans, under Lopez, and the allied army of Brazil, Argentina and Uruguay, under General Camera. Camera attacked Lopez's entrenchments and drove him out, forcing him to take refuge in the mountains with the small remnant of his troops.

San Jacinto (Texan Rising).

Fought April 2, 1836, when the Mexican army, under Santa Anna, about 5,000 strong, was routed and almost destroyed by the Texans, under General Houston. The survivors, with Santa Anna and his staff, were taken prisoners, and Texas was freed from the Mexican yoke.

San Jacinto.

Fought February 12, 1867, between the adherents of the Emperor Maximilian, under Miramon, and the Mexican Constitutionalists, under Escobedo. Miramon was defeated, and his army surrendered, he himself escaping with difficulty from the field.

San Juan. *See* El Caney.

San Lazaro (War of the Austrian Succession).

Fought June, 1746, between the Austrians, 40,000 strong, under Prince Lichtenstein, and the French and Spaniards, under Marshal Maillebois. The allies attacked the Austrian entrenched camp, and after an obstinate conflict, lasting nine hours, were repulsed with a loss of 10,000 killed and wounded.

Sanna's Post (Second Boer War).

Fought March 31, 1900, when a force of cavalry, with 2 R.H.A. batteries and a considerable convoy, under Colonel Broadwood, was ambushed by a party of Boers, under De Wet, while crossing a donga. The guns were just entering the donga when the Boers opened fire, and 4 guns of Q battery succeeded in getting clear and opening fire, stuck to their work till only 10 men of the battery were left standing. Broadwood succeeded in extricating his force, but at a cost of 19 officers and 136 men killed and wounded, 426 prisoners, 7 guns, and the whole of his convoy. General Colville's column was within a few miles, but though the firing was heard, he failed to relieve. This is also known as the action of Kornspruit.

San Sebastian (Peninsular War).

This town was besieged July 10, 1813, by the British, under General Graham, and was defended by a French garrison, under General Rey. An assault on July 25 was repulsed, and pending the arrival of heavy guns from England, the siege resolved itself into a blockade. Active operations were resumed, and on the 31st the town was taken by storm. Rey, however, still held out in the citadel, and it was only after further bombardment that he surrendered on September 9. The besiegers' losses amounted to over 2,500 killed and wounded.

San Sebastian (First Carlist War).

This fortress, held by a garrison of Cristinos and a small detachment of the British legion, under Colonel Wylde, was besieged by the Carlists, under Sagastibelza, February, 1836. The siege was carried on in desultory fashion, with constant fighting between the outposts, till June, 1836, when General Evans, with 10,000 British and Spanish troops, occupied the advanced Carlist positions, and forced them to withdraw.

Santa Lucia (Rio Grande Rising).

Fought 1842, between the Brazilian Government troops, under General Caxias, and the rebels, 6,000 strong, under Feliciano. The rebels were totally defeated.

Santarem (Dom Miguel's Rebellion).

Fought February 18, 1834, when the Portuguese Government troops, under Marshal

Saldanha, totally defeated the "Miguelists," under Dom Miguel.

Santa Vittoria (War of Spanish Succession).

Fought July 26, 1702, w 4 regiments of Prince Euge army, under General Visc were attacked by 15, French and Spaniards, un the Duc de Vendôme. The perialists were forced to ab don their camp and retire w the loss of their baggage, but l only 500 men, while their qua fied success cost the allies near. 2,000 killed and wounded.

Santiago (Spanish - American War).

Fought July 3, 1898, between the American fleet of 4 battleships and 3 cruisers, under Admiral W. T. Sampson, and the Spanish fleet of 4 armoured cruisers and 3 torpedo-boats, under Admiral Cervera. The Spaniards endeavoured to escape from the blockaded harbour of Santiago, but were unsuccessful, the whole squadron being destroyed. The Americans suffered hardly any damage, the Spanish gunnery being very inefficient, and lost only 1 man killed.

Sapienza (Ottoman Wars).

Fought 1490 between the Turkish fleet, under Kemal Reis, and the Venetians. The Venetians suffered a severe reverse, this being the first naval victory of the Turks in the Mediterranean.

Saragossa (War of the Spanish Succession).

Fought August 20, 1700, between 25,000 Spaniards, and a force of Austrians, British, Dutch and Portuguese troops, 23,000 in number, under the Archduke Charles. The Portuguese in the right wing gave way, leading a large force of Spaniards in pursuit, but the 'eft and centre stood their round, and finally repulsed e enemy, with a loss of 4,000 soners, besides killed and nded. The Archduke at took possession of Sara-

sa (Peninsular War).

ne, 1808, siege was laid city by the French, under arshal Lefebvre. A successful defence was made, and the marshal's forces being insufficient to effect a prompt capture, he raised the siege in August. In December of the same year it was again besieged by the French, under Moncey and Mortier, and defended by a Spanish garrison, under Palafox. A most heroic defence was made, notable for the bravery of Agostina, the maid of Saragossa, who took the place of her wounded lover on the ramparts, and helped to serve the guns, but despite all the efforts of Palafox, the place was stormed, and, after very severe house to house fighting, captured, February 21, 1809.

Saratoga. *See* Stillwater.

Sardis (Wars of Alexander's Successors).

Fought B.C. 280, between the troops of Pergamus, under Eumenes, and the Syrians, under Antigonus Soter. Eumenes gained a signal victory, and annexed a large part of the dominions of Antigonus.

Sárkány (Hungarian Rising).

Fought December 30, 1848, between the Austrians, under Windischgrätz, and the Hungarians, under General Perczel. Perczel had been entrusted by Görgey with the defence of the Sárkány defile, but on being attacked by the Austrians, his division made little resistance, and fled in disorder, thus forcing Görgey to retire from the line he had chosen to defend.

Sauchie Barn (Rebellion of the Barons).

Fought June 18, 1488, between the rebel Barons, under Angus "Bell-the-Cat," and the troops of James III of Scotland, under the king. The royal army was totally defeated and James slain.

Saucourt (Norse Invasion of France).

Fought 861 between the Neustrians, under Louis III, and the invading Norsemen, when Louis gained a brilliant victory.

Sauroren (Peninsular War).

Fought July 28, 1813, between the French, 25,000 strong, under Soult, and the British, 12,000 strong, under Wellington. Soult attempted to turn the British left in order to drive them from a strong position, but after severe fighting he was repulsed, with a loss of about 3,000. The British losses were about 2,600. Soult renewed his attempt to force Wellington's lines on the 30th, but was again repulsed, with a loss of 2,000 killed and wounded and 3,000 prisoners. The British loss amounted to 1,900.

Savage's Station. *See* Seven Days' Battle.

Savandroog (Second Mysore War).

Siege was laid to this place December 10, 1791, by a column of Lord Cornwallis' army, about 4,000 strong,. It was defended by a strong garrison of Mysoris, and was considered impregnable, but a practicable breach having been effected, it was taken by storm eleven days later, the garrison offering little resistance. The assailants did not lose a man.

Saxa Rubra (Revolt of Maxentius).

Fought October 28, 312, between the Imperial troops, under Constantine, and the legions of Italy, under Maxentius. The Italian cavalry, posted on the wings, was routed by Constantine's horse ; the infantry, thus left unsupported, fled from the field, only the Pretorians making a brave resistance, and dying where they stood. Maxentius escaped, but crosing the Tiber into Rome by the Milvian Bridge, was forced by the crowd of fugitives into the river and drowned.

Scarpheia (War of the Achæan League).

Fought B.C. 146, between the Romans, under Matellus, and the Achæans, under Critolaus. The Greeks were totally defeated with heavy loss, Critolaus being killed.

Scio (Ottoman Wars).

Fought July 5, 1769, between a Russian fleet of 10 sail of the line, under Admiral Spiritoff, and 15 Turkish ships, with some small vessels, under the Capitan

Pasha. After a severe engagement, in which both the flagships were blown up, the Turks were driven into the Bay of Tchesme, where a few days later their fleet was destroyed by fire-ships.

Schipka Pass (Russo - Turkish War).

Fought August 21, 1877, and following days, when the Russians, 7,000 strong, under General Darozhinsky, holding the pass, were attacked by 25,000 Turks, under Suleiman Pasha. The Russians were driven from point after point of their defences, and were on the verge of being overwhelmed, when the arrival of reinforcements enabled them to assume the offensive and recover their lost positions, and on the 26th fighting ceased. The Russian losses amounted to 4,000, including Darozhinsky, while the Turks lost about 11,500.

On September 16 Suleiman, reinforced to 40,000 men, made an attempt to carry the Russian position on Mount St. Nicholas, but was repulsed with a loss of 3,000, the Russians losing 31 officers and about 1,000 rank and file.

By January 8, 1878, the Russian force in the Schipka had been increased to 60,000 men, under General Radetski, while the Turks, numbering 40,000 were under Vessil Pasha. General Mirsky, with 25,000 men, attacked the Turkish entrenchments and drove them out of all their positions, and on the following day Vessil Pasha surrendered with 36,000 men and 93 guns. The Russians lost 5,000.

Schwechat (Hungarian Rising).

Fought October 30, 1848, between the Austrians, under Prince Windischgrätz, and the Hungarians, under General Moga. The Hungarian militia made a very feeble stand against the Austrian regulars, and were driven back all along the line with considerable loss.

Scutari (Ottoman Wars).

This place, held by a Venetian garrison, under Antonio Loredano, was besieged by the Turks, under Suleiman Pasha, May, 1474. The garrison held out stoutly till the middle of August, when Suleiman raised the siege.

Four years later, in June, 1478, Mohammed II invested it, the garrison now being under the command of Antonio di Lezze. Though few in numbers, the Venetians withstood a continuous bombardment, repulsing two serious assaults, until September 8, when Mohammed retired, leaving behind him only a blockading force. When on the conclusion of peace the place was handed over to the Turks only 450 men and 150 women were alive in the town. In the first assault the Turks lost 12,000 men, and an even greater number, it is said, in the second.

Sebastopol (Crimean War).

This fortress was besieged by the allied French and British armies, under Marshal St. Arnaud and Lord Raglan, September 28, 1854. It was defended by a large force of Russians, under Prince Mentschikoff, with General Todleben as his principal engineer officer.

The besiegers were too few for a complete investment, and though the harbour was closed by the British fleet, under Sir Edmund Lyons, the Russians were throughout the siege enabled to obtain reinforcements and provisions from the north side. The batteries opened on October 17, and from that time till September 8, 1855, the town was more or less continuously bombarded. On that day the Malakoff, an important part of the southern defences, was stormed by the French, and the place became untenable, the allies entering it unopposed on the following day. The Russians, during the later days of the bombardment, are said to have lost as many as 3,000 men a day.

Secchia, The (War of the Polish Succession).

Fought September 14, 1734, when the Imperialists, under Count Köningsegg, surprised the camp of the French army, under the Duc de Broglie, capturing 5,000 prisoners, 100 guns and the whole of the stores, baggage and ammunition.

Secessionville (American Civil War).

Fought June 15, 1862, when 6,000 Federals, under General Benham, attacked the strong position of Secessionville, covering the road to Charleston, which was held by 2,000 Confederates, under General Evans. The Federals were repulsed with a loss of 600 men, the Confederates losing 200.

Secunderbagh (Indian Mutiny).

Fought November 16, 1857, during the second relief of Lucknow, by Sir Colin Campbell. The Secunderbagh, a walled enclosure of strong masonry, held by a large body of rebels, was, after a bombardment of about an hour and a half, taken by storm by the 93rd Highlanders and the 4th Punjabis, with very heavy loss to the enemy, over 2,000 dead bodies being afterwards carried out of the enclosure.

Sedan (Franco-German War).

This battle, the most decisive of the war, was fought September 1, 1870, The French, under Marshal Macmahon, who was wounded early in the action, were driven from all their positions by the Germans, under the King of Prussia, and compelled to retire into Sedan, where they laid down their arms. The Emperor Napoleon III was among the prisoners, and one of the results of the surrender was his dethronement and the proclamation of a republic in Paris. The battle is remarkable for the charge of the Chasseurs d'Afrique, under General Margueritte, in the neighbourhood of Floing. The brigade was cut to pieces and the general killed. The Germans lost in the action 460 officers and 8,500 men ; the French 3,000 killed, 14,000 wounded, and 21,000 prisoners, while 83,000 subsequently surrendered in Sedan. The Germans took 419 guns, 139 fortress guns and 66,000 rifles.

Sedgemoor (Monmouth's Rebellion).

Fought July 5, 1685, between the Royal troops, under the Earl of Faversham, and the

Q

rebels, under James, Duke of Monmouth. Monmouth attempted a night attack on Faversham's camp, but the alarm was given, and the Royal troops falling upon their assailants, put Monmouth's cavalry to flight, and though his infantry made a sturdy resistance they were at length overpowered and routed with heavy loss. This defeat put an end to the rebellion.

Segeswár (Hungarian Rising).

Fought July 31, 1849, between the Hungarians, under General Bem, and the Russians, under General Lüders. The Russians, after a severe engagement, were totally defeated.

Segikahara (Rebellion of Hideyori).

Fought September 16, 1600, between the troops of the Shogun Tokugawa Tyeyasa, 80,000 strong, and 130,000 rebels, under Mitsunari. The rebels were utterly routed with the loss of 30,000 killed, among whom was Mitsunari, and the rebellion was suppressed.

Seine Mouth (Hundred Years' War).

Fought August 15, 1416, when the English fleet, under Bedford, sailed into the Seine with the object of revictualling Harfleur, which the French were besieging. The blockading force, consisting of 8 large Genoese carracks, besides smaller vessels, attacked the English fleet, and after six hours' hard fighting were totally defeated, with a loss of 5 carracks and 5 other ships, while Bedford succeeded in throwing supplies into the town.

Selby (Civil War).

Fought April 11, 1644, between the Royalists, 3,300 strong, under Colonel John Bellasis, and a slightly superior force of Parliamentarians, under Sir Thomas Fairfax. Bellasis had occupied Selby with the object of preventing a junction between Fairfax's troops and those of the Scots at Durham. He was attacked by Fairfax and totally defeated, with the loss of 1,600 men and all his artillery and baggage.

Selinus (Second Carthaginian Invasion of Sicily).

This city was besieged by the Carthaginians, 100,000 strong, under Hannibal, B.C. 409. An attempt by the Syracusans, under Diocles, to relieve came too late, for after resisting stubbornly for nine days, the garrison, hopelessly outnumbered, were overpowered ; and the place stormed and sacked, all the survivors being carried off into captivity.

Seminara (Italian Wars).

Fought 1495 between 6,000 Spaniards and Neapolitans, under Gonsalvo de Cordova and Ferdinand of Naples, and a largely superior French army, under D'Aubigny. The Neapolitans fled almost without striking a blow, and though the Spaniards fought well, they were overpowered by numbers, and in the end totally routed, only Gonsalvo with 400 Spanish cavalry making an orderly retreat.

Sempach (War of Sempach).

Fought July 9, 1386, between 6,000 Austrians, under Duke

Leopold, and 1,500 Swiss Confederates. The Swiss gained a complete victory, the Austrians losing 1,500 killed and wounded, while only 120 Swiss fell. The battle is celebrated for the heroic action of Arnold von Winkelried, who broke the line of the Austrian spearmen at the cost of his life, and enabled his followers to penetrate their phalanx.

Seneff (Wars of Louis XIV).

Fought August 11, 1674, between the French, 45,000 strong, under Condé, and the Flemings and Spaniards, 60,000 strong, under the Prince of Orange. Orange, finding Condé's position too strong to attack, began a retreat towards Le Quesnay, thereby exposing his flank. Condé took instant advantage of this error, and dispersed the vanguard of the allies, but the Prince took up a strong position at Seneff, from which Condé was unable to dislodge him, and the conflict ended in a drawn battle, after seventeen hours' hard fighting.

Senegal (Napoleonic Wars).

The French garrison of this place surrendered, July 13, 1809, to a British force of 1 frigate and 2 brigs, with some transports carrying troops, under Captain G. H. Columbine.

Senekal (Second Boer War).

Fought May 29, 1900, when a British force, under General Rundle, attacked the Boers, strongly posted on the Biddulphsberg. The attack was made amidst great bush fires, in which many of the wounded perished, and was unsuccessful, the British losses amounting to 7 officers and 177 men killed and wounded.

Senlac. *See* Hastings.

Sentinum (Third Samnite War).

Fought B.C. 298, between five Roman legions, under Q. Fabius Maximus and Publius Decius, and the Samnites and Gauls, under Gellius Equatius. The Roman left was disordered by the war-chariots of the Gauls, but was rallied by Decius, who restored the battle, but at the cost of his life. On the right the Samnites were routed, and Fabius then fell upon the Gauls in flank, and broke them. Meanwhile the Samnite camp was attacked, and Equatius slain, the Romans gaining a signal victory. The losses of the victors amounted to 8,200, while the Gauls and Samnites lost 25,000 killed and 8,000 prisoners.

Sepeia (Argive War).

Fought B.C. 494, between the Spartans, under Cleomenes, and the Argives. The Spartans, by a ruse, succeeded in surprising the Argives while the soldiers were dining, and totally routed them. This defeat deprived Argos of the paramountcy in the Peloponnesus.

Seringapatam (Second Mysore War).

This city was besieged, February 5, 1792, by 22,000 British and native troops, with 86 guns, under Lord Cornwallis, and defended by a Mysori garrison, under Tippu Sahib. On the 6th an assault upon the outlying works was successful, all the redoubts commanding the city being carried, at a cost to the assailants of 530, while the

Mysoris lost 20,000. On the approach of reinforcements, under General Abercromby, on the 16th, Tippu consented to treat, and peace was signed in the following month.

Seringapatam (Third Mysore War).

The second siege by General Harris, opened April 6, 1799, when the city was defended by a garrison of 20,000, under Tippu. On May 3, the breach was declared practicable, and the place was stormed by 4,000 men, under General Baird. Tippu was slain in the rout which followed the assault. The British losses during the siege amounted to 1,464. About 8,000 Mysoris fell in the assault.

Seringham (Seven Years' War).

Fought 1753, between 1,000 British troops, under Major Laurence, and the French, with their Mahratta and Mysori allies, under M. Astruc. The French attacked in force an isolated post, held by 200 Sepoys, and carried it before Major Laurence could come up. He then attacked, and in turn carried the position, driving off the French, and the Mahrattas who came up to their support, and captured three guns.

Seskar (Russo-Swedish Wars).

Fought 1790, between the Swedish fleet, under the Duke of Sudermanland, and a Russian squadron, under Admiral Kruze. The Swedes were totally defeated, after a severe engagement, which lasted from daybreak till far into the night.

Seta (Yoshinaka's Rebellion).

Fought 1183, between the army of Yoritomo, under his brothers Noriyori and Yoshitsune, and that of Yoshinaka. The rebels were completely defeated, and Yoshinaka killed.

Seven Days' Battles (American Civil War).

A series of actions fought by General Lee, with 100,000 Confederates, against General M'Clellan, with 95,000 Federals, Lee's object being to relieve Richmond. On June 26, 1862, General Hill, with 1,400 Confederates, attacked M'Call's division, in a strong position at **Beaver's Dam Creek**, which attack M'Call repulsed, at small cost to his force. On the 27th, General Porter, 35,000 strong, posted on the Chickahominy at **Gaines' Mill**, was attacked by 54,000 Confederates, under Lee in person. The Southerners advanced under a heavy artillery fire, and after severe fighting, drove the Federals across the river, and captured 20 guns. On the 28th, M'Clellan prepared to withdraw to the James River, his centre having been pierced, and commenced his retreat. On the 29th, 4 Confederate divisions, under Longstreet, aided by an armoured train, came up with Sumner's corps at **Savage's Station**, but was repulsed, Sumner thus inflicting a serious check upon the pursuing columns. On the 30th, 3 divisions, under General Jackson, overtook the Federal rearguard, under General French, near the **White Oak Swamp**, and an artillery duel followed, which cost the Federals some guns. Two divisions, under Longstreet, also attacked M'Call's division, and routed it, M'Call being captured. By the evening of the 30th, M'Clellan reached **Malvern Hill,** overlooking the James River, and determined to oppose here the further advance of the Confederates, On July 1st, the Confederates attacked, but the Federals held their ground throughout the day, and on the 2nd retired in good order and practically unmolested. The Federals admit a loss of 15,249 men and 25 guns during the operations, but Confederate accounts put the figures much higher, and claim 51 guns. The losses of the Southerners were also very heavy, especially at Malvern Hill, but Lee's object was accomplished, and Richmond was relieved.

Sevenoaks (Cade's Rebellion).

Fought June 18, 1450, between the rebels, under Cade, and the royal troops, under Sir Humphrey Stafford. The force under Stafford was quite inadequate for the work in hand, and was routed, Stafford being killed.

Seven Pines. *See* Fair Oaks.

Shahjehan (Tartar Invasion of Kharismia.)

This city was besieged 1221, by the Tartars, under Tuli Khan, and was obstinately defended by the garrison under a Turkish general named Bugha. For twenty-one successive days the besiegers delivered assaults, which were repulsed, but finally the inhabitants made terms with Tuli Khan, and opened the gates

Shaldiran (Ottoman Wars).

Fought August 24, 1514, between 120,000 Turks, under Selim I, and about 80,000 Persians, under the Shah Ismael.

The wing led by the Shah in person was victorious, but the Persian left was totally routed, and in endeavouring to restore the battle on that side. Ismael was wounded, whereupon the army was seized with panic, and took to flight.

Shannon and Chesapeake (Second American War).

A famous frigate action, fought May 29, 1813, between the British frigate *Shannon*, of 38 guns, commanded by Captain Broke, and the American frigate *Chesapeake*, also of 38 guns, under Captain John Lawrence. The *Chesapeake* sailed out of Boston Harbour to attack the *Shannon*, and after a brisk action was taken by the board by the British. The *Shannon* lost 4 officers and 21 men killed, and 3 officers and 56 men wounded ; the *Chesapeake*, 8 officers and 39 men killed, and 9 officers and 106 men wounded. Captain Lawrence was killed and Captain Broke wounded.

Sheerness (Dutch Wars).

Fought June 7, 1667, and following days, when the Dutch fleet, under de Ruyter, sailed up the Medway as far as Upnor Castle, and destroyed 7 ships of war.

Sheriffmuir (Rebellion of the Fifteen).

Fought November 13, 1715, between 3,500 royal troops, under the Duke of Argyle, and 9,000 Highlanders, under the Earl of Mar. Argyle's left wing was routed by the Macdonalds, and his left and centre, though at first they held their own, were in the end compelled to retire, and Argyle effected a retreat in good order to Stirling.

Sherstone (Danish Invasion).

Fought 1016, between Edmund Ironside, and Knut, the rival claimants to the throne. The battle was indecisive.

Shijo Nawate (War of the Northern and Southern Empires).

Fought 1339, between the army of the Northern Emperor, under Takaugi and Tadayoshi, and the troops of the Southern Emperor, under Kusunoki Masatsura. Masatsura was attacked at Yoshino, which place was temporarily the Imperial residence. Feeling that he was too weak to defend it, he marched out with his whole force to meet his assailants, and fell fighting to the last, the Northern troops gaining a complete victory. Japan was soon afterwards again united, under the rule of the Northern line.

Shiloh (American Civil War).

Fought April 6 and 7, 1862, between the Confederates, 43,000 strong, under General Johnston, and the Federals, 40,000 strong, under General Grant. The Confederates attacked Grant's position on the west of the Tennessee river, and surprised the Federals, driving back the first line in confusion. By nightfall, Grant was practically defeated, but Johnston failed to take advantage of his opportunity, and Grant being reinforced by 20,000 men during the night, was able on the 7th to assume the offensive. After severe fighting the Southerners were driven from the field with a loss of 9,740 killed and wounded and 959 prisoners, General Johnston be-

ing among the killed. The Federals lost 9,617 killed and wounded, and 4,044 prisoners.

Shinowara (Yoshinaka's Rebellion).

Fought April, 1183, between the troops of the rebel Daimio Yoshinaka, and the Japanese Imperial army, consisting of 100,000 horsemen, under Taira-no-Kore. The Imperial troops were defeated with a loss of 20,000 killed.

Shirogawa (Satsuma Rebellion).

Fought September 24, 1876. when the last remnants of the rebels, under Saigo, were defeated by the Imperial army, under Prince Taruhito. The rebels were practically annihilated, and most of the leaders of the revolt killed. Saigo, after the defeat, committed *Hara-kiri* on the field.

Sholapur (Third Mahratta War).

Fought May 10, 1818, when a body of cavalry, under General Pritzen, forming part of General Monro's force, attacked and dispersed the retreating remnant of the Peshwa's army. Sholapur surrendered on the 15th, the operations having cost the British only 97 killed and wounded, while the loss of the Mahrattas exceeded 800 killed.

Sholingur (First Mysore War).

Fought September 27, 1781, between the British, 10,000 strong, under Sir Eyre Coote, and the Mysoris, numbering about 80,000, under Hyder Ali. Hyder was surprised in the act of striking camp, and though a series of cavalry charges enabled him to withdraw his guns in safety, it was at a cost of 5,000 men that he eventually made good his retreat. The British loss did not exceed 100.

Shrewsbury (Percy's Rebellion).

Fought July 21, 1403, when the royalists, under Henry IV, met and defeated the insurgents, under Hotspur. Hotspur was killed, and Douglas and Worcester taken prisoners. The battle was the baptism of fire of Henry, Prince of Wales (Henry V), who displayed great bravery, and was severely wounded.

Sidassir (Third Mysore War).

Fought March 6, 1799, between the advance guard of General Stuart's force, composed of three regiments, under Colonel Montresor, and 12,000 Mysoris, under Tippu Sahib. Montresor's small force withstood the attack of Tippu's troops for over six hours, and their ammunition was all but exhausted when Stuart came up, and drove back the enemy with a loss of 2,000 men. The British lost 143 killed and wounded.

Sievershausen.

Fought July 9, 1553, between the Germans, under Maurice, Elector of Saxony, and the Brandenburgers, under the Margrave Albert. The Brandenburgers were defeated, but Maurice was wounded in the action, and died two days later

Siffin.

A series of actions extending over a hundred days, in 656, between the Moslems, under the Caliph Ali, and the adherents Moawiyeh, the son of Abu Sophian, a pretender to the Caliphate. In the course of these engagements Ali lost 25,000, and Moawiyeh 45,000 men, but the latter was undefeated, and the sanguinary conflict was ended by an unsatisfactory compromise.

Sikajoki (Finland War).

Fought April 18, 1808, between the Swedes, under General Klingspor, and the Russians, under General Bouxhoevden. The Russians endeavoured to outflank the Swedes by moving out on to the ice at the mouth of the Sikajoki river, at the same time assailing them in front. Both attacks were repulsed, and after eight hours fighting, Klingspor took the offensive, and drove the Russians from the field, with heavy loss. The Swedes lost 1,000 killed and wounded.

Silistria (Crimean War).

This fortress was besieged by the Russians in 1854, and was defended by a Turkish garrison, who received valuable assistance from two English officers, Captain Buller and Lieutenant Nasmyth. Many attempts to storm the place were repulsed, and though no efforts were made to relieve them, the garrison held out until June 22, when the Russians raised the siege, having suffered a loss of over 12,000 men.

Silpia. *See* Elinga.

Simnitza (Russo-Turkish War).

Fought June 26, 1877, between the Russians, under the Grand Duke Nicholas, and the Turkish garrison of Sistova. On the night of the 26th, the Russian advance-guard, 15,000 strong, under Dragomiroff, crossed the Danube in boats, and then, under Skobeleff, drove the Turks headlong from their entrenchments. On the morning of the 27th, Sistova was occupied, the Russians having lost 820 only in the operations.

Singara (Persian Wars).

Fought 348, between the Romans, under Constantius, and the Persians, in largely superior force, under Sapor II. The Persian king, having posted the major part of his army on the heights overlooking Singara, engaged the Romans with a comparatively small force of light-armed troops, who were easily routed by the legionaries. The pursuit, however, was carried too far, and when night fell, the Romans, exhausted by their efforts, bivouacked under the heights. During the night, Sapor led his best troops to the attack, and routed the weary Romans, with terrible slaughter.

Singara (Persian Wars).

This fortress, held by a Roman garrison, was captured, after a brief siege, by the Persians, under Sapor II, in 360. The garrison was sent into captivity and the fortress dismantled.

Sinnaca (Parthian War).

At this place the remnants of the army of Crassus, after the battle of Carrhæ, B.C. 53, surrendered to the Parthians. Only 5,000 men were with the eagles.

Sinope (Crimean War).

Fought 1853, when the Russian fleet attacked the Turkish fleet of 9 sail, lying in the harbour of Sinope. No quarter was given, and the Turkish fleet was totally destroyed.

Over 4,000 Turks were killed, and it is said that only 400, almost all wounded, escaped the massacre.

Sinzheim (Wars of Louis XIV).

Fought October 4, 1674, between the French, under Turenne, and the Imperialists, under General Caprara and the Duke of Lorraine. The French gained a signal victory. This action is also known as the Battle of Entzheim.

Sitabaldi (Third Mahratta War).

Fought November 24, 1817, between a small force of Madras native troops, and some Bengal cavalry, in all about 1,300 men, under Colonel Scott, and the army of Nappa Sahib, Rajah of Nagpur, 18,000 strong, with 36 guns. The Sepoys held their ground for 18 hours, and eventually beat off their assailants, at a cost to themselves of about 300 men.

Skalitz (Seven Weeks' War).

Fought June 28, 1866, between the 5th Prussian Army Corps, under General Steinmetz, and the 6th and 8th Austrian Corps, under General Ramming. The Austrians were defeated, and Skalitz occupied by the Prussians, who captured 4,000 prisoners and 8 guns.

Slivnitza (Servo-Bulgarian War).

Fought November 17, 18 and 19, 1885, between the Servians, 28,000 strong, under King Milan, and Bulgarians, at first 10,000 in number, but reinforced on the night of the 17th and during the 18th, by a further 5,000, under Prince Alexander. On the 17th, Prince Alexander, who occupied a position strong against a frontal attack, but very vulnerable on his left, made a strong attack on the Servian left, to distract attention from his weak flank. This attack was repulsed, and on the following day the Servians attacked Alexander's left. Having been reinforced, however, he was able to beat them off, while a frontal attack was also repulsed with loss. On the 19th the Servian attacks were again unsuccessful, and by 3 p.m. they were in full retreat, pursued by the Bulgarians. The Servians lost about 2,000, the victors 3,000 in killed and wounded, in the three days.

Sluys (Hundred Years' War).

Fought June 24, 1340, when the English fleet of 250 sail, under Sir Robert Morley and Richard Fitzalan, attacked the French fleet of about 200 sail, under Hugues Quiéret, lying in Sluys Harbour. Practically the whole of the French fleet was captured or destroyed, and Quiéret was killed. The French lost 25,000 men, the English 4,000.

Smolensko (Russo - Swedish Wars).

Fought September 22, 1708, when Charles XII of Sweden, with 4,000 infantry and 6 regiments of cavalry, attacked a force of 16,000 Cossacks and Tartars. The king with one regiment was in the course of the action cut off from the rest of his troops by a body of Tartars, and had a narrow escape. His immediate following was reduced to 5 men, when he was rescued by a cavalry charge. In the end the Swedes routed the Cossacks with heavy loss.

Smolensko (Campaign of Moscow).

Fought August 17, 1812, between 175,000 French, under Napoleon, and 130,000 Russians, under Bagration, of whom about 50,000 and 60,000 respectively were actually engaged. Bagration's corps occupied the town of Smolensko, which Napoleon attacked, carrying two of the suburbs. During the night the Russians set fire to the place, and evacuated it, having lost in the action about 10,000 killed and wounded. The French lost 9,000.

Sobraon (First Sikh War).

Fought February 10, 1846, between the British, about 15,000 strong, and 25,000 Sikhs, under Runjur Singh. The Sikhs were strongly entrenched on the Sutlej, and Sir Hugh Gough, with feigned attacks on their centre and right, succeeded in pushing home his assault on their left, and after hard fighting drove the defenders to the river, where many perished. The British lost 2,383, the Sikhs about 8,000.

Soczawa (Ottoman Wars).

Fought 1676, between the Poles, under John Sobieski and the Turks, under Mohammed IV. The Poles, who had been reinforced by the Lithuanians, under Paz, totally routed the Turks, who were greatly superior in numbers, and drove them in confusion into Kaminiec, with the exception of which fortress, the whole of Poland was thus freed from the Ottoman invaders.

Sohr (War of the Austrian Succession).

Fought September 30, 1745,

between 18,000 Prussians, under Frederick the Great, and 35,000 Austrians, under Prince Charles of Lorraine. The Prussians attacked the Austrian position and the Austrians, failing to display their usual courage made no stand against the steady advance of the Prussian infantry, and were driven back in confusion, with a loss of 6,000 killed, wounded and prisoners, and 22 guns. The Prussians lost between three and four thousand men.

Soissons.

Fought 486, and notable as the first military exploit of Clovis, the founder of the Merovingian dynasty, who here defeated Syagrius, Count of Soissons, and annexed his dominions.

Solebay (Dutch Wars).

Fought May 28, 1672, when the French and English fleets, together about 140 sail, under the Comte d'Estrées and the Duke of York, were surprised at anchor, by a Dutch fleet of 115 ships, under de Ruyter. The French were first attacked, but soon edged out of the fight, and the bulk of the work fell to the English. The battle was indecisive, for though the Dutch lost five or more ships, and the English one only, the allied fleet was too crippled to take the offensive for over a month after the action.

Solferino (Franco-Austrian War).

Fought June 24, 1859, between 150,000 Austrians, under the Emperor Francis Joseph, with Generals Wimpffen and Scholick in actual command. and the French and Piedmontese, under Napoleon III and Victor Emmanuel. The French attacked the Austrian position on the heights round Solferino, which were held by Scholick, and after very hard fighting, they were captured by the corps of Macmahon and Baraguay d'Hilliers. Meanwhile Wimpffen, with three Army Corps, attacked the French left, but was held at bay throughout the day by Marshal Niel's corps, and when night fell, the Austrian centre being broken, Francis Joseph had no option but to retreat, and consequently recrossed the Mincio. The Austrians lost 22,000 killed, wounded and missing. The allies' losses were 18,000, of which number the Piedmontese corps of 25,000 lost 4,000.

Solway Moss (Scottish Wars).

Fought December 14, 1542, between the Scottish invading army, under Oliver Sinclair, and a band of 500 English borderers, under Thomas Dacre and John Musgrave. The Scots were totally defeated, and many important nobles captured.

Somnauth (Mahmud's Twelfth Invasion of India).

This city, one of the holy places of India, was captured by the Afghans, under Sultan Mahmud of Ghuzni, in 1024. According to tradition, he carried off the great gates of the city to Ghuzni; and certain gates purporting to be the same, but which afterwards proved to be of later date, were brought back to India with a flourish of trumpets, after the capture of Ghuzni by the British in 1842.

Son-Tai (Tongking War).

This fortress, defended by a

garrison of 25,000 Chinese, including 10,000 " Black Flags," under Lin Yung Ku, was attacked by the French, under Admiral Courbet, with 7 river gun-boats and force of 7,000 men, December 14, 1883. On this day the outer defences were carried, and the garrison driven into the citadel. During the night the French were surprised by a sortie, which however they repulsed, after severe fighting. On the 16th they stormed the citadel, losing in the three days 92 officers and 318 men killed and wounded. The Chinese lost about 1,000.

Sorata (Inca Rising).

This city was besieged, 1780, by the revolted Peruvians, under Andrés, the last of the Incas. The fortifications, well provided with artillery, proved impregnable, but Andrés diverted certain mountain torrents against the walls, and thus opened a large breach, through which the Peruvians entered the city, and massacred the whole of the garrison and inhabitants. Of 20,000 souls, it is said that only one priest escaped.

South Mountain (American Civil War).

Fought September 14, 1862, between the Federals, under General M'Clellan, and the Confederates, under General Lee. Lee's object was to hold M'Clellan in check while Jackson captured Harper's Ferry, and to this end he posted General D. Hill with 15,000 on South Mountain. Here Hill was attacked, and driven to the upper slopes, but being reinforced by a portion of Longstreet's command, he main-tained his position there, withdrawing on the morning of the 15th. Each side lost about 2,500 men, but Lee had gained his object, as the delay to M'Clellan ensured the capture of Harper's Ferry.

Southwark (Cade's Rebellion).

Fought July 5, 1450, between the rebels, under Cade, and the citizens of London, under Matthew Gough. The Londoners endeavoured to hold London Bridge, to prevent the plundering expeditions of Cade's followers into the city, but were driven back, and the central drawbridge set on fire. The Londoners lost heavily, among the killed being Gough.

Southwold Bay (Dutch Wars).

Fought 1665, between the English fleet, under the Duke of York, and the Dutch fleet, under Admiral Opdam. The English were completely victorious, the Dutch losing 18 ships and 7,000 men. The English lost one ship only, and 700 men.

Spanish Galleons. *See* Vigo Bay.

Sphacteria. *See* Pylos.

Spicheren (Franco - German War).

Fought August 6, 1870, between the Germans, under Von Alvensleben, and a superior French force, under General Frossard. After an obstinate encounter, the French were driven from all their positions with heavy loss, and compelled to retreat on Metz. The Germans lost 223 officers and 4,648 men. The battle is remarkable for the storming of the Rote Berg by 1 company of the 39th Regiment and 4 companies of the 74th Regiment, under General von François, who was killed. These 5 companies maintained their position throughout the afternoon, in face of a vastly superior force. This action is also known as the Battle of Forbach.

Spion Kop (Second Boer War).

General Buller's second attempt to break through the Boer lines on the Tugela, and relieve Ladysmith, is known by this name. The operations commenced on the 19th, 24,000 men being employed. On that day Sir Charles Warren's division commenced to turn the Boer right, and gradually drove them from ridge to ridge till the evening of the 22nd, when by a night surprise, Spion Kop, the centre of the position, was seized. It was, however, found impossible to get artillery up the steep slopes, and the brigade holding the hill lost about a third of their strength in the course of the 23rd, including the Brigadier, General Woodgate. At nightfall, Colonel Thorneycroft, who had been appointed to the command, abandoned the hill, and on the following day General Buller decided to recross the Tugela. The British losses during the operations amounted to 87 officers and 1,647 men.

Spira (War of the Spanish Succession).

Fought November 15, 1703, between the French, under Marshal Tallard, and the Imperialists, under the Prince of Hesse, each side being about 20,000 strong. After a severe engagement, the Imperialists were overpowered by the French cavalry, and totally defeated with a loss of 6,000 killed, wounded and missing. Among the prisoners was the Prince of Hesse.

Splitter (Swedish Invasion of Brandenburg).

Fought January, 1679, between 16,000 Swedes, under Field-Marshal Horn, and 10,000 Brandenburgers, under the Elector Frederick William. The Swedes were utterly routed, Horn being taken prisoner, and not more than 1,500 succeeded in making their way to Riga.

Spottsylvania (American Civil War).

A continuation of the Battle of the Wilderness, fought May 10 to 12, 1864, between the Confederates, under General Lee, and the Federals, under General Grant. Lee's position covering Richmond was attacked on the 10th by Grant, and the day ended with both armies in their original positions, while the losses, especially on the side of the assailants, were very heavy. On the 12th Grant renewed the attack, and General Hancock, on the right surprised the first line of the Confederate defences, and compelled General Johnson and his division to surrender. With this exception, entailing the loss of about a mile of ground Lee held his own throughout the day, and Grant had suffered too severely to renew the attack. The losses from the 5th, the date of the first Battle of the Wilderness, to the 12th inclusive, were : Federals, about 50,000 killed and wounded, Confederates, about 12,000.

Spurs. *See* **Courtrai.**

Spurs. *See* **Guinegate.**

Stadtlohn (Thirty Years' War).

Fought August 9, 1623, between the army of the Protestant Princes of Germany, about 22,000 strong, under Duke Christian of Brunswick, and the Imperialists, under Tilly. The Protestants were utterly routed and dispersed, Christian fleeing to Holland.

Staffarda (War of the Revolution).

Fought 1690, between the French, under Marshal Catinat, and the Imperialists, under Victor Amadeus of Savoy. The Imperialists met with a crushing defeat.

Stamford Bridge.

Fought September 25, 1066, between the English, under Harold, and the Norse invaders, under Harold Hardrada and Tostig. The Norsemen were surprised by Harold in their camp, and totally defeated, both Hardrada and Tostig being killed, and the survivors driven to their ships.

Stamford Bridge (Wars of the Roses).

An encounter between the retainers of Sir Thomas Neville, and those of Lord Egremont, which developed into a pitched battle, in August, 1453. It is considered to be the beginning of the Wars of the Roses.

Standard, The (Scottish Wars).

Fought at Luton Moor, near Northallerton, in 1138, between the Scots, under David, and the English, under Thurstan, Archbishop of York, and Raoul,

Bishop of Durham. The Scots were routed, and fled in disorder. The battle derives its name from the fact that the banner of St. Cuthbert of Durham, which was held to ensure victory, that of St. Peter of York, and those of other saints, were carried in a waggon in the midst of the English army.

Stavrichani (Ottoman Wars).

Fought August 28, 1739, between 30,000 Russians, under General Münnich, and the Turkish army, under Veli Pasha. The Russians stormed the Turkish entrenched camp, driving the Turks headlong into the Danube, where thousands perished, and capturing all their guns and baggage. Münnich followed up this success by the capture of Choczin.

Steinkirk (War of the Revolution).

Fought August 8, 1692, between the English, under William III, and the French ,under Marshal Luxembourg. The English attacked the French camp at daybreak, and broke and dispersed a brigade. Luxembourg, however, rallied his troops, and after a severe engagement, repulsed the English attack, though William was able to withdraw his forces in good order.

Stillwater (American War of Independence).

Fought October 7, 1777, between the British, 6,000 strong, under General Burgoyne, and the Americans, under General Gates. The Americans occupied a strongly entrenched position, which was attacked by

Burgoyne. After a severe encounter, the attack was repulsed at all points, and the British driven back upon their camp at Saratoga, with heavy loss, including General Fraser, mortally wounded. The Americans followed up their success by an assault upon the British camp, in which they succeeded in effecting a lodgement, and on the following day, Burgoyne withdrew, and took up a fresh position on the heights near the Hudson. On October 15, Burgoyne, surrounded by the Americans, and finding that no aid could reach him, surrendered with 5,790 men, his total losses during the campaign having amounted to 4,689.

Stirling (Scottish Wars).

Fought September 11, 1297, between the Scots, under Sir William Wallace, and the English, 50,000 strong, under the Earl of Surrey. Wallace fell upon the English army as it was crossing a narrow bridge over the Forth, and practically annihilated it, This battle is also called the Battle of Cambuskenneth

Stockack (Wars of the French Revolution).

Fought 1799, between the French, under Jourdan, and the Austrians, 60,000 strong, under the Archduke Charles. The French were defeated and driven back upon the Rhine.

Stoke (Lambert Simnel's Rebellion).

Fought June 16, 1487, between the royal troops, under Henry VII, and the rebels, under John de la Pole, Earl of Lincoln, who was aided by 2,000 German mercenaries, under Martin Schwarz. The King, whose force was superior in numbers, completely defeated the rebels, Simnel and all the rebel leaders being taken prisoners.

Stolhoffen (War of the Spanish Succession).

Fought May 22, 1707, when Marshal Villars, with 45 French battalions, stormed and captured the lines of Stolhoffen, which were held by the Imperialists, under the Marquis of Baireuth. The French took 50 guns.

Stone Creek. *See* Murfreesboro.

Stormberg (Second Boer War).

Fought December 10, 1899, when General Gatacre, with about 3,000 men, made a night march to attack the Boer position at Stormberg. He was misled by his guides, and came unexpectedly under a heavy Boer fire. The position was too strong to carry, and Gatacre was forced to retire, with a loss of 89 killed and wounded, and 633 prisoners.

Stralsund (Thirty Years' War).

This place was besieged, July 5, 1628, by the Imperialists, under Wallenstein, who had sworn to take it in three days. It was defended mainly by the inhabitants, aided by a small garrison of Swedes and Scots. An assault on the 8th was repulsed, and though on the 9th some of the outworks were gained, the town still held out, and finally, after a siege of 11 weeks, Wallenstein was compelled to withdraw his troops, having suffered a loss of over 12,000 men.

Stralsund (Dano-Swedish Wars).

The town was again besieged, October 19, 1715, by an army of Prussians and Danes, 36,000 strong, under Frederick William III of Prussia and Frederick IV of Denmark, and was defended by a Swedish garrison, under Charles XII. At the end of three months, the besiegers succeeded in seizing the island of Rugen, which commanded the town, and an attempt by Charles to retake it ended disastrously, the king escaping with difficulty, and severely wounded, while the whole of his force was killed or captured. On October 10, the allies captured the hornwork, and on the 20th, the place being no longer defensible, Charles left the town and embarked for Sweden on the only ship remaining in the harbour. The garrison immediately afterwards surrendered.

Stratton (Civil War).

Fought May 16, 1643, between the Parliamentary troops, under General Chudleigh, and the Cornish Royalists, under Sir Ralph Hopton. The Royalists attacked the Parliamentarian position on Stratton Hill, and after severe fighting defeated them, capturing 1,700 prisoners, including Chudleigh, 13 guns and all their baggage and munitions of war.

Suero, The (Civil War of Sertorius).

Fought B.C. 75, between the rebels, under Sertorius, and the Roman army, under Pompey. The Roman right, under Pompey, was broken and defeated, but Afranius turned defeat into victory, capturing the Sertorian camp, and routing and dispersing the rebel army.

Suddusain (Second Sikh War).

Fought July 1, 1848, when a force of Bhawalpuris and British 18,000 strong, under Lieutenant Edwardes, encountered 12,000 Sikhs, under Malraj. The Sikhs attacked, but were beaten off, largely owing to the superiority of the British artillery, and defeated with heavy loss.

Sudley Springs (American Civil War).

Fought August 29, 1862, between the Federals, under General Pope, and the Confederates, under Jackson. Jackson, by a forced march, had succeeded in taking up a strong position in Pope's rear, and defied all attempts to dislodge him, repulsing the Federal attacks with a loss of over 8,000 men.

Sugar-loaf Rock (Seven Years' War).

Fought September 20, 1753, between the British, about 3,000 strong, under Major Laurence, and the French army which was besieging Trichinopoly, under M. Astruc. Laurence attacked before daybreak, and the native auxiliaries with the French army were seized with a panic and fled, leaving the Europeans unsupported. In the end the French were defeated, with a loss of 100 killed and 200 prisoners, including Astruc. The British lost 40 killed and wounded.

Surinam (Napoleonic Wars).

This place, held by a Dutch garrison, was captured, May 5, 1804, by a British squadron, under Commander Hood, together with 2,000 troops, under Sir Charles Green.

Sursuti, The (Mohammed Ghori's Invasion).

Fought 1191, between the Aghans, under Mohammed Ghori, and the Hindus, under the King of Delhi, with 200,000 horse and 300 elephants. The Afghans, who were greatly outnumbered, were surrounded, and utterly routed, Mohammed Ghori escaping with difficulty from the field.

Sursuti, The (Mohammed Ghori's Invasion).

Fought 1192, when Mohammed Ghori, on the field where he had suffered defeat in the previous year, encountered the Rajputs and Delhi men, under the Rajah of Ajmir. The Afghans, numbering 120,000, completely routed the Rajputs, and captured the Rajah.

Sveaborg (Finland War).

This place was besieged by the Russians, under General Suchtelen, in February, 1808, and was defended by a garrison of 7,000 Swedes and Finns, under Admiral Cronstedt. The siege was conducted under considerable difficulties, the transport of breaching guns being almost impossible. However, lack of supplies compelled the Admiral to sign an armistice, on April 3, by which he agreed to surrender if not relieved by at least five ships of war on May 3. This being still unbroken at that date, he handed over the town to the Russians, with 200 guns, and 2 frigates and 19 transports, which were ice-bound in the harbour.

Sveaborg (Crimean War).

The town, which had become an important Russian arsenal, was bombarded by a British fleet, under Admiral Dundas, August 9 to 11, 1854. By the latter date, the arsenal and storehouses had been destroyed, and Dundas withdrew, making no further attempt to destroy the fortifications.

Sybota.

Fought 433 B.C., between a Corinthian fleet of 150 sail, and a Corcyrean fleet of 110 sail, aided by 10 Athenian triremes. The Corcyrean right wing was defeated, and would have been destroyed, but for the assistance of the Athenians, and the arrival of a reinforcement of 20 Athenian ships caused the Corinthians to retire. The Corcyreans offered battle on the following day, but the Corinthians declined. Both sides claimed the victory, but the advantage lay with the Corinthians, who captured several ships.

Syracuse (Athenian Expedition to Sicily).

Siege was laid to this city by the Athenians, under Alcibiades, Lamachus and Nicias, who with a fleet of 134 galleys, took possession of the harbour and effected a landing in the autumn of 415 B.C. Alcibiades was soon recalled, and Lamachas killed in a skirmish, while Nicias proved weak and incompetent. The siege works were not pressed and in the following year, Gylippus of Sparta succeeded in getting through the Athenian lines, and bringing a considerable force to the aid of the Syracusans, capturing at the same time the advanced positions of the besiegers. Early in 413, Demosthenes arrived from Athens, with a fleet of 73 triremes, and made a desperate attempt to recover the lost ground. He was, however, totally defeated, and in a series of sea-fights which followed, the Athenian fleet was completely destroyed. This disaster forced the Athenians to raise the siege, and was, in addition, a death-blow to the naval supremacy of Athens.

Syracuse (Second Carthaginian Invasion).

Syracuse was again besieged, B.C. 387, by about 80,000 Carthaginians, under Himilco, aided by a powerful fleet, and defended by Dionysius, with about an equal number of troops. A fleet of 30 Lacedæmonian triremes arrived to the succour of the Syracusans, and meanwhile a pestilence had carried off thousands in the besiegers' camp. At this juncture Dionysius decided on a joint sea and land attack upon the Carthaginians, which was completely successful. Leptinus, with 80 galleys, surprised the Carthaginian fleet while the crews were ashore, and completely destroyed it, while Dionysius stormed Himilco's defences, and utterly routed the besiegers, Himilco and his principal officers escaping from Sicily, and leaving the army to its fate.

Syracuse (Second Punic War).

In 213 B.C. Syracuse, then in the hands of the pro-Carthaginian faction, was besieged by the Romans, 25,000 strong, under M. Marcellus, and a fleet

under Appius Claudius. The city was defended by a garrison under Hippocrates. The siege is specially notable for the presence in the city of Archimedes, whose military engines played an important part in the defence, especially against the fleet. During the winter, the revolt of other Sicilian towns drew off a portion of the besiegers, and during the spring and early summer of 212, only a partial blockade could be maintained. Then however, taking advantage of a festival in the city, Marcellus stormed and captured the upper portion of the town. An attempt to force the Roman lines by a Carthaginian relieving force, under Himilco, was repulsed, and shortly afterwards the rest of the city was captured by assault.

Szigeth (Ottoman Wars).

This small place, held by a Hungarian garrison, under Count Zrinyi, was besieged by the Turks, under Solyman the Magnificent, in 1566. The siege was prosecuted with vigour but was fatal to the great Sultan, who died on the night of September 4. On the following day, however, the Turks stormed and sacked the town, and Count Zrinyi and his little garrison perished in the flames.

T

Tabraca (Revolt of Gildo).

Fought 398, between 5,000 picked Roman legionaries, under Mascazel, and the revolted Africans, 70,000 strong, under

Gildo. At the first onslaught of the legionaries, all the Roman soldiers serving under Gildo deserted, and the Africans taking to flight, Mascazel gained an almost bloodless victory. Gildo was captured and committed suicide in prison.

Taçna (Peruvio-Chilian War).

Fought May 26, 1880, between the Chilians, under General Baquedano, and the Peruvians, the Chilians gaining a signal victory. The Peruvian losses were very heavy, including 197 officers. Following up their victory, the Chilians captured the fortress of Ariça.

Tacubaya (Mexican Liberal Rising).

Fought April 11, 1859, between the Mexican Government troops, under Marquez, and the Liberals, under Degollado. The Liberals were completely routed, with the loss of all their artillery and munitions of war.

Tagina (Second Gothic War).

Fought July, 552, between the Goths, under Totila, King of Italy, and 30,000 Imperial troops, under Narses. The Romans withstood the charge of the Goths, broke their cavalry, and then drove their infantry from the field, with a loss of about 6,000. Totila was overtaken and slain in the pursuit.

Tagliacozzo (Guelfs and Ghibellines).

Fought 1268, between the Guelf party, under Charles of Anjou, the usurper of the throne of Naples, and the Ghibellines, under Conradin, the rightful heir, and Frederick, Duke of Austria. The Ghibellines were utterly routed, and their leaders, including Conradin and the Duke, captured and beheaded.

Taiken Gate (Hogen Insurrection).

Fought 1157, between the Japanese rebels, under Shitoku, and the Imperial troops, under Bifukumonia and Tadamichi. The rebels were utterly routed. This battle is remarkable for the fratricidal nature of the conflict, many of the greatest families of Japan having representatives in both armies.

Taillebourg.

Fought 1242, between the French, under Louis IX, and the English, under Henry III, with whom were allied the rebellious vassals of the French crown, the Comtes de Marche and de Foix. The allies were defeated, and Henry withdrew his forces from France.

Takashima (Chinese Invasion of Japan).

After the wreck of the Chinese fleet, in 1281, the survivors, under Chang Pak, took refuge on the island of Takashima. Here they were attacked by the troops of Kiushiu, under Shoni Kagesuke. They were almost without exception killed or captured, only three out of the vast host returning to China.

Taku Forts (Second China War).

Fought June 25, 1859, when an attempt was made by the British to carry the forts at the mouth of the Peiho River. Eleven light-draught gunboats crossed the bar, and tried to silence the batteries, but without success, and at 5 p.m. an attempt was made to carry the defences by a land attack. A force of 600 marines and blue-jackets, under Captain Van-sittart, was landed, but after severe fighting was driven back to the boats, with a loss of 68 killed, and nearly 300 wounded. Six of the gunboats were sunk or disabled, and their crews also suffered heavily.

On August 21, 1860, a second and successful assault was made on the forts by a force of 11,000 British and 7,000 French troops, under Sir Hope Grant. After a brief bombardment, the small north fort, garrisoned by 500 Chinese, was stormed by 2,500 British, and 400 French, 400 of the garrison falling, while the British lost 21 killed and 184 wounded. In the course of the day the remaining forts sur-rendered without further fight-ing.

Talana Hill (Second Boer War).

Fought October 20, 1899, between 4,000 Boers, under General Lucas Meyer, and a British force of equal strength, under General Symons. The Boers occupied a strong position on the heights of Dundee, from which they were dislodged by the British infantry, with a loss of about 300. The British lost 19 officers, 142 men killed and wounded, and 331 prisoners, the latter a detachment of cavalry and mounted infantry, who were surrounded by a superior force of Boers, and surrendered. General Symons was mortally wounded. The action is also called the battle of Dundee.

Talavera (Peninsular War).

Fought July 28, 1809, be-tween 19,000 British and 34,000 Spaniards, under Sir Arthur Wellesley, and 50,000 French, under Marshals Jourdan and Victor, with Joseph Buonaparte in nominal command. The British repulsed all the attacks on their position, at a cost of 6,200 killed and wounded. The Spanish losses were returned at 1,200, but the figures are doubt-ful, as they took practically no part in the fighting. The French lost 7,389 killed, wounded and missing, and 17 guns.

Talkhan (Tartar Invasion of Khorassan).

This fortress was captured, 1221, by the Tartars, under Genghiz Khan, after an obstin-ate defence of seven months, in which thousands perished on both sides.

Talneer (Third Mahratta War).

By the treaty of January 6, 1818, this fortress was sur-rendered by Holkar to the British, but on Sir Thomas Hislop, with a British force, arriving to take possession, on February 17, the commandant refused to hand it over. Though warned of the consequences, he fired upon the British, where-upon Hislop opened fire, and in the afternoon of the same day the place surrendered. By some misunderstanding, how-ever, the Arab garrison of 300, were drawn up at one of the gates, and on the approach of two British officers and some Sepoys, cut them down. No quarter was then given, the garrison being killed to a man, and the commandant hanged.

Tamai (Soudan Campaigns).

Fought March 13, 1884, when 4,000 British, under General Graham, attacked and defeated the Mahdists, under Osman Digna, destroying their camp. The British fought in two squares, one of which was momentarily broken by the Mahdists, who captured the naval guns. The second square, however, moved up in support, and the Mahdists were repulsed and the guns recovered. The British lost 10 officers and 204 men killed and wounded ; the Dervishes over 2,000 killed.

Tanagra.

Fought 457 B.C., between the Spartans, and their Peloponnesian allies, and about 14,000 Athenians and others, including a body of Thessalian cavalry. The battle was stubbornly contested, both sides losing heavily, but the desertion during the action of the Thessalians turned the scale, and the Spartans were victorious, though at a cost which deterred them from their intended attack upon Athens.

Tanjore (Seven Years' War).

This place was besieged, August, 1758, by the French, under Lally-Tollendal, and was defended by a garrison, under Monacji. After five days' bombardment, the walls were still insufficiently breached, and owing to lack of ammunition, Lally determined to retire. Hearing this, Monacji made a sortie, and nearly succeeded in surprising the French camp. He was with difficulty beaten off, and the French withdrew, with the loss of all their siege guns and heavy baggage.

Tanjore.

The fortress was besieged, August 20, 1773, by a British force, under General Joseph Smith, and defended by a garrison of 20,000 men, under the Rajah, Laljaji, and his Vizier Monacji. On September 16, a breach having been effected, the besiegers delivered an assault at midday, when their garrison were taking their usual noonday rest, and meeting with little opposition, made themselves masters of the place.

Tansara Saka (Satsuma Rebellion).

Fought 1876, when the rebels in a very strong position were attacked by the Imperial troops, under Prince Taruhito, and after very severe fighting, driven out with enormous loss. The Imperialists also suffered severely.

Tarapaca (Peruvio-Chilian War).

Fought November 17, 1879, and resulted in the defeat of the Peruvians with heavy loss.

Tarento (Italian Wars).

This fortress, held by a Neapolitan garrison, under the Conde di Potenza, was besieged by about 5,000 Spaniards, under Gonsalvo de Cordova, in August, 1501. Gonsalvo endeavoured to reduce the place by blockade, but found his forces melting away by desertion, and was forced to have recourse to more active measures. The north front of Tarento being bounded by a lake, was unfortified, and Gonsalvo, with incredible labour, transported overland some of the smaller vessels of the Spanish fleet lying in the Bay of

Tarento, and launched them on the lake. The town was then at his mercy, and surrendered, being entered by the Spaniards, March 1, 1502

Tarragona (Peninsular War).

This city was besieged by the French, 40,000 strong, under General Suchet, in May, 1811, and defended by a garrison but little inferior in numbers. The outer defences were stormed one by one, and by June 21, the besiegers had effected a lodgement in the lower town. On the 28th, the upper town was taken by storm, and the survivors of the garrison, 8,000 in number, laid down their arms. The French lost about 6,000 during the siege.

Tashkessen (Russo - Turkish War).

Fought December 28, 1877, between 2,000 Turks, under Valentine Baker Pasha, and a Russian division, under General Kourloff. In order to cover Shakir Pasha's retirement from the Shandurnik heights, Baker's greatly inferior force withstood throughout the day, the determined onslaughts of the Russians, when Baker finally withdrew, having effected his object. He had lost 800 men, and had inflicted a loss on his assailants of 32 officers and over 1,000 men.

Tauris (Civil War of Cæsar and Pompey).

Fought B.C. 47, between the Pompeian fleet, under Marcus Octavius, and the Cæsareans, under Publius Vatinius. The Cæsarean fleet consisted of merchant vessels, temporarily equipped with beaks, but Vatinius, though his ships were inferior both in number and quality, boldly attacked the Pompeians, and after severe fighting, completely defeated them, compelling Octavius to abandon the Adriatic.

Taus (Hussite Wars).

Fought August 14, 1431, between the Hussites, under John Ziska, and the Imperialists, under the Emperor Sigismund. The Hussites gained a signal victory.

Tayeizan (Japanese Revolution).

Fought 1868, when the adherents of the Shogun made their last stand in Tokyo at the Tayeizan temple in the Park of Uyeno. They were defeated after a sharp conflict, leaving the Imperialists in undisputed possession of the Shogun's capital.

Tchernaya (Crimean War).

Fought August 16, 1855, between three Russian divisions, under General Gortschakoff, and three French and one Sardinian division, under General Marmora. The Russians attacked the allies' position on the Tchernaya, and after severe fighting, were repulsed with a loss of 5,000 killed and wounded. The allies lost 1,200.

Tchesme (Ottoman Wars).

Fought July 7, 1770, between the Russian fleet of 50 sail, under Count Alexis Orloff, and the Turkish fleet of nearly 100 sail of the line, under Hassan Bey. With the exception of one ship, which was captured, the whole of the Turkish fleet was destroyed.

Tearless Battle.

Fought B.C. 368, when a force of Arcadians endeavoured to cut off a Spartan army, under Archidamus, in a narrow defile in Laconia. They were repulsed with heavy loss, and not a single Spartan was killed, whence the engagement came to be called the Tearless Battle.

Tegea.

Fought B.C. 473, when the Spartans defeated the combined forces of the Arcadian League and the Argives, under the walls of Tegea. Though victorious, the Spartans were too much reduced in numbers to venture upon the attack of Tegea, which had been the object of the expedition.

Tegyra (Bœotian War).

Fought B.C. 373, when Pelopidas, with the Sacred Band of 300 Thebans, routed a large force of Spartans in a narrow pass near Orchomenus, slaying 600, including their two generals.

Telamon (Conquest of Cisalpine Gaul).

Fought B.C. 225, when the Gauls, marching upon Rome, found themselves caught between two Roman consular armies, and though fighting desperately, were cut to pieces.

Tel-el-Kebir (Arabi's Rebellion).

Fought September 13, 1882, when the British, 17,000 strong, under Lord Wolseley, after a night march across the desert, attacked and stormed Arabi's entrenchments, which were defended by 22,000 Egyptians. The British lost 339 killed and wounded, the Egyptian loss was very heavy.

Tel-el-Mahuta (Arabi's Rebellion).

Fought August 24, 1882, when the Egyptians attempted to oppose the march of the British advance guard, under General Graham, to Kassassin. They made, however, but a feeble resistance, and were driven off with heavy loss.

Te-li-ssu (Russo-Japanese War).

Fought June 14 and 15, 1904, between 35,000 Russians, under Baron de Stakelberg, and about 40,000 Japanese, under General Oku. The Japanese attacked the Russian position, but the Russians held their ground throughout the 14th, at a cost of about 350 killed and wounded. On the 15th, however, their flank was turned, and after hard fighting in which they suffered heavily, two batteries of artillery being absolutely cut to pieces, they retreated in some disorder, leaving over 1,500 dead on the field. The Japanese, who lost 1,163 in the two days, captured 300 prisoners and 14 guns. The total Russian losses were about 10,000.

Tellicherry (First Mysore War).

This place, held by a small British garrison, and very imperfectly fortified, was besieged June, 1780, by a Mysore force, under Sirdar Ali Khan. Aid was sent to the garrison from Bombay, and a most gallant defence was made till January 18, 1782, when reinforcements arrived, under Major Abington, who, aided by the garrison, stormed the Mysori entrenchments, capturing all their guns, 60 in number, and 1,200 prisoners, among whom was Sirdar Ali.

Temesvar (Hungarian Rising).

Fought August 9, 1849, between the Austrians, under Haynau, and the Hungarians, under Dembinski. The latter was totally routed, and his army dispersed, this being the last stand made by the Hungarians in the war. On the 13th, Görgey and his army surrendered to the Russians at Villágos.

Tenchebrai.

Fought September 28, 1106, between the English, under Henry I, and the Normans, under Robert of Normandy, Henry's brother. Robert was totally defeated and made prisoner, and Henry annexed Normandy to the crown of England.

Tergoes (Netherlands War of Independence).

This fortress was besieged, August 16, 1572, by the Dutch Patriots, 7,000 strong, under Jerome de 't Zeraerts, and was defended by a small Spanish garrison. On October 20, a force of 3,000 Spanish veterans, under Colonel Mondragon, succeeded in crossing the "Drowned Land," with a loss of only 9 men drowned, and relieved the town, 't Zeraert's troops refusing to face this unexpected attack.

Testry.

Fought 687, between the Neustrians, under Thierry III, and the Austrasians, under Pepin d'Héristal, the Maire du Palais. The Neustrians were routed, and Thierry captured.

Tettenhall (Danish Invasion).

Fought 910, between the Danish invaders, and the West Saxons, under Edward the Elder. The Danes were defeated.

Tetuan (Morocco War).

Fought February 4, 1860, when 30,000 Spaniards, under Marshal O'Donnell, stormed the Moorish entrenchments outside Tetuan, held by about 40,000 Moors. Three days later Tetuan was entered by the Spaniards.

Teuttingen (Thirty Years' War).

Fought November, 1643, between the French, under the Maréchal de Rantzau, and the Imperialists, under the Count de Merci. The Imperialists surprised the French camp, and totally routed them, Rantzau, being captured with most of his superior officers, and all his artillery and baggage.

Tewkesbury (Wars of the Roses).

Fought May 4, 1471, when the Yorkists, under Edward IV, defeated the Lancastrians, under Prince Edward, Somerset and others, with heavy loss. Prince Edward and other leading Lancastrians were killed, and Margaret of Anjou promptly surrendered.

Texel (Dutch Wars).

Fought June 2, 1653, between a British fleet, under Monk, and a Dutch fleet, under Van Tromp. The action was undecided, but on the following day, Monk having been reinforced by 18 ships, under Admiral Blake, renewed the attack, and signally defeated Van Tromp, with a loss of 11 ships and 1,300 prisoners taken, and 6 ships sunk. The British lost 20 ships and 363 killed and wounded.

Thala (Numidian Revolt).

In the year 22, this fortress, defended by no more than 500 Roman veterans, was attacked by a large force of nomads, under Tacfarinas. The Romans sallied out, and inflicted so severe a defeat upon Tacfarinas that his army was dispersed.

Thapsus (Civil War of Cæsar and Pompey).

Fought April 6, B.C. 46, between the Cæsareans, consisting of 10 legions, under Julius Cæsar, and the Pompeians, 14 legions, in addition to cavalry, light troops, and 100 elephants, under Metellus Scipio and Juba.

Thebes.

This city was captured by the Macedonians, under Alexander the Great, in September, 335 B.C. The Thebans were blockading the Macedonian garrison, which held the citadel, and the Cadmea; Perdiccas, one of Alexander's captains, without orders, broke through the earthworks outside the city. Before the Thebans could shut the gates, Perdiccas effected an entrance into the city, and being joined by the garrison of the Cadmea, soon overcame the resistance of the Thebans. Six thousand of the inhabitants were massacred, and the city was razed to the ground.

Thermopylæ (Third Persian Invasion).

Fought 480 B.C., when 300 Spartans and 700 Thespians, under Leonidas, defended the pass of Thermopylæ, leading southwards out of Thessaly, against the Persian host, under Xerxes. They kept the Persians at bay until a considerable force having passed the mountains by another part, they were attacked in the rear. They then retired to a hillock, and fought till the last man fell.

Thermopylæ (War with Antiochus).

Fought B.C. 191, between 40,000 Romans, under Glabrio, and the army of Antiochus the Great, King of Asia, Antiochus was entrenched at Thermopylæ, where he was attacked by the Romans, and a post held by 2,000 Ætolians being surprised, his flank was turned, and he was disastrously defeated. Antiochus escaped from the field with barely 500 men.

Thetford (Danish Invasion).

Fought 870, between the Danish invaders, and the East Anglians, under Edward. The latter were defeated and Edward killed.

Thorn (Russo-Swedish War).

Siege was laid to this place by the Swedes, under Charles XII, September 22, 1702. It was defended by a garrison of 5,000 Poles, under General Robel, who made a gallant defence, but after a month's siege, he was compelled by famine to surrender.

Thurii.

Fought B.C. 282, when a Roman consular army, under Caius Fabricius, routed the Lucanians and Bruttians, who were besieging Thurii. The siege was raised, and the Tarentine coalition temporarily broken up.

Tiberias.

Fought July, 1187, between the Saracens, under Saladin, and the Christians of Jerusalem, under Guy de Lusignan. Saladin gained a signal victory, capturing the King, the Grand Master of the Templars, and the Marquis de Montferrat. Following up his success, Saladin recovered in succession, Acre, Jaffa, and other important places, and in the month of October of the same year, recaptured Jerusalem.

Ticinus (Second Punic War).

Fought B.C. 218, between 26,000 Carthaginians, under Hannibal, and 25,000 Romans, under P. Cornelius Scipio (the Elder). The Romans were defeated with heavy loss, Scipio being severely wounded.

Ticonderoga (Seven Years' War).

Fought July 8, 1758, between Montcalm, with 3,600 French and Canadians, and the British, 15,000 strong, including 6,000 regulars, under General James Abercromby. Montcalm was strongly intrenched on a ridge in front of Fort Ticonderoga, his position being furthered strengthened by an abatis. Abercromby made no attempt to turn the position, but without waiting for his guns, ordered the regulars to take the lines by storm. Notwithstanding the gallantry of the troops, who advanced six times to the assault, the position proved impregnable, and Abercromby was forced to withdraw, with a loss of 19,44 killed and wounded, the French losing 377 only. The 42nd Regiment (Black Watch) showed conspicuous bravery,

losing half the rank and file, and 25 officers killed and wounded.

On July 22, 1759, a British force of 11,000 men under General Amherst, arrived before Ticonderoga, which was held by about 3,500 French and Canadians, under Bourlamaque. On the 23rd, Bourlemaque withdrew to the Isle-aux-Noix, on Lake Champlain, leaving only 400 men, under Hébécourt, with instructions to hold Amherst before the place as long as possible. On the 26th, however, Hébécourt set fire to the magazine and retired.

Ticonderoga (American War of Independence).

This place was invested, June 22, 1777, by the British, under General Burgoyne, and was defended by 5,000 Americans, under General St. Clair. After a brief siege, the Americans evacuated the Fort, July 5.

Tiflis (Tartar Invasion of the Caucasus).

Fought 1386, between the Tartars, under Tamerlane, and the troops of the Caucasian tribes, under the Queen of Georgia. The Queen issued from Tiflis to offer battle to the Tartars, but her forces could not stand against them, and were cut to pieces.

Tigranocerta (Third Mithridatic War).

Fought B.C. 69, when the Romans, 10,000 strong, under Lucullus, who was besieging the city, were attacked by 200,000 Pontic and Armenian troops, under Tigranes. ¹Tigranes had failed to occupy some high ground which commanded the position of his cavalry. This Lucullus seized, and attacking the Pontic cavalry in rear, broke it, He then attacked and routed the infantry, with a loss according to the Roman account of 100,000. The Romans lost 5 men only.

Tigris (Persian Wars).

Fought 363, when the Romans under Julian, crossed the Tigris in the face of a large Persian army, strongly entrenched on the opposite bank. At the first assault, though an attempt at a surprise failed, the Romans stormed the Persian lines, and after 12 hours' fighting, drove them from the field. The Romans only admitted a loss of 75 men, while they claimed that the Persians lost 6,000 killed.

Tippermuir (Civil War).

Fought September 1, 1644, between the Covenanters, 6,700 strong, under Lord Elcho, and about 3,000 Scottish Royalists, under Montrose. The Covenanters were totally defeated, with a loss variously estimated at from 1,300 to 2,000 killed, and 800 prisoners, while the Royalist loss was trifling. Following up his victory Montrose occupied Perth.

Toba (Japanese Revolution).

Fought 1868, between the troops of Aiza and Kuwana, under the Shogun Yoshinobu, and the army of Satsuma and Choshu. The Shogun was totally defeated, and abandoned his invasion of Satsuma, returning with his troops to Yedo by sea, surrendering shortly afterwards to the Imperial forces.

Tofrek (Soudan Campaigns).

Fought March 22, 1885, when

General McNeill, with 3 battalions of Indian, and 1½ of British troops, was surprised in his zariba, by about 5,000 Mahdists. One of the native regiments broke and fled, but the Berkshires and Marines, made a gallant defence, though the zariba was forced, as did the other native regiments. After twenty minutes' fighting the attack was beaten off, the Mahdists leaving 1,500 dead on the field. The British lost 294 combatants and 176 campfollowers, killed, wounded and missing.

Tolbiac.

Fought 496, between the Franks, under Clovis, and the Alemanni. The Franks, after a desperate conflict, began to give way, but were rallied by Clovis, who leading a charge in person, utterly routed the Alemanni. This victory gave the Franks undisputed possession of the territory west of the Rhine.

Tolentino (Hundred Days).

Fought May 2, 1815, between 50,000 Italians, under Murat, and 60,000 Austrians, under General Bianchi. The Italians were routed and dispersed, and Murat compelled to flee from Italy.

Tolenus (Social War).

Fought B.C. 90, between the Romans, under Lupus, and the revolted Marsians. Lupus was attacked while crossing the Tolenus, and totally routed with a loss of 8,000 men.

Tondeman's Woods (Seven Years' War).

Fought February 14, 1754, when a convoy to revictual

Trichinopoly, escorted by 180 British and 800 native troops, was attacked by 12,000 Mysore and Mahratta horse, under Hyder Ali and Morari Rao, supported by a small French force. The Sepoys at once laid down their arms, but the Europeans made a gallant defence, until the arrival of the French force, when, hopelessly outnumbered, they also surrendered. The convoy and the whole detachment were captured.

Torgau (Seven Years' War).

Fought November 3, 1760, between the Prussians, under Frederick the Great, and the Austrians, under Count Daun. The Austrians, besides being numerically superior, occupied a strong position at Torgau. Frederick divided his forces, and while one portion, under Ziethen, attacked in front, he himself led the rest of his army round the position, and fell upon the Austrian rear. Both attacks were repulsed, but during the night, Ziethen, finding the heights badly guarded, gained them, and seized the batteries, turning a defeat into a signal victory. The Austrians lost 20,000, the Prussians, 13,000, and the victory gave Frederick possession of the whole of Saxony.

Toro (War of the Castilian Succession).

Fought March 1, 1476, between the Portuguese, and the Spanish supporters of Joanna for the throne of Castile, 8,500 strong, under Alfonso of Portugal, and the adherents of Isabella, about equal in numbers, under Ferdinand the Catholic. Ferdinand, after a long march,

attacked the Portuguese at 4 p.m., and at the end of two hours' fighting, signally defeated them with heavy loss.

Toulon (War of the Spanish Succession).

An attack was made upon the fortress by a combined Dutch and British fleet, under Sir Cloudesley Shovel, July 17, 1707. The allies failed to gain a footing in the town, but 8 French ships lying in the harbour and 130 houses were destroyed by fire.

Toulon (War of the Austrian Succession).

Fought February 11, 1744, between a British fleet of 27 sail of the line, and 8 frigates, under Admiral Matthews, and a combined French and Spanish fleet of 28 line-of-battle ships. The British fleet suffered a serious reverse, in consequence of which the Admiral and four captains were tried by court-martial and cashiered. The British lost 274 killed and wounded, the allies about 1,000.

Toulon (Wars of the French Revolution).

On August 29, 1793, Toulon, which had opened its gates to the British, and was held by a small garrison, under Lord Mulgrave, was besieged by the French, under Dugommier. By December 18, most of the landward defences had been carried, and the place having become untenable, Lord Mulgrave carried off his troops by sea. This siege is chiefly memorable as being the first important appearance of Napoleon, who commanded the artillery.

Toulouse (Peninsular War).

Fought April 10, 1814, between 38,000 French, under Soult, and 24,000 British and Spaniards, under Wellington. The French entrenchments in front of Toulouse were attacked by the British, who after severe fighting captured some of the outworks. The victory, however, was incomplete, and was in effect of no value, as Napoleon had on this date already surrendered to the allies in Paris. The French lost about 3,000 killed and wounded, the allies, 4,659, of whom 2,000 were Spaniards.

Tournay (Netherlands War of Independence).

This place was besieged, October 1, 1581, by the Royal troops, under Alexander of Parma, and in the absence of the Governor, Prince Espinay, was gallantly defended by the Princess, who held out until November 30, when, by an honourable capitulation, she was allowed to march out at the head of the garrison, with all the honours of war.

Tournay (War of the Spanish Succession).

The town was besieged by the British, under the Duke of Marlborough, July 8, 1709, and was defended by a French garrison under M. de Surville. After 56 days of open trenches, the garrison surrendered, having suffered a loss of 3,000 men.

Tours (Moslem Invasion of France).

Fought 732, between the Franks, under Charles Martel, and the Saracens, under Abderrahman Ibu Abdillah. The battle lasted several days—according to the Arab chroniclers, two, while the Christian accounts say seven—and ended in the fall of Abderrahman, when the Saracens, discouraged by the death of their leader, owned defeat, and fled, losing heavily in the pursuit.

Towton (Wars of the Roses).

Fought March 29, 1461, when Edward IV, immediately after his proclamation, marched against the Lancastrians, under Henry VI, and vigorously attacked their entrenched position at Towton. Aided by a heavy snowstorm, blowing in the faces of the defenders, Edward defeated them all along the line, with heavy loss, among the killed being Northumberland, Dacre and de Mauley. Henry and Margaret escaped from the field, and fled northward.

Trafalgar (Napoleonic Wars).

Fought October 21, 1805, between the British fleet of 27 sail of the line and 4 frigates, under Nelson, with Collingwood second in command, and the combined French and Spanish fleets, numbering 33 sail of the line and 7 frigates, under Admiral Villeneuve. Nelson attacked in two lines, and destroying the enemy's formation, completely defeated them, 20 ships striking their colours. Nelson fell in the moment of victory, while the Spanish Admiral was killed, and Villeneuve captured. Most of the prizes were lost in a heavy gale which sprang up after the battle, but the destruction of Villeneuve's fleet put an end to Napoleon's scheme for an invasion of England. The British lost 1,587 killed and wounded, the losses of the allies being far heavier.

Trautenau (Seven Weeks' War).

Fought June 27, 1866, between the First Prussian Army Corps, under General von Bonin, and the 10th Austrian corps, under General Gablenz. The Prussians at first drove back the Austrians, but General Gablenz advancing in force, fell upon the Prussians, wearied with a long march, and compelled them to retreat, with a loss of 1,277 killed and wounded. Owing to the superiority of the needle-gun, the Austrians, though victorious, suffered a loss of 5,732.

Travancore (Second Mysore War).

Fought December 28, 1789, when Tippu Sahib, with about 15,000 Mysoris, made a night attack upon the British lines. Having thrown down a portion of the rampart, a small advance party were hastening to open the gate, when they were assailed by a detachment of the garrison, and hurled back into the trench. This repulse threw the advancing troops into confusion, and they were routed with a loss of over 2,000.

Trebbia (Second Punic War).

Fought December B.C. 218, between 26,000 Cathaginians, 6,000 being cavalry, under Hannibal, and 40,000 Romans under the Consul Sempronius. Sempronius' colleague, Scipio, had been wounded a few days before in a skirmish, and Sempronius, contrary to his advice, being in sole command, crossed the Trebbia to attack the Carthaginians. The Romans fought with determination, and the issue was for some time in doubt, but finally a charge of the Carthaginian horse, under Mago, against their left flank, threw the legionaries into confusion, and they were routed with enormous loss.

Trebbia (Wars of the French Revolution).

Fought June 19 to 21, 1799, between the French, under Macdonald, and the Russians, under Suwaroff. After a severe conflict the French were totally defeated and driven beyond the Apennines, being obliged shortly afterwards to evacuate Italy.

Trebizond (Ottoman Wars).

This city, where the last representative of the family of Comnenus had taken refuge after the fall of Constantinople, was besieged by the Turks, under Mohammed II, in 1461. After a brief resistance the city surrendered, and the last vestige of the Empire of the East was swept away.

Treveri (Gallic War).

Fought B.C. 55, between the Romans, 50,000 strong, under Julius Cæsar, and 300,000 Asipetes, a German tribe, who had made a raid into Gaul. The Germans were routed with enormous loss ; indeed, the action was less a battle than a massacre, and very few succeeded in recrossing the Rhine.

Tricameron (Invasion of the Vandals).

Fought November, 533, between the Romans, under Belisarius, and the Vandals, under

Gelimer and Zano. The Romans were drawn up behind a stream, and were attacked by the Vandals, though only the wing under Zano displayed any vigour in the assault. In the end the Vandals were defeated with a loss of 800, the Romans losing 50 only. This defeat put an end to the Vandal domination in Africa.

Trichinopoly.

This place was captured, after a three months' siege, by the Mahrattas, March 26, 1741. It had been provisioned for a long siege by Chunda Sahib, but the Mahrattas retired to a distance of 250 miles, whereupon the avarice of Chunda Sahib impelled him to sell the grain which he had in store. The Mahrattas, who had been counting upon this, retraced their steps, and the garrison were in a very short time starved into submission.

Trincomalee (Seven Years' War).

Fought August 10, 1759, between a British squardon of 12 sail, under Admiral Pococke, and a French fleet of 14 sail, under the Comte d'Aché. After an engagement lasting two hours, the French were worsted, but sailing better than the British, as usual at this period, eluded pursuit and lost no ships.

Trincomalee (First Mysore War).

Fought September 3, 1767, between the British, under Colonel Smith, and the Mysore army, under Hyder Ali. Hyder attacked the British camp, but was beaten off with a loss of 2,000 men while the British lost 170 only.

On September 26 of the same year, a second engagement took place near Trincomalee, when Colonel Smith, with 12,000 British and native troops, came unexpectedly upon the united armies of Hyderabad and Mysore, 60,000 strong, under Hyder Ali, while rounding a hill which separated them. The superior discipline of the British enabled them to take full advantage of the surprise, and they inflicted an overwhelming defeat upon their opponents' disordered masses. Hyder Ali lost over 4,000 men and 64 guns, the British loss being 150 killed and wounded.

Trincomalee.

A naval action was fought off this place April 12, 1782, between 11 British ships, under Sir Edward Hughes, and 12 French vessels, under Suffren. After a sanguinary action with no decisive result, the two fleets, both too seriously damaged to renew the conflict, separated, the British making for Trincomalee, and the French for their base to repair damages.

On September 3, 1782, another indecisive fight took place between the same Admirals off Trincomalee, the British having 12 and the French 15 sail. Both squadrons were compelled after the action to return to their respective bases to refit.

Trinidad (Wars of the French Revolution).

This island was captured from the French, without resistance, by a naval and military expedition under Admiral John Harvey and Sir Ralph Abercrombie, February 17, 1797.

Trinkitat (Soudan Campaigns).

Fought March 29, 1884, when the British, 4,000 strong, under General Graham, totally defeated 6,000 Mahdists, under Osman Digna, after five hours' severe fighting. The British casualties amounted to 189 killed and wounded ; the Mahdists lost about 2,000. This action is also known as the Battle of El Teb.

Tripoli (Moslem Conquest of Africa).

Fought 647, between the invading Moslems, under Abdallah, and 120,000 Imperial troops and African levies, under the Prefect, Gregory. The Moslems gained a signal victory, Gregory being among the slain.

Trivadi (Seven Years' War).

Fought 1760, between 5,000 Mysoris, under Hyder Ali, and a British force of 230 European and 2,700 native troops, under Major Moore, Notwithstanding his inferior numbers, Moore attempted to prevent the junction of Hyder Ali with the French, and was totally defeated.

Trout Brook (Seven Years' War).

A small skirmish, in which the advance guard of Abercromby's army, marching on Ticonderoga, fell in with a French scouting column, 350 strong, under Langy, July 6, 1758. The French lost 150 killed and wounded and 148 prisoners, and the affair would be without importance but for the fact that Lord Howe, who was the brain of Abercromby's staff, was killed in the fight. His death was followed by the disaster of Ticonderoga, and as Parkman says (*Montcalm and Wolfe*, chap. xx.) : " The death of one man was the ruin of fifteen thousand."

Troy.

The siege and destruction of this city by the Hellenes, though all the details are legendary, may be accepted as a historical fact, and the date may be put approximately at 1100 B.C.

Truceia.

Fought 593, between the Neustrians, under Queen Fredegond, and the Austrasians, under Childebert II. The Austrasian army was totally routed and fled from the field.

Tsushima (Mongol Invasion of Japan).

Fought 1419 between the Chinese and Koreans, and the ships of the Barons of Kiushiu. The Japanese gained a signal victory, and from that time were no more troubled by foreign invasion.

Tudela (Peninsular War).

Fought November 23, 1808, between 30,000 French, under Lannes, and 45,000 Spaniards, under Castaños and Palafox. The Spaniards were totally defeated, with a loss of about 9,000 killed and wounded, 3,000 prisoners and 30 guns. The French losses were small.

Tunis (First Punic War).

Fought B.C. 255 between 15,000 Romans, under Regulus, and 16,000 Carthaginians, of whom 4,000 were cavalry, with 100 elephants, under Xanthippus, the Spartan. The Romans were broken by a cavalry charge, and their rout was completed by the elephants, and all but 2,500 fell on the field. Regulus was captured, and Tunis at once occupied by the Carthaginians.

Tunis (Ninth Crusade).

This city was besieged by the French Crusaders, under Louis IX in 1270. While before the walls of the place, which offered an obstinate resistance, Louis died of a fever, and the crusaders at once raised the siege and retired.

Turbigo (Franco-Austrian War).

Fought June 3, 1859, when the advance guard of Marshal Macmahon's corps, under the Marshal in person, was attacked by a portion of the Austrian division of Clam-Gallas, while simultaneously 4,000 Austrians assailed the bridge over the canal near the Ticino, which the French main body was crossing. After severe fighting both attacks were repulsed with considerable loss.

Turcoing (Wars of the French Revolution).

Fought 1794 between the French, under Souham, and the British, under the Duke of York. The British were defeated and driven back upon Tournay.

Turin (Revolt of Maxentius).

Fought 312, between the legions of Gaul, 40,000 strong, under Constantine, and the troops of Maxentius, considerably superior in number. The charge of Maxentius' heavy cavalry failed, and he was driven back into Turin with enormous loss.

Turin ((War of the Spanish Succession).

This place, held by an Im-

perialist garrison, 10,000 strong, under the Duke of Savoy, was besieged by a French army of 68 battalions and 80 squadrons, with artillery and engineers, under the Duc de la Feuillade, May 26, 1706. On June 17 the Duke of Savoy left the city to orgainse a relief force, Count Daun taking the command. The garrison held out stoutly till September 7, when the approach of a large relieving force under Prince Eugene compelled the French to raise the siege. About 5,000 of the garrison perished either in action or by disease. In the action which preceded the retirement of the French, the Imperialists lost 1,500, the French 2,000 killed and wounded and 6,000 prisoners.

Turnhout (Netherlands War of Independence).

Fought August 22, 1597, between the Dutch, under Prince Maurice of Nassau, and the Spaniards under the Archduke Albert. The Spaniards were totally defeated, and this victory may be said to have set the seal of the Independence of the Netherlands.

Tyre (Alexander's Asiatic Campaigns).

This strongly fortified city, built on an island separated from the mainland by a channel 1,000 yards wide, was besieged by the Macedonians under Alexander the Great, B.C., 332. Alexander at once commenced the construction of a mole across the channel but was much hampered by the Phœnician galleys, which issued from the two fortified harbours, and de•

stroyed his military engines. He therefore collected in Sidon a fleet of 250 ships from the captured Phœnician cities, and holding the Tyrian galleys in check, completed his mole. It was some time, however, before a breach could be effected, but in August, 332, an assault was delivered, headed by Alexander in person, and the city was stormed and taken. Eight thousand Tyrians fell in the storm, and about 30,000 were sold into slavery.

U

Ucles (Mohammedan Empire in Spain).
Fought 1109, between the Spaniards, under Don Sancho of Castile, and the Moors, under Ali. The Spaniards were defeated, with a heavy loss of the Christian chivalry, among the killed being Don Sancho.

Uji (Taira War).
Fought 1180 between the adherents of the Taira clan, under Shigehira, and the Japanese, who had risen against the domination of the Taira at the Court of the Emperor Antoku, under Prince Yukiiye and Yorimasa. The Taira gained a complete victory, Yukiiye being killed, while Yorimasa committed suicide in the field.

Ulundi (Zulu War).
The last battle of the war, fought August, 1879, between 5,000 British, under Lord Chelmsford, and about 20,000 Zulus. The Zulus were routed with a loss of over 1,500, the British losing only 15 killed and 78 wounded.

Upsala (Dano-Swedish Wars).
Fought 1520, between the Danes, under Otho of Krumpen, and the Swedes, under Christina Gyllenstierna, widow of the Administrator, Sten Sture. The Danes, in superior force, were strongly entrenched at Upsala. They were vigorously attacked, but the advantage of position and numbers enabled them to beat off their assailants with heavy loss, though only after severe fighting.

Upsala (Dano-Swedish Wars).
Fought 1521, when 3,000 Swedes, under Gustavus Vasa, defeated the troops of the Bishop of Upsala, who was holding the city in the Danish interest. After his victory Gustavus occupied the city.

Urosan (Invasion of Korea).
This place, held by a Japanese garrison under Kiyomasa, was besieged 1595 by the Chinese and Koreans, under Tik Ho. The garrison had been reduced to such straits that they had eaten their horses, when the approach of a relieving force, under Toyotomo Hideaki and Mori Hidemoto, forced Tik Ho to withdraw. While retreating, however, he was attacked by the Japanese and totally routed.

Ushant (Wars of the French Revolution).
This action, generally known as the " Glorious First of June," was fought June 1, 1794, between a British fleet of 25 sail of the line, under Lord Howe, and 26 French ships, under Villaret. After four hours' fighting the French were defeated, with a loss of 6 ships

captured, and one, the *Vengeur*, sunk. The sinking of this ship was elaborated by the French into a fable, to the effect that she refused to surrender, and went down with all hands and colours flying. She had, however, undoubtedly struck her colours, and her captain and over 200 of her crew were rescued by the boats of the British fleet. The French admitted a loss of 3,000 men, besides prisoners, while the British lost 922 killed and wounded.

Utica (Civil War of Cæsar and Pompey).

Fought B.C. 49 between the Pompeians, under Varus, and the Cæsarians, under Curio. Varus sallied from his entrenchments to attack the Cæsarians, but was signally defeated, his troops fleeing in disorder, and opening the way for the occupation of Utica by Varus.

Utica (Moslem Conquest of Africa).

Fought 694 between 40,000 Moslems, under Hassan, and a large force of Greeks and Goths in the Imperial service. The Imperialists were defeated and driven out of Africa, and Hassan followed up his victory by the destruction of Carthage, which thenceforth ceased to exist, except as an obscure village.

Utsonomiya (Japanese Revolution).

Fought 1868, between the forces of the Shogun, under Otori Keisuke, and the Imperial troops, under Saigo Takamori. The Imperialists were completely victorious.

V

Vaalkranz (Second Boer War).

General Buller's third attempt to pierce the Boer lines on the Tugela. On February 5, 1900, he seized Vaalkranz, under cover of a feint attack at Brakfontein towards the Boer right. The hill was held by a brigade during the 6th and 7th, but finding further progress impossible, Buller again recrossed the Tugela. The British losses amounted to 374 killed and wounded.

Valenciennes (Netherlands War of Independence).

Siege was laid to this place in December, 1566, by a force of Spaniards and Germans, mercenaries, under Noircarmes. The operations were somewhat indolently conducted, insomuch that he and his six lieutenants were derided as the " Seven Sleepers," but towards the end of February Noircarmes began to press on his siege works, and on March 23 his batteries opened fire, the city surrendering on the following day.

Valenciennes.

Defended by a Spanish garrison under Francisco de Manesses, Valenciennes was besieged June, 1566, by the French, under Turenne and La Ferté. The French encamped in two divisions on the opposite side of the Scheldt, and when the city was on the point of surrendering, La Ferté's division was attacked by 20,000 Spaniards, under Condé, and totally routed with a loss of 400 officers and 4,000 men, before Turenne could come to his assistance.

In consequence of this defeat, Turenne was forced to abandon the siege and retire.

Val-ès-Dunes.

Fought 1047, between the Normans, under William of Normandy, with aid from Henri I of France, and the rebel Norman Barons. The rebels were totally defeated.

Valetta (Wars of the French Revolution).

The capital of Malta, held by a French garrison, 60,000 strong, under General Vaubois, was besieged September, 1798, by a force of British and Maltese, under Sir Alexander Ball. Vaubois held out for two years, but on September 5, 1800, was compelled by famine to surrender. The Maltese lost during the siege 20,000 men.

Valmy (Wars of the French Revolution).

Fought September 20, 1792, between the French, 70,000 strong, under Dumouriez, and the Prussians, under the Duke of Brunswick. The battle consisted in the main of an artillery duel, in which the French had the upper hand, and after nightfall the Prussians retired, recrossing the frontier two days later.

Valparaiso.

This city, entirely open and undefended, was bombarded March 31, 1866, by the Spanish fleet under Mendez Nuñez. By this disgraceful action Valparaiso was reduced to ashes.

Valutinagora (Moscow Campaign).

Fought August 19, 1812, between Ney's corps, about 30,000 strong, and a strong rear-guard of Barclay de Tolly's army, about 40,000 strong, under Barclay de Tolly in person. The Russians were strongly posted in marshy ground, protected by a small stream. The French, attacking resolutely, carried the Russian position in the face of enormous natural difficulties. Each side lost about 7,000 men.

Varaville.

Fought 1058, between the Normans, under William of Normandy, and the French and Angevins, under Henri I of France. The Normans gained a complete victory, and the French king shortly afterwards made peace.

Varese (Italian Rising of 1858).

Fought May 25, 1859, between 3,000 Garibaldians, under Garibaldi, and 5,000 Austrians, under General Urban. The Austrians were repulsed after hard fighting, and suffered considerable loss. This action is also known as the Battle of Malnate.

Varmas (South-American War of Independence).

Fought 1813 between the Colombian Patriots, under Bolivar, and the Spanish Royalists. The latter were defeated.

Varna (Ottoman Wars).

Fought November 10, 1444, between the Turks, under Amurath II, and the Hungarians, under King Ladislaus. The Hungarians attacked the Turkish camp, but were beaten off with heavy loss, the King being killed. On the following day Amurath stormed the Hungarian entrenchments, practically the whole of the defenders being put to the sword.

Varna (Ottoman Wars).

This fortress, held by a Turkish garrison of 20,000 men, was besieged July, 1828, by the Russians, under Prince Mentschikoff, and though a feeble attempt to relieve it was made by Omar Vrione Pasha, the place was taken by storm on October 11.

Varus. Defeat of (Germanic Wars).

The site of this famous battle is supposed to be between the rivers Ems and Lippe, not far from the modern Detmoldt. In A.D. 9 the Roman army, under Quintilius Varus, was attacked while on the march and encumbered by a heavy baggage-train, by the Germans, under Arminius or Hermann. The country was thickly wooded and marshy, and the Romans could make but little defence, with the result that they were almost annihilated. Varus committed suicide on the field to avoid falling into the hands of the victors.

Vasaq (Ottoman Wars).

Fought 1442, between 80,000 Turks, under Shiabeddin Pasha, and 15,000 Hungarians, under John Huniades. The Turks were utterly routed, with a loss of 20,000 killed and wounded, and 5,000 prisoners, including the Pasha.

Vauchamps.

See Champ-Aubert.

Veii.

This city was besieged B.C. 400 by the Romans, the siege being carried on in a desultory fashion for seven years. At the end of this period the citizens of Capua and Valerii made an attack upon the Roman camp, and inflicted a signal defeat upon the besiegers. M. Furius Camillus was then appointed dictator, and a determined attempt was made to end the siege, with the result that Veii fell B.C. 393. Rome's greatest rival in Italy was thus destroyed.

Veleneze (Hungarian Rising).

Fought September 29, 1848, between the Hungarians, under General Móga, and the Croats, under the Ban, Jellachich. The battle was indecisive, and was followed by a three days' armistice.

Velestinos (Greco-Turkish War).

Fought May 5, 1897, between a Turkish division under Hakki Pasha, and the Greeks, 9,000, under Colonel Smolenski. The Greeks occupied a strong position at Velestinos, where they were attacked by the Turks, but held their own throughout the day. After nightfall, however his line of retreat being threatened, Colonel Smolenski withdrew to Volo, where he embarked his troops on the 7th.

Velletri (Italian Rising of 1848).

Fought May 19, 1849, between 10,000 Garibaldians, under Roselli, and the Neapolitans, 10,000 strong, under Ferdinand, King of Naples. The advance guard, under Garibaldi, attacked the town of Velletri, which made a poor defence, and was evacuated during the night. The losses of the Garibaldians were small.

Vercellæ (Cimbric War).

Fought July 30, 101 B.C., between 50,000 Romans, under Marius, and the Cimbri, under Boiorix. The Cimbri were almost annihilated, and their king slain.

Verneuil (Hundred Years' War)

Fought August 18, 1424, between 3,000 English, under the Duke of Bedford, and 18,000 French and Scots, under the Constable Buchan and the Earl of Douglas. The men-at-arms on both sides fought dismounted, but the French could make no impression upon the English archers, who were protected by a barricade of stakes, and in the end were utterly routed, leaving over 4,000 dead on the field, among them Buchan and Douglas. The Duc d'Alencon was taken prisoner.

Verona (Revolt of Maxentius).

This place was besieged 312 by Constantine, with the legions of Gaul, and was defended by a body of rebels, under Pompeianus. After a sortie had been repulsed, Pompeianus escaped through Constantine's lines, and raised a force for the relief of the city. He was, however, met and defeated by Constantine, many thousands of the Italians, including their leader, falling, and Verona at once surrendered.

Veseris (Latin War).

Fought near Mount Vesuvius, B.C. 339, between the Romans, under Manlius Torquatus and Decius Mus, and the Latin army. The Roman left was repulsed, but Decius Mus, sacrificing himself for the army, sprang into the midst of the enemy and was slain, and his soldiers following him, renewed the conflict. Manlius now brought up his veteran reserve, and the Romans breaking the Latin line, slew or captured nearly three-fourths of their opponents. The Roman loss, however, was so heavy, that they were unable to pursue.

Viborg.

Fought 1157, between the adherents of Sweyn III of Denmark, and those of his successor Waldemar. Sweyn was totally defeated and fled, but falling into a morass in his flight was overtaken and slain.

Vicksburg (American Civil War).

This city, held by a Confederate garrison, was invested June 24, 1862, by a fleet of 13 Federal gunboats, under Admiral Farragut, aided by a land force of 4,000 men, under General Williams. After a bombardment which made no impression on the defences, Farragut reimbarked the troops, and withdrew, July 24. In the course of the siege Captain Brown with the *Arkansas*, a small river steamer, coated with iron, and carrying eight guns, attacked the Federal flotilla, which mounted 200 guns, and ran the gauntlet successfully, losing 14 men killed and wounded. The Federals lost 82.

On January 9, 1863, the city was again invested by two Federal corps, under General M'Clernand, aided by a flotilla of gunboats, under Admiral Porter. It was defended by a garrison of 3,000 Confederates, under General Churchill. On the 11th an attack by the combined forces overpowered the garrison of the fort, but the town defences still held out, and the siege was not pressed. On May 18, the siege was renewed by three army corps of General Grant's army, the garrison being now commanded by General Pemberton. On the 22nd an unsuccessful assault cost the Federals 2,500, and a regular siege commenced, with the result that on July 4, Pemberton surrendered with 25,000 men and 90 guns.

Vienna (Ottoman Wars).

This city, held by a garrison of 16,000 men, under Count de Salm, was besieged by Solyman the Magnificent, at the head of 120,000 Turks, in September, 1529. From the 27th of that month till October 14, the garrison withstood a series of assaults, culminating in an attempt to storm the breach, which were repulsed with heavy loss. Solyman thereupon raised the siege and withdrew.

Vienna (Ottoman Wars).

Fought September 12, 1683, between 300,000 Turks, under Kara Mustapha Pasha, and 70,000 Christians, under John Sobieski. The Turks were besieging Vienna, and Sobieski marched to its relief, with 30,000, bringing up the available forces to 70,000, of which he was given the command. With this army he attacked the Turkish lines, and after a sanguinary engagement, lasting throughout the day, routed the Turks with enormous loss. Six Pashas were killed, and Mustapha only escaped capture by a precipitate flight.

Vigo Bay (War of the Spanish Succession).

Fought October 12, 1702, when the combined fleet of 30 British and 20 Dutch ships, under Sir George Rooke, forced the boom at the entrance to Vigo Harbour and destroyed the French and Spanish fleet anchored therein. Of the men-of-war, 11 were burnt and 10 captured, while 11 Spanish galleons, with treasure, were taken. This action is generally called the affair of the Spanish Galleons.

Villach (Ottoman Wars).

Fought 1492, between the Turks, under Ali Pasha, and a Christian army, under Rudolph de Khevenhuller. During the battle 15,000 Christian prisoners in the Turkish camp broke out, and fell upon the rear of the Turks, who were in consequence totally defeated. The Christians lost 7,000 killed, the Turks 10,000 killed and 7,000 prisoners, including Ali.

Villa Viciosa (War of the Spanish Succession).

Fought December 10, 1710, when 13,000 Imperialists, under Staremberg, retreating into Catalonia, after the defeat of Stanhope at Brihnega, were attacked by 20,000 French, under Philip of Anjou and Marshal Vendôme. Staremberg's left wing was cut to pieces, but his right and centre more than held their own, driving back the French with considerable loss, and capturing some guns. Staremberg was, however, too weak to take advantage of this partial success, and continued his retreat after the action.

Villeta (Paraguayan War).

Fought December 11, 1868, between the Paraguayans, under Lopez, and the armies of Brazil, Uruguay and Argentina. Overwhelmed by vastly superior numbers, Lopez was forced to withdraw his forces to the entrenched camp at Angostura.

Villiers (Franco-German War).

A determined sortie from Paris, under General Ducrot, on November 30, 1870, directed against the Wurtembergers. The operations lasted till December 3. The French, who had at first gained some successes, were finally repulsed, with a loss of 424 officers and 9,053 men. The Germans lost 156 officers and 3,373 men.

Vindalium.

Fought B.C. 121, between the Romans, under Q. Fabius Maximus, and the Arverni. The Arverni were completely defeated, and compelled to sue for peace.

Vinegar Hill (Irish Rebellion).

Fought June 20, 1798, when the British regulars, under General Lake, attacked the camp of the Irish rebels, 16,000 strong, under Father Murphy. Little resistance was made, and the rebels were driven out of their camp with a loss of 4,000 killed and wounded, and 13 guns.

Vimiera (Peninsular War).

Fought August 21, 1808, between 18,000 British and Portuguese, under Sir Arthur Wellesley, and 14,000 French, under Junot. The French were signally defeated, losing 2,000 men and 13 guns, but the victory was not followed up by Sir Harry Burrard, who was in supreme command, and the French were allowed to evacuate Portugal unmolested, under the Convention of Cintra. The British lost 720 killed and wounded.

Viney.

Fought 717, between the Austrasians, under Charles Martel and the Neustrians, under Chilperic II. The Neustrians were defeated.

Vionville.

See Mars La Tour.

Vittoria (Peninsular War).

Fought June 21, 1813, between 80,000 British, Portuguese and Spanish troops, under Wellington, and about 70,000 French, under Joseph Buonaparte. After severe fighting the French were defeated at all points and made a somewhat disorderly retreat, losing 6,000 killed, wounded, and prisoners, 143 guns, and almost all their baggage and treasure. The allies lost 5,000. This battle finally closed the era of French domination in Spain, and opened to Wellington the road to the Pyrenees.

Vögelinseck (Appenzel Rebellion).

Fought May 15, 1402, between 5,000 troops, of the Swiss Imperial towns, and 900 rebels of Appenzel and Schwyz. After a brief engagement, the rebels were driven from the field, with a loss of 250 men.

Volconda.

Fought April, 1751, between Mohammed Ali's army, 5,600 strong, under Abdul Wahab Khan, aided by 1,600 British, under Captain Gingen, and Chunda Sahib's troops, 17,000 strong, together with a battalion of Frenchmen. Captain Gingen, though greatly outnumbered, insisted on attacking, but was repulsed, his Europeans not showing their usual steadiness, and forced to retreat with considerable loss,

Volturno (Unification of Italy).

Fought October 1, 1860, between 20,000 Italians, under Garibaldi, and 40,000 Neapolitans, under Afan de Riva. Garibaldi's position in front of Capua was attacked by the Neapolitans, who, after hard fighting, were repulsed all along the line, with heavy loss. The Garibaldian casualties were 2,023 killed and wounded. The Neapolitans lost 2,070 prisoners, but their losses in killed and wounded are unknown. In consequence of this victory, Garibaldi almost immediately captured Capua.

Vouillé.

Fought 507, between the Franks, under Clovis, and the Visigoths, under Alaric II. Alaric was endeavouring to effect a junction with Theodoric, King of the Ostrogoths, when he was attacked by Clovis, and totally defeated. Alaric fell in the battle.

W

Wagram (Campaign of Wagram).

Fought July 6, 1809, between 150,000 French, under Napoleon, and 140,000 Austrians, under the Archduke Charles. Na-

poleon crossed the lesser arm of the Danube from the Island of Lobau, on the night of the 4th and 5th July, and driving the Austrian advanced posts before him, prepared to attack their main position. An attack upon them on the evening of the 5th was repulsed. On the 6th the Austrians attacked the French right, under Davoust, but were unsuccessful ; later, however, the French centre and left were compelled to give ground, but Napoleon bringing up the artillery of the Guard and Macdonald's corps, checked the Austrian advance, while Davoust carried the heights on the Austrian left, outflanking them, and rendering their position untenable. By three o'clock they were in full retreat, having lost about 24,000 killed and wounded, 9,000 prisoners, including 12 generals, and 20 guns. The French lost 18,000 killed and wounded.

Waizan (Hungarian Rising).

Fought April 10, 1849, between the 3rd Hungarian corps, under Damjanics, about 7,000 strong, and two Austrian brigades, under Götz and Jablonowski. Damjanics attacked the Austrians and drove them out of Waizan with heavy loss, among those who fell being General Götz.

Wakamatsu (Japanese Revolulution).

The last stand of the Shogun's followers was made at the Castle of Wakamatsu, which was stormed by the Imperialists, September 22, 1868, The resistance to the new régime was thus completely broken.

Wakefield (Wars of the Roses).

Fought December 30, 1460, between the Lancastrians, under Somerset, and the Yorkists, under Richard, Duke of York. The Lancastrians advanced from Pontefract and offered battle to Richard, who, though weakened by the absence of foraging parties, accepted the challenge. Somerset prepared an ambush, into which the Duke fell as he marched out of Wakefield, and the Yorkists were defeated with heavy loss. The Duke and many other nobles were killed, and Salisbury captured and beheaded.

Waltersdorf (Campaign of Friedland).

Fought February 5, 1807, between the French, under Ney, and the Prussian corps of Lestocq. The Prussians were defeated with a loss of about 3,000 killed, wounded and missing.

Wandewash (Seven Years' War).

Fought January 22, 1760, between the British, with 1,900 European and 3,350 native troops, under Colonel Coote, and the French, 2,250 Europeans and 1,300 natives, under Lally-Tollendal. The French army was accompanied by 3,000 Mahratta horse, who took no part in the action. After severe fighting Lally was defeated, with a loss of 600 Europeans, besides natives, the British losing 190 only.

Wandewash (First Mysore War).

This fort, defended by a small native garrison, under Lieutenant Flint, who had only one other European with him, was besieged, December, 1780, by the Mysoris, under Hyder Ali.

Flint held out with the utmost gallantry till January 22, 1781, when the approach of Sir Eyre Coote forced Hyder Ali to raise the siege. The garrison had then only one day's ammunition left.

Warburg (Seven Years' War).

Fought July 31, 1759, between the French, 35,000 strong, under the Chevalier de May, and a largely superior force of Prussians and British, under Prince Ferdinand. The French were in danger of their flanks being turned, and after a brief engagement, retired, having lost 1,500 killed and wounded and 1,500 prisoners.

Warsaw (Second Polish Rising).

This city, which was held by a garrison of 30,000 Poles, under General Dembinski, was attacked by the Russians, 60,000 strong, under General Paskiewitsch. The first onslaught on the Polish entrenchments was made on the 6th September, 1831, and the Poles, were driven from their first line. On the 7th a further assault was made, notable for the defence of the Wola redoubt, where, when it was finally captured by the Russians, only eleven men remained alive out of a garrison of 3,000. On the 8th the last defences were overcome, and the city capitulated. The Poles had 9,000 killed in the defence. The Russians admitted a loss of 63 officers and 3,000 men killed, and 445 officers and 7,000 men wounded.

Wartemberg (Campaign of Leipsic).

Fought October 3, 1813, when Blucher, with 60,000 Prussians, defeated 16,000 French, under Bertrand, posted in a very strong position, protected by a dyke and a swamp. Aided by the ground, the French withstood the Prussian attack for over four hours, but finally Blucher turned their right flank and drove them from their position. The Prussians lost about 5,000. The French admit a loss of 500 only.

Wartzburg (Wars of the French Revolution).

Fought 1796, between the French, under Jourdan, and the Austrians, under the Archduke Charles. The Archduke interposed between the armies of Jourdan and Moreau, who were endeavouring to effect a junction, and inflicted a severe defeat upon Jourdan, forcing him to retire to the Rhine.

Waterloo (Hundred Days).

Fought June 18, 1815, between 24,000 British, and 43,500 Dutch, Belgians and Nassauers, in all 67,655 men, with 156 guns, under the Duke of Wellington, and the French, 71,947 strong, with 246 guns, under Napoleon. Wellington posted his troops along the line of heights covering the road to Brussels, with advanced posts at the farms of Hougoumont and La Haye Sainte. Napoleon attacked this position with the utmost resolution, but the British squares held their ground against the French cavalry and artillery throughout the day, and though the French captured La Haye Sainte, and obtained a footing in Hougoumont, the arrival of Blucher, with the Prussian army, on the French right,

enabled Wellington at last to assume the offensive, and drive the enemy headlong from the field, utterly routed. The British lost about 15,000, the Prussians 7,000 in the battle. The losses of the Dutch and Belgians were very small, as they left the field early in the day. The French loss was never officially stated, but it was doubtless enormous, and the army practically ceased to exist as an organized force.

Watigaon (First Burmah War).

Fought November 15, 1825, when Brigadier-General M'-Donell, with four native regiments, advanced in three columns, against a large force of Burmans, under Maha Nemyo. The columns failed to keep touch, and were repulsed in detail, with a loss of 200 men, including the Brigadier.

Watrelots (Netherlands War of Independence).

Fought January, 1567, between 1,200 Flemish Protestants, under Teriel, and 600 Spaniards, under the Seigneur de Rassinghem. The Protestants were defeated and 600 took refuge in an old graveyard, where they held out till the last man had fallen.

Wattignies (Wars of the French Revolution).

Fought October, 1793, when the French, under Jourdan, attacked the Austrians, under the Duke of Coburg, and drove him from his position, forcing him to raise the siege of Maubeuge.

Wavre (Hundred Days).

Fought June 18, 1815, between

the French, under Grouchy, and the Prussians, 27,000 strong, under Thielmann, who had been entrusted by Blucher with the task of containing Grouchy, while the main Prussian army marched on Waterloo. Grouchy, who was anxiously expected at Waterlooo, mistook his instructions, and wasted the day in attacking Thielmann, whom he defeated, but uselessly.

Wednesfield (Danish Invasion).

Fought in 911, between the Danes and the West Saxons, under Edward the Elder. The Danes were defeated.

Wei-hai-Wei (Chino - Japanese War).

On February 4, 1895, the boom protecting Wei-hai-Wei harbour was cut, and the Chinese fleet attacked by 10 Japanese torpedo-boats, who succeeded in sinking one battleship, at the cost of two torpedo-boats. On the following night the attack was renewed by four boats, and three Chinese ships were sunk. On the 9th another battleship was sunk by the Japanese land batteries, whereupon Admiral Ting, the Chinese commander, surrendered, and he and his principal officers committed suicide.

Weissenburg (Franco-German War).

The opening engagement of the campaign, fought August 4, 1870, between the advance-guard of the Third German Army, under the Crown Prince of Prussia, and a portion of Marshal Macmahon's army, under General Abel Douay, who fell in the battle. The Germans carried the French position, and captured the town of Weissenburg, at a cost of 91 officers and 1,460 men. The French lost 2,300 killed, wounded and prisoners.

Wepener (Second Boer War).

This place was invested by a strong force of Boers, under De Wet, April 9, 1900, and was defended by 1,700 men of the Colonial Division, under Colonel Dalgety. Notwithstanding the Boer's great preponderance in artillery, and a succession of bold assaults on the trenches, the garrison held out gallantly till April 25, when they were relieved by General Rundle, having lost 300 killed and wounded in the course of the operations.

Werben (Thirty Years' War).

Fought July 22, 1631, between the Swedes, 16,000 strong, under Gustavus Adolphus, and 26,000 Imperialists, under Count Tilly. Tilly attacked Gustavus' entrenchments in front of Werben, but his troops could not face the fire of the Swedish batteries, and being thrown into disorder, were then charged by the cavalry, under Baudissen, and repulsed. The attack was renewed a few days later with a similar result, and Tilly then drew off his forces, having suffered a loss of 6,000 men.

Wertingen (Campaign of Austerlitz).

Fought October, 1805, between the cavalry of Murat's corps, and nine Austrian battalions, strongly posted in and round Wertingen. The Austrians were defeated, losing 2,000 prisoners and several guns, and had the French infantry been nearer at hand, it is probable that the whole force would have been captured.

White Oak Swamp.

See Seven Days' Battles.

Wiazma (Moscow Campaign).

Fought November 3, 1812, when the corps of Eugène Beauharnais and Davoust were attacked during the retreat from Moscow, by the Russians, under Kutusoff, and suffered a loss of 4,000 men.

Wilderness, The (American Civil War).

Fought May 5 to 8, 1864, between the Army of the Potomac, 150,000 strong, under General Grant, and 53,000 Confederates, under General Lee. Lee's object was to intercept Grant's advance on Richmond, and early on the morning of the 5th he attacked the approaching Federal columns, and after a hard-fought day, succeeded in arresting the progress of Grant's right wing. On the 6th, Lee almost succeeded in breaking Grant's centre, but at the critical moment, Longstreet, who was to lead the attack, was fired upon and dangerously wounded by his own troops. The Federal right wing, however, was driven back in confusion, and Lee on his side lost no ground. The two following days minor skirmishes took place, leading up to the great battle of Spottsylvania. The Confederates lost about 8,000 in the two days' fighting. The Federal losses were far heavier, amounting to 15,000 in the second day alone.

Williamsburg (American Civil War).

Fought May 5, 1862, between the Confederates, under General Magruder, and the Federals, under General M'Clellan. Magruder occupied a very strong position and held the Federals at bay throughout the day, but being greatly outnumbered, withdrew during the night. The Federals lost 2,228 killed, wounded and missing, the Confederate loss being much smaller.

Wilson's Creek (American Civil War).

Fought August 6, 1861, between 6,000 Federals, under General Lyon, and 16,000 Confederates, under General M'-Culloch. General Lyon divided his force into two columns, for the attack on M'Culloch's position, and that led by himself surprised the Southerners, and gained a partial success. They rallied, however, and beat him off, Lyon falling, the other column being also repulsed. The Federals lost 1,236, and the Confederates 1,095 killed, wounded and missing.

Wimpfen (Thirty Years' War).

Fought April 26, 1622, between 14,000 Palatinate troops, under the Margrave of Baden, and the Imperialists, under Count Tilly and Gonsalvo de Cordova. Tilly attacked the. Margrave's camp, which was not entrenched, and though a brilliant cavalry charge captured his guns, it was not supported by the Palatine infantry, and the Imperialists rallying, drove off the cavalry in disorder, recovered the guns, and then routed the infantry, with a loss of 2,000 killed and wounded, and all their artillery, baggage and camp equipment.

Winchester (American Civil War).

Fought June 14, 1863, when 7,000 Federals, under General Milroy, were defeated by three Confederate divisions, under General Ewell, and forced to retreat with heavy loss, including 3,700 prisoners and 30 guns.

Winkovo (Moscow Campaign).

Fought October 18, 1812, when Murat, with 30,000 men, forming the advance-guard of the retiring French army, was attacked by the Russians, under Count Orloff Dennizoff, and driven from his position, with a loss of 2,000 killed, 1,500 prisoners, and all his baggage and artillery.

Wisby (Dano-Swedish Wars).

A three days' battle, fought 1613, between the fleet of Gustavus Adolphus of Sweden, and that of Christian IV, of Denmark. The action was very obstinately contested, and finally the fleets separated without any decisive result.

Wisloch (Thirty Years' War).

Fought April 16, 1622, between the troops of the Count Palatine, under the Count von Mansfeldt, and the Imperialists, under Count Tilly. Tilly attacked and drove in the Palatinate rearguard, but failing to check the pursuit, was confronted by the main body, and defeated with a loss of 3,000 killed and wounded, and all his guns. This victory enabled Mansfeldt to effect a junction with the army of the Margrave of Baden.

Worcester (Civil War).

Fought September 3, 1651, between 12,000 Royalists, under Charles II, and about 30,000 Parliamentarians, under Cromwell. Charles attacked Cromwell's wing, and was repulsed and driven into Worcester, where he was met by the other wing of the Parliamentary army, under Fleetwood. The Royalists were utterly routed and dispersed, losing 3,000 killed, among whom was the Duke of Hamilton, and a large number of prisoners, including Lords Derby, Lauderdale and Kenmure, and five generals. Charles himself escaped with difficulty. This was the last pitched battle of the Civil War.

Worth (Franco-German War).

Fought August 6, 1870, between the Third German Army, under the Crown Prince of Prussia, and the French, under Marshal Macmahon. After a closely contested engagement, the French were driven from all their positions, and made a hasty retreat beyond the Vosges. The Cuirassier division of General Bonnemain was completely cut to pieces in charging the German infantry, near Elsasshausen. The German losses amounted to 489 officers, and 10,153 men, while the French lost 10,000 killed and wounded, 6,000 prisoners, 28 guns and 5 mitrailleuses.

Wrotham Heath (Wyatt's Insurrection).

Fought January, 1554, when the Kentish insurgents, under Sir Henry Isley, were totally defeated by the Royal troops, under Lord Abergavenny.

Wargaom (First Mahratta War).

Fought January 12, 1779, when a British force, 2,600 strong, under Colonel Cockburn, retreating from Poonah, was attacked by the Mahratta army, under Mahadaji Sindhia, and Hari Pant. The British succeeded in beating off the attack, and making good their position in the village of Wargaom, but at a loss of 352, including 15 officers, and ultimately a convention was signed by Sindhia, under which the British retired unmolested.

Wynandael (Napoleonic Wars).

Fought September 28, 1808, between the British, under General Webb, and the French under the Comte de la Motte. The French, with 40 battalions and 40 squadrons, attempted to intercept a convoy of supplies for the army besieging Lille, and were totally defeated, by a far inferior force, with a loss of 7,000 men.

X

Xeres (Moslem Empire in Spain).

Fought July 19 to 26, 711, between 90,000 Spaniards, under Roderic, and 12,000 Moslems, with a numerous force of African auxiliaries, under Tarik. On the fourth day the Moslems suffered a severe repulse, leaving 16,000 dead on the field, but the defection of Count Julian, with a large part of the King's forces, revived their courage, and finally the Christians were routed and dispersed. Roderic fled from the field, but was drowned in crossing the Guadalquivir. This victory marks the fall of the Gothic monarchy, and the beginning of the Moorish domination in Spain.

Y

Yalu (Chino-Japanese War).

Fought September 17, 1894, between the Chinese fleet of 2 battleships and 8 cruisers, under Admiral Ting, and the Japanese fleet of 10 cruisers, and 2 gunboats, under Admiral Ito. The two fleets met at the mouth of the Yalu, the Chinese steaming out in line abreast. Ito attacked in line ahead, using his superior speed to circle round the enemy's ships. Two of the Chinese vessels hauled out of the line and fled without coming into action, while two more were set on fire, and made for the shore. The remaining 6 ships fought well, and a little before sundown Ito retired, leaving the crippled Chinese fleet to make its way to Port Arthur. The Japanese lost 294 killed and wounded, of whom 107 fell on the flagship, the *Matsushima*, while the *Chiyada*, which was the next ship in the line, had not a man touched. The Chinese losses are unknown.

Yalu. *See* Kiu-lien-cheng.

Yamazaki.

Fought 1582, between the adherents of the Ota family, then predominant in Japan, and the followers of the rebel Mitsuhide. Mitsuhide sustained a crushing defeat.

Yashima (Taira War).

Fought 1184, between the adherents of the Taira family,

and the rebels, under Yoshitsune. The Taira forces were defeated.

Yawata (War of the Northern and Southern Empires).

Fought January, 1353, between the armies of the Northern and Southern Emperors of Japan. The army of the latter, led by Moroushi, gained a signal victory.

Yenikale, Gulf of (Ottoman Wars).

Fought July, 1790, between the Turkish fleet, and the Russians, under Admiral Onschakoff. The battle was fiercely contested, but eventually both fleets drew off without any decisive result.

Yermuk (Moslem Invasion of Syria).

Fought November, 636, between 140,000 Imperial troops, under Manuel, the General of Heraclius, and 50,000 Moslems, under Khaled. The Moslem attack was thrice repulsed, but they returned to the charge, and after a long and sanguinary engagement, drove their opponents from the field with enormous loss. The Moslems lost 4,030 killed.

Yorktown (American War of Independence).

The entrenched position of Lord Cornwallis, with 6,000 British troops at this place, was invested by Washington, with 7,000 French and 12,000 Americans, in September, 1781. The British held out until October 19, when, surrounded and outnumbered, Cornwallis surrendered, having lost during the operations, 12 officers and

469 rank and file, killed and wounded.

Yorktown (American Civil War).

This small village gives its name to the entrenched position occupied by General Magruder with 11,000 Confederates, which was invested by 105,000 Federal troops, with 103 siege guns, April 5, 1862. On the 16th, an unsuccessful attack was made upon Magruder's lines, and both sides having been reinforced, M'Clellan set about the erection of batteries. On May 4, the Federals were about to open fire, when it was found that the Confederates had abandoned the position and retired.

Youghiogany (Seven Years' War).

A skirmish of no importance in itself, but notable as being " the shot fired in America which gave the signal that set Europe in a blaze " (*Voltaire, Louis XV*), and was in a sense the cause of the Seven Years' War. On May 27, 1754, Washington, with 40 Virginians, surprised a small French detachment, under Coulon de Jumonville, despatched probably as a reconnaissance by Contrecœur from Fort Duquesne. The detachment, with one exception, was killed or captured.

Z

Zab, The (Bahram's Revolt).

Fought 590, between the troops of the Persian usurper Bahram, and the army of the Emperor Maurice, under Narses. The usurper's forces were totally routed, and Chosroes II restored to the throne of Persia.

Zalaka (Moorish Empire in Spain).

Fought October 26, 1086, between 40,000 Moors, under Almoravid, and 300,000 Christians, under Alfonso VI of Castile. The Spaniards were utterly routed, with enormous loss. Alfonso, at the head of 500 horse, cut his way out, and with difficulty escaped.

Zama (Second Punic War).

Fought B.C. 202, between the Carthaginians, under Hannibal, and the Romans, under Scipio Africanus. The Carthaginians began to attack with their elephants, 80 in number, but some of these became unmanageable, and fell back upon the cavalry, throwing them into disorder, while the legionaries opened out and allowed the others to pass down the lanes between their ranks. The infantry then closed, and after severe fighting, the Romans gained a complete victory, 20,000 Carthaginians falling, while as many more were made prisoners. Hannibal escaped from the field at the end of the day.

Zamora (Moorish Empire in Spain).

Fought 901, between the Spaniards, under Alfonso the Great, King of the Asturias, and the Moors, under Abdallah, King of Cordova. The Moors were utterly routed, with heavy loss, Alfonso thereby extending his dominions as far as the Guadiana.

Zeim (Russo-Turkish War).

Fought April 20, 1877, between the Russians, under Loris Melikoff, and the Turks, under Mukhtar Pasha. Melikoff attacked the Turks in a strongly entrenched position, but was repulsed with considerable loss.

Zendecan (Turkish Invasion of Afghanistan).

Fought 1039, between the Seljuks, under Moghrul Beg, and the Afghans, under Musrud, Sultan of Ghuzni. The Afghans were defeated, and Musrud compelled to retire on his capital.

Zeugminum (Hungarian War).

Fought 1168, between the Greeks, under Manuel I, Emperor of Constantinople, and the Hungarian invaders. The Hungarians were signally defeated, and the war, which had lasted for five years, came to an end.

Zeuta (Ottoman Wars).

Fought September 11, 1679, between the Austrians, under Prince Eugene, and the Turks, under Elwas Mohammed, the Grand Vizier. Eugene attacked the Turkish army as it was crossing a temporary bridge over the Theiss, and the cavalry being already across, cut it in two, and completely routed the infantry, driving them into the river. The Turks lost 29,000 men. The Austrians 500 only.

Ziela (Third Mithridatic War).

Fought B.C. 67, between the Romans, under Triarius, and the Pontic army, under Mithridates. The King attacked the Roman camp, and practically annihilated them, though himself dangerously wounded in the assault.

Ziela.

Fought August 2, B.C. 47, between 7 Roman legions, with

some Asiatic auxiliaries, under Julius Cæsar, and the Bosporans, under Pharnaces. Pharnaces attacked the Romans while they were pitching camp, but the legionaries quickly formed up, and utterly routed their assailants. This is the occasion of Cæsar's famous despatch, " Veni, vidi, vici."

Ziezicksee (Flemish War).

Fought 1302, when the Genoese galleys, in the service of Philip IV of France, under Grimaldi and Filipo di Rieti, utterly destroyed the Flemish fleet.

Zlotsow (Ottoman Wars).

Fought 1676, between the Poles, under John Sobieski, and 20,000 Turks and Tartars, under Mohammed IV. The Turks were signally defeated.

Znaim (Campaign of Wagram).

Fought July 14, 1809, when Masséna, with 8,000 French, attacked 30,000 Austrians, under the Prince of Reuss, and drove them into Znaim with considerable loss, including 800 prisoners.

Zorndorf (Seven Years' War).

Fought August 25, 1758, between the Prussians, 25,000 strong, under Frederick the Great, and a Russian army, under Fermor, which was besieging Custria. Frederick attacked the Russian entrenchments, and drove them out, with a loss of 19,000 forcing them to relinquish the siege. The Prussians lost about 11,000.

Zummerhausen (Thirty Years' War).

Fought 1647, when the French

and Swedes, under Turenne and Wrangel, inflicted a decisive defeat upon the Imperialists.

Zurakow (Ottoman War).

In 1676, John Sobieski, with 10,000 Poles, was besieged by 200,000 Turks and Tartars, under Ibrahim Pasha (Shaitan). Having 63 guns, Sobieski made a sturdy defence, and by constant sorties inflicted enormous loss on the besiegers. At last, being unable to make any impression on the defence, and finding his army wasting away, Ibrahim consented to treat, and withdrew his forces from Polish territory. The Turks lost enormous numbers during the siege ; the Poles lost 3,000.

Zutphen (Netherlands War of Independence).

Fought September 22, 1586, between the Spaniards, under Prince Alexander of Parma, and the English, under the Earl of Leicester. The Spaniards endeavoured to throw a convoy of provisions into Zutphen, which Leicester was besieging. He attempted to intercept it, but without success, and was forced to retire after suffering conderable loss. Among those who fell on the English side was Sir Philip Sydney.

Zuyder Zee (Netherlands War of Independence).

Fought October 11, 1573, between 30 Spanish ships, under Bossu, and 25 Dutch ships, under Admiral Dirkzoon. The Spanish fleet fled, after losing 5 ships, only Bossu standing his ground. His ship, however, was eventually captured, after losing three-fourths of her crew.

T

INDEX

A

275

U